ISLAND TOURISM

ISLAND TOURISM

Vikash Choudhary

CENTRUM PRESS
NEW DELHI-110002 (INDIA)

CENTRUM PRESS
H.O.: 4360/4, Ansari Road, Daryaganj,
New Delhi-110002 (India)
Tel: 23278000, 23261597, 23255577, 23286875
B.O.: No. 1015, Ist Main Road, BSK IIIrd Stage,
IIIrd Phase, IIIrd Block, Bangalore-560085 (INDIA)
Tel: 080-41723429
Email: centrumpress@gmail.com
Visit us at: www.centrumpress.com

Island Tourism

First Edition, 2010

PRINTED IN INDIA

Printed at Mehra Offset Press, Delhi

Contents

Preface *vii*

1. Tourism as a Geographical Phenomenon 1
2. Sustainable Tourism Development in Small Island 52
3. The "Backpacker" Phenomenon and the "Spaniard" 80
4. Kangaroo Island Tourism 104
5. Ecotourism in the Wider Caribbean Region 128
6. Contribution of the Tourism Sector to the Economy 147
7. Balancing Water, Religion and Tourism on Redang Island, Malaysia 160
8. The Challenges to Sustainability in Island Tourism 189
9. Tourism Development in Indonesia 216
10. Ecotourism in Southeast Asia 275
11. Climate Change Threatens Island Tourism 309
12. Island Tourism Development 332

Bibliography 339

Index 343

Preface

Islands are special places with a natural attraction for tourists and a special challenge to sustainability. The thousands of islands on the face of the earth include some of the finest and most sought after destinations, such as the Balearic Islands, the Hawaiian Islands, the Galapagos Islands, the Canary Islands, the French Polynesian Islands, and the Caribbean islands. The mystique associated with islands is dependent on a blend of different lifestyles, indigenous cultures, unique land formations, flora and fauna, and ocean and coastal resources. To keep that mystique alive and thriving, islands must implement sustainable tourism policies in all areas including environmental, economic and socio-cultural. This paper will examine the unique challenges that islands face as they attempt to build sustainability into their tourism development policies. It will also propose policies to assist in attaining and maintaining quality island tourism.

Islands vary in many ways, and understanding the various types clarifies for the decision-makers the policies that need to be used. One classification is islands' climate which can be cold, temperate or tropical. Even though tropical islands (Caribbean, Hawaii, French Polynesia) tend to have most allure for tourists, cold and temperate islands also have environmental or cultural features and lifestyles that attract tourism – for example the Shetland islands off the coast of Scotland. Baum 1997 describes the general attractivity of North Atlantic islands, including their remoteness, their small size, the slower pace of life, the chance to go back-in-time, the wilderness environment, the water-focused society and the sense of difference yet fam. Very cold islands such as Iceland and Greenland offer unique landscapes and flora and fauna and are alternate destinations often attracting scientists, photographers and other specialized travellers.

Another island classification is the proximity to the related mainland and also its size. Islands that are more remote and distant face more challenging accessibility and transportation issues due to their isolation. Visitors will tend to stay longer in islands that are remote and larger, whereas those close to the mainland and smaller may experience more excursionist tourism. For example, Cousin Island in the Seychelles, hosts only day visitors that leave the island at the end of each day. The island's choice to host excursionists versus stay-over visitors requires a careful evaluation of the strengths and weaknesses of each type of tourism.

The latest advancements in tourism theory and thinking, retaining the thoroughness of content, diversity of applications, regional and international issues, economic significance, tourism operators and the role of technology in the tourism industry etc. are also described elaborately. Numerous regional and global case studies and examples are included to provide an appropriately broad geographic context. This work will be highly informative and useful to students, researchers, policy makers, managers and working groups of travel and tourism industry."

—*Vikash Choudhary*

1

Tourism as a Geographical Phenomenon

Tourism is an inherently geographical phenomenon. Tourism's concepts are embedded in the physical and cultural attributes of a visited place and the movement of people from the realm of the known to the realm of the unfamiliar or exotic. Each destination is important, as it holds some physical or cultural attribute that is distinctive to that place and thus the tourist seeks out this distinctiveness on the Earth's surface. Tourism also holds particular spatial characteristics that lure tourists, such as different climates, physical landscapes, cultural landscapes, and often ethnic variation. These spatial characteristics are an important quality to a specific region's tourism industry.

Geographers have approached tourism studies using spatial-analytical methods that helped to identify historical connections to contemporary patterns. This approach enabled scholars to forecast possible changes to the physical and cultural landscapes of a particular place resulting from tourists flows and activities.

The geographical scope and economic size of modern tourism encompasses a wide range of disciplines. Thus, the body of literature covering tourism related topics is enormous. In this chapter we will review some of the early literature that is important in understanding the ways in which tourism research has taken place. We will also discuss tourism as a modern industry in three separate but equally important and over lapping categories, world tourism, in Central America, and tourism in Honduras. We will also discuss my research methodologies in the field and the geographical perspectives we used as we conducted my fieldwork on one very small island.

Review of the Literature

Geographers became interested in tourism as a subject of research in the 1930s. *Ralph Brown (1935:471)*, in an article in the Geographical Review, offered "an invitation to geographers" writing "From the geographical point of view the study of tourism offers inviting possibilities for the development of new and ingenious techniques for research, for discovery of facts of value in their social implications in what is virtually a virgin field." However, as *Campbell (1966)* noted, this so called invitation, was accepted by only a few geographers and therefore techniques for collection, analysis, interpretation, and cartographic representation of tourism data lagged. After World War II, however, those who began conducting tourism studies did so under the guise of economic geography, and looked at the regional and destination economic impacts of tourism as well as travel routes. American geographers such as *Cooper (1947)* were involved in discussions concerning seasonality and travel motivations which became a major precursor to works conducted in the 1980s and 1990s. By the 1950s, although many scholars felt tourism studies had not yet received the proper attention by geographers, *McMurray (1954)* included tourism studies in a chapter in an overview text on the state of geography in the United States.

American geographers were not the only scholars conducting tourism research during these initial decades. In Britain and Canada, Gilbert and Wolfe, also delved into tourism studies. *Gilbert (1939, 1949)* published articles concerning British seaside resorts while *Wolfe (1951)* conducted research on "cottaging" in Ontario. Wolf's studies created a base for later works on second home development. After Gilbert's initial work little other research was conducted in the United Kingdom until the 1960s. During the 1960s geographical research on tourism accelerated and continued to grow rapidly over the next decade. Several influential reviews were produced in the 1960s such as, *Murphy (1963)*, *Winsberg (1966)*, *Wolfe (1967)*, and *Mitchell (1969a and b)*. These authors focused on the geography of the tourism industry which led to works conducted by regional geographers such as *Guthrie (1961)*, *Christaller (1963)* and *Piperoglou (1966)*. However, as *Williams and Zelinsky (1970:549)* noted, "virtually all the scholarship in the domain of tourism has been confined to intra-national description and analysis...In view of its great and increasing economic import, the probable significance of tourism in diffusing information and attitudes, and its even greater future potential for modifying patterns of migration, balance of payments, land use, and general socio-economic structure with the introduction of third-generation jet transport and other innovations in travel, it is startling to discover how little attention the circulation of tourists has been accorded by geographers, demographers, and other social scientists."

The concerns of Williams and Zelinsky are at the forefront of tourism geography today, as well as the growing concern of the increases in leisure time world wide. *Mercer (1970)* suggested a discussion of the increase in leisure time in the affluent countries of the world in the 1970s and commented that, "leisure still remains a sadly neglected area of study in geography." Whether a dearth still exists today in this aspect in geographical studies is open for discussion, however, few can argue that it is important in determining source regions for tourist.

Several influential publications appeared during the 1970s and 1980s that indicated tourism studies in geography were increasing. Geographers such as *Cosgrove and Jackson (1972)*, *Lavery (1971)*, *McCannell (1973)*, *Robinson (1976)*, *Coppock (1977)*, *Butler (1980)*, *Pearce (1981, 1987a)*, *Mathieson and Wall (1982)*, *Patmore (1983)*, *Pigram (1983)*, and *Smith (1983)* published articles and texts concerning the new field. However, as *Mitchell (1979:235)* noted in the introduction to a special issue of Annals of Tourism Research, "the geography of tourism is limited by a dearth of published research in geographical journals." Likewise, *Pearce (1979, 1995)* commented that the geography of tourism was not coherent and lacked a conceptual and theoretical base. Perhaps he was unaware that *Butler (1980; 1991)* had modelled cycles of evolution of destinations in the 1980s and has published on this topic into the 1990s.

While the study of the geography of tourism remains on the periphery of geography in general, this subject does not occur in, "isolation from wider trends in geography and academic discourse nor of the society of which we are a part". A large degree of the research conducted by geographers has used techniques inherent in spatial analysis and applied geography (ibid). *Hall and Page (1999)* suggested that the three most influential works on the geography of tourism written in the last two decades approached their research from a spatial perspective with a small emphasis on the role of behavioural research. However in the 1990s geographers such as *Shaw and Williams (1994)* took a more critical approach to tourism studies and showed the importance of other factors such as the political economy, production, consumption, commodification and globalization in the ever shifting character of tourism. This perspective shift is important, because tourism studies connect with many other aspects of geography. Tourism as its own phenomenon engages topics beyond what can be seen and experienced in the natural environment of a particular place. As *Matley (1976:5)* observed, "There is scarcely an aspect of tourism which does not have some geographical implications and there are few branches of geography which do not have some contribution to make to the study of the phenomenon of tourism."

Tourism as a World Phenomenon

Tourism is the world's largest industry and continues to grow. Total gross expenditures for travel and tourism were $3.2 trillion in 1993 or, approximately six percent of the global GNP *(WTTC 1993)*. By 2005 the number of tourism related jobs is expected to exceed 350 million *(ibid)*. In the 1990s more than 200 million people were directly or indirectly employed in the global tourism industry and 20,000 jobs are created for every 1 million dollars of revenue generated. Tourism accounts for more than 11 percent of all consumer spending world wide *(ibid)*. In the 1990s, in the United States, tourism produced 13.4 percent of the nation's GNP, generated $50 billion in tax revenue and employed 11 million people.

According to the World Tourism Organization (WTO) international tourist arrivals grew from 93 million in 1963 to 284 million in 1981 *(WTO 1997)*. By 1990 arrivals had reached 456 million and are expected to double by 2010 *(WTO 1997)*. However, after the recent international terrorist events these expectations are not likely to be met. It appears that the stage is set for the continued growth of tourism in the developed world in the quaternary sector of the economy. Many developing nations are also moving towards a more service-based economy as governments begin to comprehend the potential economic magnitude of the industry. In recent years the most rapid growth of the tourism industry has been in the developing world. In these countries tourism makes up a substantial portion of their gross national and gross domestic products as well as a major portion of their foreign earnings. Many scholars feel these countries show the greatest prospects for continued growth. However, tourism is not a panacea for the economic crises of the developing world although it has become an economic fact in today's society.

Tourism in Central America

Central America's reputation for political unrest and inadequate transportation and infrastructure has caused an uneven growth in tourism since the 1960's. However, in 1965 the Central American Bank for Economic Integration, in conjunction with the U.S. Agency for International Development's regional office for Central America, commissioned Porter International Company to examine the possibilities of the development and promotion of tourism in the region. According to Ritchie and his associates,

> *"The objective was that the conclusions and recommendations reached could serve as a basis for a Master Plan of Tourism, which would permit the promotion, financing, and execution of specific investment projects for the development of a tourism industry in Central America."*

For each country specific locations were designated as having qualities favorable for tourism. These qualities included important historical-cultural sites, such as Esquipulas in Guatemala, and areas where the physical geography was conducive to tourists, such as the Bay Islands of Honduras. David Weaver (1994), some three decades later, discussed characteristics of tourism development that followed the recommendations of Ritchie and his associates. Weaver suggested that tourism development in Central America was based on physical and cultural geographical factors. The insular region, according to *Weaver (1994)*, attracts tourists because of its appealing climate, extensive beaches, developed resorts, and its close proximity to the tourism markets of the United States. In this region the traditional "3s" (sand, sea and sunshine) type of tourism takes place. The mainland region of Central America relies on the extensive culture-history of the Maya and other pre-Colombian tribes and the more recent colonial additions for its tourism draw. However, this region also has the "3s" attraction along with more highly diverse natural areas and ecosystems *(ibid)*.

The number of tourist visiting Central America from 1960 to 1970 grew from 124,000 to 744,000 *(WTO 1993, 1994, 1996, 1997)*. This growth followed the international trend during this period. Annual tourist arrivals between 1970 and 1975 in this region rose from 744,000 to nearly 1.7 million *(WTO 1993)*. This increase surpassed the global rate of growth, which was documented at 134 percent, as well as the rate of the growth to the Americas (118%) and to Mexico (143%) *(WTO 1993)*. The next decade (1975-1985), however, did not follow this trend. Total tourist arrivals to the region dropped from 1.7 million to 1.1 million annually. The decline was associated with the highly publicized escalating violence throughout the isthmus. Guatemala, Nicaragua, and El Salvador, the countries with the most widespread public violence, lost the most tourists.

However, Costa Rica, the country with the most stable reputation, was also affected to a lesser extent by the regional drop. Honduras' international tourist arrivals during this time were slightly lower than the other countries in the region and remained relatively constant. Panama, the hub for air and sea travel in the region, according the West and *Augelli (1989)*, had always enjoyed a steady flow of tourists. During the regional lull in tourism Panama's arrivals increased. Susan *Stonich (2000)* associates this increase with the inclusion of U.S. military personal and their families in the national statistics.

Since the 1980s the governments of the Central America countries have been in the process of strengthening their economies through new avenues of development. Stonich suggested that these avenues are designed to "integrate their economies, diversify exports, promote foreign investment, and increase foreign exchange earnings". One of the most important of these tactics has been the promotion of international tourism. However, because these countries are still considered developing relying on tourism as a means to fix their economics remains problematic. Tourism is cyclical in nature and in many developing countries disasters have ensued as tourism becomes a leading economic component. Much like the product cycle of economic theory, the product cycle of tourism development of a given area or the development of a specific type of tourism must pass through specific stages *(ibid)*.

The first stage of development, like that of a new product, begins as a relatively unknown place with just a trickle of visitors over a given period *(ibid)*. As it becomes better known its popularity grows until it reaches its popularity peak. Once this happens, visitation to this site will reach a saturation point and them it will begin its decline. Destination can take steps to overcome the likelihood of decline as suggested by Robert *Butler (1991)* that will reinvent the site and continue to attract tourists. However, further complicating the tourism product cycle is the capricious nature of the tourist. It has been suggested that tourists often favour the in-style, most publicly advertised places, and move on to new sites once the fad has dissipated. Unless the site can reinvent itself the likelihood of decline is probable.

Among other drawbacks discussed widely, and one of the most important for this discussion, is the possibility of economic leakage. Economic leakages occur most often in developing countries because unfettered foreign development and investment are allowed in hopes of gaining significant revenues from tourism growth. Leakages arise as a result of large ownership percentages held by foreigners or corporations and thus much of the revenue generated leaves the host country and returns to the country of investment origination. External labour brought into a host country by foreign investors can exacerbate leakage problems. John *Beekhuis (1981)* calculated that Central America's leakage rates ranged from 30 percent to 50 percent while in Cancún, Mexico estimates were as high as 90 percent. In 1994 Erlit *Cater (1994)* suggested that 90 percent of the coastal development in Belize was foreign owned thus leakage rates were much higher.

Under the leadership of Mexico, in 1988, the presidents of El Salvador, Belize, Guatemala, and Honduras began one of the region's earliest attempts at promoting regional tourism with the creation of El Mundo Maya. Relying upon the financial assistance of groups in the United States and Europe the five presidents signed a joint tourism promotion pact. The group's first goal was to secure financial and technical assistance from the European Community to expand both the public and private tourism sectors in the five countries *(ibid).*

The goal of the project, as stated by Mexico's Minister of Tourism was to, "showcase the history and culture of the entire region as one entity without borders. Cancún would become the "doorway" for the world to the project *(ibid).* In 1991 the European Community loaned the group $1 million and the project began. In each country three types of tourism were endorsed: cultural/historical tourism, coastal tourism, and ecotourism or adventure tourism. Fourteen tourism circuits were established, each containing one of the three types of tourism *(ibid).*

Examples of three of the circuits established in Honduras were the Copán ruins (cultural/historical tourism), Roatán Island (coastal beach tourism) and la Mosquitia/Río Plátano Biosphere Reserve (eco/adventure tourism). The inclusion of Roatán and la Mosquitia are ironic because these two sites have never been inhabited by the Maya, although it is likely that Maya might have visited these places. However, these areas have become popular tourist attractions for Honduras and have been featured in several articles promoting Honduran tourism.

Other projects were planned, along with the initial circuits, which included infrastructural improvements (airports, roads and marinas), increased hotel construction and international marketing. In El Salvador and Chiapas, Mexico archeological projects were initiated and upon completion were to be included in El Mundo Maya *(ibid).* More than two million international tourists visited Central America annually during the 1990s exceeding the arrivals from the previous decades *(WTTC 2001)*. The promotion of Central America as a single tourism region has become a trend in the 1990s. The joint initiative first began with the creation of El Mundo Maya and then in 1996 the Central American presidents signed the Declaration of Montelimar II. The declaration designated the tourism industry as the principal growth strategy for the isthmus and it emphasized the necessity for cooperative efforts among all the Central American countries in making the region a single tourism destination. The promotion of these initiatives has been supported financially by several international donors such as the World Bank, the International Development Bank, the United Nations, and USAID.

In 1996 tourism contributed approximately $1.6 billion to Central America's foreign exchange earnings and more than 2.6 million tourists visited the region that year *(WTO 1997)*. 2001 estimates have suggested tourist arrivals reached 4 million and created $3 billion in foreign exchange earnings making tourism a viable component in the Central American economy *(WTO 2001)*.

Tourism in Honduras

The Honduran government began actively promoting tourism as a national development strategy in the late 1960s. Emphasis was placed on the development of three separate physical and cultural geographical areas: the Mayan archeological site of Copán, the beaches and colonial history of the North Coast, and the coral reefs of the Bay Islands *(ibid)*. La Mosquitia and the Río Plátano Biosphere Reserve were added as ecotourism became a popular world trend in the 1990s.

The government of Honduras, in the 1980s, established a set of laws creating special "tourism zones." These zones helped attract foreign investments by providing liberal tax and import incentives. However, Article 107 of the Honduran Constitution prohibited foreign ownership of land 40 km from the Caribbean Sea and Gulf of Fonseca or the international borders of Nicaragua, El Salvador, and Guatemala. Recognizing this barrier, the Honduran National Congress, in 1990, passed Decree Law 90/90 to allow foreign property purchases in designated tourism zones, established by the Ministry of Tourism, in order to build permanent or vacation homes.

Areas along the North Coast and the Bay Island were among the most popular for investment. Continued acceleration of these "neoliberal" economic policies occurred during the 1990s specifically with the creation of Tourism Free Zones in 1993. Tourism investors were given the same benefits as the private Export Processing Zones including; 100% foreign ownership of property, federal and municipal tax exemptions, tax free imports for any materials needed to further the industry (including boats, planes, and worn equipment).

During the first five months of 1995 the tourism industry in Honduras generated US $90 million which was a 62% increase from all of 1994. The Bay Islands accounted for almost one-fourth of this total *(ibid)*. According to Maria Callejas de *Durón (1995)*, Senior Commercial Officer for Honduras, in 1995 tourism ranked fifth in the revenue generation for the country and had not reached its full potential. Aside from the tourist attractions offered by the continuous "summer-like weather," *Durón (1995)* felt that the country still lacked additional attractions in the areas where the flow of foreign visitors was greatest. However, with the institution of the Tourism Free Zone Law, ecotourism programs, and the national demand for additional tourism projects, she felt tourism had the potential to become the country's leading industry.

By 1997 tourism ranked third in foreign exchange earnings (US $ 143 million) behind coffee (US $330 million) and bananas.

Following the Tourism Free Zone Laws, in 1999 the Law of Tourism Incentives was passed. The National Congress stated their intentions with this new law; it was to continue to:

> *"facilitate the development of the nation's tourism sector by providing fiscal incentives that will encourage greater participation by private investors, both local and foreign, in the development of tourism products, thereby stimulating the creation of jobs, promoting investment, and increasing the nation's intake of currency and tax revenue"."*

The incentives granted under this law included: a ten year exoneration from income tax payments, exoneration from payment of taxes and tariffs on the import of goods and services including printed advertising materials, and exoneration from the payment of taxes, fees or any other kind of financial obligation on cultural presentations and shows. Tourism was also considered by the Honduran government to be an economic activity that would be closely linked to the cultural and social development of the Honduran people. Projects devoted to rescuing cultural heritage and conserving natural landscapes were given an added exoneration from the payment of municipal property taxes *(ibid)*. According to the Ministry of Tourism, all activities carried out under the stipulations of this law were to comply with the sustainable development of the entire nation *(ibid)*. Tourism was to have only minimal impacts on the cultural and natural resources of Honduras but being of maximum benefits to the Honduran people *(ibid)*. In 2001 tourism brought an estimated US $300 million to the economy of Honduras making it the third greatest financial generator of income for the country. According to the Honduran Institute of Tourism (2000) within an estimated four years tourism will be the number one source of dollars for Honduras. After Hurricane Mitch the tourism sector had 92% of its infrastructure intact and 90% of the country's natural and cultural attractions were unaffected. This well surpassed the countries leading dollar producer, agriculture, which suffered sever setbacks. These figures illustrate the overwhelming resilience of the industry and its potential for the future.

Specific Aims of the Study and Methodology

The purpose of this research is to document the development of tourism on the island of Utila, Honduras and the affects this new industry is having on the social, economic, and environmental aspects of the island. Traditionally, Bay Islanders have been culturally and economically oriented to the sea. Livelihoods once depended on agriculture and fishing and, more recently, merchant sailing. Documenting the shift from the merchant sailing economy to a tourism economy on Utila will be a major focus. In addition, because nearly two-thirds of Utila is mangrove swamp and tourism development is expanding into this area, ecological alterations will be documented.

Being the smallest of the three major Bay Islands, Utila has historically drawn a different type of tourist. Those not interested in big resorts and lavish facilities, looking for a fairly "cheap" way to see Central America and the Caribbean, find their way to this island. It would seem that this type of tourist has determined the character of tourism facilities on Utila. In the literature, a similar type of tourist population has been documented, gives an example of this type of tourist in a small fishing village in Brazil, and discusses the affects these tourists have on the economics, society, and cultural. As a subsidiary to the core of my research documenting a similar type of tourist and their effects on the island will also be addressed. Understanding how this new tourist economy has affected and potentially will affect the island's landscape also enters the research question. In addition to the international "backpacker" phenomena associated with tourism on Utila, the component of mainland Hondurans is growing. Documentation of this growth will also be discussed.

During the summer of 1999, as an undergraduate student, I visited Utila for the first time. During this trip this project began to take shape. Although we were in the country to observe the reconstruction efforts of the Honduran people after Hurricane Mitch, the week spent on Utila lead to the realization that the Bay Islands functioned much differently than the rest of Honduras. It was evident that tourism was the primary income producer for the island. However, the type of tourist visiting Utila was quite different than on the other two major islands and led me to expand this thesis to include a chapter on this character.

Over a three month period from May until August 2001, I lived and worked on the island. During this time I came to know many of the islanders and tourists and through these personal interactions gathered much of the information for this paper. There is a definite and distinct link between the islanders and their environment that is played out in social and economic interactions. Understanding this link and the ways in which the islanders manipulate these interactions to fit personal needs and gains is an important part of this research. Global factors, apparent during my visit on the island, continue to play a role in the economic and social lives of the islanders. Therefore, it was necessary to blend the theories of cultural ecology and political ecology in an attempt to make sense of the social, economic, and natural environmental state of the island.

Location and Size of the Bay Islands

The Bay Islands comprise one of the fifteen departamentos in the Republic of Honduras. Situated in an arc 29 to 60 kilometres off the north coast, the Bay Islands consist of three major islands, five minor islands and sixty-five cays. The largest and most predominant of these islands, in terms of land and population, are Roatán, Guanaja, and Utila is the smallest of the major islands, approximately eleven kilometres long and five kilometres wide. East Harbour is the only agglomerated settlement, however, twelve populated cays are located off the southwestern end of the island. The total land area of the Bay Islands is approximated at 238 square kilometres *(ibid)*. Roatán, the central island accounts for over one-half of the islands total.

Topography

The islands are the above water appearance of the Bonacca Ridge, which forms the northern edge of the continental shelf in the Caribbean. The ridge is a non-continuous underwater extension of the Sierra de

Omoa. This mainland mountain range, located near the southern escarpment of the Bartlett Trough, disappears into the Caribbean Sea near Puerto Cortés *(Banks and Richards 1969).*

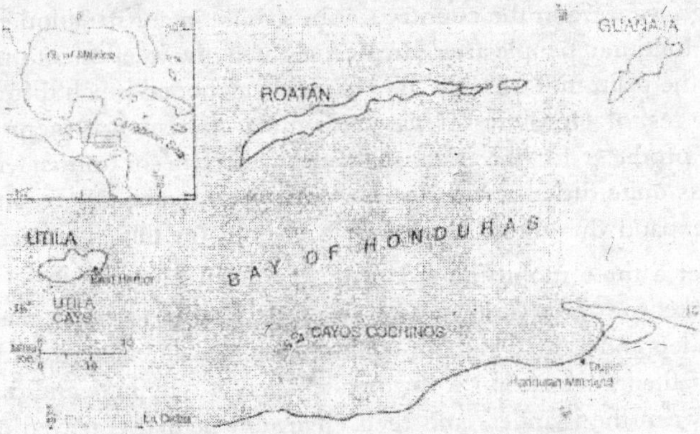

Figure 1: The Bay Island's of Honduras

On Utila this geological base is capped with coralline limestone. Thus, nearly two-thirds of the island is hardly more than a swampy basin, perfect for catching rainwater and in some places this limestone has eroded to sea level. Utila is also composed of volcanic materials that make up another important part of the island's topography. Pumpkin Hill, located near the eastern end of the island is the remnant of an ancient volcano that creating the ragged terrain in this area. This limestone and volcanic base has much to do with the western sloping perspective of Utila. And the creation of a cultural lingo associated with directions on the island. If one travels from the western end of Utila towards East Harbour, one is said to be going "up town"; to the west is "down." Moving eastward from Utila the elevations of the islands generally increase, with the eastern island of Guanaja having the tallest peak at approximately 415 meters. In addition to the increase in elevation as one moves eastward, so to does the terrain grow steeper, the vegetation and wildlife become more diverse, and the amount of fresh water resources increases.

The number of streams differs greatly on each of the three major islands. This also affects drainage patterns on the islands. Roatán has a number of run-off routes. These routes, however, do not retain water for any length of time after rain because of the steep slopes. Standing water on the island can only be found near the shoreline where the land generally becomes flat (ibid). This water is not good for human consumption because tidal variations and long-shore drift make it brackish *(ibid)*. Guanaja has the steepest slopes and on the northeast portion of the island, two major streams carry fresh water year-round. Utila differs from the other two major islands because it is flatter and has not developed any significant gulling. Rain seeps downward into limestone caverns and into the centrally located mangrove swamps. One small stream, located in the southeast of the island, seems to play only a minor role in the drainage process. Natural deposition of sediment on Guanaja and Roatán can be found where the hills near the shoreline and the slopes become gentler. Utila's dominating swampy area also accumulates upslope sediment.

Climate

Honduras has three major climate types. The Bay Islands, like the adjacent mainland coast, have a humid tropical climate. In the tropics rainfall, not temperature, determines seasonality. Two-thirds of the islands' rainfall normally occurs between October and January. Changing wind direction associated with North American cold fronts is a major cause of this winter rainfall. As is expected in the tropics, temperature variation is relatively slight. Average mean monthly temperature ranges normally do not exceed four degrees Celsius. However, a climatic phenomenon that occurs along the east coast of Central America from the Yucatán to Colombia, called veranillo, brings a short early midsummer rainfall increase and a slight drop in the July temperatures.

The Bay Islands are located in the belt of the trade-winds. Winds normally blow from the east, roughly parallel to the north coast of Honduras. Velocities range from thirty-two to forty kilometres per hour *(Cry 1965)*. In August, as noted by islanders, calm periods of up to five days occur. During the winter months, North American cold fronts cause winds to shift and come from the north and west. This creates the extended rainfall characteristic of the region. Like elevation on Utila, wind direction is also important in local lingo. Winds normally blow from east to west and therefore, walking into east winds (up-wind) correlates with up slope and going "up town."

Because Utilians are oriented to the sea ocean currents are an important part of local life. In this region, currents normally have an easterly flow along the southern portions and between the islands. Which makes westerly travel slower. However, during the winter months, there is a weakening of this easterly current because of the reversal of the current that flows north of the islands.

During the last century nearly 20 hurricanes have affected the Bay Islands. How the Bay Islands are situated in the Bay of Honduras, their distances from the mountains on the mainland of Central America, and the general northwestwardly paths of these storms, are all factors that reduce storm strengths. Davidson suggested that although the Bay of Honduras has seen developments of large storm systems only every ten years do these storms mature into hurricanes. The most destructive hurricanes that affect the islands, such as Hurricane Francelia in 1969 and Hurricane Mitch in 1998, develop in the open ocean and then strike the islands uncharacteristically from the north.

Marine Environment

In the Bay of Honduras reef systems are of two types: barrier and fringing. A barrier reef is a coral wall separated from the land by a lagoon. A fringing reef however, begins adjacent to the shore, often with only small breaks that might allow small boat passage. Many people make the mistake and assume that the barrier reef system off the coast of Belize is connected to that of the Bay Islands. This is an incorrect notion passed along primarily in tourism literature. Not only does the Bartlett Trough separate the two distinct systems, the Bay Islands reef is a fringing reef.

On the northern sides of Roatán and Guanaja the reef encloses much of the islands. Only small breaks allow for passage into tidal inlets associated with stream mouths *(ibid)*. Guanaja's reef begins about one mile offshore in places, farther than on the other two islands. Utila's northern reef exposes itself as iron shore that extends from the central portion of the island almost continuously around the eastern tip *(ibid)*. Utila's north side reef is characterized by "steep escarpments and spur and groove formations" *(ibid)*. In the middle of the north side is a small break in the coral that has become the entrance to a canal that extends across the island into Oyster Bay Lagoon.

Utila's eastern side, much like the north side, is covered by fossilized coral and low cliffs referred to as iron shore *(Harborne et al 1999)*. This side of the island has long and shallow fore reefs and large sandy areas *(ibid)*. Additionally, the eastern end of the island faces a deep trench that separates Utila and Roatán and is one of the few places in the world where whale sharks can be seen *(ibid)*.

The southern side of Utila, facing the Honduran mainland, is the more developed portion of the island. The southern reef is dominated by a sloping fore reef that is the widest of the reef zones *(Harborne et al 1999)*. Also characteristic of the southern reef are some spur and groove formations *(ibid)*. The back reef consists of exposed bedrock and sand and covers a smaller area and is much less diverse in coral types and topographic features *(ibid)*. East Harbour, located on southeastern Utila, is protected by an uplift of the southern reef. Roatán's south side reef is similar and runs almost the entire length of the island *(Jacobson 1992)*. Guanaja also has an expansive southern reef where the two cays of Bannaca Town are located.

The western end of Utila is dominated by fringing reefs. The southwestern reef supports Utila's twelve cays. Also found in this area are patch reefs and expansive sea grass habitants that surround the cays. Inside the reefs Utila also has a number of bays, bights, and harbours that interrupt the shoreline. These include, Spotted Bay, Carey Bay, Turtle Harbour, Rock Harbour, Jack's Bight, Swan Bay, Big Bight, East Harbour, and Little Bight, which provide anchorage for shallow vessels.

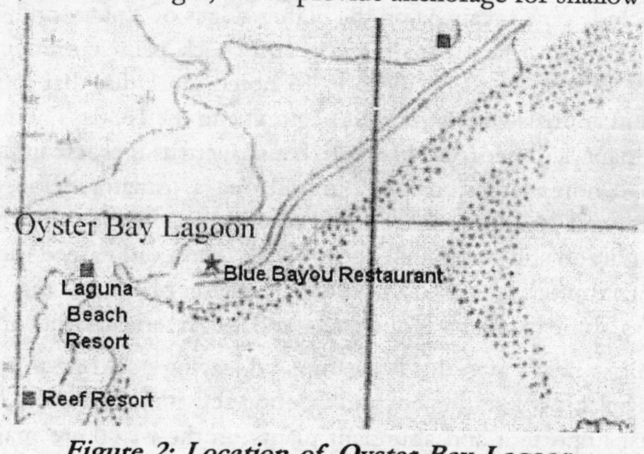

Figure 2: Location of Oyster Bay Lagoon

East Harbour, however, is the only place on Utila where large watercrafts such as shrimpers, sail boats, and cargo and passenger ships can safely moor. These factors were probably taken into consideration when the original founders settled in East Harbour. Perhaps because of the reefs the Bay Islands are known for their diverse tropical fish and other marine populations. These fish include porgies, old wife, black fin, wahoo, red snapper, dogteeth snapper, hogfish, and the whale shark. Conch, crawfish, and four species of turtles can also be found around the islands. These marine species have been historically important to the economy of the islands and recently many have become of interest to sport fishermen. The islanders have long depended on the sea to sustain them. The reef provides a place for the abundant fish population to feed and survive. It also provides the islanders with protection from the dynamic ocean. More importantly, in recent years, the reefs have been the major draw for the developing tourism industry.

Flora and Fauna

Island vegetation has been altered drastically since first recorded by Christopher Columbus on his fourth voyage to the New World in 1502. Although Columbus and his crew did not provide detailed descriptions, they did mention the presence of pine trees on Guanaja and named the island "isla de pinos". Although pines are still present, they have undoubtedly been depleted since this first account because of human needs, for ship building and house construction, and environmental destruction, especially from fires and hurricanes. Today, as noted by the Bay Island Conservation Association, the main vegetation types include pine savannas on the higher ridges of Roatán and Guanaja and tropical dry forests, mangroves, and beach plant communities on the three major islands. In 1975 Lord noted, on Utila, that most food plants and animals were imported beginning in the 1830s. These include mango, papaya, breadfruit, plantain, banana, citrus (grapefruit, lime and orange), canop, mamey, mamea, almond, guava, tomato, melon, cassava, cocoyam, and star apple *(ibid)*. Most of these plants are still present on the islands and still very much part of local diet. Lord named the groups that contributed to the cultivation of these plants as the Cayman Islanders, some mainland Hondurans, and the American fruit companies.

Utila is nearly two-thirds swampland leaving only one-third of the island available for settlement and farming activities. Therefore, perhaps the most important and abundant plants on the island are mangroves. Utila has three species of mangrove; white mangrove (Laguncularia racemosa), red mangrove (Rhizophora mangle), and black mangrove (Avicennia germinaus). These plants have adapted to saline coastal environments in the tropics and subtropics *(West 1998)*. They can live in a wide variety of water types, from fresh to salt, but tend to do best in brackish water (salinities from 10 to 20 parts per thousand) *(ibid)*. Mangrove are associated with tidal zones where they form a cover that ranges from shrubs to taller trees *(ibid)*. On Utila these plants can be found in both brackish (to the interior) and along ocean-fronts protected by the fringing reef. The mangrove is important for natural land building on the island. They also act as nurseries and spawning grounds for many species of open ocean marine life *(ibid)*. Additionally, growths associated with interior swamp and marsh areas are an important feeding ground for various species of crabs and snails. Thus large accumulations of these species can be found here and attract other fauna such as turtles and iguanas which have been traditionally important to the Utilian diet and economy. In recent years, associated with the growing tourism economy, large portions of Utila's mangrove have been destroyed.

The Bay Islands also have an abundant wildlife population that has been suggested as an additional resource for the further diversification of the island's tourism industry. In a conservation plan prepared by Tropical Research and Development, Inc. the authors identified potential trials for hiking, bird-watching, and horseback riding that would allow alternatives to scuba diving which is the current draw for the islands *(ibid)*. One of the biggest limiting factors to human use of Utila is its size and topography. Although agriculture has become less important to Utilian life the lack of available arable land has forced the islanders to turn to the sea for survival. Recently, as tourism has become an important part of the economy on the islands, the surrounding ocean has been the strongest draw for international tourists.

Utila's Cultural History

The cultural landscape is fashioned from the natural landscape by a cultural group. Culture is the agent, the natural area is the medium, the cultural landscape the result. The Bay Islands, including Utila, have a distinctive and diverse cultural heritage. The mélange of ethnicities stemming from its settlement history has created the diverse population seen today. As noted by William Davidson in his 1974 publication of these past and present populations, seven distinct groups have inhabited the islands. Before European contact, Paya Indians probably occupied the islands. After Contact, Spaniards, buccaneers, Garífuna, English, English-descended Antilleans, African-descended Antilleans, and North Americans have settled for varying time periods on the islands.

Utila was inhabited by only six of these groups because the Garífuna only settled on Roatán. In recent years, however, other ethnic groups have found their way to the island, specifically European tourists and Mainland Hondurans. As mentioned in the introduction, in the 1960s Honduras became interested in the sustainable development of its tourist industry. Since this time the ethnic make up of Utila has changed. This chapter will discuss the historical and modern populations that settled on the island.

Pre-Columbian Inhabitants

Just prior to Spanish Contact the north coast of Honduras, including the Bay Islands, appeared to be sparsely inhabited by aboriginal tribes. In Central America the pre-Colombian populations are designated as "high" and "low" cultural groups. Geographical boundaries that separate these groups have some relationship to the islands. The high cultural groups included the Maya and Aztec. These people lived primarily in the southern Central Plateau of Mexico and the Yucatán, and the highlands and Pacific lowlands of Central America *(ibid)*.

They could be distinguished from other populations in the area because they lived in agglomerated settlements comparable to modern cities, their agriculture could support the large numbers of people in the settlements and was much more advanced than the low cultural groups, and their economy was controlled by social organizations and theocratic states. The presence of large temples and ceremonial centres were also characteristic of these "high cultures" *(ibid)*. In contrast, the "low cultures" of Middle America inhabited the West Indies, much of the Central American lowlands, and northern Mexico.

These groups included the Chichimecas of northern Mexico, the Caribs of the West Indies, and the many tribes of the Central American lowlands such as the Paya and Jicaque. Characteristics of these groups included, smaller much less organized, dispersed settlements, simpler agricultural techniques, tubers as the primary food source, and lack of large ceremonial centres. It should be noted that these two groups did have contact with each other. Aztec and Mayan traders probably travelled throughout much of the isthmus and to many of the islands off the coast.

The Paya have been suggested as the first inhabitants of the Bay Islands. The boundaries for this group on the mainland were established as being from Trujillo to Cape Gracias a Dios. William Strong and William Davidson, among others, seem to believe that this aboriginal group extended its boundaries to include the Bay Islands. Others have suggested that islanders were Maya, Lenca, and Jicaque. For this paper, we will support Davidson and Strong's notion that the aboriginal population was Paya. Evidence presented alludes to similarities between the mainland Paya populations and sites found on the Bay Islands. These island sites have been classified in three categories with the addition of a fourth focusing on burials. The first of these three are residential sites. Archeologists pinpoint residential sites when the presence of kitchen ware and shards are prevalent. Sites containing these items have been found on Roatán, Utila, and Guanaja of the larger islands and Helene of the smaller islands in this region.

The largest of these main sites is found at "80 Acre" on Utila and encompasses forty acres of land *(ibid)*. Locations are generally forty to sixty feet above sea level, on sloping land, a few hundred yards from the beach *(ibid)*. Davidson suggested that these aboriginal populations located their villages at these specific elevations and distance from the shore to escape mosquitoes and sand flies *(ibid)*. In addition, it seems reasonable to assume that these people relied heavily on the ocean therefore making site location close to the water important.

Ceremonial sites, being the second in this list of site classifications, are located near the large residential areas of Utila and Guanaja. These sites, however, are in no way comparable to the sites associated with the Maya and Aztec of mainland Mesoamerica. No large ceremonial structures, such as temples, have been located on any of the Bay Islands. However, there are identifiable artifacts associated with this type of site, such as large stone monoliths, earth mounds, stone mounds, and stone causeways. Utila had one a site located on Stewart's Hill. This site is supposedly the origination point of an aboriginal paved road system on the island *(ibid)*.

The third site classification deals with the deposition of offerings. These offertory sites, lacking the monuments found in ceremonial locations, have objects that have been placed in nature and elicit help from a higher power. Artifacts ranging from shell ornaments to clay figurines can be found in association with these sites. The largest in the Bay Islands are on the island of Roatán and the smaller island of Barbaret. Nearly every occurrence of these sites where located on tops of hills. Although a separate category, burial sites on the islands seem to be located close to and hypothetically in conjunction with offertory sites. However, on islands such as Utila, burials were located on sandy beaches There is no archeological evidence that offertory sites were located on Utila.

Eight known burial sites exist on the Bay Islands. They have been located in three different physical settings; beach, hilltop, and refuse heaps. Utila has three of these eight sites and all of them were located on the beach *(ibid)*. Characteristics of these beach sites include slate slab coverings, multiple burials, skulls placed in large urns, with bones and other goods nearby *(ibid)*.

The Paya Indians apparently lived in only a few settlements with one residential area on the major islands. Artifacts and residential patterns resemble those of their mainland Paya neighbours, making it possible to hypothesize that the groups were related. Trade seemed to be occurring between these groups as well as with other aboriginal groups from the mainland, showing that the Bay Islanders were not living in cultural seclusion. It seems the Paya were the first of many ethnic populations to call the islands home.

Christopher Columbus and the Encomenderos

Christopher Columbus made contact with the aboriginal populations on the Bay Islands on his fourth voyage in 1502. Hence, Utila and the rest of the Bay Islands became a part of history on July 30, 1502, when Columbus and his crew anchored off the north shore of Guanaja. Columbus documented the island's appearance and subsequently called it Isla de Pinos, for the large pine stands located there. For nearly 136 years the Spanish crown held virtually uncontested rule over the Bay Islands

The Paya populations on the Bay Islands were inevitably subjected to slaving raids. Queen Isabella of Spain, however, commanded her conquistadores to make slaves of only those aboriginal populations who were unwilling to become Christians or those designated as "cannibals". Even though the populations of the Bay Islands were noted as being relatively peaceful it served the purposes of the conquistadores based in Cuba to inform the Queen that the Bay Islanders were hostile, cannibalistic, and opposed to Christianity.

In 1516, Queen Isabella allowed Diego Velasquez to remove the aboriginal populations on the Bay Islands to be used on plantations in Cuba where populations had already been exterminated. Allegedly only two raids took place in the Bay Islands and according to Sauer, it was during the second in 1525 that the name Utila appeared for the first time. Although some islanders survived slaving seeds had been planted for future Spanish settlement.

The Roman Catholic Church had little influence on the Bay Islands unlike other places in Latin America. A seemingly more important landscape and cultural change occurred with the institution of the encomienda initiated in Honduras in 153. This system called for Spanish occupation of the islands where the encomenderos would Christianize the Indians. Utila obtained only one. The encomienda brought the islanders into constant contact with the Spanish encomenderos, thus changing the lifestyles of the natives.

Buccaneering, Early English Inhabitants, and the Garífuna

As the Spanish made their presence known in the New World other European explorers began to see the potential of the Caribbean and Central America as a whole. Yet another cultural group saw the opportunity to carve its name in the ethnic history of the Bay Islands. By 1536 the French had appeared in the western Caribbean and the Dutch soon after in 1594. The English, however, were the most successful in disrupting the Spanish shipping routes and appeared sometime in the 1560s. The English, French, and Dutch realized that the Bay Islands were in a strategic position to loot Spanish vessels. The islands had fresh water and protected natural harbours that the freebooters valued.

Although the pirate settlements had no lasting impressions on the natural landscape, they did create myths that still exist among islanders. Myths of sunken treasures draw amateur relic hunters and tourists to the islands today. Town names found on Roatán (Coxen Hole) and business names on Utila (Captain Morgan's Dive Shop and the Bucket of Blood Bar) are also reminders of the pirate presence from earlier days. Ironically, Utila was not one of the popular hideouts for the pirates and has not been mentioned in the literature as having any involvement with these scallywags.

By 1639, however, the harassment caused by the pirates towards the Spanish became intolerable. Buccaneers had completely disrupted the role the Bay Islands were playing in Spanish shipping. Consequently, the Spanish Crown ordered the Indians removed so they could no longer provide for the pirates. The Spanish hoped that the removal of the natives would deter the pirates from hiding on the islands. However, the opposite occurred, and instead of leaving the Bay of Honduras, the British intensified their efforts to settle the islands. By the late 1600s however, buccaneering reached its zenith in the Bay of Honduras and Spanish shipping had been significantly disrupted. The English became the most successful in this pirating trade and eventually had the longest lasting impact on the Bay Islands. Among the most famous English pirates who took refuge on the islands were Morgan, Jackson, Coxen, Sharpe and Low. These names are still present on the islands as last names, settlement names, and business names.

The Bay of Honduras was in constant turmoil because of the many conflicts the Spanish were having with other European nations. Between 1638 and 1782 Spanish colonists constantly were hassled at the hands of the English. The Spanish and the British, for the next 150 years, struggled for control over the Bay Islands. This struggle left lasting impressions on the islands. In the late 1630s, the first English colonists attempted to establish permanent settlements on the Islands, specifically on Roatán. A Puritan-based company, Providence Company, laid the foundations for this settlement and assigned a North American colonial, William Claiborne, to Roatán. The English renamed the island Rich Island after Lord Henry Rich, Earl of Holland. However the specific settlement location has never been determined. Apparently engaged in agricultural, these colonists set the stage for another ethnic transition.

The first military occupations of the Bay Islands by the English began in 1742 and lasted seven years. It was the intentions of the British to take control of the entire Atlantic Coast. Fortifications were constructed on the Island of Roatán and at the mouth of the Río Negro (up the coast east of Trujillo). The forts built on Roatán were to provided a base to provoke rebellion on the mainland, so that the English could keep control of the logwood trade and that their cutters from Belize and Mosquitia had a place to go when the Spanish became aggressive. On numerous occasions Spanish colonists tried unsuccessfully to remove the English. In 1744 negotiations began to rid Roatán of its unwelcome English guests. However, it was not until late 1749 that the English finally evacuated the island in accordance with the Peace of Aix-la-Chapelle signed by Britain and Spain in 1748.

A second English occupation of the Bay Islands began thirty years later. During the period between these separate occupations little change was documented on the islands. In 1779, in an attempt to reach Lake Nicaragua, the English used the existing Fort George on Roatán as a military base. In 1782 the English were finally disposed of at the Battle of Port Royal Roatán. Fort George was burned, and the Spanish forces captured the remaining inhabitants of the island. Once again the Bay Islands were left to nature. Neither the English nor the Spanish formed permanent colonial settlements that have survived until the present.

In 1797 the Bay Islands received its first permanent settlers. Again Roatán was the site for this settlement. These permanent settlers were the Garífuna (Black Caribs). A colonial tribe, the Garífuna, evolved over 300 years ago on the island of St. Vincent in the Lesser Antilles. In the seventeenth century an English slave vessel shipwrecked off the island, and the African born slaves escaped. Carib Indians already inhabited the island, and the cultures began to mix.

This new ethnic group proved to be intolerable for the English settlers, and in 1797, over 2,000 Black Caribs were removed from the island and exiled to the Bay of Honduras. They were first abandoned on the uninhabited island of Roatán. The Spanish feared this was an attempt by the English to reestablish control and therefore moved the Garífuna to Trujillo. However, some managed to stay on the island and formed the settlement now known as Punta Gorda. In 1980, there were fifty-four villages along the Caribbean coast extending from northern Nicaragua to southern Belize.

The British and the Spanish continued to have sporadic conflicts until September 15, 1821 when the Central American Federation proclaimed its independence from Spain. Of the two European countries colonizing in this region during this time, Spain was the weaker, thus allowing Britain unhindered expansion along the Caribbean Coast from what is now Belize to Mosquitia.

Utila, led a rather quiet existence during the colonial conflicts of the seventeenth and eighteenth centuries. However, early in the nineteenth century, Utila began attracting "people who were basically farmers interested in good, free land that they could cultivate for subsistence crops". It has been suggested that the quiet existence of the island, was one of the attractions that lead these new settlers to relocate on Utila's Cays, and by the 1830s nearly a dozen people migrate.

Antillean Populations

In the nineteenth century the modern landscape of the Bay Islands began. Black Caribs, a few Spanish soldiers, two Americans, and two French families made permanent residences on the islands. Honduras, including the Bay Islands, became a sovereign state and the official position of the English was to adhere to this sovereignty. However, the Bay Islands were still seen as strategic for the domination of the Bay of Honduras. The Cayman Islanders became important in the British quest for the Bay Islands.

Established as British colonies, the Cayman Islands had developed an agrarian economy. With this reliance on agriculture slave labour was necessary. By 1830 the Angelo-Antillean settlers of the Cayman's were outnumbered 5 to 1 by its slave populations. The British Crown, in this same decade, began its abolition of slavery. The English on the Cayman

Islands, fearing the break down of their society, decided to relocate. They resettled in Belize and the Bay Islands. Suc-Suc Cay, Utila, and Coxen Hole, Roatán where the first settlements made by these people. Lord documents the first family of Cayman Islanders to settle on Utila in his 1975 work as follows,

> *"Joseph Cooper, his wife and nine children— two boys and seven girls— came to Utila from the Caymans by way of Belize. He was apparently one of the many land hungry British subjects of peasant or working class extraction that found the British isles too constricting. The Cooper family and an American named Samuel Warren who had been born in Massachusetts and served with Perry in the Battle of Lake Erie formed the nucleus of Utila's future populations. Warren and another American surnamed Joshua (who early dropped out of the historical picture) were already cultivating small plantations in the cays. Cooper also settled there to avoid the clouds of mosquitoes and sandflies that infested the bush-covered main island."*

A few years later, other families such as the Thompsons, Morgans, Boddens, Diamonds (or Dimon), Howells, and Gabourels had settled on Utila's Cays.

Subsequently, within a few years of the white landholding Cayman Islanders immigrating to Utila, many of the former Cayman slaves also moved to the Bay Islands. Likewise, settlers from the United States, British Honduras, Germany and Sweden took up residence on Utila. As 1858 came to a close so did the British colonial era on the Bay Islands. The islands legally became a part of greater Honduras. Many of the islanders left when this change took place but their culture has lasted until today.

Twentieth Century Utila

As Utila rounded the corner of the nineteenth century and entered into a new millennium, the ethnic and cultural melting pot that the island had become with the Anglo and Afro Cayman populations, Americans and Europeans, particular social stratifications were becoming evident. In 1975 when Lord was conducting his research on the remittance system on Utila he also paid particular attention to this developing phenomenon. He pointed out two key factors in understanding the social organizations that had arisen on the island. The first was that there were, and still are, three locally recognized strata based on ethnicity, and the second dealt more with gradations of prestige, that were present in these strata, based on income and lifestyle.

Social Stratification

In Utilian society, social distinctions are not simply a matter of socioeconomic differences between societal sectors. Rather, these strata lie in skin pigmentations that have created ethnic prejudices and stereotyping that are basic to the ordering of Utilians social existence. Lord compared these strata to the caste system of India, where a person is born into a certain caste and carries this distinction for life *(ibid)*. However, marriage into the highest strata is allowed, but those who married in are still second class to those who were born into that class. Utila's social hierarchy, according to *Lord (1975)*, developed in much the same way focusing on three colour based classes.

At the top of the social hierarchy are the "whites" of Utila. This position is based primarily on skin colour and with it comes social prestige, important local leadership roles, wealth, and occupation of prime real estate. Most of this segment of society came from the British West Indies colonies and made up the original founders of the modern settlement on Utila and its related cays. In 1975 nearly three-fifths of Utila's population was considered part of this class *(ibid)*.

The second tier of the social stratification system noted by Lord was made up of those Utilians with Afro-Antillean ancestry. In 1975, this group was collectively called "coloured" *(ibid)*. However, during my research on the island I did not hear this term used, rather the general term "black" was used to refer to this group, perhaps reflecting modern contacts with the United States. In 1975, as Lord documented, the "white" Utilians did not feel that the "black" Utilians were "mentally or morally inferior," however, he did note that, "there was a qualitative difference between themselves and coloureds that would forever separate the two groups even though they lived side by side". This attitude or these first two ethnic strata still exist on Utila maybe problematic, however there still is a geographic component related to these ethnic groups.

The third stratum, the more recent migrants from the mainland, is still very much present on the island. Since the mid 1960s Spanish Hondurans have become another part of the cultural mélange present on the Utila. Although native-born islanders see themselves as having no relation to these "Spaniards," this group is nevertheless carving its niche.

This group makes up the third rung of the social ladder on Utila. The term "Spaniard" denotes both an ethnic group and a derogatory epithet on the island. In the 1970s Spaniards were, "individuals of Spanish heritage (usually from mainland Honduras) who bear Spanish surnames, speak little or no English, and are common labourers recently arrived on Utila". This group is generally poorer than native Utilians, thus they live in the worst housing on the island and subsequently exist in some of the most extreme conditions. Locals see them as, "immoral…uncouth and uncivilized". Often times the term "Indian" is used interchangeably with Spaniard, not to denote differing physical characteristics but to further emphasize their perceived "uncivilized" behaviour *(ibid)*.

In 1975 Lord noted little interaction between the Spaniard and other Utilians. However, in recent years many young Utilian men have married mainland women. One such marriage occurred during the summer of 2001. Additionally, Lord did extensive research focused on marriages since 1881, and noted that only two "white"/"black" marriages had been documented *(ibid)*. He further remarked that the white men were not Utilians and had come with the merchant fleets because there seemed to be a standing consensus among islanders that "blacks" and "whites" did not marry. Similarly, the recent "black"/"white" marriages on the island had young black Utilian men marrying young white European women. As tourism continues to grow, these isolated incidences might be expected to become more common.

Geographical Boundaries

The social stratifications of Utila also manifest themselves geographically. Lord noted this phenomenon in 1975 and it was still present in 2001. There were six ethnically derived barrios or neighbourhoods in East Harbour and one on the combined two populated cays (Pigeon and Suc-Suc). Today, East Harbour has three more. Barrios on Utila were initially established for identification in official documents such as birth and death certificates and maps. However, islanders began using them as geographical identifications for what kind of Utilian one was, based on the strata discussed above.

In 1975 the barrios in order by size were, Punta Calienta, (the Point), Aldea de los Cayitos (the Cays), Cola de Mico (Monkey's Tail), La Loma (the Hill), Main Street, Sandy Bay and Holland. In the preliminary figures for the 2000 Honduran Census, the barrios listed in order of size were; Sandy Bay, La Punta (The Point), Cola Mico (Monkey Tail), Los Cayos (the Cays), El Centro (Main Street or the Centre of Town), Mamey Lane, La Loma (the Hill), Lozano, Camponado, and Holland (Figure). The number of houses in a given barrio determines size.

However, as *Lord (1975)* noted, size was not the important factor for these neighbourhoods. Instead the ethnic composition became the dominant factor when islanders would discuss the barrios. In 1975, Sandy Bay was almost exclusively "black," as it is today. A section of Cola de Mico was also "black." Main Street was completely "white" with the exception of one Spanish household *(ibid)*. The Point was made up of transplanted Cayans (a term used to distinguish those who live on the Cays from those who live on Utila) with a few scattered Spaniards and "blacks" *(ibid)*. The Cays consisted of only "whites" as did La Loma because this was the first area settled when the original Cayman Islanders moved from the Cays to the main island of Utila. Lord also noted other landscape features that came into play in areas of mixed ethnicity such as Cola de Mico. In this neighbourhood the Bucket of Blood Bar (which is still in operation) was a reference point in the landscape. Those that lived below the bar were either white or upper class "blacks," in contrast to those that lived above the bar who were manly lower class "blacks". Today many of these same general ethnic distinctions exist on Utila, with the inclusion of one predominantly Spanish neighbourhood, Camponado.

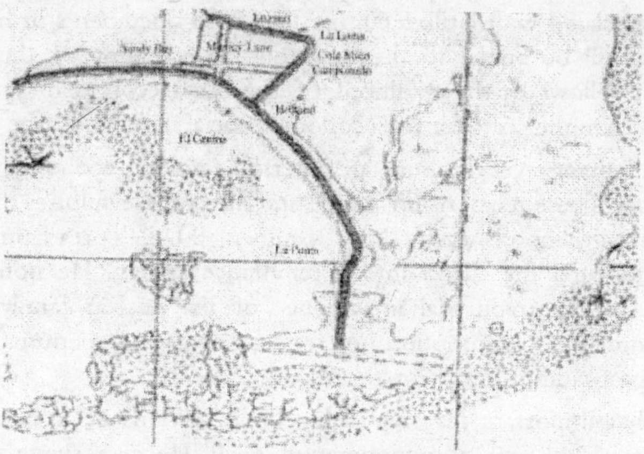

Figure 3: Neighbourhood Locations on Utila

However, because of the general increase in population and the new economic dependence on tourism, the 1990s the predominantly "white" and "black" areas of Utila became more diverse. For example, the Cays are no longer totally "white" but have a few Spanish and "black" families. Additionally, economics do not seem to play a major role in the original neighbourhoods, rather families seem to stay in place generation upon generation with little heed to their economic situations. The biggest changes that are taking place in relation to neighbourhoods have little to do with the islanders and more to do with developers who have followed the tourism industry.

Utila, and the other Bay Islands, have established themselves as a cultural hearth culminating into a distinct landscape apparent to modern visitors. From the Paya to the various European invaders an imposition of cultural identities has influenced this development. It seems that the geographic location of the islands made them more vulnerable to these landscape changes.

Economic History of Utila as a Precursor to Tourism

Utila has a diverse economic history. The islands' pre-Columbian inhabitants relied primarily on subsistence agriculture and, more importantly, were oriented to the sea. This seaward orientation also can be linked to all post-Columbian settlers of the island. This chapter will discuss the economic history of Utila as it relates to the different cultural groups that inhabited the island. These economic escapades can also be related to landscape change on the island. The unique cultural traits associated with Utilian culture that Lord documents in his work in 1975 will be linked to the new tourism economy of the island. Tourism follows in the traditions of the other economic systems as being yet another catalyst for economic, social, and landscape change.

Underlying every culture are interfaces among economy, society, and polity. These relationships shape and direct these cultures into their respective livelihoods. *Lord (1975)* documented Utila's preadaptive traits that stimulated the island into a remittance system. He noted such things as, "the traditional importance of the nuclear family as the production and consumption unit, and a heritage of maritime activity in shipping and fishing" on the island.

Other important features included orientations of individualism, commercialism, and non-cooperation *(ibid).* He also suggested that because of the nature of a remittance system (i.e. men being absent from the island for months at a time) the men enjoyed a level of indulgence and relaxing of laws and social norms when they return from sea. Therefore, an atmosphere of "rest and recreation" developed on the island as the men participate in "heavy partying and drinking". These pre-adaptive traits formed an easy transition from an economy based in agriculture to one dependent on maritime service *(ibid)*. These traits also helped in the development of the tourism industry on Utila today.

Pre-Columbian Economy

Only scant archeological evidence exists of the indigenous island cultures. However, documentation is available on the locations of settlement sites and the initial contact Columbus had with the indigenous people and their lands. The "80-Acre" site on Utila provides evidence that Indians lived and worked on the island. According to Columbus's notes on Bay Islands' vegetation and what is present today, early islanders probably hunted, cultivated local vegetation, and fished. In addition, his brother Bartholomew, who went ashore on the island of Guanaja, briefly described the local peoples and their "white grain from which they made a fine bread and the most perfect beer".

From the account of Columbus with the indigenous trader it is probable that islanders had contact with their mainland neighbours as well as with the other inhabited islands. According to Diaz del Castillo, while Cortés was visiting Trujillo, twenty years later fish and turkeys were brought to him that were found in abundance on the islands.

The archeological records and reports from the Spanish conquistadors suggest that the original Bay Islanders did not live in cultural seclusion. Instead, they traded with the mainland tribes close to Trujillo and possibly farther. These first inhabitants mastered the fine art of beer making as well as bread and possibly metallurgy. After Spanish Contact, for the next 136 years, the Bay Islanders were subjected to, and treated like, many other Caribbean populations. Following the initial slave raids religious "crusades" sought labourers to transport to plantations on Cuba and the Central American mainland. For the next 400 years the Bay Islands went through many economic transitions.

Encomiendas and Buccaneering

The Bay Islanders, unlike many other unfortunate indigenous Caribbean populations, survived initial contact with the Spanish only to be forced into servitude most likely on the Spanish encomiendas. The original economic components of the aboriginal Bay Islands, such as fishing, farming and trading, were not abandoned. These activities, especially farming, were probably expanded to fit the inclinations of the new Spanish colonial systems. Spanish needs not related to food production, such as craft production, were also begun.

Many of the initial reports concerning the physical geography of the islands characterized them as being fertile. The Spanish, who were based in Trujillo less than twenty-five years after contact, viewed the islands as a potential source for food. In addition, European livestock such as chickens and hogs were introduced to the islands, further diversifying the economy. This increase in diversity and eventual productivity gave the islanders prominence as the lone agricultural supporters of the port of Trujillo.

Some suggest that this increase in production was related to the introduction of encomienda system. This economic institution was initiated in Honduras in 1536 by Pedro de Alvarado and was documented in Trujillo in 1539. Early encomiendas were associated with significant landscape and cultural change on the islands as well as elsewhere in the New World. This system regulated all aspects of the indigenous persons' life from dwelling size and land standardization to religion and language.

Another change that took place because of this economic system dealt with the ways in which the islands were used and seen by the Spanish. Before the institution of the encomienda, the Bay Islands were treated as a single unit and the islanders were closely tied to each other in terms of production of goods and services to the mainland. However, this system broke the cohesion between the islands, and Utila was no longer attached to Trujillo. Instead, probably because of its geographical location, Utila was first attached to Puerto Caballos and then to Munguiche, coastal towns located farther to the west. At this time, Trujillo and Puerto Caballos were the major ports in this region and by 1582 the Bay Islands were producing sufficient foodstuffs to support the Spanish ports and ships returning to the Spanish homeland.

While the Spanish were successfully exploiting their new territories other European countries began to understand the value of the New World possessions. Spain's rivals thought that the best way to reap quick benefits would be to intercept Spanish ships of New World goods as they left their Central American ports. In 1643 the Bay Islands became a strategic point of interception because of their location in the Bay of Honduras.

As the Spanish encomienda system was thriving, the freebooters from France, Netherlands and mainly England found refuge in the islands. Because of the pirating activities, which began in the 1600s, the Spanish eventually called for the complete removal of the Bay Islands' population as well as any significant economic activity on the islands.

For Utila, it was nearly one hundred years before any real economic activity resurfaced.

Agricultural Phase and the Cayman Islanders

Unlike the other nearby islands, Utila had a relatively quiet existence during the Spanish and Buccaneering period. Although *Lord (1975)* found evidence of an encomienda present on the island there was not much in the way of pirate activity because of the island's physical geography.

Utila had fewer places for the pirates to hide and it was much more difficult for them to penetrate the surrounding reef. It has been suggested that, as England considered the abolition of slavery, plantation owners of the Caymen Islands began to look elsewhere to settle. Utila and its cays were an inviting possibility. The early 1830s brought a new culture and subsequently a new economic agenda to the island.

The Cayman Islanders were one of the first groups to settle permanently on the Bay Islands. The first wave of islanders chose the Utila Cays as their final destination. It has been documented that nearly a dozen people migrated here. These farmers were looking for a place to go that had free land so they could cultivate subsistence crops. Because these new residents were of British origin they began to create ties, mostly commercial in nature, with the closest British outpost in British Honduras (Belize). However, Utila was fairly autonomous during its first years after permanent settlement. Not until 1849 did the Bay Islands petition the Crown to be included in the British Empire. Their first attempts were directed unsuccessfully towards Belize but three years later the islanders were successful. The political compact did little to improve Utila's economy. Development began only in 1868 when the small island gained a relationship with the United States, one that lasts until the present. About 1854 the islanders began to cultivate coconuts and bananas, among other things, to sell to a few ports around the Bay of Honduras. This growing trade relationship spurred the original Cayman settlers to relocate to Utila (now East Harbour) where land was more plentiful for plantation agriculture. This new Utilian economy based on export farm production coincided with the United States agricultural import interests, especially fruit that took Utila's economy to a new level.

According to *Lord (1975)*, economic expansion occurred in 1868 when two schooners from Portland, Maine arrived on Utila to buy bananas and coconuts for sale in New Orleans. Limes, bananas, coconuts, and other tropical fruits were also exported to New York, Tampa, and Boston. As shown in table as late as 1881 Utila was shipping goods to the United States. However by the end of the nineteenth century, the much larger United States fruit companies such as Standard Fruit and United Fruit overwhelmed the small operations from Utila.

Table 1: Utilian Goods exported to New Orleans, 1881

Coconut	Banana	Plantain	Mango	Lime	Pineapple
950	1880 bunches	5000	5 lbs	1 lb	16 dozen

The initial fruit operation on Utila was much different than that which developed later. The system that was prominent in the mid 1800s relied on "pickups". The Bay Islands were just one of many tropical ports that these companies visited to support their business. However these "pickups" were time consuming and gave the companies little control over the quality of product they received. Therefore, by the early 1900s the precursors of the United Fruit in Tela and Standard Fruit in La Ceiba had clearly made themselves the new fruit ports and the "pickup" ports, like Utila and the rest of the Bay Islands, had become obsolete. In 1872, Utila's economy suffered another blow when the Bay Islands became a department of Honduras. Although the islands continued to govern themselves, Honduras wanted to enforce the Wyke-Cruz Treaty. In doing this, the Honduran government was essentially curtailing the islands' relationship with the United States. Rose commented on the situation as follows:

> *"...the (ensuing) change of laws gave a crippling blow, for some time, to the industries in the islands and to the hopes of the people. There was general discontent chiefly on account of the high import duties imposed under the new laws. And this discontent was perhaps excusable, because the people had always been accustomed to very low tariffs."*

The islanders honored the stipulations of the treaty to a certain extent, but many believed that they could continue living under English common law. This was a mistake on their part, and in 1902 the islands were visited by the H.M.S. Psyche, a vessel sent to inform the Bay Islanders that they were no longer British citizens. The islands did not prosper from the fruit business that was booming on the mainland, instead, the islanders, for the next 40 years, struggled to reverse the slump they had entered into at the turn of the century.

On Utila islanders were forced to begin making concessions, both socially and economically, while trying to regain their former lifestyles *(Rose 1904)*. American imported luxury items, which the islanders had become accustomed to purchasing, were no longer economically possible. Specialized plantation crops that were sold during the "pickup" period were diversified to fit the available markets. From 1929 to 1939, these agricultural markets declined; wage labour was scarce because little craft specialization had taken place on the island, and the shipping industry was defunct *(ibid)*. Thus, in 1929 the "Coconut Oil" years began on Utila *(ibid)*. Coconuts were one of the crops that had become more important after the brief fruit trade business ended and became the island's primary income producer. The process of making coconut oil was time consuming, labour intensive, and rather arduous *(ibid)*. The population of Utila became very resourceful during this time of economic depression and certain social and cultural traits began to form. In fact, the beginning of the next decade was a turning point for Utilian society.

In the words of *Lord (1975:36)*, "the decade of the 1940s marked a dramatic turning point in Utila's history, and two events in particular at the beginning of this period coloured the socio-cultural systems in Utila today." More importantly, for the purposes of this work, this new economic system and the cultural adaptations which developed out of it have been influential in the development of the tourism industry that dominates the island's economy today.

The Remittance Period

Although the coconut industry on Utila did see a veritable boom period and islanders began aspiring to travel and become educated in the United States, reality struck as the price of coconut dropped to only 5 US cents each in the 1950s. Yet another economic slump ensued on the island. However, large scale merchant shipping had reached the Bay of Honduras by the 1940s, and the versatile islanders, who were already competent and experienced sailors, took advantage of the opportunity. The heritage of Utila's men going to sea to fish and to carry products to market coupled with their attachment to Anglo-America, made the transition from farming and fishing to maritime service a logical and easy step. Additionally, the labour intensive cash crop farming in the insect-infested bush and the poor market conditions of the "post bellum" economy ensured that fishing and agriculture would never again be more than a part time income source for most Utilians. Many of Utila's banana and coconut plantations by 1950 had been destroyed by disease and hurricanes *(ibid)*. Therefore, the maritime service industry, which began during the 1940s, became the primary economic institution on the island.

In Charles Wilson's 1968 work, he discusses the beginnings of the merchant marine service in the Bay Islands. He traced its origins to World War II, when the United States, in 1940, leased some of the larger and better equipped banana ships for emergency defence duty *(ibid).*

By 1941, the United Fruit Company began sending representatives to Utila and the other islands to sign up men to work on their steamship lines. Shortly, some of the men found themselves working in the United States merchant shipping service. Neither Lord nor Wilson were clear on whether United Fruit was involved in the emergency leasing program or if they were simply training a reserve of sailors for their own use, nevertheless scores of Utilian men were acquiring marketable skills as the coconut industry dwindled. The remittance period in Utila's economic history was born out of necessity both for the Utilians and the United States. After World War II adult males ranging in age from 18 to 55, on regular basis left their island home to sail the open ocean. For periods of nine to twelve months, men would work for various shipping lines, sending their wages home *(ibid).* These jobs were a dependable source of income for the men and their families. Additionally, the fringe benefits while on the ships secured this occupation as a lasting economic industry for Utila. During this time, Utila again oriented itself to the United States.

The USA became the land of opportunity for many Utilians. Children were sent to New Orleans for schooling and many families subsequently moved to the United States. New York and New Orleans have large Utilian communities today. As the merchant business of the 1940s took off, many locals realized that trying to make a living solely on agriculture and reclaiming the lifestyle before the introduction of the remittance system was unrealistic. This fact was reinforced in 1961 when Hurricane Anna struck the Bay of Honduras. Although the hurricane did not strike Utila directly, according to Lord, some 75,000 coconut palms were destroyed approximately one-third of the islands' total *(ibid).* He also reported, for nearly two years following the event not a single plantain could be found growing on the island *(ibid).* Subsequently, few men were inclined to repair the damage and hopes of reestablishing an agricultural market on the island were dashed. Utila settled into the remittance system that still exists in some form, but tourism has become of increasing importance.

Many traditional elements of Utila's society pre-adapted it for the remittance system and more importantly for this discussion, for the developing tourism industry today. These traditions include an emphasis on individualism, commercialism, and consumerism or non-cooperation. Lord suggested that these pre-adaptations are intimately interrelated and share equal importance in motivating the islanders into economic situations *(ibid)*. Since the Cayman Islanders first began farming on the island a shared attitude of independent economic, social, and political action has created the basis for the cultural trait of individualism *(ibid)*. The first farmers were generally independent of their neighbours. The lack of inter-family dependency allowed men to leave the islands to take part in the remittance system because families were so independent.

As tourism began to develop as a viable industry on the island very little cooperative effort was seen and businesses started, and continue to run, as family operations. Commercialism and consumerism follow along these same lines in that it is rare to see any sort of cooperative work ventures. This attitude is still present today, and is evident in the constant price wars between dive shops and hotel owners and the general skepticism that has occurred when ideas of creating regulations on prices are introduced by foreign owners. Additionally social and political actions tend to be more self-serving. Since the time of the original settlers, one's prestige and other accomplishments have been considered a function of individual effort, thus preserving the ideas of non-cooperation *(ibid)*. These traits can still be seen as islanders only get "up-in-arms" if their personal businesses are being effect by another's actions. More importantly for this discussion were the adaptations islanders made during the remittance period concerning attitudes of "rest and relaxation" for the men who returned home from sea. In total the economic history of Utila has had many peaks and valleys, from subsistence agriculture to commercial agriculture to the remittance period and now tourism. However, these endeavours have fostered certain traits that have helped the islanders to survive.

Tourism Development on Utila

The tourist development of the Bay Islands is a forgone conclusion. No area of such beauty and such accessibility can remain undiscovered and unexploited. To yield their full potential, however, careful planning is indicated…It would be most unfortunate if the beauty of the Bay Islands was not available to all visitors to—and residents of—Central America. Nature has not created comparable attractions along the

Caribbean coasts of Guatemala, Nicaragua or Costa Rica. The Bay Islands are a truly regional resource. Before beginning a discussion of the history of the tourism industry on Utila, perhaps a note on tourist types is appropriate. Paul *Fussell (1980)* distinguished the tourist from three other types of people who take trips. His first classification is the explorer. Explorers seek the undiscovered and believe that no others have gone before. Christopher Columbus and his crew and the many other conquistadors who visited this part of the world during the colonial period are early examples. Travellers, Fussell's second type follow the explorers and attempt to learn about the newly discovered areas through study and experience. In the Bay Islands, people such as Mitchell-Hedges and his associates and William Duncan Strong, the first ethnologists and archeologists to visit the Bay Islands, are considered among this group. Travellers did not make it to the islands until early in the 20th century.

Fussell's definition of the tourist differs from the others because they seek areas already discovered by businesses and publicized by the media. People who want nothing to do with the mass stereotypical tourist destinations and seek only the most remote of places that they perceive to be more authentic Fussell labels the antitourist. These people, he believes, imagine themselves as travellers, however, the days of the explorer and traveller are long past because few places on Earth have not been visited by humans.

Fussell's typology lacks a category for the scoundrels, fugitives, and scallywags who visited the islands before they were developed by the modern Bay Islanders. Further, he does not suggest where academic researchers fit into this scheme. Still, utilizing his discussion, it is possible to determine when the first modern tourist reached Utila and that travellers came to the island well before tourism become a major economic component of the world market after World War II. The Bay Islands remained relatively remote until well into the twentieth century. Although they were accessible to wealthy explorers, scholars and the occasional fugitive, for the modern tourist, getting to the islands was difficult because the only transportation from the mainland was by small dories and fishing boats. Travellers such as Mitchell-Hedges gave accounts that portrayed images of a rustic, savage place with extensive reefs that held ship wrecks.

The possibility of pirate treasures hidden in the reefs lured the first major wave of tourists to the islands in the late 1970s. However, Utila's potential for tourism did not go unnoted by Rose in 1904, well before tourist began visiting the island. Ritchie, Davidson and Lord in the 1960s and 1970s, when an infant industry was beginning to develop on the islands, also noted the possibilities an economy based on tourism could bring to the islanders. Nevertheless, for Utila, it would be well into the 1980s before tourism became a significant component of their island economy. The conclusion of World War II brought a world boom in tourism and travel world wide. The Bay Islands and much of the western Caribbean, however, did not participate in the tourism explosion. Inadequate transportation, infrastructure, and boarding facilities were among the primary reasons for this lack of participation. The region also had acquired a reputation as being politically unstable.

In the late 1960s a diminutive modern tourism industry emerged in the islands as regular airline service from the mainland was initiated. In this same decade several popular periodicals suggested that the islands were perfect places for the adventuresome traveller who found sailing, diving and treasure hunting appropriate activities. Also fundamental in development of the tourism industry on the Bay Islands were the Honduran legislative actions taken in the 1980s to help the existing economic crisis. Additionally, the political unrest during the 1970s was resolved and a perception of peace throughout Central America contributed to the growing industry.

Though a modern tourism industry emerged in the 1960s it grew fairly slowly until the 1990s. Roatán had the largest number of hotels in 1960, while Utila and Guanaja each had only one. By 1989 Roatán's numbers had decreased by two leaving the island with only ten hotels while Guanaja's numbers had increased to four and Utila's to three. The inhibiting factors present during the 1960s, such as in adequate facilities and accessible transportation remained unresolved well into the 1980s.

Table 2 : Hotels on the Bay Islands from 1960-2001

	Roatan		***Guanaja***		***Utila***	
Year	***Hotels***	***Rooms***	***Hotels***	***Rooms***	***Hotels***	***Rooms***
1960-1969	12	81	1	H" 4	1	H" 2
1970-1979	11		4	H" 46	1	H" 5
1980-1989	10	168	4	46	3	34
1990-2001	59	953	18	178	28	330

A ferry service between La Ceiba and the island settlements of Utila, Oak Ridge, and French Harbour had been established but the transportation infrastructure on the islands improved very little. For example, Utila had no paved roads until the late 1990s aside from a small portion of Main Street that was paved in the early 1970s.

In 1988 through international assistance, Roatán's small airstrip outside Coxen Hole was enhanced to handle jet aircraft *(ibid)*. In that same year, Honduras's airline Tan Sahsa began offering regular airline services between the mainland and the island, from several Central American countries, and from Miami, New Orleans, and Houston *(ibid)*. Service into the United States lasted only a few years because in 1994 the United States banned the airline because of safety violations *(ibid)*.

Utila's airport is the smallest of the three islands and is currently unpaved, therefore no international flights have flown into the island. As of 2001 only two airlines service Utila, Sosa and Atlantic. Isleña Airlines recently discontinued services because the dirt runway was damaging the airplanes. Currently Utila has five daily flights, two in the morning, one at midday, and two in the early evening before dark. There are no scheduled flights after dark on the island because the runway is not equipped with properly lighted.

Figure 4 : Old Airport on Utila

In 1974 approximately 1,000 tourist visited the Bay Islands, however by 1988 this number had risen to approximately 15,000. The 1990s has been the decade for the Bay Islands' tourism industry. In 1997 roughly 93,000 tourists visited the islands. This number was nearly quadruple the islands population total in the 1988 census.

In the early 1990s approximately 11% of the islands' total labour force was employed in service sector jobs *(ibid)*. By the end of the decade nearly 80% of the islands' population was directly or indirectly dependent on the tourism industry *(ibid)*. Most islanders were employed as service personal with little or no training and those in management or executive positions were mostly foreign *(ibid)*.

The number of tourist facilities from 1985 to 1996 also grew substantially from 17 to 80 for all the islands. Utila's proportion of hotels increased from 18% to 30%; total number of rooms increased from 34 to 199. Of course, Roatán still attracts the greatest number of tourist. Roatán also has the greatest price range for hotels; 10$ to $1500 daily. Guanaja has the highest mean price for daily lodging $94.25, and as might be expected Utila is the least expensive ($18.04). Since 1996 Utila has experienced an even greater spurt of development and continues to grow today.

Table 5 : Tourists arrivals for the Bay Islands, 1970-2000

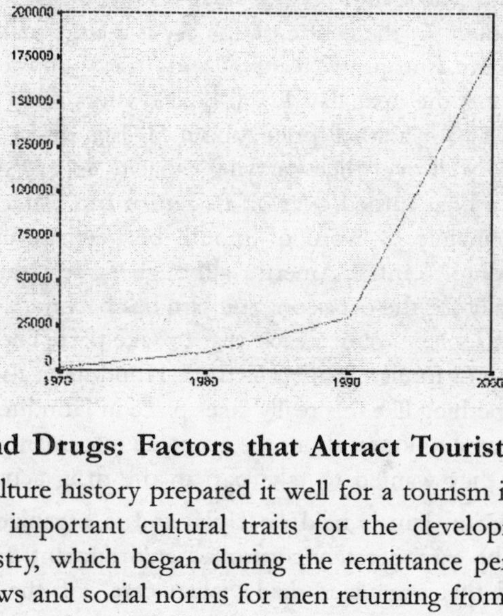

Sea, Sun and Drugs: Factors that Attract Tourists to Utila

Utila's culture history prepared it well for a tourism industry. One of the most important cultural traits for the development of the tourism industry, which began during the remittance period, was the relaxing of laws and social norms for men returning from sea. Because of this, an atmosphere of "heavy partying and drinking" became a common occurrence on the island.

These relaxed social laws have been important in drawing tourists to the island. Women are free to walk around in swimsuits and men in shorts without being harassed by locals as might occur on the mainland. Alcohol and drugs are easily accessible on the islands and local law enforcement officials rarely make arrests for public drunkenness or drug possession. When they do, however, if the suspect can pay their fine, they are released within 24 hours. Utila has become so well known for its drug activity that an event was created to play off of this reputation. In August of 1998, Utilians hosted the first Sun Jam festival on Water Cay. In only four years the event has become the epitome of drinking, drugs, and partying on the island. People from all over the world visit Utila to take part in the festival. It has become so popular that the organizers feel having another in the spring could be financially beneficial for the island.

There are two main organizers (one local and one local foreign) although many others on the island participate. The organizers start receiving shipments of drugs weeks in advance as they prepare for the masses of tourists who are expected to participate (personal communications). These organizers also section off the small cay to local businesses who want to set up small booths to sell food and drinks (mostly alcoholic). At the centre of the cay is a large makeshift bar and D.J. booth where European "techno" and "trans" music can be heard playing well into the next day. Local boat owners ferry tourist to and from Water Cay for a small price (about 50 Lps or $3 US). They are usually packed well over their carrying capacity as was shown the year before when a boat turned over on its return trip. Advertising for the event occurs mainly by word of mouth between groups of tourists travelling through Central America although there is an Internet site set up especially for the occasion. Sun Jam has become a cult-like event as many "Sun Jamers" return each year to take part. The festival is not solely made up of foreign tourists as many Hondurans also visited Utila, "to see if something like this really takes place in Honduras." No matter how people came to know about the event, all informants had one thing in common, they wanted to take part in the drug activity.

Because Sun Jam is held on Utila, and is organized by locals, it appeared to be a moderately controlled environment. For example, it was reported that organizers had "taken care" of the police well in advance so that none were seen on Water Cay during the festival. This sense of security may also play a part in the popularity of Sun Jam as many informants expressed their reservation about taking part in drug activities in other places in Central America. However, on the Friday before the festival, an American military helicopter landed on the island. It was never confirmed why it had come and no one ever saw military walking around the island, but many suspected a major international drug bust. An attempt was made to determine the number of tourists on the island during this event. One local hotel and dive shop owner said that all rooms on the island were occupied so Many "Sun Jamers" where leaving for Water Cay the day before the event started to set up tents and hammocks. One estimate of the number of partiers was over 500. This number seems possible if all the hotel rooms were filled because at least 330 rooms are now available on the island and more than half of these are able to sleep more than one person. Additionally, a number of multiple occupant apartments are available. All included, the total occupant load of the island is well above 500.

The Sun Jam festival makes up a sizable portion of the summer tourism economy. There was no other time during the summer of 2001 that all the hotels were full and lines would form outside restaurants. Although it last only a weekend, the financial potentials for the local industry has become an important part of the summer tourism season.

The drinking and partying atmosphere is not the only draw for Utila. In fact before drugs were a major part of the Utilian allure, small groups of people were visiting the islands to explore, dive and fish the reefs. In the 1960s the islands' reefs and the possibility of "sunken treasures" attracted groups of American and European tourists to the island.Long before the local diving industry was established, fully equipped groups would visit the island and pay locals to take them to the reefs and lead them on underwater expeditions. On occasion these early divers initiated destructive practices when they removed objects hidden in the reefs. One diver reportedly used dynamite to reach the Spanish treasures that had been encased in the reefs. However, the Bay Islander's have also been accused of destroying the reefs.

Other tourists were more interested in fishing the still plentiful waters surrounding the island and discovering Utila's "pristine" island environment. By 1980 Utila had entered into its present economic phase.

Emergence of the Present Tourism Industry

From about 1960 onward a small but relevant tourism industry was beginning to form on the island. As early as 1965, in the report by Ritchie and his associates, Utila was recognized for its inexpensive appeal. The group wrote,

> *"The initial development of Utila should attempt to maintain a balance between the bargain appeal (the present boarding house charges $3 dollars per day American plan) and accommodations of quality that can be promoted by U.S. travel agencies...Design should be of high*

standards and in keeping with the architecture of the town. The objective is first-class comfort and housekeeping, without luxuries."

These first tourists were made up of recreational sailors, fishermen, and SCUBA divers along with the occasional "hippie". In 1971, when Davidson carried out his survey of the Bay Islands tourism facilities, Utila had only one small hotel, the Jimenéz. A few years later, when Lord conducted his research on Utila he noted the presence of three local bars, including the most famous and the only one still in operation: the Bucket of Blood Bar. As shown in Figure, just a handful of facilities existed before 1980. However, when the Honduran Government realized the islands' potential as a means to end the economic crisis of the 1980s, Utila, along with the other three islands, began to reap the economic benefits of new governmental legislation.

The periods of the most intensive growth can be linked to the establishment of these policies. The implications of these policies for landscape and cultural change have been important in this discussion. However, in this section, I will reconstruct the emergence of the industry on the island using dates acquired from locals and other documents from local tourism facilities.

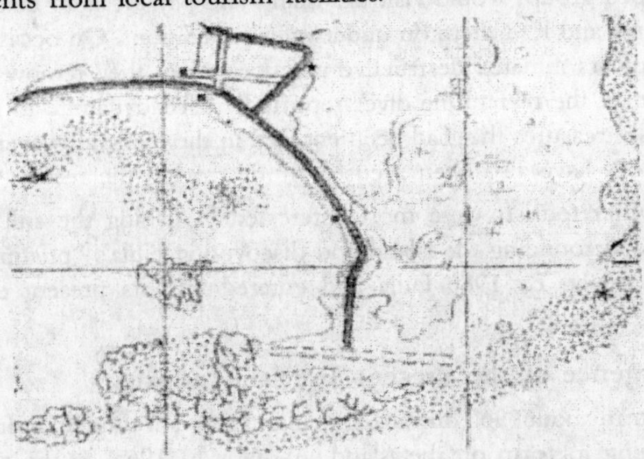

Figure 6 : Tourism facilities on Utila before 1980

Aside from Hotel Jimenéz, before 1980 Utila had one other family owned hotel, Hotel Trudy. A second hotel was begun sometime in the mid 1970s but was never finished. Its skeleton is visible on a ridge west of town. Locals say that an American named Duncan began the hotel. However, he ran out of money and left the island, "never to be seen again" *(Rafeal 2001).* Now, the hill site is known by locals as Duncan

Hill. As one of the few high outcrops of coral on the island the view is panoramic over the entire settlement of East Harbour. The hotel ruins are now home to ladino squatters. In addition to the two boarding facilities, Utila had one travel agency, (Morgan's Travel) (site unknown), two restaurants (site unknown), a general store (site unknown), three bars and an airstrip. As figure shows, before 1980, tourism facilities on Utila were rare and the industry was still in its infancy. The situation changed during the 1980s.

As SCUBA diving became more popular worldwide after the 1970s the flow of tourist increased to the island. The first organized dive schools were established during the 1980s and included, Cross Creek Dive Centre, Utila Water Sports, and Utila Dive Centre. Three new hotels were also built, Cross Creek Hotel, Celena, and Blueberry Hill, and the first small resort was built in East Harbour (Utila Lodge). However, Utila Lodge was not advertised as a resort until the mid 1990s.

Cross Creek Hotel began a trend that has been followed in recent years, that is, dive shops build their own hotels or establish contracts with existing hotels for rooms. This arrangement allows the dive schools to advertise packages that give their clients cheaper rates on rooms. These arrangements have caused conflicts among locally owned dive shops and foreign owned dive shops. Cross Creek, along with its dive shop and hotel, also constructed a restaurant to complete its tourism complex.

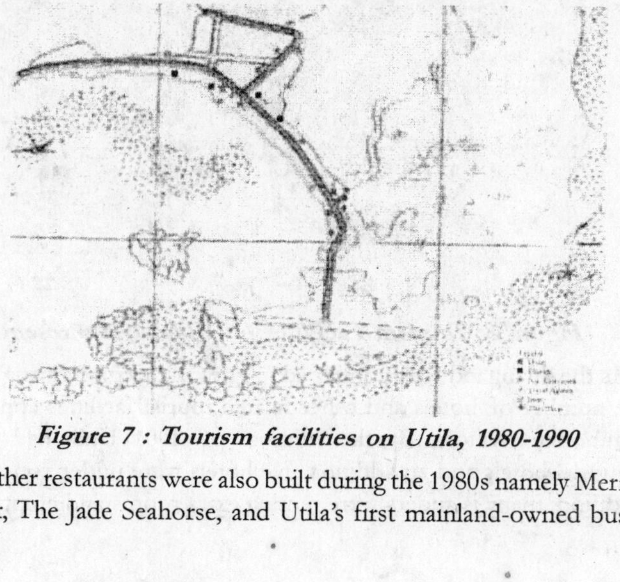

Figure 7 : Tourism facilities on Utila, 1980-1990

Other restaurants were also built during the 1980s namely Mermaid's Corner, The Jade Seahorse, and Utila's first mainland-owned business,

Las Delicias. Additionally, a second travel agency was built, as well as a bank, Hondutel telecommunications office, and two supermarkets. As Figure shows, the decade of the 1980s began the escalation of the modern industry, with diving being its primary attraction.

Utila is known worldwide for being one of the "cheapest" places in the world to dive and thus attracts a certain type of tourist. The establishment of the first dive centres and the understanding of the type of tourist the island was attracting created a more coherent industry. Local businesses focused their attention and efforts towards building on this attraction. As each new diving school was built a hotel soon followed. With the exception of the three resorts, all of the other tourist related businesses stayed within the "unspoken" price parameters.

The 1990s brought the greatest changes to Utila's tourism industry and by the summer of 2001 Utila had developed into a thriving diving-oriented tourist centre. Today the island has 11 dive shops, reduced from a high of 14. Two dive shops, Sea Eye Dive Centre and Reef Resort Dive Shop, closed shortly after opening because of internal competition. After the Reef Resort Dive Shop closed in 1997 the owners converted the building into the Reef Cinema, one of two places on the island where films can be viewed. Within an eight year period eight dive shops have opened and are flourishing on the island (figure).

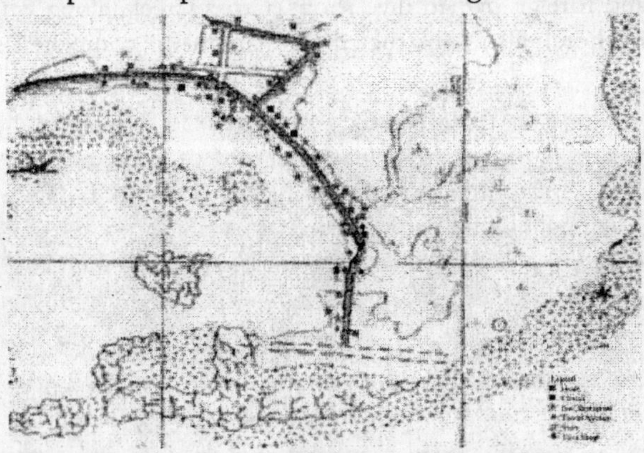

Figure 8: Tourism Facilities on Utila. 1990-Present

As the diving industry continued to grow, an accompanying increase in the number of hotels and other related tourist facilities appeared to accommodate visitors. By the summer of 2001 Utila had 28 fully operational hotels and an addition five hotels were under construction. In addition, many islanders were renting extra rooms and empty houses to tourists who wanted to stay on the island for longer periods of time. Some 19 new restaurants, bars, and cafés were also constructed between 1990 and 2001. These new facilities were built especially for the growing tourist industry. In addition to the new dive shops, hotels and restaurants that were established in the last 11 years some 23 other tourist related facilities have also been built. These businesses include three internet shops, two bicycle rental shops, several souvenir shops, several laundry services, several boutiques, two community health centres, several household good stores and two bottled water businesses.

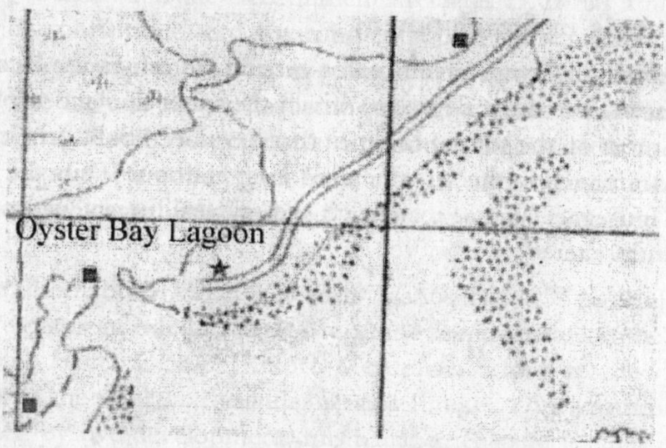

Figure 9: Oyster Bay Lagoon with % Hotels and * Restaurant

The bottled water business beginnings are in direct correlation with the escalating numbers of tourist to the island. Before the 1990s Utilians used well water and cistern water for drinking and other related needs. Imported bottled water was available for consumption on the island, however, when large numbers of foreigners start visiting the island locals saw the potential for personal profit. Therefore the two businesses began operation. Since 1970 nearly 49% of the tourist related facilities constructed, were built in the settlement of East Harbour on unoccupied land. While 51% of the facilities were placed in existing buildings or on land formally occupied. Of this 51%, 25% of the new facilities were housed in converted private dwellings. Although only 49% of the new buildings were built on unoccupied land the landscape and land-use patterns existent on Utila before tourism became an important economic factor were beginning to undergoing change.

Utila does not have the infrastructure that the other islands possess, such as 24-hour electricity or island-wide sewage disposal or plumbing. The island's electricity comes from a diesel powered-generator. In 1965 the generator ran only during the early morning and early evening, less than nine hours a day. Many islanders remember this time and joked that if the generator came on during the night it meant someone had died. A generator still produces the power on the island. It normally runs from six in the morning until midnight. Because of fuel shortages and frequent mechanical problems, neighbourhood outages often occur. Such inconsistencies required that tourist facilities have their own generators to guarantee their services.

New Trends in Development

Previous observers have noted a general pattern to the location of tourist facilities and the degree to which they alter the landscape. Until recently most of the tourist facilities that have been built on Utila have been concentrated in the settlement of East Harbour. Thus the islands' natural landscape, such as mangrove and tropical forests, had not been significantly altered.

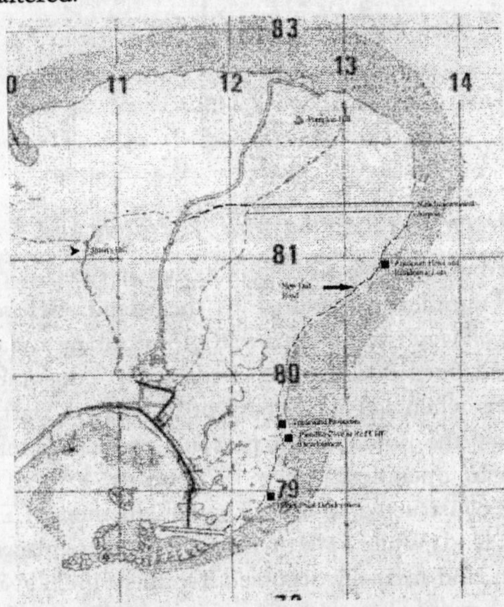

Figure 10: Development on the Eastern end of Utila

However, the new trend to locate tourist facilities and residential areas away from the existing settlement of East Harbour has caused drastic changes to the natural landscape. These new developments have been constructed to cater to higher paying clientele and provide services beyond room and board. In the 1990s Utila acquired its first two resorts of this nature, the Laguna Beach Resort and the Reef Resort. Additionally, by the end of the decade two residential development projects had been started that have significantly altered the natural landscape.

There are two areas on Utila in which these developers have located: on the eastern tip of the island where the fragile iron shore is located and along the southwestern shore facing the cays. The development underway on the eastern tip of the island incorporates four different sites, including "Rocky Point Estates," "Paradise Cove at Red Cliff," an unnamed site, and "Aquarium" hotel and residential lots. However, for the purpose of this discussion, this area will be referred to as one site. Both developments incorporate beach-front property in otherwise uninhabited parts of the island. It seems these developers bought large chunks of land for a relatively low price and then cleared the natural vegetation so that they could section the land off into smaller lots to sell to foreign tourists. We specify foreign tourists because, as many islanders explained to me, they can not afford to buy these lots from the developers. An estimated price of one such lot on the eastern tip was about $ 80,000 US dollars. These properties are being brokered through locally owned Alton's Real Estate, and American-owned Utila Island Properties.

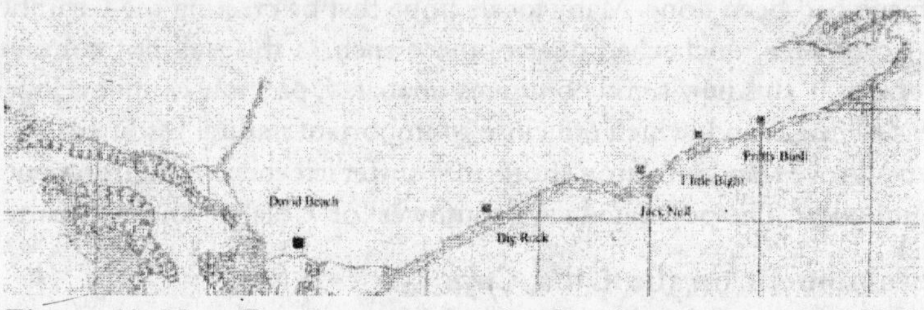

Figure 11: New Development on the Southwestern end of Utila

The development on the southwestern section of the island was purchased and developed first, and already has attracted foreign buyers. Advertised prices for lots, including small houses, begin at $100,000 US dollars. The second development, on the eastern tip, came with the construction of the new airport. When the large machines were brought to the island to be used in the airport's construction, contractors soon realized the roads in the existing community were not strong enough or wide enough to allow passage. Therefore, a new road was cut beginning at the northern end of the old airport and wrapping around the northeastern coastline of the island. The real estate development began soon after this road was cut because, before, this area was virtually inaccessible except by boat. Essentially these areas will become foreign enclaves, well separated both geographically and economically, from the rest of the community on Utila. Additionally, if this development continues unchecked, a previously undeveloped area, close to mangrove habitant, tropical forests, and the delicate iron shore, may well suffer irreversible damage. During the summer of 2001, many locals became aware of the possible negative implications of these new developments. However, they soon discovered they had little say in the way in which land was sold and developed on the island. Therefore, fearing what had happened on Roatán, many local business owners petitioned the local government officials to create a Chamber of Commerce. This surge of local community participation was fueled by one of the owners of the sites on the eastern tip of the island.

An American man had begun developing land in this area, however, his land did not have direct access to the water because of the presence of the iron shore. Additionally, he had already sold the land near the iron shore and begun cutting paths to the beach without going through the proper channels and without acquiring the proper permits. Soon after he was fined and had to replace the coral he removed but the damage had been done. Many locals hope that by creating the Chamber of Commerce, unchecked development such as this will not continue to occur. If this new trend continues unabated, previously undeveloped areas of the island, which are close to important natural resources such as mangrove stands and iron shore, may suffer irreversible environmental degradation. The populated cays southwest of Utila are another matter.

Development on the Utila Cays

The two largest cays, Suc-Suc and Pigeon, have developed into a thriving fishing community separate from Utila. During the first surveys of the area in the 1970s, no tourism facilities were documented. However, since 1980 three small hotels have been constructed: Hotel Kayla, Lone Star Hotel, and Vicky's Rooms (found above Vicky's General Store). There is also a small house for rent at the west end of Pigeon Cay.

Many Cayens (This term is meant to distinguish those people who live on the cays fro those who live on Utila. It is a term that is used by Cayens and Utilians.) expressed that they serve as a day excursion spot for the tourists who are staying on Utila. One business owner expressed that much of her daily business comes from the diving boats.

She said, "We are close to one of their favourite dive spots, so the instructors bring their divers here for lunch instead of going all the way back to Utila." Rarely, however, are the Cayen hotels full. It was suggested that their tourism lags behind the main island because they lack sufficient resources. For example, no fresh water wells exist on the cays and the closest well on Utila is not potable. Rain cisterns are present on the cays, which provide minimal water for washing purposes, but bottled drinking water has to be imported from the mainland or from the main island. Allowing large numbers of tourist onto the cays, many Cayens feel, could be detrimental to their water supply. Garbage disposal, which is already a problem, would also be magnified, if tourism were to expand. Many Cayens expressed their contentment with their tourism status.

Figure 12: Pigeon and Suc-Suc Cay

The ten smaller, uninhabited cays, however, have become popular tourist spots. These include Diamond Cay, Jack O'Neil's Cay and Water Cay. Diamond Cay, just off the south eastern tip of Suc-Suc Cay, once housed the Utila Cay's Dive Shop and Hotel. Tourists can now rent or buy the abandoned structures. Jack Neil's Cay, Morgan Cay and Sandy Cay can also be rented (house included) for about 400 Lps a day ($27 US). Water Cay has become a favourite spot for tourists and islanders and has earned the reputation as being the "party island." To access the cay a caretaker charges one lempira a day. Hammocks are also available to rent from the caretaker's house for ten Lps. Utila's cays did not participate in the tourism boom found on the main island. Although, they do receive some business from the tourists that visit Utila, their economy has not become as dependent on this industry. Instead, this community continues to rely on the sea for its livelihood.

Defining Utila's Tourism Source Regions

The diversity of tourists that visit Utila is increasing. While discussing tourism issues with a few locals during the summer of 2001 this subject was broached. From their statements it seemed reasonable to infer that it was no longer just North Americans who were making up Utila's tourist population (or at least those staying in hotels).

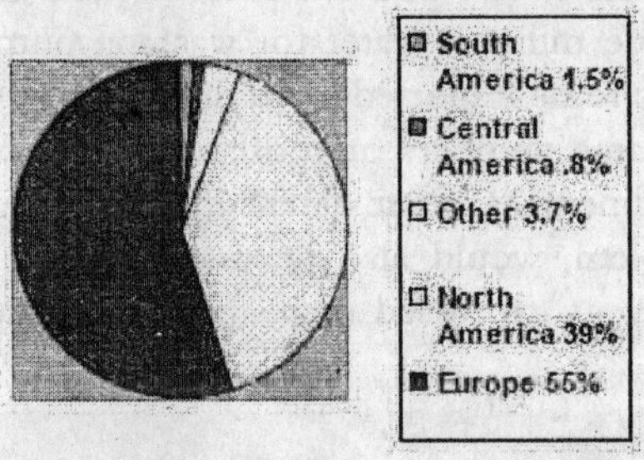

Table 13: Tourists Percentages for 1999 on Utila

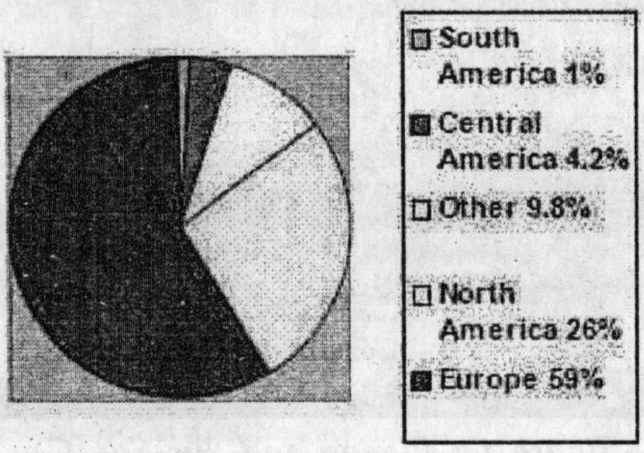

Table 14: Tourist Percentages for 2000 on Utila

This differs from documentation taken in the early years of the industry for the islands and especially the mainland. North Americans, more specifically those from the United States, have been documented as the major group visiting the North Coast and Bay Islands. However, today Europeans seem to make up the largest group on the island. Therefore, in trying to prove this shift I looked at several hotel records to try and determine places of origin for the island's tourists. By law each operating hotel on the island must keep a logbook that has all pertinent information about their visitors, such as, names, dates staying, place of passport issue, and where the tourist came from before arriving on Utila. I surveyed five of the local hotels ranging from the least expensive on the island to one of the higher priced hotels. It seemed important to do this to get an accurate view of the island's situation.

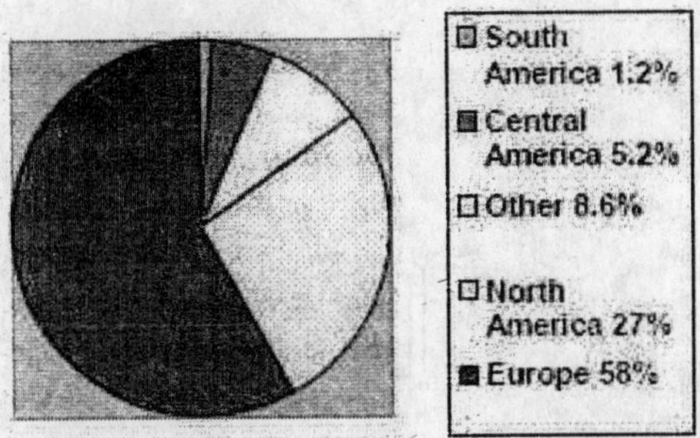

Table 15: Tourist Percentages for 2001 (Jan-Aug) on Utila

However, hotel owners either do not keep or would not divulge records any earlier than 1999. For each hotel it was necessary to make tallies of each person according to country. From the information gathered five categories seemed appropriate to get an accurate representation. The term "other" was used to group all persons not from Europe, North American, Central American, or South American because there were so few people not from one of the other categories. However, the diversity of this group is definitely increasing. The largest group visiting the island originated in Europe. North Americans were second. The stream of Central Americans is gradually increasing.

From the first travellers that ventured to the island, to the modern tourist, Utila's distinctive culture and impressive natural environment has spurred an economically prosperous industry. As the islanders realized this potential prosperity, tourism has become a significant economic factor. The most rapid phase of development occurred during the period from 1990 to 2001. The industry continues to grow, as is exemplified by the five hotels under construction.

However, until recently, development has been confined to the existing settlement of East Harbour and minimal landscape and land-use change has taken place. At the end of the last decade, Utila entered into a new phase of development that mimics the practices in other popular tourism sites such as Cancun and Jamaica. These practices include the building of larger more lavish resorts and housing developments away from the existing local community. In conjunction with the islands prosperity and as this new phase begins, large numbers of migrants have been flocking to the island seeking steady work. These groups bring cultural attributes that are different from those already in existence.

2

Sustainable Tourism Development in Small Island

Experience Gained and Problems Encountered by Small Island Developing States in Tourism

Economic Impact

Overview of Performance: Tourism is often identified as a promising growth sector in small island developing States. It offers one of the few opportunities for economic diversification in very small islands. Tourism has many linkages with other economic sectors, and if integrated into national development plans with adequate provisions for inter. sectorial linkages, it can contribute to the growth of all tourism-related activities in all of the major economic sectors-agriculture, including fishing, industry and services, including transportation. At present, the extent of tourism activities in small island developing States varies widely between geographical regions as well as between countries within regions. Likewise, the economic benefits derived from tourism are diverse. In some small island developing States, tourism has become the major contributor to the gross domestic product GDP), while in others it is still relatively undeveloped.

It is well known that in small island developing States, the scope for economic diversification and growth is limited. Their key constraints are small land areas and small populations. The relatively larger ones have the human resources potential to support a number of economic sectors viably and thus to benefit from linkages of those sectors with the tourism sector. The smaller ones, however, do not have such potential and will therefore have to be more reliant on imports to meet the material demands of the tourism sector. Other things remaining equal; the net benefits, i.e., domestic value-added per visitor, derived by the smaller islands from tourism will be relatively smaller.

The main objectives of the promotion of tourism as a growth sector are to accelerate the growth of national incomes, gainful employment, foreign exchange earnings and government tax revenues. A thorough evaluation of the contribution of tourism in small island developing States with respect to these parameters is at present hampered by the incompleteness of data. In a sample of 29 small island developing States for which data are available, gross direct receipts from tourism as a percentage of GDP ranged from a meagre 1 per cent to 88 percent on the average during the period 1989-1993. In this sample of countries, tourism and tourism-related activities have become the mainstay of the economy in Antigua and Barbuda, Aruba, Barbados, Saint Lucia, the Bahamas, Saint Kitts and Nevis and Seychelles, or mostly in the small island developing States in the Caribbean. Important exceptions apart, tourism makes the least contribution to national income in most of the African and Pacific small island developing States.

With a few exceptions, most small island developing States have realized a fast, although diverse, pace of growth of gross tourism receipts in nominal terms in recent years. During the period 1989-1993, in 24 out of 34 for which data are available, the growth of gross receipts from tourism ranged from 2 per cent to 61 per cent per annum on the average. In most, it exceeded 10 per cent and in 9 it was 15 per cent or more. Generally, but not universally, the fast pace of growth reflects low initial levels of receipts from tourism. Even among those with low initial levels, several countries did not do so well.

In view of the constraints faced by small island developing States in promoting exports of goods in an increasingly competitive and fast-changing international economy, by and large, these States are giving increasing importance to tourism as a source of raising their foreign exchange earnings. The available data show that during the period 1980-1992, for a sample of 26 small island developing States, the percentage increase in the ratio of foreign exchange earnings from tourism to total export earnings ranged from 2 per cent to 453 per cent, In 10 of them, it exceeded 50 per cent. In 1992, the contribution of tourism to total export earnings in 23 countries ranged from a meagre 2 per cent to 83 per cent; in 13 of them it exceeded 25 per cent.

The data on average daily expenditures per visitor for 10 countries ranged from US$ 41 to $304 in 1992. In 1989, average daily expenditures per visitor for 23 small island developing States ranged from $37 to $226. The diversity of performance even in these small samples is significant. It suggests that those countries that want to promote tourism as a growth sector need, in addition to adequate investments in tourism infrastructure, to make greater efforts to enhance the diversity and quality of goods and services they sell to visitors.

Countries that have relatively full employment are less interested in the employment potential of expansion of tourism than those that have substantial unemployment. The employment advantages of tourism are twofold: first, the industry is labour-intensive, and secondly, much of the employment is relatively unskilled. Consequently, investment in tourism produces a higher and faster increase in employment than equal investment in other activities. Tourism creates employment directly in the tourism industry as well as in industries providing goods and services to the tourism industry. Data on direct employment in the tourism industry is extremely scanty. It may be inferred, however, that the impact of tourism on employment in small island developing States, where tourism makes an important contribution to national income, is considerable. In 15 Caribbean tourist destinations, a total of 77,319 hotel rooms accounted for 88,697 jobs, equivalent to 1.15 jobs per room. With the recent decline in the agriculture sector, in particular sugar and bananas, the relative share of tourism in employment has risen. In the South Pacific, tourism generated 27,500 jobs in direct employment in 1991 in the 10 member countries of the Tourism Council of the South Pacific (TCSP), with a population of about 5 million. Fiji accounted for 10,340 of this amount. In the Mediterranean region, overall employment in Cyprus exhibited an upward trend during the period 1980-1992, with the fastest growth occurring in tourism and related services. Employment in these occupations doubled from 33,000 jobs in 1980 to 64,000 in 1992. Hotels, restaurants and retail trade increased their share of employment from 17.9 per cent in 1980 to 24.3 per cent in 1992. In 1993, the total contribution of tourism to employment in Malta was roughly estimated at about 17 per cent of the labour force. In the African region, the available data for Mauritius and Seychelles indicate that during the period 1990-1994, the share of direct employment in tourism in total employment rose from 3.4 per cent to 4.8 per cent in Mauritius and remained stable at about 18 per cent in Seychelles.

While the employment objective remains important for several small island developing States, the level of wages in the tourism industry is also important. The available information indicates that most jobs created in tourism are low-paying. This is to be expected in countries with high rates of unemployment, particularly of unskilled labour. The creation of low-paying jobs in the tourism sector in countries with relatively high rates of employment is the result of the strong pull factor of the relatively less physically demanding jobs in the tourism sector from more arduous jobs in the primary sector. This process exerts pressure on producers in the primary sector to modernize and increase capital intensity so as to permit a rising level of real wages; otherwise, the sector will lose its labour force and dwindle. This could marginalize important productive activities such as agriculture and fishing, and weaken the linkages of other sectors with tourism reducing the benefits derived from the tourism industry.

Tourism is likely to play an even more important role in the growth and development of small island developing States if appropriate measures are taken to invigorate other sectors, in particular agriculture and fishing, so that they can more adequately meet tourist demand for consumer goods from domestic sources. Except for the very small ones, small island developing States can, with careful planning and provision of adequate facilities such as credit for mechanization, modernization and diversification, where necessary, support viable agricultural and fishing activities, as well as light manufacturing in addition to tourism. As inter sectorial competition raises wage rates and incomes and reduces labour supply to the tourism sector, emphasis can be shifted to up-market tourism, with reliance on a slower rate of growth but of higher-spending visitors.

In evaluating the direct contribution of tourism to national income, gross levels of incomes or gross foreign exchange earnings are much less significant than net earnings after deductions have been made for all necessary foreign exchange expenditures of the tourism industry. The primary leakages of foreign exchange earnings from direct tourist expenditures arise from: (a) imports of materials and equipment for construction, (b) imports of consumer goods, particularly food and drink, (c) repatriation of profits earned by foreign investors, (d) overseas promotional expenditures and (e) amortization of external debt incurred in the development of hotels and resorts. The impact of these leakages varies greatly from country to country depending on the ability of countries to produce the goods and services necessary to meet the needs of the tourism industry. The estimates available for 17 countries or territories presented below show that the higher leakages pertain to small island economies.

Leakage of foreign exchange from gross tourism receipts (Percentage)

1.	Fiji	56
2.	Cook Islands	50
3.	Saint Lucia	45
4.	Mauritius	43
5.	Aruba	41
6.	Hong Kong	41
7.	Jamaica	40
8.	United States Virgin Islands	36
9.	Seychelles	30
10.	Sri Lanka	27
11.	Antigua and Barbuda	25
12.	Cyprus	25
13.	Kenya	22
14.	Republic of Korea	20
15.	New Zealand	12
16.	Yugoslavia	11
17.	Philippines	11

Source: Travel and Tourism Analyst No. 3

Direct income from tourism provides only a partial picture of the contribution of tourism to national income. A complete picture would call for the estimation of tourism income multipliers in each small island developing State.

Since expenditures of tourists give rise to the generation of additional incomes throughout the economy, the incomes and the associated employment thus induced can be considerable. Aside from the savings propensity of the local population, the size of the tourism income multiplier in a particular small island developing State depends on the extent of leakages of tourist expenditures overseas. The less the leakage of direct tourist expenditures, the higher the tourism income multiplier. Because of the complexities relating to the requisite data, however, the estimation of tourism income multipliers is beyond the scope of the present report.

Regional Perspectives

At the regional level, the development of the tourism industry is more advanced in the Mediterranean and Caribbean small island developing States than in those located in the Asia-Pacific and African regions. The two Mediterranean small island developing States, Cyprus and Malta, have experienced brisk expansion of tourism in the past, which is reflected by the high share of tourism in their GDP and their total foreign exchange earnings. In both of them, however, industry remains the dominant sector. The good performance of tourism in these countries is explained in part by their advantageous location in the vicinity of high-income European countries, particularly the United Kingdom of Great Britain and Northern Ireland, their main source market.

In the Caribbean, with a larger number of small island developing States, the pattern of economic performance has become closely linked to the performance of the tourism industry. The direct contribution of tourism in terms of its share in GDP and export earnings is high in most of them. In the wider Caribbean, travel and tourism is the largest relative contributor to the regional economy, at 31.5 per cent of GDP. While in some, the economic base is relatively diversified, in the majority of them most other activities have become increasingly linked to tourism, with agriculture and industry lagging behind. This is particularly the case in the smaller islands which have become essentially service economies. The development of tourism in the Caribbean has been helped by considerable amounts of foreign investments and the fact that they are located in the tropics but in proximity to high-income North America.

The level of development of tourism and its contribution to economic development is more uneven and generally much lower in small island developing States of the Asia-Pacific region than in those in the Mediterranean and Caribbean. In most of them, the level of general economic development is also much lower. Six of them-Maldives, Samoa, Vanuatu, Tuvalu, Kiribati, and Solomon Islands-are actually classified as least developed. Tourism activities are concentrated in only a few. The contribution of tourism to national income is significant only in Fiji, Vanuatu, Samoa, Cook Islands and Maldives. By and large, in small island developing States of this region, agriculture and related activities predominate. Development of tourism in the region has been slow because of low levels of development of physical infrastructures and human resources in most of them, particularly the smaller ones, isolation from the major sources of tourists, problems of communal landownership, extremely weak aviation and communication links, and heavy reliance on foreign investment, with foreign investors concentrating on the most profitable destinations. In the African region, considerable progress has been achieved in tourism development in Seychelles and Mauritius. In the other three African small island developing States, Sao Tome and Principe, Cape Verde and the Comoros, all of which are classified as least developed, the development of tourism is still in an incipient stage. The slow pace of development of tourism in these countries is attributable to the slow pace of general economic development, and of the development of social and physical infrastructures and human resources in particular, as well as the inadequate importance attached to tourism as a growth sector in the past.

Emerging Trends

The future development of tourism in small island developing States will be affected by two principal current global trends. First, global travel and tourism is expected to grow more rapidly in the coming years, outpacing the growth of world economic output. Between 1995 and 2005, travel and tourism is projected to grow by an annual average rate of 5.5 per cent in real terms and create 12.5 million new direct and indirect jobs annually on the average.

In the wider Caribbean, travel and tourism output is projected to grow at an annual average rate of 3.6 per cent in real terms between 1995 and 2005 and to create 2.7 million jobs. For sustaining Caribbean tourism, the secretariat of the Caribbean Tourism Organization has identified a number of areas of action at the regional level, notably, maintenance of product quality, including the integrity of the natural environment; enhancement of profitability; provision of air access at competitive rates from major tourist markets; provision of a secure environment for the industry by combating crime and drugs; strengthening intersectoral linkages and creation of a regional competitive force through regional collaboration, particularly in the area of overseas marketing and promotion; and creation of social acceptability of the further expansion of tourism by the local population.

A similar trend is expected for Asia and the Pacific. The region as a whole is projected to be the fastest growing area in world tourism activities up to the year 2005. Between 1995 and 2005, the annual average real rate of growth of travel and tourism output in the region is estimated at 8.0 per cent. The South Pacific is expected to share in this growth through further growth of its traditional destinations, as well as through the gradual development of as yet untapped potentials in other islands. In most of the small island developing States of the South Pacific, the growth of tourism will require the removal of several major internal constraints, including the following: shortages of trained staff; inadequacy and infrequency of air transportation; low level and quality of supporting infrastructure-airport facilities, tour operation, restaurants; low budgets for marketing and promotion; lack of investment capital; and restriction on landownership. By far the greatest challenge for the expansion of tourism in the South Pacific small island developing States will be their ability to achieve international competitiveness.

In the African region, Mauritius and Seychelles have planned for further growth but have opted for up-market tourism. They have consequently banned charter flight operations and hope to achieve a slower rate of growth of visitors, with emphasis on higher-spending visitors on scheduled flights. Of particular concern to these countries is the spread of drugs and of diseases such as the human immunodeficiency virus/acquired immunodeficiency syndrome (HIV/AIDS), which can impact very severely on their small populations. The other three African small island developing States have considerable room for growth and are just beginning to develop tourism as a growth sector.

In Malta and Cyprus, the rate of growth of tourist arrivals has slowed down in the recent past. This is attributable in part to capacity constraints and in part to deliberate policies to slow down expansion in order to deal with environmental and other adverse impacts of previous rapid expansion. Both countries plan to place considerable importance on tourism as a growth sector for quite some time to come, but have opted for up-market tourism.

A second discernible trend that will shape tourism development in small island developing States in coming years is the growing interest in and demand for speciality tourism. Underlying this trend is greater environmental awareness globally, greater health consciousness, and a growing preference by travellers to experience unspoilt environmental surroundings. In tandem with this trend, many small island developing States have embarked on a gradual policy of diversification of the tourism package emphasizing to a greater extent other natural assets than the beach and the sea. Diversification of the tourism product also reflects the realization on the part of the authorities in small island developing States of the need to innovate in order to remain competitive.

Risks of Over-reliance on Tourism

Over-reliance on tourism, especially mass tourism, carries significant risks. Economic recession in industrialized countries, their major source of tourists, and the impacts of tropical storms and cyclones to which many of them are particularly prone have devastating effects on the tourism sector and hence on tourism-based island economies. Mass tourism, unlike up-market tourism, is characterized by relatively high income elasticity of demand and is likely to fall off suddenly as a result of economic recessions in the source markets. Excessive reliance on a single major source of tourists, as in Cyprus and Malta on the United Kingdom market, is extremely risky as economic difficulties in the source country have direct adverse impacts on the receiving countries.

In small islands, there is a tendency for fast growth of tourism to be accompanied by inflationary pressures. Prices of real estate, particularly land suitable for building, which is extremely scarce, quickly rise beyond the reach of the local population. Inflationary pressures build up throughout the economy as the prices of locally produced construction materials and consumer goods rise. Although this process means higher profit margins in bottleneck sectors and could stimulate more inward investment, overly accommodating monetary policy could generalize the inflation with adverse consequences for international competitiveness and future investment.

Social and Cultural Impacts

Sudden, rapid development of tourism can cause significant social disruptions in small island States. Pressures are exerted on households and communities by the upward pressure on land prices and prices of foodstuffs and household items. Among other things, potential long-run effects could be a reduction in the living standards of high proportions of island populations and a sense of alienation brought about by their lack of access to limited land resources. Many small island populations also suffer a loss of access to beaches and important leisure areas because of exclusive rights granted to developers. This, in some cases, also translates into economic losses as fishermen and others are adversely affected by loss of access to the sea. Furthermore, excessively high visibility of foreigners can lead to anxieties on the part of the local people and a tendency to blame local problems on them, and thus to a social rejection of the growth of tourism. An important factor in sustainable tourism development in small island States is the tourist carrying capacity of these societies, in both environmental and social terms. At peak periods, visitors are known to outnumber nationals by multiples in several of the smaller islands. In larger islands such as Jamaica or Fiji, local concentration of tourism often leads to localized problems of carrying capacity, such as overcrowding of beaches, traffic congestion, noise pollution, increased incidence of drugs and crime, and the spread of diseases brought in from outside. The ratios of tourists to local population for a number of small island developing States in 1993. While optimal carrying capacity cannot be quantified with any exactitude, it is generally contended that the population to tourists ratio, i.e., the inverse of what is shown in the table, should be kept at a level that does not exceed social tolerance limits, which may differ from country to country.

Island tourism is invariably centred on sun, sea and sand. However, to the extent that some interaction occurs with local customs and traditions, tourism is sometimes believed to exert a negative sociocultural influence on small island States. A high level of tourism can lead to commercialization, which is thought to cheapen local customs and traditions. Local arts and crafts and cultural practices are sometimes adapted to suit foreign tastes, which leads to the creation of contrived cultural products.

Some research conducted in the Asia-Pacific and Caribbean regions, however, has failed to produce much evidence of major destruction of local cultures as a result of the influence of tourists. On the contrary, the findings indicate that tourism can assist in preserving customs and cultures by providing incentives to invest in and promote them. If properly managed and promoted, local cultures can be given an impetus by the presence of tourists. It is contended, for instance, that the popularization of Jamaican reggae and carnival festivals of Trinidad and Tobago and similar cultural forms in other small island States is a direct result of the influence of tourism.

Environmental Impacts

The fragile ecosystems of small island States and their generally more limited scope for action in development alternatives make concerns for the environmental impact of tourism very acute, particularly because the sector, which is almost totally dependent on the natural environment, is viewed by many small island developing States as a fast route to social and economic development. Intensive tourism development and tourism activities often have very quick and severe impacts on their natural resources. The principal tourism-related environmental difficulties confronting small island developing States are several.

Land Resources and Terrestrial Biological Diversity

The environmental impacts of tourism are attributable to the development of tourism infrastructures and facilities and to the impacts of tourists' activities. In small islands, even more so than elsewhere, there is strong competition for the use of land between tourism and other competing uses. Rising prices of building land increase the pressure to build on agricultural land. Deforestation and intensified or unsuitable use of land cause erosion and loss of biological diversity. In many small island developing States, ecosystems are now being threatened as a result of the development of tourism, which has intensified human interference with vegetation and wildlife. This can lead to irreversible damage to their valuable ecosystems and to traditional activities such as fishing.

Waste Management

For small island developing States, treatment and disposal of liquid and solid wastes constitute a major problem. With limited physical infrastructure, the capacity of many small island States is already strained. This is exacerbated by wastes generated by tourism activities. Examples abound of damages caused by the disposal of untreated effluents into surrounding areas of land and sea. Pollution of scarce inland freshwater resources is one such example. The loss of valuable marine life, the destruction of coral reefs and the silting and erosion of coastal beaches, on which island tourism highly depends, are others. Pollution from ship-generated wastes is also a major cause for concern for small island developing States. One dimension of this particular threat is the dumping of oily waste, sewage, garbage and cargo residues, which cause marine and beach pollution, by merchant ships plying their seas. Another dimension, particularly for the Caribbean, is the frequency of tourist cruise ships plying that region's seas and generating substantial volumes of liquid and solid wastes for disposal at the ports of call. The following factors have been cited as impeding corrective action: inadequate infrastructure; weak institutional, legislative and enforcement capacities; the absence of a regional consensus on appropriate criteria for sewage, effluents and coastal water standards; and the inability of small island developing States to require cruise ships and other vessels to comply with the provisions of the International Convention for the Prevention of Pollution from Ships regarding generation and disposal of ship wastes.

Coastal Area Degradation

Tourism as a mainly coastal development has already had a number of adverse impacts on small island developing States. In Mauritius, Seychelles, Malta, Cyprus and several islands in the Caribbean, the previously unchecked construction of tourism facilities along their coastlines resulted in the despoliation of much of the originally pristine beauty of these areas. In order to halt the degradation, the Governments of a number of these countries have, of late, taken steps through legislation to restrict and control coastal construction. Stipulations of building size, with limits on height and room capacity, and specifications of design and materials used in construction have been instituted in an effort to correct past errors and ensure better harmony with the natural environment. Beach destruction caused by intensive sand mining for tourism-related construction is also a feature of many coastal areas. This practice has recently been curtailed in Maldives, Seychelles, Mauritius, the Bahamas and Cook Islands, among other States. Beaches destroyed by sand quarrying are not being naturally replenished because of the destruction of coral reefs by sewage and other types of pollution. Erosion owing to tourism facilities and infrastructures built too close to the coast also contributes to beach destruction and coastal degradation. Another common feature of coastal area destruction in small island developing States is the removal of valuable mangrove forests, which act as nesting places for birds and other animal life in addition to their function as a natural barrier against encroachment of the sea. Indiscriminate diving, fishing and boating activities associated with tourism may further contribute to this disturbance. For a detailed discussion of coastal area issues in small island developing States, see the report of the Secretary-General on coastal area management in small island developing States.

Freshwater Resources

The problem of freshwater availability is most severe in the low-lying atolls that have the least opportunity for surface-water catchment and storage. Several other small island developing States also suffer from frequent droughts and chronic water scarcity. On the high volcanic islands, rainfall is in many cases abundant but access to freshwater is often limited by lack of adequate storage facilities and delivery systems.

The supply of freshwater relative to the growing demand from agriculture, industry and households is becoming an acute problem in many small island developing States. Added to this is the growing competition of limited water resources from tourism, which is extremely water-intensive.

Climate Change and Sealevel Rise

Island tourism is a climate-sensitive industry, and being largely concentrated in coastal locations is susceptible to sealevel rise. An analysis of data by the Intergovernmental Panel on Climate Change has confirmed a trend in global warming, with increases in temperatures of 0.3 to 0.6 degrees centigrade occurring since the late nineteenth century, much of which has occurred in the past 40 years. The effect of this trend is a rise of mean sealevels at a rate of 1.5 millimetres per year. In small islands and coastal areas in general, that would cause the inundation of coastal and some inland areas, threatening sanitation systems and freshwater supplies as seawater infiltrates subterranean water tables, with possibly catastrophic consequences for island tourism. An erosion of shorelines would undoubtedly bring about severe stress and damage to both natural and built environments, the overall economic consequences of which are currently inestimable. In addition, damages from tropical storms with a possible link to changes in weather patterns have been increasing in recent years. Small island developing States that are especially vulnerable to these phenomena now experience considerable difficulty securing insurance coverage. Reliable sunshine is one of the major tourism assets of tropical islands. Potential threats of climate change, which are beginning to appear in greater health risks from direct exposure to sunlight, may undermine this asset.

Policies, Finance, Capacity-building, Technology and Infrastructure

The present section discusses some of the main policy issues in the area of sustainable development of tourism at the national, regional and international levels. Emphasis is placed on legislation, finance, capacity-building, and sustainable tourism infrastructure and policies as necessary means of implementing the provisions of the Programme of Action.

At the National Level

Development Policy Framework

Tourism development has been incorporated into the overall development plans of some small islands. Some Caribbean island authorities have established tourism master plans, with links to national development plans, and have created national sustainable development commissions or, as in the case of Saint Lucia, a National Sustainable Tourism Commission. In the South Pacific, tourism development plans and policies have been formulated in several small island developing States. However, the level of policy commitment to sustainable tourism development differs from country to country, which in turn influences the degree of action in this area. According to a study by the Economic and Social Commission for Asia and the Pacific (ESCAP), this uneven commitment in the South Pacific can serve as an impediment to the promotion of sustainability at the regional level. By and large, a long-term national policy for sustainable tourism development, with emphasis on natural resource conservation, has yet to evolve. The focus of policies generally continues to be on: (a) creating and improving conditions for attracting foreign investment in tourism; (b) marketing and promotion of tourism to achieve maximum growth in arrivals; and (c) designing the type of legislative framework that would further those objectives. The prevalence of this situation points to the urgent need for a policy framework for sustainable tourism development in most small island developing States.

Legislative Framework

A necessary requirement for the pursuit of sustainable tourism development is an effective legislative framework. A wide range of laws have been enacted in small island developing States, in many instances since the conclusion of the United Nations Conference on Environment and Development, establishing standards for land use in tourism development, tourism facilities and investment in tourism. Despite progress in the enactment of environmental legislation, its effectiveness continues to be impaired by weaknesses in the institutional frameworks for enforcing legislation, lack of standardization of legislation and the obscurity of regulations. Consequently, the level of enforcement of regulations to ensure sustainability in tourism in many small island developing States leaves much to be desired. Regulations for coastal zone management and the creation of protected areas, both marine and land-based, present a case in point. Their enforcement, particularly in the Caribbean, remains very weak.

Investment

The majority of small island developing States suffer from a lack of local capital for bulky investments and, in many cases, the absence of a significant local entrepreneurial class. The financing required for the development of the tourism sector is therefore obtained largely through foreign investment. Special efforts are made by Governments of small island developing States to attract foreign capital through the provision of tax breaks, tax holidays, building concessions and other incentives to foreign investors. While that may well be necessary to some extent, competition among small island developing States to attract foreign capital for tourism development often leads to the provision of over-generous financial incentives to foreign investors which deprive all these States of part of the income from tourism. Moreover, since small island developing States are over-reliant on foreign capital, they are unable to impose environmental sustainability conditions on foreign investors. Both to derive the maximum benefits from tourism and to avoid environmental deterioration from tourism activities, there is a need for small island developing States to jointly adopt uniform incentive and environmental policies, at least at the regional level.

While efforts at encouraging local investment and participation in the sector have increased in many small island developing States, considerably more effort is needed. Such efforts are, in many cases, hampered by the inability of the private sector in most small island developing States to raise adequate capital. A judicious mix of foreign and local investment, and especially the encouragement of joint ventures, would be one way of ensuring the adequacy of capital resources for sustainable tourism development and the fuller participation of nationals in the sector.

Aside from foreign direct investment in tourism, the bulk of tourism-related services are also known to be largely in the control of foreign operators in a number of small island developing States. Overseas sales and marketing, and promotion of tourism packages for most small island developing States, are undertaken by outside entities. Several domestic operations are also handled by foreigners. In this area, there is a need for increased investments in the training of nationals for greater participation in tourism.

In order to supplement the efforts of the private sector at ensuring sustainability in the tourism sector, greater non-governmental organization/government partnerships in tourism development could be developed. Such partnerships can be useful, especially in the restoration, development and maintenance of cultural and historical sites, while ensuring conservation and profitability. Funds for investment in such activities could be raised through mechanisms already existing in many cases, such as increases in airport taxes and airline ticket taxes, as long as they meet International Civil Aviation Organization (ICAO) stipulations, and entrance fees for tourism sites.

Human and Institutional Capacity

45. Most small island States face the persistent problem of inadequate supply of trained manpower, particularly in government agencies responsible for the implementation and monitoring of standards and environmental regulations in tourism. The shortage of skilled human resources is compounded by the dispersion in some States of roles and responsibilities among several government agencies. To address these weaknesses, an integrated approach to tourism planning and environmental conservation, coupled with training at all levels, needs immediate attention in all small island States. A system for monitoring the implementation of sustainable tourism policies must also form part of an integrated approach to tourism planning and the building up of institutional capacity. A study by ESCAP found that national tourism organizations, important mechanisms in the development and implementation of sustainable tourism policies, are largely under-staffed and underfunded. The study also found that attempts by individual small island States to market their tourism product themselves have not been significantly effective in most cases because of the high costs involved and the lack of skilled human resources. Overall, the shortcomings of capacity could be better addressed through greater regional collaboration.

Infrastructure

The main physical infrastructural requirements for tourism development include the following: effective transportation facilities, including airports and air and/or sea carrier links; reasonably good road networks; telecommunication links; reliable energy supply systems; freshwater supply systems; accommodation facilities; restaurants and entertainment sites. For many small island developing States, the inadequacy of these infrastructures is an obstacle to the development of the sector. In some of the smaller Pacific islands in this category, efforts are being made to build new airport facilities. This is regarded as a necessary initial step to their fuller participation in tourism. In the Caribbean, where the sector is more developed, air links to long-haul markets such as Germany, Italy and France are being extended.

Many small island developing States are confronted with severe infrastructural inadequacies consequent to the growth of tourism. Many of them suffer from chronic shortages of freshwater supply for their own use, a problem that is further aggravated by the high demand of large tourist populations. Liquid and solid waste disposal present a colossal problem to all small island developing States but especially to those that are tourism-based. Another dimension is added to this problem by the requirement of facilities to handle waste brought to their ports by cruise lines which frequent small island destinations.

The diversification of the tourism product through the development of nature and cultural tourism also necessitates additional infrastructural and environmental requirements. Some sites are remote and may require additional access routes and other infrastructures such as those for the supply of water and electricity, and new accommodation. These requirements are particularly burdensome to the archipelagic small island developing States. Generally, when developing infrastructure, the issue of the carrying capacity of the destination must also be considered.

Technology

Sector-specific technology needs of small island developing States are discussed in various reports to the Commission on Sustainable Development at its fourth session which highlight the need for the introduction or more widespread use of certain technologies by tourism enterprises and Governments of small island developing States, as appropriate. Some examples are: (a) solar technology for cooling of hotels and for water heating; (b) environmentally sound technologies for the treatment, recycling and disposal of solid wastes generated by tourism facilities and those brought to port by cruise ships; (c) telecommunications technologies for the fuller integration of small island developing States into global telecommunications networks to enhance their marketing and promotion operations; and (d) electronic information technologies to enhance day-to-day tourism operations, such as reservations.

At the Regional Level

The need for greater collaboration among small island developing States on issues of sustainable tourism development is well recognized. Collaboration and cooperation could lead to greater long-term benefits for the environment and the economies of small island developing States, particularly in an increasingly competitive global arena. The harmonization of standards and regulations, including legislative actions to govern tourism, has been identified as a critical need in the Programme of Action for the Sustainable Development of Small Island Developing States and by some regional authorities. Integrated tourism development planning, marketing and promotion can increase both effectiveness and efficiency. Joint overseas marketing and promotion would help achieve benefits of economies of scale and increased value-added in the tourism sector. Overseas marketing and promotion by individual small island developing States entail a heavy cost to each of these States and reduce significantly their net foreign exchange earnings from tourism.

The Programme of Action provides for the pursuit of regional initiatives in: (a) the harmonization of standards and regulations to ensure that tourism and the environment are mutually supportive; (b) the promotion of cooperation in developing potential complementarities in the tourism sector; and (c) the establishment of mechanisms for information exchange and sharing of experiences, particularly through existing regional tourism organizations. The ESCAP report cited above has identified, in addition to those measures, the need for regional collaboration in: (a) integrating tourism development planning, including concerted market development and promotion; (b) strengthening and expanding the roles of national and regional tourism institutions and organs; and (c) promoting joint training and manpower development in tourism.

In recent years, attempts have been made, particularly in the two main regions-the Pacific and the Caribbean-to consolidate efforts in sustainable tourism development by forging common regional approaches for the sector. The necessary institutional framework currently exists for these regions in the form of the Tourism Council of the South Pacific and the Caribbean Tourism Organization. These institutions have been mandated by the respective regional political forums-the South Pacific Forum and the Caribbean Community (CARICOM)-to strengthen regional cooperation in tourism development, planning and promotion. Provision for some financial support has been made for both institutions under the Caribbean and Pacific regional tourism development programmes funded by the Lome' Convention concluded between the European Community and the African, Caribbean and Pacific States.

In spite of many difficulties, the Tourism Council of the South Pacific has been successful as a regional agency in the area of marketing and promotion of the South Pacific as a tourist destination, but not in the area of strategy and planning. For the Caribbean small island developing States, the political framework was consolidated with the formation in 1995 of the Association of Caribbean States (ACS), which has identified the tourism sector as one of three areas for high-priority measures for wider regional cooperation. Regional cooperation in the area of tourism has been further strengthened by the formation of the Caribbean Coalition for Tourism, with the goal of creating the largest possible pool of resources for cooperative marketing by drawing on the resources of the widest range of players both in the public and in the private sectors. Resource constraint has been recognized as an impediment for both TCSP and CTO to adequately cover the broad range of activities that they must undertake to increase market awareness, promote sustainability, develop human resources and carry out marketing and promotion. External assistance is seen as essential to the viability of both institutions. Increased support for these bodies, aside from regional Governments, will be contingent upon increased involvement of the private sector in their work. The inadequacy of political will to cooperate meaningfully is also seen as a major impediment to effective cooperation in both regions.

In the African region, there is little evidence of meaningful effort at regional cooperation in the area of tourism development. This may be due in large part to the dispersion of the African small island developing States, three off the east coast and two off the west coast of Africa, and the considerable disparity in development and policy emphasis on tourism among these countries. Given the recognized potential for tourism development, however, there is a need to begin efforts within this region for a common approach to sustainable tourism development through an integrated subregional policy.

In the areas of joint training and manpower development, tourism research and experience-sharing efforts at regional collaboration have been made to varying extents within the regions. The pooling within each region of the limited financial and technical resources of individual small island developing States for capacity-building would be immensely beneficial to all those States. Collaboration in information exchange and research could be achieved through the strengthening of regional tourism institutions. A priority need in this respect is for training in the use of state-of-the-art information technologies at the regional level for the monitoring of environmental impacts of tourism, and for the establishment and operation of central reservation systems.

A major area for regional cooperation is air transportation. Two considerations are worthy of note in this connection. First, small island developing States cannot depend solely on foreign carriers, which must make decisions in the best interest of their owners regarding services, routes and schedules. Such decisions may not always coincide with the best interest of the countries. Besides, even a major airline serving small island developing States in a region can suddenly disappear. Secondly, small island developing States, except for a few, cannot each maintain a viable airline. An effective solution from the point of view of cost and adequacy of air transportation for the tourism industry would be regionally owned and managed carriers, with provision for regional functional cooperation. For a detailed discussion on air transport needs for small island developing States, see the report of the Secretary-General on air transport in small island developing.

Country Experiences

The economic prospects of many small island developing States depend significantly on a productive tourism sector. For the States, generally, the furtherance of sustainable tourism development is an economic as well as a socio-environmental imperative. In these countries, tourism actually provides an economic rationale for safeguarding the natural environment.

Many of the policies that underpin sustainable development were recognized and elaborated in a number of small island developing States prior to the United Nations Conference on Environment and Development and were given further impetus by it and by the Barbados Conference. For instance, Maldives, concerned about sustainability in the wake of rapid tourism development, recognized the need for the establishment of a National Environment Council to address those concerns as far back as 1985. The preparation of a national environment action programme, as well as a related work programme, was completed in 1989, with provision for the systematic inclusion of environmental issues in the country's national development plan. Specific policies have been adopted to promote sustainable tourism development, particularly in the areas of waste disposal, use of coral reefs and construction in coastal sites and for the type and diversity of accommodation.

Policies aimed at the creation of national parks and the encouragement of visits to wildlife refuges, bird sanctuaries and other natural beauty spots have been put in place in Seychelles and Mauritius as a means of diversifying the tourism product with a possible spin-off benefit for the protection and conservation of these sites. The drive for product diversification and the enhancement of natural endowments is also very strong in the Caribbean. Several legislative acts have been passed in individual countries of this region with the objective of addressing environmental problems. For example, in Saint Lucia, a National Sustainable Tourism Commission was established and a National Environmental Action Plan was prepared for implementation in 1994. A Minimum Standards Act was scheduled for adoption in 1995, with a view to addressing all areas of hotel, restaurant and tourist carrying capacity. A Development Control Act has also been approved by the Saint Lucia authorities, making the conduct of environmental impact assessment and its incorporation into all decision-making processes mandatory. Jamaica recently carried out a review of existing environmental legislation. The review resulted in the passage of new legislation requiring the conduct of environmental impact assessment for all new developments. In some small island developing States where rapid tourism expansion has given rise to problems of sustainability and over-reliance on tourism as a major sector, several measures have been taken in an attempt to overcome such problems. A case in point is Cyprus, where pollution, beach erosion, physical carrying capacity and difficulties of competitive pressures on other economic sectors have been felt. Efforts have been made through the use of economic instruments and legislation to achieve sustainability and balance. Various new tax incentives have been introduced to diversify and upgrade the tourism product and a new marketing strategy focus is directed at improving tourist quality. Additionally, fiscal instruments are now being used to encourage sound land use and coastal zone practices aimed particularly at slowing down and improving coastal development and efficient allocation and use of water and other resources. Simultaneously, a policy of economic restructuring in the manufacturing and agriculture sectors have been put in place in order to improve their overall competitiveness and linkages with tourism.

Diversification within or away from tourism has been undertaken in many small island developing States, notably in Cyprus and Malta. Several constraining factors have been recognized, including a generally limited scope and capacity for novel forms of tourism development in small islands, a usually small proportion of visitors interested in other forms of activity, and more importantly, the fact that all aspects of tourism accommodation and other facilities have been geared towards traditional forms of tourism. The authorities in Mauritius and Seychelles have also adopted some policies for diversification within tourism, particularly in targeting high-spending visitors and in encouraging to some extent inland and nature tourism. In the foreseeable future, however, the need for continued mass tourism is acknowledged largely because of an existing over-capacity in tourism. A spin-off benefit of the thrust for quality has been a general upgrading of facilities and greater attention to avoiding negative impacts. Mauritius has been relatively successful in achieving some degree of economic diversification and balanced growth through the development of export processing zones and, to a lesser extent, agricultural modernization and diversification.

In the Comoros and Cape Verde, the Governments and private sector have recently demonstrated heightened interest in tourism development. The institutional groundwork has been prepared in the Comoros with the adoption in 1994 of a national environmental policy document and an environmental plan of action, and the creation in 1995 of the Association Touristique Comorienne. The implementation of these plans, however, is subject to a number of constraints, including poor levels of infrastructure development, particularly hotels, poor air and communication links with tourist-generating areas and some degree of political instability. Recent initiatives in Cape Verde include the adoption of a tourism development plan and the establishment of a National Institute for Tourism. The main constraints identified are the following: a lack of interest by the local and foreign private sector; a lack of demonstrated support by donors for the tourism development plan; and limited domestic financial resources.

Dominica has formally launched eco-tourism as the main form of tourism development. The island is mountainous, boasts few beaches but has 60 per cent forest cover containing many endemic species of plants, animals and birds. Two large national parks, two forest reserves and a Carib Indian reservation form the basis of eco-tourism attractions. The Government of Dominica has enacted legislation to ensure heritage and natural resource preservation, and the creation of linkages with local economic activities. While no scientific assessment has been conducted of the impact of increased human activity on the natural environment, several negative trends have been observed, among which are the accumulation of litter and garbage around nature sites, the extraction of plants from protected areas and the effects of the use of soap by local people in rivers and natural pools. Based on the experience of Dominica, concerns have been expressed regarding issues of carrying capacity and the impact of large numbers of tourists on environmentally sensitive ecologies. Although the adoption of regulations and policy guidelines can be seen as an indication of government commitment to sustainability, weaknesses persist in the management and policing of protected areas and tourism sites. Another unique feature of the experience of Dominica is the emphasis on participation by the local population through tax exemptions for local shareholder participation in hotels and other ventures.

Experiences of Major Groups and Non-governmental Organizations

Private Sector

A survey conducted by the World Travel and Tourism Council indicates that in much of the private sector, the pursuit of sustainability measures in tourism is gradually becoming a matter of sound business practice. Little by little, recognition of the link between conservation measures on the one hand and profitability and competitiveness on the other is taking hold. Some private sector companies involved in travel and tourism have reported positive results from conservation measures, in the form of increased profitability, a rise in staff morale and an enhanced image among their clientele. In order to develop voluntary practice approaches, tourism industry associations have emphasized the use of voluntary environmental codes of conduct and guidelines. Through a survey and publication, the United Nations Environment Programme (UNEP)Industry and Environment Programme Activities Centre has identified more than 30 codes, among them, those prepared by main industry associations such as the World Travel and Tourism Council, the Pacific Asia Travel Association, the American Society of Travel and the International Hotels Environment Initiative.

An emerging feature among some multinational businesses, particularly in the hotel sector, is resort to voluntary measures for conservation, primarily with a view to securing strategic advantages, but also as a means of precluding more costly retrofitting that may be required by future government regulations. However, to date, most efforts have focused on energy and water conservation, waste minimization and product purchase. New tourism developments should more often incorporate improved plant designs, and improved energy-efficient features that will enable greater natural lighting, natural cooling of accommodation facilities, and waste treatment and water recycling.

Already, some progress can be noted: hotel staff are being trained to adopt energy-and water-saving, and waste-minimization measures during cleaning; and hotel guests are being encouraged to minimize water use by the reuse of towels and linens. Product purchase measures are being instituted, for example, through switching from phosphate-free cleaning products to those known to have less harmful properties. In the Asia-Pacific region, the development of integrated resorts is setting a new trend in resort development with the key objective of exercising greater control over environmental quality as a means of providing a guarantee of quality to guests. New complexes are built with all facilities on site, with particular emphasis on water conservation and recycling, energy supply and conservation, and waste management.

Non-governmental Organization and Community Involvement

The growing trend of environmental awareness globally is accompanied by an increase in international and national environmental movements in tourism development. For instance, at the international level, the International Scientific Council for Island Development, with the support of the Government of Spain and the sponsorship of several organizations, spearheaded the convening of the World Conference on Sustainable Tourism at Lanzarote, Canary Islands, in April 1995. The Conference adopted a Charter for Sustainable Tourism which affirms, inter alia, that: (a) tourism must be sustainable and integrated with the natural, cultural and human environment; (b) the achievement of sustainability is contingent upon integrated planning and cooperation at all levels; (c) tourism development must contribute to local economic development and improve the quality of life of all people; and (d) the benefits and burdens of tourism must be more equitably distributed.

In consequence of the Conference, a follow-up committee responsible for the dissemination of the Charter and for the promotion of related studies, projects and actions was established; and the launching of a European network for sustainable tourism development in islands and coastal zones was proposed. The objective of the network is to generate and diffuse information and know-how on the promotion of environmentally sound tourism. Like industry associations, non-governmental organizations such as the Ecotourism Society and the World Wide Fund for Nature Tourism Concern have also developed codes of conduct and guidelines for tourism. At the regional level, the Caribbean Conference on Sustainable Tourism, which was held at Punta Cana, Dominican Republic, towards the end of 1995, under the sponsorship of Earthkind International and the Earth Pledge Foundation, explored a wide range of issues relating to sustainable tourism in that region. A similar conference is planned for the South Pacific in 1996.

At the local level, the involvement of non-governmental organizations, community groups and local authorities in the promotion and development of sustainable tourism policies is just beginning but a discernible trend is apparent in some small island developing States. The following are examples of recent initiatives: in Trinidad and Tobago, a project has been put in place at Matura Beach to train community youths as tour guides, with the goal of preventing poaching of leather back turtles, an endangered species; in Jamaica, resort boards, which include representatives of non-governmental organizations, the local community and business enterprises, have been established in the main tourism areas of Ocho Rios, Montego Bay, Negril and Port Antonio for overseeing all aspects of tourism policy, practice and development; in Mauritius, the authorities have published The Mauritian Code of Ethics for Tourism: For Mauritians. The Code, which focuses largely on the social and cultural aspects of tourism, presents guidelines for use by the local community in their dealings with tourists.

Activities and Experiences in International Cooperation in Sustainable Tourism Development

Organs of the United Nations System

A number of organizations and bodies of the United Nations system have reported plans and activities in the area of tourism development, in keeping with the Programme of Action. The United Nations Development Programme has reported that its programme of assistance in the South Pacific and in some small island developing States in the other regions addresses issues relating to sustainable tourism development within the overall national environmental plans of the countries concerned. The Economic Commission for Latin America and the Caribbean (ECLAC) and ESCAP have planned or recently implemented specific activities in tourism. ECLAC has reported that proposals for environmental codes of conduct for the tourism sector, which it recently developed, are now being carried out by the Caribbean Tourism Organization. ESCAP has reported that in 1995, it convened a workshop on integrated tourism planning in Pacific island countries and published a set of studies on foreign investment in the tourism sector in Samoa and Vanuatu. The United Nations University is currently undertaking a study to examine indicators of sustainability for the tourism sector in small islands, along with a project on eco-tourism. It is expected that the results of these two undertakings will be useful to small island developing States.

In 1992-1993, the World Heritage Convention, sponsored by the United Nations Educational, Scientific and Cultural Organization (UNESCO), in collaboration with UNEP, carried out surveys on tourism management in natural and mixed heritage sites and subsequently convened an international seminar which helped formulate a set of general principles for tourism development in natural heritage sites. During 1994-1995, UNESCO collaborated with several regional initiatives on tourism in the Asia-Pacific region. The Earth Sciences Division of UNESCO has undertaken modelling of human-induced geomorphologic change to serve as a guide to improved planning of human settlements. In addition, UNESCO has planned a world heritage promotion seminar for the Caribbean, and a pilot project on water supply problems and community attitudes in the South Pacific islands, as well as studies with reference to the Caribbean on the interrelationships between tourism, population pressures, pollution and natural hazards. In 1993, through the Pan American Health Organization Regional Office, the World Health Organization collaborated with a number of regional organizations to launch the Environmental Health and Sustainable Tourism Development Initiative for the Caribbean and to convene the Regional Conference on Environmental Health and Sustainable Development in the Caribbean. UNEP is making efforts to promote integrated coastal zone management in small island developing States through its regional seas programme. The Mediterranean Action Plan and the Caribbean Action Plan have in particular addressed tourism issues. The Industry and Environment Office of UNEP has developed fruitful partnerships with industry associations at the international level to inform about and disseminate examples of good environmental practices, in particular on codes of conduct and environment management of hotels. The Food and Agriculture Organization of the United Nations has planned two regional workshops in 1996, one for the Caribbean and one for the South Pacific small island developing States. One of the items on the agenda of both workshops will be linkages of tourism with agriculture, forestry and fisheries.

Other Intergovernmental Bodies

In addition to the Tourism Council of the South Pacific and the

Caribbean Tourism Organization, both of which are intergovernmental bodies whose activities have been discussed above, the Organization of American States (OAS) and the European Union have been active in promoting sustainable tourism development in small island developing States. OAS has assisted Caribbean small island developing States in various policy studies on sustainable tourism. The European Union has provided assistance, under ongoing cooperation arrangements, in carrying out a number of tourism development projects in African, Caribbean and Pacific small island developing States.

Main Findings

Tourism already makes an important contribution to economic growth, employment and foreign exchange earnings in the majority of small island developing States. It provides an opportunity to most of them for economic diversification and growth.

Looking to the future, there are indications that the development of tourism in small island developing States will be subject to two current global trends. First, global travel and tourism output is expected to grow more rapidly in coming years, outpacing the growth of world economic output. This trend is expected to reinforce current trends in small island developing States. Secondly, tourism development in these countries will be shaped by the growing interest in, and demand for, speciality tourism, particularly nature tourism propelled by growing environmental awareness. To these trends may be added another, namely, an apparent upward trend in global warming and sealevel rise, the persistence of which would have devastating impacts on island tourism.

From the point of view of the future course of action, the following findings on the economic, social and environmental aspects of tourism in small island developing States are worthy of note:

(a) Economic aspects. (i) Generally, the leakages through imports out of direct tourist expenditures to meet the needs of the tourism sector itself are extremely high in these countries; (ii) the daily expenditures per visitor vary from country to country but are generally low; (iii) excessive reliance on tourism carries many risks, including excessive exposure to international economic shocks and weakening of intersectoral linkages which, inter alia, reduce the potential benefits from tourism;

(b) Social aspects. Rapid development of tourism, particularly mass tourism, can have significant adverse social impacts in small islands. The following are of particular significance: (i) persistent inflationary pressures pose the danger of significantly worsening the household distribution of income; (ii) the social carrying capacity of small islands quickly reaches its limits of tolerance as the ratio of visitors to the local population rises, causing overcrowding of beaches, noise pollution and exacerbating traffic congestion; (iii) prolonged growth of mass tourism may be accompanied by increased incidence of crime, and spread of drugs and diseases, including HIV/AIDS;

(c) Environmental aspects. Intensive tourism development and tourism activities, particularly if not properly planned and managed, can very quickly cause environmental damages in small island developing States. The most notable impacts are observable in (i) land degradation and loss of terrestrial and marine biodiversity; (ii) increased levels of pollution from dumping of solid and liquid wastes generated by tourism activities on land and in the sea; (iii) coastal zone degradation through intensive sand mining, removal of mangrove forests and destruction of coral reefs, erosion and destruction of landscape owing to tourism facilities and associated infrastructures; (iv) freshwater shortages aggravated by the demand from the water-intensive tourism industry, excessive groundwater pumping and consequent lowering of water tables.

3

The "Backpacker" Phenomenon and the "Spaniard"

Although tourists have visited the island for nearly a century, only since 1990 has consistent, rapid development taken place. Documentation of this development by academics has primarily focused on the environmental impacts that the industry has had and potentially could have on the islands. More specifically this attention has focused on Roatán because development has been concentrated there.

This chapter explores the human consequences of the expanding tourism industry on the diverse cultural heritage of Utila. Two specific tourists groups, the "backpacker" and "the Spaniard," will be discussed. Particular questions will be addressed concerning the origin of these groups, their reasons for choosing Utila, and how they have or have not affected the local economy. Nearly 30 years ago in the conclusion of his historical geography of the Bay Islands, Davidson questioned whether the Bay Islands British West Indian culture, having emerged from years of Anglo-Hispanic conflict, could survive the new migrations of the ladinos from mainland Honduras and more North-American visitors. Today these two groups come to the island for very different reasons and subsequently have different impacts. As tourism has become more pronounced on Utila, the island is also grappling with another group-the "backpacker" or "ticks" as the islanders like to call them. Similar groups have been documented in fishing-based villages elsewhere in South America.

The "Backpacker"

Utila was predestined to attract a certain type of tourist, one not looking for expensive resorts, rather, one looking for a fairly cheap place to dive and experience Central America and the western Caribbean. This type of tourist I have dubbed the "Backpacker." This term has been used to describe young European tourists but, in this work, it will be extended to all cultural groups that travel in this fashion. Before the development of the 1990s, Utilians were slow to construct adequate housing and other tourist related facilities. Therefore, when groups of young, budget tourists came to the island they camped on the beaches. To further reduce their costs backpackers often bought only "coconut bread and beer". Tourism in this form kept interactions with local populations to a minimum and only slight contributions were made to the local economy.

Activities of this nature were documented by many locals during the early 1990s when adequate facilities had been constructed. It was apparent that the backpackers' incentives had little to do with the lack of facilities on the island. Rather, much like *Kottak (1998)* noted in Brazil, backpackers activities stemmed from an economic necessity and longing for social interactions.

Although Kottak called the group he observed "hippies," they essentially began their travels for the same reasons and had similar effects on the local population in Arembepe, Brazil. For the tourists that I have distinguished as the backpacker class, many of them are young and travelling on small budgets. As they travel, they meet other backpackers and form small groups. Through these groups and through other backpacker groups, they learn of economic and social havens. These havens establish reputations within the backpacker society because of their flexible law enforcement. The groups are able to find short-term work without acquiring expensive permits. However, as might be expected, animosity often arises between the backpackers and locals who might be competing for the same jobs. Utila has established this reputation.

The relationship between the islanders and the backpackers began to deteriorate in the early 1990s when it became clear that the visitors had little intention of changing their behaviour. Many local businessmen resented these tourists because while visiting they made only minimal contributions to the newly established economy. Thus, many of the island's businessmen petitioned the alcalde (mayor) to make beach camping illegal. The backpackers, much like Kottak's hippies, first moved farther away from the local settlement so that they could continue staying on the island. However, pressure from locals enforced the law and by 1999, backpacker camps had been eradicated. As greater numbers of tourists visited Utila, a related increase in job opportunities and income levels followed. Jobs such as diving instructors and bartenders were in high demand. Diving is one of the Utila's most important tourist attractions. The island is known for being the cheapest place in the Caribbean to earn SCUBA-diving certification.

During the summer of 2001 eleven diving establishments were in operation. Of these over half are owned and managed by foreigners. In most cases these owners and managers were not backpackers. They decided on Utila because of its reputation in diving circles and its beauty. However, nearly all of the support staff are backpackers who came to the island with little intention of staying. The steady work in a beautiful, cheap place persuaded many of these backpackers to make Utila their home, at least temporarily. Most stay no longer than six months. Except for three Bay Island instructors, the rest are non-Honduran.

Table 1: Countries of Origin of Utila's Dive Instructors

	Honduras	**US**	**Europe**	**Other**
Dive Shop				
Alton's Dive Shop	2	0	2	1
Utila Dive Centre	0	0	4	2
Under Water Vision	0	1	2	2
Utila Watersports	0	0	1	2
Cross Creek	0	0	2	2
Captain Morgan's Dive Centre	0	0	2	1
Parrot's Dive Centre	1	1	1	0
Bay Islands College of Diving	2	1	0	0
Paradise Divers	1	0	0	2
Gunter's Ecomarine	0	0	3	3
Totals	**6**	**3**	**17**	**15**

Of the backpackers interviewed many gave the same general story about how they had come to Utila and why they stayed. For most of them, they had heard about the island on the mainland of Central America and decided to "check it out." Realizing the possibilities Utila offered for employment and general relaxation they decided to become certified divers. Most of these backpackers were not divers before they came to the island. To pay for this certification many of them worked either for the dive shops or in local bars. After becoming certified they would stay for a short while until they saved enough money to continue their travels. From my research I believe this has become a pattern for the many of the backpackers that visit Utila.

Over the last five years many local attitudes have slowly changed and the backpackers have become "just another source of income and labour".

This is illustrated in a conversation with one such businessman:

F: So what do you think about all these foreigners on Utila now?

B: Me, man, I have no problem with the foreign guys being here. Now some do. Like those old men down there (points down the street where a group of older island men have gathered). I bet if you went down there and asked them that question they would tell you a different answer. But not me, man. Just as long as they don't take away from my business and keep giving me business I don't care how long they stay….Man, the jobs that the tourists take are the ones that the locals don't want or can't do anyway, man.

F: Even if they don't have their papers.

B: Well, man, you know most of them don't, and well, man, I don't care about that either. Some do though. Just the other day some local, and I won't name names, went and complained to the police that there were lots of illegals working here. So the mayor had to crack down, but give it a couple of weeks and it will be right back to the way it was before. That kind of thing happens all the time, man, when one guy gets jealous of another guy making more money or something and then they go and tell but it doesn't last for long. Really it only hurts them because they're the ones hiring the foreign guys. Not me, man, I have no need for them.

A minority of islanders, however, still hold bitter feelings. Although "ticks" are contributing to the economy in general, by renting rooms and houses and buying food and other locally produced goods and services, some feel these backpackers are taking jobs from locals. But as shown in the above conversation, most of the jobs the backpackers take are jobs that locals, "don't want or can't do." It must be stressed that those who dislike the backpackers are those who benefit the least from them living on Utila.

Additionally, some also feel that as tourism has become the

predominant industry and more foreigners are living on the island for extended periods of time, crime rates, drug use, and general disorderly conduct have increased. Proof of these accusations was never provided, nor observed. From time to time, when competition and jealousy reach a breaking point, the local government is called in to control the illegal workers. This enforcement last only a short time before backpackers are working again.

The "Spaniard"

The Bay Islanders have always harboured bitter feelings towards the mainland "Spanish" populations. As documented by *Davidson (1974)* three decades ago, these feelings stem from the many feuds between the English and Spanish throughout the settlement history of the islands, as well as the many cultural differences, and the general lack of communication between the Bay Islanders and the Hondurans. As I spent time with many older Utilians it became clear that the resentment lingers as they told me stories about when they were. Their stories were riddled with profanities and harsh generalizations, as my informants described experiences with the mainland Hondurans.

In each case, the Utilians described episodes of harassment and ridicule at the hands of the mainlanders. Many of them said they would be called, "uneducated, uncultured, thieves" by the Hondurans. Perhaps it is not surprising to see similar attitudes expressed about the ladinos who are no living on the island. A reversal of harassment and ridicule has now surfaced against the ladinos who have recently made Utila their home.

The first wave of Honduran migrants came to the islands in the 1960s. This group however, preceded the economic boom associated with the tourism industry that has been blamed for the recent influx. *Davidson (1974)* concluded that the initial intrusion was fueled by the favorable economic conditions on the islands associated with shipping and merchant marine industries at the time. Ladinos would come to the islands and start businesses selling Honduran made goods as well as work in the other industries on the islands. In 1968, Guanaja seemed to be the island that was drawing the largest portion of ladinos. This cultural group made up approximately eight percent of the island's total. Surprisingly, Roatán's ladino population made up only three percent of its much larger total. Utila, although involved in the merchant sailing business, probably was not producing as much income because the islanders had not developed a large shipbuilding industry like the other islands and therefore, in 1968, only .8% of Utila's population was ladino.

As the tourism industry began to take hold on the island, the trickle of ladinos escalated to a steady pour. The first ladino owned businesses on the island, namely Comedor Dilicia, Mario's Place, Captain Jack's, Commerca Mantoya, Delco Bike Hire, Raimundo and the two banks opened during the 1990s. Previously, the only businesses on Utila that were run by ladinos were those whose spouses were Bay Islanders.

During my surveys of 2001, businesses owned by Bay Islander and ladino couples were considered Bay Island establishments. These businesses included, The Sea Breaker, Covemen, and Samantha's 7-11. Nothing in their facades indicated they were owned by ladinos. In 1999, the first street venders pervasive elsewhere in Latin America, appeared on Utila. "Baliada Ladies" selected the cross-roads of Main Street and Main Line Road, where the municipal dock and municipal buildings are located, as their location. These ladies have been noted in many travel guides published around this same time. The "Baliada Ladies" only sold food and had not expanded into the market style shops located on the mainland.

During the summer of 2001, however, a Latin America market structure appeared on Utila. As shown in figure, items ranging from shoes to hammocks, are sold from stalls that are essentially similar to those on the mainland.

Figure 1 : Baliada Ladies found at the Municipal Dock Figure : Ladino Street Vender on Utila

Many local Utilians give two reasons for the recent influx of ladinos, the tourism industry and the alcalde. Much like the perceived economic opportunities Davidson noted in the late 1960s and early 1970s, the tourism industry on Utila has given the island a reputation with many mainlanders as a place to improve their standard of living.

Although, very few ladinos work directly in the tourism industry a few have employment in hotels as maids, on construction crews building houses and roads, and as trash collectors. They are heavily involved in the construction of the new airport, perhaps because that deal was negotiated on the mainland. Stonich noted this same phenomenon on Roatán.

Most ladinos cannot take part fully in the tourism industry because they do not have the extra income or personal contacts it takes to start businesses on the island. Subsequently, the jobs they do take, when they are available, have increased negative local attitudes towards them. Many islanders feel that since the ladinos have come to the island wages have been inflated because this group will work for much less than local residents.

Additionally, there seems to be a local attitude concerning hunting and collecting fruits from the bush that most islanders seem to follow like an unspoken law. Hunting for one's family is acceptable as well as collecting only enough fruits that can be carried out of the bush by hand. However, many ladinos have been caught hunting iguanas, turtles, and other local wildlife, which they then take to the markets on the mainland to sell. Many islanders also attest to seeing ladino families coming out of the bush with bags full of fruits and plants. The market in the adjacent coastal city of La Ceiba does have signs that advertise iguana and turtle eggs for sale. Whether ladino gathering on Utila is the source of La Ceiba's sales is unknown, but these rumours are adding to the already strained relationship between islanders and ladinos.

Figure 2 a and b: Crude Lot Separation in Camponado Neighbourhood

Beginning in 1997, when the present mayor came into power, he, in conjunction with the government of Honduras, began a project to offer poor landless Hondurans from the mainland affordable land and housing. Utila, and the other Bay Islands, offer an outlet to establish such a project because of the perceived availability of work and other monetary prospects. Those mainlanders, who had already come to

Utila, suggested that they knew the islanders were wealthier than they, and believed the prospects for work would be better on the islands because of the tourism industry. What they did not foresee was the higher cost of living on the islands and the irregularity of work because of the seasonal aspect of tourism. Nevertheless, in 1997, an area located in the interior mangrove swamp on the eastern end of the island off Cola Mico Road behind the Bucket of Blood Bar, was cleared, separated into lots and sold at "very low prices" to mainlanders (actual prices were never discussed during my research).

Camponado, the islanders' name for this new barrio, by the summer of 2001, had become a well populated area. In the preliminary 2000 census figures, the neighbourhood contained 68 houses. Two distinct areas exist in Camponado. The older one begins behind the Bucket of Blood Bar. This area has concrete sidewalks and standard Bay Island's houses and English is still spoken. This section extends approximately 30 yards from the road and does not enter the swamp. However, where the swamp water begins, concrete is replaced by wood planks and English is replaced by Spanish. This is the younger part of the neighbourhood, settled by mainlanders in 1997.

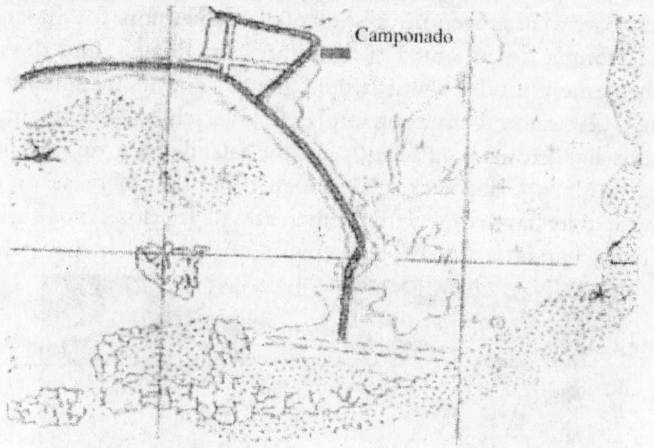

Figure 3: Location of Camponado on Utila

Land building on Utila has been a process carried out by islanders for generations. Because nearly two-thirds of the island is mangrove swamp, drying land or constructing artificial land is a common practice among islanders. New land is made from a variety of materials such as trash, fossilized coral, sand and concrete. In Camponado, land building is being carried out in a furious effort so that construction of more permanent houses can take place. However, some houses have been built in areas still under water. Without rules for sewage disposal, raw human refuse is deposited directly into the water. Trash and other materials are also thrown into the swamp reducing the environmental quality in this barrio. This type of environment is a breeding ground for many diseases such as cholera, malaria, dysentery, hepatitis and dengue fever. If regulations are not set for the continued growth of this neighbourhood, an outbreak of disease will most likely occur.

Figure 4: Land Building in Camponado Figure 6: Ladino House in Camponado

This barrio has become a source of contention for most local Utilians. Stonich documented such an area on Roatán, and described much the same attitudes towards the "ghetto" and its inhabitants. Not only has Utila's natural environment been adversely altered, the number of ladinos has grown significantly on the island since this barrio has been open. Many Utilians expressed their belief that increases in crime and drug activity have come with the increases of ladinos. As one islander said, "Their hands is full of glue, anything they touch they take".

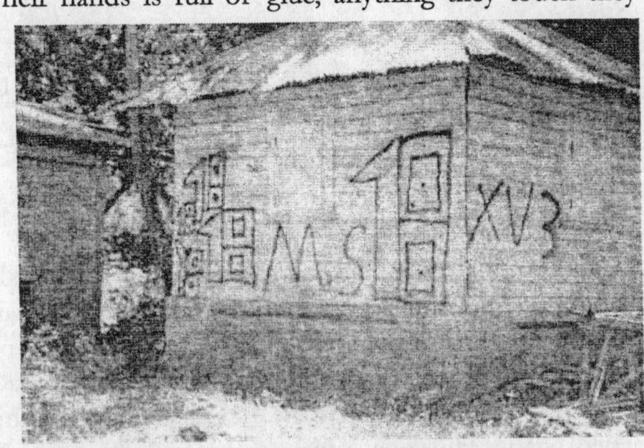

Figure 5: Mainland Honduran Gang Tags found on Utila

Many young Utilians voiced concerns about the presence of mainland gang activity on the island. Mainland gang insignia, representative of the Diez y Ocho's and the Salva Truchnas are now appearing on Utila. If gang members are on the island is not known for certain and some suspect the tags were copied by local children. Unlike the attitudes Utilians have towards the involvement of the backpackers in the tourism industry, ladinos are seen as bad for the economic livelihoods of the locals.

A local man said: "Man, those Spaniards need to go! They come here and don't work and they just steal from us. They rape tourists and then give our island a bad name....the ones that do come to our island and work, take our jobs because they will work for less than we will. The foreigners that hire them don't know that they do bad work and will end up stealing from them."

In 2001, many ladinos were seen working on construction crews, building houses and roads. Others were working to clear and clean the new foreign owned land developments on the island. Primarily, Spaniards are working on the new airport, which is being built on the eastern side of the island. Still, many ladinos are without work and until local attitudes change, finding will continue to be difficult. However, they continue to come to the island under the pretext that the perceived tourism industry boom will provide opportunities for them. The ladinos have and will continue to have an affect on the island both culturally and environmentally and the Anglo-Hispanic conflict Davidson noted nearly 30 years ago is still very much a part of Utilian life.

Utila, like many other small island tourism destinations, is beginning to experience new cultural flows that follow its growing industry. Although there was resentment in the beginning, locals are slowly tolerating these groups. The backpackers today seem to be the most accepted group. This acceptance is not unanimous but as long as the "ticks" do not interfere with local business, they are allowed to stay.

However, the new mainland families moving to the island are still under constant scrutiny Although, today intermarriages between Utilians and ladinos are common place, those families that have come to settle on the island still hold the lowest place in the social hierarchy. They have become the local scapegoat for many of the problems that have occurred since tourism became the predominate economic institution on the island.

Effects of Tourism Development on Utila

The perceived image of Utila as a place for economic opportunity has been the major catalyst for the recent, population, economic, landscape and environmental changes on the island. The perceptions are widespread throughout Central America and coincide with larger global expectations of growth in the tourism industry. The rapid transformation on Utila, if left unmanaged, will begin to challenge terrestrial and marine resources, as well as other cultural attributes of the island and may begin to undermine any long-term economic prospects for the island's residents.The potential population and cultural consequences of the developing tourism industry on Utila. These groups coupled with general visitation rates have begun to create stress on the island's resources. They have also begun to influence the island's cultural and physical landscape as well as the natural environment. This chapter will discuss changes that have occurred as a result of the developing tourism industry especially those related to population, economics, landscape and environment.

Population Growth and Composition

During the last two decades island population has increased significantly and the composition has changed drastically. Since 1980, the population has virtually doubled. This date coincides with the national decision to push tourism as a means for economic prosperity. From the mid-1800s to the mid 1970s the total population of the islands grew at about 3.5% per year. This growth corresponded with the approximate annual growth on the mainland.

According to the 1988 census, the annually growth rate for the Bay Islands had reached a high of 4.5% and increased to about 5% between 1988 and 1996 *(ibid)*. The islands' growth rate differed significantly from the mainland where population increase has never exceeded 3.5% annually *(ibid)*. According to *Stonich (2000)*, in 1991 Bay Island population was 24,000, with Utila contributing less than 10%, or about 2,200. Preliminary figures from the 2000 census placed Utila's population at about 6,500, indicating a significant contribution from in-migration.

As might be expected with the recent population increases, population composition has also changed. According to *Stonich (2000)*, the percentage of ladinos on the Bay Islands increased from 7% in 1970, to 12% in 1981, and by 1988 this group made up nearly 16% of the islanders. This acceleration of migration by this group has begun to shift the ethnic composition and distribution of settlements on the islands. Bay Islanders historically located their settlements along coastlines in a linear form. However, as the mainlanders migrated to the islands they tend to live away from the existing settlements in marginalized areas, such as Camponado on Utila. This new pattern is related to their social status on the islands. For traditional Bay Islanders, social place is related to physical space. Those who have property on coastlines or nearby the water generally hold higher social positions than those who are relegated to marginalized areas such as swamps and other interior places. Thus, as migration continues ethnic composition and distribution of human settlements will continue to change.

Economic Change

As both *Davidson (1974)* and *Lord (1975)* chronicled, the Bay Islanders have developed a type of "economic resilience" throughout their history. Utila's inhabitants have survived throughout periods of slavery, piracy, boom and bust cycles of the fruit trade, fishing, fish processing, and remittances. Indeed this economic resilience is fostered by the adaptability of the islanders. As Lord suggested with his critique of the remittance system, the islanders developed traits that helped them create and rebound from the inevitability of economic boom and bust cycles. Although there has not been a bust cycle in the merchant sailing business per se there has been a world boom in tourism. Tourism, the world's largest industry, is, according to the World Travel and Tourism Council, growing at a rate 23% faster then the world economy *(WTO 2000)*. Although some islanders still participant in the remittance system, many are now depend on tourism.

Susan *Place (1988)*, in her work documenting the establishment of Tortuguero National Park in Costa Rica, identified several consequences associated with tourism expansion in this region. Among the most important she pointed out were the socioeconomic differentiation of the local population, the placement of local populace into menial jobs, inflation, and increased foreign ownership of local resources *(ibid)*. She also recognized that those who benefited most from the local community were the wealthier residents who could take advantage of expanding opportunities *(ibid)*.

This is also the case on Utila. The gap between the rich and poor on the island continues to grow. The population of migrants from the mainland, as one might expect, make up the lower end of the spectrum. Those families who prospered most from earlier economic systems have been more able to take advantage of the opportunities presented by tourism. However, those residents who came later to the island or those who have not acquired the monetary or land resources from past economic endeavours are relegated to menial jobs in the developing industry. Foreign ownership of land and valuable resources has also become a problem as liberal investment policies are instituted by the national government to help facilitate the growing tourism industry.

Perhaps this new economic endeavour in tourism is a continuation of past sporadic trends. However, none of these past periodic expansions had the capability to so thoroughly undermine the island's resource base or so rapidly change the availability of resources on Utila. Now the dependence on tourism is most evident and through continued policy expansions by the national government this industry will probably continue to grow. However, if tourism proceeds at its current rate and remains unregulated as it is now, the future of the island's economic and environmental landscapes might be in jeopardy.

Cultural Landscape Change

Lord (1975) suggested that the first people to inhabit Utila proper located away from the shoreline and out of the range of the sandfly. However, because of lack of infrastructure and the islanders' dependence on the sea for transportation and economic purposes they were forced to reestablished their settlement along the coastline.

Figure 6 a and b: Rain Cisterns Found on the Island used for Collecting Water

This pattern dictated a linear settlement formation. As such, houses were normally built on stilts out over the water, so that they could not only have unobstructed access to the ocean and daily sea breezes but also they were out of the range of the sandfly and mosquito *(ibid)*. In 1974 Davidson noted that nearly 83% of the houses in the Bay Islands were, "on stilts with wooden floors, lumber walls, and zinc roofs". He also noted that most houses were built in a box-like fashion with shuttered windows and porches that extended half way or completely across the front of the structure. Rain cisterns were also characteristic of Utilian houses before water systems where installed and still can be seen today. Outhouses on stilts with walkways that extend over the water which were sometimes used as temporary docks are also characteristic of Utila's landscape. These structures were present on Utila in 2001 but most were in great disrepair.

Family owned docks and boathouses were also an important feature to the many Utilians and remain part of the modern landscape. Other architectural styles adopted from the British West Indian Victorian house were also present on the landscape in the 1970s as seen in figure. Originally the structure was a family owned house, however, it is now owned by an American and houses two separate businesses.

Figure 7 a and b: Traditional British West Indian House Type found on Utila

The initial settlement of East Harbour, in terms of architectural style, has not undergone much change because of the developing tourism industry. However, beginning in the 1970s as North American influences increased with the initial development of the industry, local response to these foreign developers created, as Davidson's put it, a "new American resident-tourist landscape". Most important to this landscape was the construction of tourist related facilities for lodging and meals. On Utila the first facilities built were incorporated into local houses. New structures related to the industry were not constructed until the 1980s. However, these facilities were constructed in fashions that resemble existing buildings and houses on the island. Recently, as foreign, less expensive construction materials become more readily available, developers have shifted structures from wood (the traditional building material) to concrete blocks, brick, and cement.

Figure 8 : Brick Hotel found near old Airport Figure : Concrete Structure Located in Cola del Mico

Figure 9 : Hotel under Construction near old Airport

As foreign capital and foreign developers become more prevalent on the island, larger and more Americanized structures have appeared in East Harbour. Since 1990, a few houses have been constructed away from the initial settlement of East Harbour, in a fashion that differs from traditional local styles. In 1995 John *Pigram (208)* wrote, "Tourism is, to a large degree, a resource-based activity, interacting with natural systems and with the capacity to initiate far-reaching changes on the environment". Tourism projects are not solely responsible when discussing environmental damage caused by human activity, however management of these issues has become central to tourism planning in both developing and developed worlds.

Figure 10 : New Structure built in 2000 near the centre of Town

Figure 11 : House found near Blue Bayou Figure : House found on the Southwestern end of the Island

Physical Landscape Change

As the industry has grown in recent years, island environments have incurred drastic development because these locations offer popular attractions for tourist. Tourism development impacts on these environments, such as Utila, are exacerbated, because these places are small and incorporate fragile ecosystems. The Hol Chan Marine Reserve in Belize has become a popular diving site. In Carter's discussion of this site, he discussed the deterioration that over-diving has caused to the local reef.Other environmental problems have been documented specifically associated with tourism such as: water pollution and subsequent decline of potable water, air pollution, waste disposal problems, ecological disruption, and land use changes. Because of the demands of an escalating human population caused by migration and the unfettered development of the tourism industry, Utila's fragile ecosystem has incurred unprecedented stress and decline. In this section we will discuss particular attributes of Utila's industry that are at the root of these problems as well as the effects of their development.

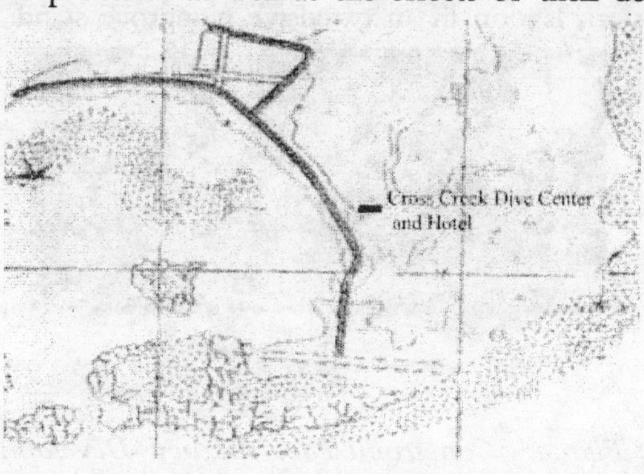

Figure 12 : Location of Cross Creek Dive Centre and Hotel on Utila

As Davidson noted in 1974, implications for the most drastic landscape change occur when developers, both local and foreign, begin constructing tourism facilities and residential areas away from the existing community.

The most palpable alterations on Utila have included the clearing of vegetation, especially mangrove on the water front and along the outer edges of the interior lagoons, draining and land building in these wetland areas, the construction of larger more lavish facilities for boarding higher paying tourists, dredging canals for travel inside the reef, construction of larger docks so that the bigger dive boats can be docked, the building of artificial beaches along the northeastern shore and the planting of palms and other ornamental plants in this area, and the cutting of horse trails and hiking paths through the bush.

Figure 13 a and b: New Development in the Interior Lagoon Associated with Cross Creek Dive Centre

The first major physical landscape alterations related to tourism began in 1988 with the construction of Cross Creek Dive Centre and Hotel. The facility was built on the interior side of the main road back into the eastern lagoon in an extensive mangrove stand.

Figure 14 : Planters Constructed for the new Development site on the Eastern Shore

The area had been filled with mangrove and as the business expanded land filling projects took place as more area of the swamp was needed. Today this area not only incorporates Cross Creek Dive Centre but residential houses have also been built.

The majority of the tourism-related businesses that have developed on Utila since 1970 have been constructed on otherwise unoccupied land showing that tourism has begun to have an effect on the island's physical landscape and land-use patterns. However, these facilities tended to stay within the existing settled area of East Harbour until the 1990s, when expansion into uninhabited parts of the island began.

Figure 15 : Coral Walls Constructed for the new Development site on the Eastern Shore

The expansion incurred during the 1990s has caused more striking alteration and can be directly linked to both the foreign owned residential developments that have appeared on the island in recent years and the building of the first two resorts. A discussion of the recent foreign owned residential developments began to describe some of the landscape alterations that have taken place. Destruction of the iron shore on the northeastern portion of the island and the removal of the natural vegetation in this area are but a few of the changes.

As shown in above figures this area is now lined with palms and other ornamental decorations such as the coral walls and planters. Scenes such as this are a reminder of the close connection Utila has with the United States, because such landscape ornamentation is popular in beach communities in the United States. The development on the southwestern area of the island, in an otherwise uninhabited location, is currently only accessible by boat. Plans are being discussed to cut a canal through the interior of the island (in a seasonal swampy region) and connect it with Oyster Bay Lagoon, thus creating direct sheltered access for the residents. Ecological damage, such as salt water intrusion into the lagoon as water is siphoned out for the canal and large amounts of sediment deposition on either ends of the canal have been addressed during recent island discussions. Currently, the Bay Islands Conservation Association, along with many local Utilians, has organized to make a protected area of the interior of the island directly behind the settlement to prevent the canal from being constructed. Along with the developing foreign residential communities, the construction of two resorts has also been responsible for physical landscape change. *Davidson (1974)* recognized a pattern to expanding tourism industries and noted that significant changes occur when larger resorts, which cater to higher paying clientele with services beyond just room and board are built, away from the existing settlements.

Utila Reef Resort and Laguna Beach Resort. These resorts were constructed in uninhabited parts of the island. Utila Reef Resort is located near Pretty Bush, farther away from the lagoon, and has not been very profitable. In 2001 no visitors had been reported in a least a year. Because it is smaller than Laguna, very little vegetation was cleared was necessary for its construction.

Figure 15: Utila Reef Resort Located West of Oyster Bay Lagoon

However, Laguna Beach Resort sits at the edge of the lagoon and large mangrove stands and other beach vegetation were cleared for its construction. Because it is only accessible by boat, the owner constructed a large dock well into an area were the reef is present.

As the resort's reputation grew, the owner wanted to be able to moor his boats in the lagoon instead of at the larger docks in East Harbour. However, the entrance to the lagoon is very shallow, less than three feet, so dredging was required for his boats to have access.

Figure 17 : Laguna Beach Resort found at the mouth of Oyster Bay Lagoon

Now, it seems, large amounts of sediment from the lagoon are being deposited on the reef, destroying the one of the things that brings customers to the island. In addition to the two resorts that are located beyond Oyster Bay Lagoon, in 1995, a local man began constructing a large hotel in Blue Bayou. However, to construct a hotel of this magnitude in this area of Utila, extensive cutting of the interior mangrove was needed, as well as land building into the lagoon.

Figure 18 a and b: New Hotel Built near Blue Bayou

The hotel remains unfinished because of lack of funds and water damage incurred during Hurricane Mitch. Infrastructural transportation improvements, such as the construction of new roads and especially the new international airport, are also having negative impacts on the physical landscape. On Utila, roads are constructed with cement and coral.

After an area is cleared and lined with wooden two-by-fours, a layer of coral is placed between the wood as a foundation. Then cement is poured on top of the coral to make a smooth surface. The road being constructed in Figure above is privately owned and funded. It leads to an area on the south side of Stewart's Hill where a foreign developer has planned a new residential community. Construction of the community had not been set as of the summer of 2001. The men constructing the road said that the coral being used came from the new airport construction site.

Figure 19 : Traditional Road Construction on the Island

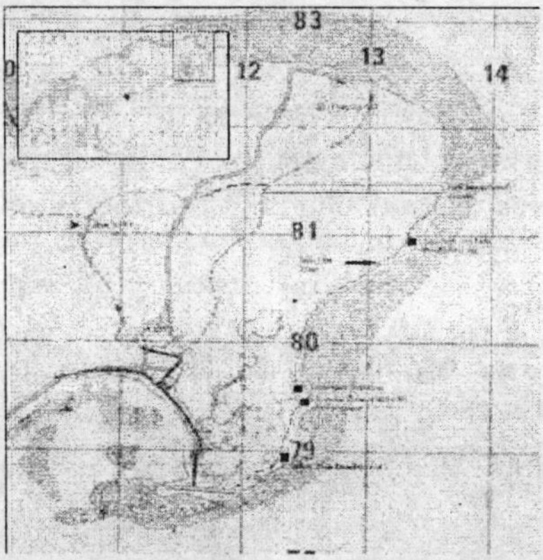

Figure 20 : Location of the New International Airport on Utila

Before the coral at the new airport site was available, or large quantities of cement were affordable, sand and gravel were taken from Pumpkin Hill Beach along with coral from the exposed reefs and iron shore. This has caused increased beach erosion in these areas *(McNab 2001)*. This type of impact has been noted elsewhere in the Caribbean and has had long-term impacts on the beach landscape.

The new international airport was a "hot topic" with the locals during the summer of 2001. It is located at Swan's Bay on the northeastern tip of the island.

Figure 21 : New Airport under Construction on Utila

Figure 22 : Natural Fresh Water Wells on Utila

Before construction, this area consisted of lush secondary tropical forest and also incorporated natural fresh water wells, it was the breeding ground for the island's iguanas as well as the nesting area for many of Utila's birds *(ibid)*. In the conservation strategy prepared by Tropical Research and Development, Inc, this area was recommended to remain undeveloped because of its ecological importance to the island's potable water and its endemic species. However, in 1999 an area approximately 1,700 meters long by 250 meters wide by 2 meters deep (some 425,000 meters squared) was bulldozed for the construction of the runway. The tropical forest was split in half, causing a condition known as fragmentation. When fragmentation occurs, important resources for local species may not be evenly distributed and corridors allowing animals to access different resources are no longer available. As a result many of the birds that use to nest on Utila are leaving and the iguana's are in decline.

Construction stopped temporarily during the summer of 2000 leaving the unprotected bare soil exposed during the ensuing rainy season. Soil loss in areas of heavy construction has been documented as being as great as 490 ton/hectares annually. While forested area losses can be as little as.02 ton/hectares annually. The reefs on this side of Utila are some of the most famous because of the natural caverns that line the shore and most well preserved because they have been hard to reach. Now they are in danger of being damaged by the erosion and sediment discharge from the airport.

Roatán experienced similar problems when minor work was done to extend its runway, as sedimentation damage to the coral reef was documented 30 meters into the sea. When the new airport is finished international aircraft can land on the island and bring more tourists per visit. Of course air and noise pollution associated with international airports will also be present.

When the equipment for the construction of the new airport was deposited on the island a new road was cut along the eastern coast. Large mangrove stands and tropical forest made up this part of the island. The new residential developments followed the construction of this road into this uninhabited area.

The new airport has also been connected with East Harbour by the small footpath leading from Bar in The Bush to Pumpkin Hill. However, it has been widened and paved, making it the island's first "highway." The airport road cleared a section of forest nearly 10 meters wide and several kilometres long making it the widest road on the island. According to *Stonich (2000)*, the principal forces behind habitat destruction on the Bay Islands are related to, "deforestation, inappropriate agricultural practices, highway building, and unsound tourist-related construction." These forces have been at work on Utila and, as shown above, they have occurred in a relatively short period of time.

Land use and land cover alterations, not solely related to tourism, are also important in this discussion. In 1993 Tropical Research and Development, Inc., conducted a comprehensive study of land use and land cover on the Bay Islands. Twelve principal categories of land cover and land use were established by the research group for the entire archipelago. These include primary forests, secondary forests, mixed forests, coniferous forests, mangroves, wetlands, brush, pastures, permanent agriculture, annual agriculture, water areas, and urban areas.

All of these specific areas have been affected by human activity on the islands. Less than two percent of the islands' primary forests remain and within this two percent many of the most desirable trees have been extracted *(ibid)*. The mangrove and wetland areas, until recently with construction of large hotels and other tourism facilities, had not been adversely affected *(ibid)*. As suggested by Tropical Research and Development (TRD), Inc., the two most common land cover types are pastures and secondary forests. TRD has stated that the islands have experienced most of its land cover clearing in the last 15 years because this is the time these land cover types became popular on the islands *(ibid)*. Pastures are the most undesirable land use option for the islands because activities associated with pastures, such as cattle and horses, yield little productivity in the Bay Islands. These activities also cause an increase in soil compaction and erosion *(ibid)*. In table Utila's land use and land cover categories are illustrated.

Table 2 : Land Use on Utila, 1993

	Area (Hectares)	Percent of Total Land
Primary Forest	0	0
Secondary Forest	802.2	19
Mixed Forest	0	0
Coniferous Forest	0	0
Mangrove	741.2	17.6
Swamps	2303.5	54.6
Brush	0	0
Pasture	206	4.9
Permanent Agriculture	69.2	1.6
Annual Crops	0	0

Utila, according to the above study, has high proportions of land that are poor for agriculture. Therefore the TDR has suggested that eighty-two percent of the islands become protected areas *(ibid)*. Aside from being of poor agricultural quality these lands also are valuable for water resource conservation as well as flora and fauna conservation *(ibid)*. Tourism, as exemplified in this section, has caused significant change in multiple areas, for Utila. The residents of Utila, only a small island in a nation undergoing extensive global economic transformations, are faced with enormous challenges as they try to broker tensions between economic development and personal conservation. It will become increasingly necessary for Utilians to stay aware of development as the industry continues to grow. Care must be taken so that the two most important attractions to the island, its culture and its environment, are not lost and completely destroyed.

4

Kangaroo Island Tourism

Introduction

This document presents a case study of the potential of incentive instruments and mechanisms designed to promote the conservation of biodiversity on Kangaroo Island. The aim of the study is to outline the biodiversity values on the island, determine the threatening processes that exist, and recommend instrument mixes to conserve the biodiversity values. In particular, the study focuses on the impact of nature-based tourism and ecotourism on biological diversity and discusses the use of incentives and instruments to minimise threats to biodiversity values by the tourism industry.

The Area

Kangaroo Island is situated 13 kilometres from the southeastern coast of South Australia and is 121 kilometres southwest of Adelaide. The island covers an area of approximately 4,300 sq km and is used primarily for conservation, tourism and agriculture. The agricultural lands still contain fragmented areas of uncleared native vegetation. The eastern part of the island has been settled and farmed since the nineteenth century. Most of the large scale clearing and settlement of the western half of the island occurred between 1947 to 1962. Sheep grazing for wool and meat is the major agricultural activity. Almost 30% of the island is within National Parks, Wilderness Protection Areas and Conservation Parks. The largest of these are in the southern and southwestern areas of the island. A number of mechanisms are used in these reserves to cope with present and projected tourist numbers.

Biodiversity Status

Kangaroo Island was isolated from the mainland approximately

9,500 years ago as the sea rose to its present level after the most recent glacial maximum which occurred about 18,000 years ago. The island has been isolated from the mainland for the majority of time since the Tertiary Period approximately 65 million years ago. As a result there are unique flora and fauna on the island as well as species common to the adjacent mainland. Aborigines disappeared from the island between 2,250 and 4,300 years ago for unknown reasons. As a result, Kangaroo Island has experienced a different fire regime to the mainland since that time. This provides an interesting comparison with the mainland, as do other factors such as freedom from foxes and rabbits. Kangaroo Island is also fortunate in that much of the roadside remnant vegetation is relatively undisturbed.

Vegetation

There has been great change to the structure and distribution of vegetation on Kangaroo Island during the last 100 years. Extensive clearing has taken place, particularly in the east, and there has been a greater fire frequency since white settlement. Selective elimination of species has taken place, for example, the grasstree Xanthorrhoea was used for resin making.

Trees of significance on the island include the Kangaroo Island Narrow-leaved Mallee (Eucalyptus cneorifolia). This species is almost entirely restricted to the eastern end of the island. The only other occurrence is in a few hectares on the Fleurieu Peninsula. The distribution of the species coincides with more productive agricultural land so has been extensively cleared. It was also favoured for the extraction of eucalyptus oil (NPWS, 1987). The Kangaroo Island Mallee Ash (Eucalyptus remota) is endemic to Kangaroo Island. It is found mainly in the western areas of the island. The E. remota open scrub alliance is considered to be poorly conserved (NPWS, 1987).

The Grasstree or Yacca (Xanthorrhoea tateana) is endemic to Kangaroo Island and the lower Fleurieu Peninsula and was extensively used in the Yacca gum stripping industry. The product, a resin, was used in the manufacture of varnish. The industry is in decline because of competition from synthetics and restrictions on vegetation clearance (NPWS, 1987). A Yacca management plan has recently been completed.

Davies (1992) listed the threatened plant species on Kangaroo Island. Species of consequence include Phebalium equestre, Olearia microdisca, Pomaderris halmaturina subsp halmaturina and Platysace heterophylla var tepperi.

Fauna

The native fauna represent one of the main attractions for visitors to Kangaroo Island.

Marine Mammals

The colony of Australian sea lions (Neophoca cinerea) at Seal Bay on the southern coast of the island is one of the island's major tourist attractions. This species is considered to be rare under the *National Parks and Wildlife Act 1972*. Estimates of the world population are between 9,300 and 11,700 individuals. Almost two-thirds of the world population occur in South Australia of which the Seal Bay population is significant. Seal Bay is the only breeding site on Kangaroo Island and it is one of only two or three breeding sites of the seal in South Australia.

Seal Bay consists of sandy beaches backed by dunes and low limestone cliffs in the east and rocky coves under sheer cliffs in the west. Most births take place in rocky coves in the western area of Seal Bay. The west is a Prohibited Area (declared under the National Parks and Wildlife Act 1972) within the whole area which is a Conservation Park. Up to one kilometre offshore is considered an Aquatic Reserve under the provisions of the Fisheries Act 1971.

At Cape du Couedic there is a colony of the New Zealand fur seal (Arctocephalus forsteri); in January 1987, 454 individuals were counted. The fur seal prefers rough and rocky sites with caves and ledges as a haul out zone, contrasting with the preference of the sea lions to haul out on sandy beaches. There is another colony of the New Zealand fur seal at Cape Gantheaume; however, this is very rarely visited by tourists. Several species of whale frequent the waters around Kangaroo Island. The Southern Right Whale visits the southern coast between June and October.

Fairy Penguins, Eudyptula minor, make their nests in the sandhills and cliffs along the coast. They can be seen after sunset along the rocks near the Penneshaw and Kingscote jetties as they return from fishing.

Large Mammals

The Tamar Wallaby (Macropus eugenii) was once common in South Australia and Western Australia. It now has a range in South Australia restricted to one mainland location on Eyre Peninsula and several offshore islands (NPWS, 1987), and also occurs in southwest Western Australia and some offshore islands. They are now abundant only on Kangaroo Island. The Kangaroo Island Kangaroo (Macropus fuliginosus fuliginosus) is a distinctive sub-species of the Western Grey Kangaroo, only found on Kangaroo Island. Both kangaroo and wallaby species are still common on the island with some farmers considering the wallaby a pest.

Small Mammals

Only one specimen of the Common Marsupial Mouse (Sminthopsis aitkenii) has been collected from the island since two specimens were collected in 1969. There is one record of the Brush-tailed Phascogale (Phascogale tatoatafa) in 1939 but this is probably now extinct. The Short-nosed Bandicoot (Isoodon obesulus) is found in forest and woodland on Kangaroo Island (Inns et al., 1979). Two species of Pigmy Possum are found on the island; the Southwestern Pigmy Possum or Mundarda (Cercartetus concinnus) is common throughout the island while the Little Pigmy Possum (C. lepidus) is uncommon. Six species of bat have been recorded but only three of these are common (Inns et al., 1979).

Monotremes

The Echidna (Tachyglossus aculeatus) is found on the island.

Birds

There are 216 species reported on the island. Kangaroo Island is the only part of South Australia where the Glossy Black Cockatoo occurs regularly. It is restricted to Casuarina woodland and is the most critically endangered vertebrate on the island. The Cockatoo feeds on the seeds of the drooping Sheoak and nests in Sugar Gum hollows. The total island population consists of about 150 birds; of these most are males (DELM, 1993). The yellow tailed Black Cockatoo is common and flocks are often seen. The Crimson Rosella is regarded as an endemic sub-species. Human activity has disrupted the birds on Kangaroo Island in a number of ways and was most likely responsible for the extinction of the Dwarf Emu. It was common when the island was discovered by Europeans in 1802. Other bird species have been introduced into Flinders Chase in the 1920's and 1930's; several of these survive. Other exotic species have colonised over the last century. The Kingscote and American River area and the Cygnet River estuary provide habitats for a number of wading birds. There are only a few extensive areas of fresh and brackish water on Kangaroo Island. Examples include the Cygnet River and Murray's and Lashmar's Lagoons. An introduced species, the Cape Barren Goose, is the most significant waterbird.

Other Animals

No reptile or amphibian species is unique to the island.

Introduced Australian Species

The Platypus (Ornithorhynchus anatinus), Koala (Phascolarctos cinereus) and the Common Ringtail (Pseudocheirus peregrinus) have all been successfully introduced to the island. They are found mainly in the western part of the island. The Common Brushtail Possum (Trichosurus vulpecula) is another introduced species. It is very common and larger than the mainland form. A number of birds have been introduced to the island including the Cape Barren Goose.

Other Introduced Species

Introduced species that have caused damage to native vegetation include the pig (Sus scrofa) and goat (Capra hircus). Domestic cats (Felis catus) and dogs (Canis familiaris) occur as feral animals. The cat has very likely had an influence on numbers and distribution of the smaller native animals. Pigs, goats and cats are found in several parks. Goats and pigs are concentrated in the western end of the island in Flinders Chase National Park.

Ecotourism, Resource-use and Conservation Objectives

Current Ecotourism

Kangaroo Island's permanent residents number about 4,000 (KISDC, 1995). The main service centres are Kingscote, with more than one thousand people, American River and Penneshaw. Accommodation for tourists is concentrated in these areas which are all located on the eastern side of the island. The west is serviced by the township of Parndana. Ecotourism and nature based tourism on Kangaroo Island is providing an alternative source of income to the local community. During 1993 there were 120,000 visitors, of which approximately one-third of visits were day trips and two-thirds stayed one night or more. It is anticipated by the South Australian Tourist Commission that visitor numbers will reach 180,000 by the year 2000. It is possible that numbers might be as high as 270,000 if marketing and development of the island is effective.

The South Australian Tourism Commission aims to promote Kangaroo Island as a pre-eminent international ecotourism destination. A number of Commonwealth, State and local policies have been developed to address the tourism development of the island.

Existing Commonwealth policies relevant to tourism development on Kangaroo Island include:

* the National Strategy for Ecologically Sustainable Development;
* the National Tourism Strategy; and
* the National Ecotourism Strategy.

Existing South Australian government policies include:

* Ecotourism: a Natural Strategy for South Australia;
* Kangaroo Island Tourism Policy; and
* Kangaroo Island Draft Sustainable Development Strategy (Working Strategy).

Prior to the arrival of car ferries from the mainland, most visitors relied on air transport and local island tourist buses. Visitor patterns have changed substantially since the introduction of car ferries and more recently with the introduction of the Super Flyte Ferry (Fast Ferry) transporting passengers only. This ferry transports visitors directly to the island from Glenelg and commenced operations in late 1994. This ferry service commenced operations with little prior notice to the island community and since it is capable of transporting 500 a day, it has the capacity to impact greatly on the type of tourism attracted to the island and the island community itself.

Island residents are concerned about the impact from the number of visitors this ferry is capable of delivering to the island. Tourism Kangaroo Island is responsible for the development, marketing and management of the tourist industry on the island. They have worked towards the development and marketing of an 'ecologically sustainable tourism model.' This encourages a nature based industry with a low environmental impact and high quality experience. Visitors are encouraged to spend longer than just a day trip. Tourism Kangaroo Island has developed the Kangaroo Island Tourism Development Policy. High delivery transport appears to be in conflict with the tourist model put forward in the Kangaroo Island Tourism Development Policy and the Sustainable Development Strategy for Kangaroo Island as it encourages:

* a high volume of day visitors who contribute little to the local island economy;
* an increase of fast hire cars and tourist buses on the roads as tourists wish to visit as many attractions as possible during one day;
* deterioration of the road network;

* a subsequent increase in road accidents and road kills of wildlife;
* pressure on existing infrastructure;
* pressure on natural attractions; and
* effects on islander lifestyle.

There are a small number of ecotourism operations on the island. These are modest operations that cater for tourists seeking a highly interpreted, nature based experience. The market is generally aimed at the top end international market and at tourists who want visits of more than one day.

Tourists visit the island to experience the coastal scenery and associated recreation opportunities as well as the natural environment and abundant wildlife. Many of these attractions occur within existing National Parks, Conservation Parks and Wilderness Protection Areas, in particular Flinders Chase National Park and Cape Gantheaume, Seal Bay and Kelly Hill Conservation Parks.

An island park pass has been developed by the managers of the National and Conservation Parks to facilitate funding for park facility infrastructure and interpretation. Major developments in the parks are limited to high visitation areas, in particular Cape Borda, Cape du Couedic, Remarkable Rocks, the Rocky River Headquarters area and Seal Bay. Developments such as viewing platforms and footpaths are important in mitigating disturbance and damage to the sites and associated flora and fauna. Infrastructure is especially important in controlling the disturbance and allowing safe viewing at the seal colonies.

Flinders Chase National Park is the largest park on the island and represents 74,000 hectares of largely undisturbed habitat. Over 70,000 tourists visit this park every year from a wide range of nationalities, with most arriving by tourist coach or car. Tourists visiting the western end of the island generally return to accommodation at the eastern end. Many island roads are unsealed. At Flinders Chase, Cape du Couedic, Remarkable Rocks and the ranger headquarters are the major destinations.

One of the problems with the increase of tourists to the island is increased pressure on sensitive sites. Camping in unsupervised areas can lead to environmental disturbance, such as increased litter, soil degradation and fire risk. About 4,000 people camp in Flinders Chase National Park every year, with most camping at the Rocky River Headquarters. There is some bush camping at Snake Lagoon, West Bay and Harveys Return. These areas only have basic facilities. There are very few visitors who camp overnight along the western coast (about 200 per year). In off-reserve areas some camping occurs along the coast in both permitted, supervised areas and also in prohibited areas. Seal Bay has attracted tourists for the last 40 years to view sea lions at close quarters on the beach. The area was dedicated as a Conservation Park in 1967. Visitor access facilities were constructed in the late 1970's. Guided tours with fees were introduced in 1987; the funds are used for management of the Island's parks. Seal Bay is promoted by the South Australian Tourist Commission and the Australian Tourist Commission as one of the major attractions in South Australia.

Up to 100,000 people visit Seal Bay each year with peak levels occurring in December and January. Of these, almost half are on the island as day visitors. During January 1995 there were 18,000 visitors to Seal Bay. The National Parks and Wildlife Service has a policy of no more than 100 visitors on the beach at any time. Guided tours are of 45 minutes duration and cater for private groups and bus tours of up to 30 people. Access to the main beach is by guided tour only. Some bus operators are trained by National Parks and are permitted to provide the required supervision of their own groups. The coastal areas adjacent to the main beach are Prohibited Areas.

In 1992 the Wool and Wilderness Interpretive Centre was developed by a community committee to provide information for tourists about the wool industry and remnant vegetation on the island.

Current Conservation Objectives

There are currently 16 National Parks and Conservation Parks and five Wilderness Protection Areas on the island. In total they cover about 30% of the island. The National and Conservation Parks and Wilderness Protection Areas are administered by the Department of the Environment and Natural Resources under the National Parks and Wildlife Act. All of the public lands are managed according to guidelines set out in management plans which have been developed for each area. As well, there are more than 100 heritage agreements listed on the island.

The South Australian Government introduced the Wilderness Protection Act in 1992. Five areas on Kangaroo Island have been identified as potential wilderness areas. The largest of these is Cape Gantheaume Wilderness Protection Area and covers an area of mallee covered dunes within the Cape Gantheaume Conservation Park. The Wilderness Code of Management establishes principles of wilderness values, ecosystems, flora and fauna, Aboriginal and non-Aboriginal cultural heritage; in addition to management of visitors, scientific research and fire in wilderness protection areas and zones (DELM, 1993).

Threats to Biodiversity Values

Ecotourism and nature based tourism pose a number of potential threats to the island's biodiversity values. Current tourist numbers already pose threats but these will be exacerbated as the number of visitors increase. The types of threats have been classified into those that result in habitat loss, habitat decline, utilisation of species and direct species loss. Tourism is a potential source of these threats but it may also provide substitute forms of land use that allow for a reduction in these threats. According to the Kangaroo Island Sustainable Development Strategy Tourism Working Paper, some of the implications of this tourist growth will be:

* a requirement for extra accommodation in the high season;
* modification of existing accommodation to accommodate market preferences;
* upgrade of roads;
* improvements in visitor management;
* improvements in island interpretation and history; and
* provision of high quality customer service.

Ecosystem and Habitat Loss

Land Clearance

Land clearance on the island was a major threat to loss of biodiversity prior to the *Native Vegetation Management Act 1995* and the *Native Vegetation Act 1991*. Broadacre clearing has now effectively ceased. Clearing of vegetation for accommodation for visitors may pose a threat to biodiversity.

Roadside vegetation clearance is still taking place as the road network is upgraded to cater, in part, for the pressure of increased tourist numbers. Recently legal action was taken by Kangaroo Island Eco-Action against the District Council of Kingscote over their treatment of roadside vegetation. An area of endangered plant species was disturbed during roadworks even though the council was aware of their presence. The court action is still proceeding.

Roadside vegetation is often a refuge for a number of threatened species and is consequently an important habitat to be conserved. Vegetation in these areas is susceptible to damage and change as a result of vehicle movement, intrusion, pedestrian access, stock, fire and roadworks. There is evidence that clearance of roadside vegetation leads to the spread of dieback fungi, Phytophthora cinnamoni, by infected machinery and soil disturbance.

Ecosystem and Habitat Decline

Human Visitation

Human visitation to sensitive sites has the potential to adversely affect biodiversity. People and vehicle movement along the coast can disturb breeding sites of birds and seal pups. A number of coastal species are threatened on the island. These include the Hooded Plover (Charadrius rubricollis) which lays its eggs on the beach and on sand dunes. Consequently they are especially vulnerable to traffic destroying their eggs. There are only about 150 birds on the island. Vegetation is also susceptible to damage from trampling by stock and people, particularly in some fragile coastal ecosystems. Dogs and cats have been responsible for a number of penguin deaths along the foreshore at Kingscote. These animals may belong to both visitors and locals, but, as tourist numbers increase, there is increased likelihood of this type of disturbance.

An example of an area that may be vulnerable to active use is Pelican Lagoon. It is very shallow and comprises extensive sand and mud tidal flats with a narrow connection to the sea. There are important areas of seagrasses (Posidonia and Zostera) in the lagoon which provides an environment for seabirds, waders and dolphins. The lagoon also provides a fish nursery and feeding ground and is gazetted as an Aquatic Reserve *within which the flora and fauna cannot be removed or the seabed disturbed or any matter discharged. At present very few boats use this area. Impacts that are likely to occur if there was an increase in the number of boats on the lagoon include:*

* stirring of fine muddy sediments resulting in sediment plumes detrimentally impacting seagrasses;
* scouring of the lagoon floor;
* attraction of gulls and predatory fish resulting from fish feeding and subsequent displacement of other seabirds;
* discharge of oil/fuel and litter;

* noise disturbance of fauna;
* destruction of seagrasses by boat propellers;
* bank erosion; and
* decline of sponges in lagoon channels.

Salinity

Salinity has become a problem in areas where groundwater recharge has increased as a result of native vegetation being cleared and replaced with shallow rooted crops. In areas where clearing took place at early settlement, salinity problems appeared in the 1920's or earlier. During the 1960's and 1970's saline seepage appeared in low lying areas and many freshwater lagoons became salty. An example of this is Murray's Lagoon. This occurred about 20 years after the native vegetation was cleared. Murray's Lagoon is a popular area to view water birds. Changes to the biodiversity of the lagoon may result if salinity of the lagoon increases. Measures to address dryland salinity on agricultural land in the Murray's Lagoon catchment may be necessary to alleviate elevated salt levels in the lagoon.

Pollution

Tourism may lead to pollution of the environment in a number of ways:

* emissions of fumes and noise from ferries, aircraft, cars and buses;
* litter;
* effluent from resorts and houses running into the ocean and rivers.

If environmental standards were developed and state of the art techniques adopted to address these problems, biodiversity values could be maintained.

Introduced Species (Weeds and Feral Animals)

The sea barrier is important in hindering the spread of exotic species from the mainland. Non-Australian species that have been introduced to the island and cause damage to native vegetation include the pig (Sus scrofa) and goat (Capra hircus). Domestic cats (Felis catus) and dogs (Canis familiaris) also occur as feral animals. The cat has very likely had an influence on numbers and distribution of the smaller native animals. It is possible that the southern brown bandicoot (Isoodon obesulus) and the Kangaroo Island endemic marsupial mouse

(Sminthopsis aitkeni) may be at risk from predation by feral cats. The cat population hosts diseases such as sarcosporidiosis which is a threat to the local meat export industry. Pigs, goats and cats are found in several of the National and Conservation Parks. Goats and pigs are concentrated in the western end of the island.

Introduced plants spread from farm land into National Parks and Conservation Areas. Bridal creeper was introduced as an ornamental plant and is now becoming a threat to biodiversity on the island. It commonly spreads along the roadways and is very difficult to control. It is a major threat as it smothers the original vegetation and has the potential to change the biodiversity of large areas of land. Exotic plants can also be introduced to parks by visitors and park staff as well as vehicles and road-working machinery.

The movement of native and feral animals across reserve and farmland boundaries also contributes to the spread of weeds. Several introduced species of birds have spread within the island as a result of the establishment of grasslands. Fragmentation of native vegetation by roads and paths may also be responsible for the spread of weeds.

Koala numbers have increased to such an extent in some areas they are now having an adverse effect on the rough barked manna gum.

Fire Management

The Black Glossy Cockatoo is the most critically endangered vertebrate on the island. Accidental fires as a result of camping and burning on farm lands may be a serious threat to this bird as its habitat is adversely affected by extreme fire events. The Cockatoo feeds on the seeds of the Drooping Sheoak and nests in Sugar Gum hollows (DELM, 1993). One of the most important long-term influences on the Drooping Sheoak is the frequency of fire. An increase in fire frequency resulting from increased tourism may detrimentally influence the viability of Sheoak stands.

Direct Species Loss

Kangaroo Island has lost a number of endemic species since European settlement, for example the Dwarf Emu. Direct species extinction may occur as a result of predation by cats, goats, pigs. Cats and dogs are responsible for the death of a number of penguins and their chicks in the Kingscote and Penneshaw areas. Dogs that attack penguins in urban areas are usually destroyed. Commercial and recreational fishermen pose a threat to the seal colonies as the seals compete for lobsters and fish and sharks. Fishermen have been known to shoot seals. Seals become entangled in lines and nets and drown or eventually die from monofilament line cutting into them.

Gene Loss

Harvesting

Legal and illegal harvesting of flora and fauna may pose a threat to biodiversity values on the island. Harvesting includes commercial and recreational fishing, collection of intertidal organisms and collection of plant species, eg. Yacca (grasstree) for gum. The small brown azure butterfly (Ogyris otanes) is a very rare species. It has a known range from northwest Victoria to southwest Western Australia. Most of the known habitats of the butterfly on both mainland South Australia and Kangaroo Island are within National or Conservation Parks. They are of value to illegal exporters.

Poaching of marron for the aquaculture industry poses a threat to biodiversity values particularly in National and Conservation Parks and Wilderness Protection Areas. Marron are an introduced species and poachers penetrate the wilderness areas in vehicles and on foot, trampling vegetation and introducing exotic weed species.

Recreational and commercial fishing may affect biodiversity of the marine environment. Recreational fishermen are often concentrated along jetties on the island. Abalones and crayfish as well as fin fish and sharks are targets for commercial fishing operations. The effect of commercial and recreational fishing on the fish stocks utilised by the seal population of the island is unknown.

Culling

At present, approximately 100 permits are issued annually to cull native animals on agricultural holdings. Permit records show wallabies make up 10,000 of the known carcasses, kangaroos between 1,000 and possums make up approximately 2,500.). The animal carcasses are left to rot where they are culled. Sport shooting is not permitted in the parks on the island.

Animal Feeding

Pelican feeding occurs as a tourist attraction at American River. Tourists are discouraged from feeding wallabies and kangaroos in Flinders Chase National Park.

Existing Regulations, Incentive Instruments and Mechanisms

Responsible Management Agencies

Private land on Kangaroo Island is administered by Kingscote and Dudley councils. National Parks, Wilderness Protection Areas and Conservation Parks are administered by the Department of Environment and Natural Resources. A tourism policy was developed by the South Australian Tourism Commission in 1991 after consultation with the local community. This was subsequently revised in 1994. It concluded that "Kangaroo Island will target high benefit-low impact-markets which are environmentally aware, enjoy nature, wildlife and retreat experiences and who like to learn about and directly experience the culture and environment of the places they visit."

Landcare on the island involves 13 groups and covers almost 60% of the island. It was initiated in 1989.

A $1 million program to address detrimental impacts on the Kangaroo Island environment was introduced in 1993. The program has included the development of formal camping areas, toilet facilities and shelters with gas barbeques, defined parking areas and access walkways and lookouts (SA SoE, 1993).

The introduction of the *Native Vegetation Management Act 1985* and the *Native Vegetation Act 1991* has meant that broadscale clearing of vegetation has virtually ceased on Kangaroo Island. The 1991 Act provides incentives and assistance to landholders to preserve native vegetation. Landholders are not automatically entitled to compensation if they apply for a clearing permit.

Management of the Seal Bay sea lion colony has been undertaken by the National Parks and Wildlife Service since 1972. In 1977 a Management Plan was developed by the National Parks and Wildlife Service to minimise the effects of visitors on the sea-lions, particularly during the breeding season. Prior to this, access and facilities were largely the responsibility of Kingscote District Council. During that period "ad hoc development of the area resulted in considerable erosion of the cliff and sand dune systems, with people inadvertently clambering through significant pup refuge areas".

The Management Plan recommended the relocation of roads and car parks, alteration of walking access routes and the provision of observation areas. These developments were opened in 1981. As the visitor facilities are about 2 km east of the seal colony, people are more inclined to visit the seals for a short period. This enables a "high volume visitation with a minimum impact on the animals". By 1985 the number of visitors to Seal Bay had reached 35,000 per year and additional strategies were required to manage the area. To control numbers and protect the animals on the beach, guided tours by rangers and trained tour operators were introduced in 1987 and entry was restricted to those tourists with a guide. Ticket sale revenue enabled the improvement of infrastructure at Seal Bay, including a visitors, reception centre and boardwalk to the beach. At peak times it has been necessary to regulate the traffic flow between the picnic area and the beach.

In addition, the Department of Environment and Natural Resources has proposed a number of new strategies at Seal Bay to cope in the short term with increasing visitor numbers. These include:

* a new boardwalk to facilitate alternative tours so that there are never more than 100 people on the beach;
* a tourist shuttle service from the Bales Beach car park in the peak season to alleviate congestion in the Seal Bay car park; and
* a booking system for tour operators.

There are two main objectives for the management of Seal Bay:

* the protection of the Australian Sea Lion and associated breeding habitat; and
* the provision of high quality interpretive programs to assist in the understanding of the ecological processes and requirement for conservation of that environment.

Potential Incentive Instruments and Mechanisms

The island community is generally in agreement that the most suitable form of tourism for the island is low impact, nature based tourism with longer visits providing business and employment for a broad spectrum of the local community. Ecotourism and nature based tourism can be seen as an opportunity to provide funding for biodiversity conservation and an incentive to the community to maintain biodiversity values. A long-term vision for the island is being addressed by the development of the Kangaroo Island Sustainable Development Strategy. Baseline information is required to assist decision making. Ecotourism and nature based tourism can be used to place a value on biodiversity. Funds can be used for biodiversity research, protection and infrastructure for tourists.

Ecosystem and habitat loss, and ecosystem and habitat decline

Policy Opportunity 1

Information and education: As better information is made available for tourists, tour operators, farmers and the council on the importance of biodiversity conservation, then it may be expected that the importance of biodiversity in a given area may become more apparent and valued. Methods of linking urban and rural dwellers should also be encouraged. Information for the tourist industry could be made available through a wide variety of outlets that include:

* an information booklet on arrival at the island;
* an information booklet at the entrance to parks and in park ranger offices;
* signs in suitable areas;
* Kangaroo Island community radio and newspaper announcements; and
* tourist operators and guides.

An interpretive centre is being constructed at Seal Bay by the National Parks and Wildlife Service. If an interpretive centre for visitors at the ferry terminal was developed to provide information for tourists on arrival, it could be used to highlight the importance of biodiversity on the island. A levy charged to visitors arriving on the island could fund such a centre. 'Hands on' experience is an excellent way of educating visitors and the local community about the importance of biodiversity. For example, visits to natural areas could be combined with tree planting on degraded sites. Research programs already in place at the Pelican Lagoon Research and Wildlife Centre such as the echidna watch program could be promoted. Experts from a range of disciplines could be brought to the island to work with the community on a range of projects.

Policy Opportunity 2

Kangaroo Island management body: At present the Kangaroo Island Sustainable Development Strategy is being drafted by the island community and State government agencies. For this to be adopted successfully there is a requirement for a highly effective local government administration with good communication links with State agencies. At present the island is administered by two local councils. Restructuring of the island's management bodies into one organisation could better facilitate the coordination of new developments within standardised island environmental guidelines. This organisation would also be responsible for planning, infrastructure and communication with State departments and be ultimately responsible for the conservation of biodiversity on the island. In general it is considered important for local government to effectively represent the community and have the capacity to coordinate effectively with State and Commonwealth agencies.

Policy Opportunity 3

Off-reserve ranger interpretation and extension officers: If off-reserve rangers and extension officers were employed they could provide information and policing at sensitive sites, and could collect camping fees in off-reserve areas. At present camping fees are often not collected in off-reserve areas. A Fishing Licence Officer could be funded to patrol boat ramps, jetties and fishing grounds to disseminate information, provide advice and enforce a fishing permit system. Camping fees and fishing licences could be used to fund these positions.

Policy Opportunity 5

Enhancement of existing community grant schemes: There are 13 active Landcare groups on the island. It is possible to extend the function of these groups by providing additional funding and expert advice to conserve biodiversity. Funding is provided to replant and fence vegetation in critical areas, but the perspective is likely to be focused on land degradation issues.

Land degradation and biodiversity protection are often integrated issues and benefit may be gained by a joint approach to both issues. Landcare and Dunecare promote a sense of responsibility for land conservation by giving communities an opportunity to deal with land use problems. It may also be possible to encourage visitors, particularly from urban areas, to participate in these projects. Community grants could be available to groups or landholders to re-establish vegetation in particular areas. Commonwealth grants similar to Landcare grants could be made to the local council and non-government organisations to clean up littered, polluted or degraded areas. An example would be dune walkways over frequently used, unstable dune areas.

Policy Opportunity 5

Feral cat eradication programs: Feral cats are a problem on the island and indeed across mainland Australia. Kangaroo Island is seen by the community to provide an ideal opportunity to be an area free of feral cats. If this was achieved it could be promoted along with the rabbit and fox free status to indicate to tourists the unique qualities of the island as a destination for nature based tourism. Possible methods of cat control might include:

* restrictions on visitors bringing cats to the island;
* a requirement for all cats to be desexed and registered;
* a cat curfew;
* investigation of the possible use of a virus control; and
* issue of cat traps to the local community.

It may be advantageous for the community to eventually have a cat ban on the island with the aim of eradicating all cats on the island. If visitors realise Kangaroo Island is making an effort to reduce the cat population, they may realise the potential threat to wildlife that cats pose in their own mainland areas.

Policy Opportunity 6

Regulation, zoning and minimum impact codes: The introduction of regulations and codes to control the impact of activities on the island will probably be necessary as tourist numbers increase. These might include:

* restrictions on camping in unsupervised areas along the coast. Specific areas could be zoned as suitable for camping;
* restrictions on the introduction of exotic plants and animals to the island including ship ballast water to help prevent disease and spread of exotics;
* restrictions on visitor numbers to the island. There are already restrictions on the number of visitors to Seal Bay. Norfolk and Lord Howe Islands use a ceiling on visitor numbers to control the impacts tourists have on the biodiversity of those islands;
* restrictions on four wheel drives in sensitive off-reserve areas. There is an increasing number of vehicles making their way off road within, and more commonly, outside National and Conservation Parks. They result in damage to the vegetation and constitute initial sites for soil degradation and weed spread. Some areas may be zoned as suitable for four wheel drives.

At Seal Bay there are prohibited zones to provide protection to the seals in the breeding coves and nursery areas. These areas are signposted and enforced with explanations as to the reasons for the restrictions. There is also another zone adjacent to the main beach called a 'sea-lion snooze zone.' This provides an area for the seals away from visitors and strong winds and also protects the foredunes from erosion. It also protects visitors from accidentally walking into dozing sea-lions on the vegetated dunes.

An Aquatic Reserve was proclaimed under the Fisheries Act in 1971 with amendments added with the *Fisheries Act 1982*. This protects the area adjacent to breeding coves from fishing, boating and swimming and in the eastern areas of Seal Bay from fishing.

Clearing regulations are applicable to roadside vegetation on the island. At present the vegetation is under the control of a new management plan developed as a result of the legal action against the Kingscote Council. Regulations could be put in place to protect this vegetation from clearance. A decrease in speed limits at night in target areas may be required to help reduce the number of road kills. Signs alerting drivers could be erected.

Legislation may be required to bind all parties to environmental impact assessments for development or change to areas on the island. This would ensure biodiversity factors are considered before any activity commences.

Policy Opportunity 7

Charges and levies: A special environmental levy, similar to the per capita charge levied by the Great Barrier Reef Marine Park Authority, may be applicable for each tourist arriving on the island. This could be collected by the island ferry operators and the island airlines as a ferry tax or an airport tax. Local residents would hold an exemption pass. To encourage longer stays, a flat rate entry fee or a reducing daily rate could be charged. However, the levy should not be used as the primary basis to exclude visitors on the basis of cost. This approach is considered inequitable and disadvantages low income earners. The levy should only be charged at a level that reflects the cost of services and amenities provided. The visitor funds could be used to:

* finance distribution of information on biodiversity on the island;
* rehabilitate and protect on and off-reserve areas of high biodiversity;
* pay for site development and infrastructure such as accommodation, walking paths, toilet facilities, fireplaces and fuel;

* pay for monitoring and research; and
* pay for visitor and fire management.

Commercial businesses are granted licences to operate within the parks. These rights could be offered under a tender process to raise funding for biodiversity conservation. This process would need to consider the needs of small local operators and care may need to be taken to avoid large businesses gaining monopoly control by accepting short-term losses.

At present, visitors entering the National Parks for guided tours and camping are required to pay a fee. An Island Pass is available for $15 per adult; this entitles visitors access to all Park guided tours and two weeks camping. The introduction of entry fees by parks allows the employment of information guides in the parks. The fee also provides facilities for visitors such as toilets and fireplaces. In areas sensitive to fire, fees could pay for gas cooking fires in the camping areas. The guiding system at Seal Bay provides funds for facility upgrades and employment of interpretation staff. Seal Bay was the first "user pays" system in South Australia and initially the proposal was heavily criticised. Funds collected at Seal Bay amounted to nearly $250,000 during 1993.

Policy Opportunity

Provision of Infrastructure

It is important to note that visitor pressure is not based solely on the number of visitors; it may be determined by a relationship that includes the number of visitors, their behaviour and the protecting or controlling infrastructure. At Seal Bay new infrastructure is being developed to cope with increasing tourist numbers in the short term. An additional boardwalk will be constructed to allow tourists to view the sea lions without having to walk on the beach. The beach tours will still operate for tourists seeking a tour with a greater degree of interpretation.

There may be grounds to provide grants to local/State authorities for the provision of such infrastructure to protect a site from degradation. Ultimately, however, consideration will need to be given to the type of experience that is desired by the visitor. Infrastructure may provide for increased visitor numbers but may limit the type of experience available. It would be expected that at some stage absolute numbers may need to be constrained.

Restrictions on Tourist Numbers

When tourist numbers are such that they are likely to adversely affect sensitive sites, particularly in peak season, a ceiling on visitor numbers may have to be introduced. This could be implemented on either a first come, first served basis, a ballot system, or on the basis of price. There are grounds on the basis of equity not to use price as a method of exclusion. Opportunities may also exist to redistribute some of the visits to off-peak seasons with special packages such as discounting or promotion of alternative experiences. This provides other benefits in the form of longer employment periods for casual staff and improved utilisation of accommodation facilities.

Monitoring and Guiding

A regular census of the sea-lion population at Seal Bay has been carried out by National Parks and Wildlife field staff over the last 25 years. More recently 'head counts' of sea-lions on the Main Beach have been conducted over 35 days of the peak tourist season, December and January 1985-87. The results showed that there was little change in the numbers of sea-lions on the beach in response to visitors; in fact there was an average increase of 33 animals arriving on the beach during the day at the peak of the tourist season. Since this study was completed there has been a large increase in visitors to Seal Bay. Further monitoring and a study need to be undertaken to look at current tourism effects on the sea lion population and the effects the proposed new boardwalk may have on the colony. The fur seal colony at Cape du Couedic could be included in this study as the new stairway at Admirals Arch takes tourists down the side of the cliff to a landing in close proximity to a pup refuge area.

Community monitoring of species and habitats may prove a worthwhile method of creating a biodiversity inventory. Schemes in other parts of Australia include Saltwatch and Waterwatch. Recreational fishermen could be encouraged to record the species and quantity of their catch and hand in their results as they leave the island.

Residents of the local community are employed by the Department of the Environment and Natural Resources as guides for a range of tours. The Department of Environment and Natural Resources provide training for these staff. More use could be made of this system particularly in off-reserve areas with staff being used as information officers at the ferry terminal and along coastal camping and fishing areas.

Ecotourism Accreditation

If ecotourism operators were licensed and accredited, a star rating indicating standard of service could be adopted with the National Parks logo used where appropriate. Codes of Conduct might be adopted which include criteria and standards of Best Practice for all aspects of tour operation to encourage appropriate interaction between operators, clients and the environment. Training for tour operators on site could be a worthwhile way of training operators unable to attend formal training courses.

Incentive to gain accreditation can be achieved whereby accredited operators are required to pay lower insurance premiums than operators who are without accreditation. This type of approach has been negotiated between the Victorian Tourist Operators Association (VTOA) and an insurance company. The discount is available to some operators outside Victoria and there may be merit in facilitating the operation of such a scheme nationally.

Visits to high impact tourist areas such as Seal Bay should be accompanied by a ranger or an accredited trained tourist operator. Income from accreditation courses and licences can go towards financing biodiversity conservation.

Cooperatives

The Tourism Promotion Board may be able to assist small tour operators by providing funding for cooperatives. This may enable small operators to promote their operations at a reduced cost so they are able to compete with the large tour operators, particularly off-island tour operators. This may also allow promotion of longer stays on the island, based on quality experience.

Charges on Discharges

Sewage discharges from tourist developments along the coastal areas can have a large impact on biodiversity values in an area by elevating nutrient levels. Charges on the amount of effluent discharged into the ocean or into sewerage works could be instigated.

Kingscote is serviced by household septic systems whereby overflow from tanks is directed into a common effluent scheme and settled in ponds at Kingscote. Other settlements are serviced only by household septic tanks with runover spilling into the ground, making its way into the groundwater and then into the ocean. If biocycle systems were introduced, then the provision of a rebate, subsidy or grant would assist in encouraging their use. Information should be provided to local councils on alternative methods of effluent disposal. Regulations may have to be introduced requiring tertiary treatment of effluent, particularly in peak tourist seasons. The building code may need modification so that new developments use environmentally sound techniques to dispose of effluent.

Management Plans

Initial assessments and management plans should be required for any new major developments and change of land use on the island. A good example of this would be an initial assessment and subsequent management plan if an operation such as the boat cruise proposal at Pelican Lagoon was to be put forward.

Management plans may be required as a precondition to development or sub-division approval including upgrades and widening of the road network. Bioregional planning could be developed for the whole island.

Subsidies and Grants

To encourage development on cleared rather than uncleared land, it would be valuable to encourage willing land holders to provide accommodation for ecotourism and nature based tourism. This would be of particular importance to areas in close proximity to the National and Conservation Parks. Commonwealth grants could be a method of encouragement, with grant conditions requiring promotion of biodiversity conservation. It would then be unnecessary to develop new resorts in previously undisturbed land adjacent to and within parks.

Performance Bonds

Performance bonds may be applicable to organisations wishing to develop certain areas on the island. Developers would be required to lodge security to cover the costs of site rehabilitation if unforeseen environmental problems occur during development. This should provide an incentive for developers to work within specific environmental guidelines.

Rewards

A reward system could be set up for people who provide early warning about incentives that appear to be failing. Other rewards might be made to tour operators who make an effort to educate their clients on the importance of biodiversity conservation and conduct tours in a sustainable manner. Awards should be given in consultation with the island community.

Limits of Acceptable Change study

If a Limits of Acceptable Change study was funded it would be able to monitor and manage visitor impacts in areas with significantly high biodiversity. According to the Kangaroo Island Sustainable Development Strategy (KISDC, 1995), this study should consider:

* determining sites of high environmental significance;
* potential threats and extent of impact; and
* establishment of monitoring programs with an initial task of collecting baseline data and determining key indicators.

Endangered Species Programs

An endangered species program has been put in place to conserve the Glossy Black Cockatoo. Other programs may have to be developed to cope with increasing pressure on island biodiversity.

Corporate Sponsorship

If corporate sponsors were attracted to sponsor biodiversity conservation or an endangered species program it would be a method of attracting funding. The solar powered building at Seal Bay is sponsored by Solarcare. Companies could pay for the privilege of using as their logos, for example, the Glossy Black Cockatoo, Australian Sea Lion or the Hooded Plover.

Gene Loss

Native Species Industry

At present the kangaroos and wallabies culled on the island are left as rotting carcasses. Culling should be undertaken by licensed shooters. A system should be set up to export this meat or provide it to local restaurants. Meat could be vacuum packaged so that tourists could return home with it.

Tourists could be encouraged to purchase kangaroo meat or products whilst visiting the island. Packaging of any products should include appropriate information for consumers that outlines the sustainable nature of the industry, to promote awareness and understanding of the issues surrounding the use of native species. Harvesting should not be genetically selective. A native species harvesting industry is being investigated by the Kangaroo Island Sustainable Development Strategy.

Relocation of juveniles to the mainland could be used as a method of addressing the problem of excess Koalas.

5

Ecotourism in the Wider Caribbean Region

Ecotourism: Scope and Definitions

Initial Considerations

At the conceptual level at least, the term ecotourism is still being used in a general way; its significance and the scope of the activity however are not the same in all instances. On the real, operative level the activities which are likened to the notion of ecotourism sometimes conflict with the actual terms of the definition in scope and meaning. There is on the other hand a dimension to ecotourism which is being imposed by the tourism industry and used as a promotional tool; the trend towards alternative forms of tourism observed in international tourism-in which certain segments of the market which in the recent past, mattered little, are beginning to assume major importance-has led to indiscriminate use of the term. Activities which have little to do with the more restricted, conservationist concept are thus labelled ecotourism. In any case, this synthesis does not propose to rule out the idea of a form of ecotourism which is decidedly economic or commercial in nature; the idea is to set aside a conceptual category for a type of small scale, conservationist, alternative tourism, which reserves an important role for the community in the provision of certain services and the protection of the area's resources, while being managed by industry agents who will hopefully specialize in handling a particular segment of the market.

It seems also, that certain sectors view ecotourism as an alternative to traditional tourism in terms of its effect on economic development. Even within the widest definitions of ecotourism, such a vision is out of place. Emphasis should instead be placed on recognizing the reality of a highly segmented tourist market in which certain segments — those which place the accent on nature, local cultures, sporting activities, family vacations, etc. — are rapidly growing and must therefore be given increasing attention when structuring the tourism product of a State or territory. On the other hand the growth of the sector referred to as sun, sea and sand tourism, made popular by the large all-inclusive resorts, is expected to slow down. To a certain extent however, the two types of tourism are not in competition and may even complement each other.

It may be posited that alternate forms of tourism are possible for a particular protected area. There is the option of ecotourism in the narrow sense, the conservationist option; there is also the option of large scale nature tourism. There can then be some measure of competition between the two options. In the case of unique protected areas where there exists a monopoly or near-monopoly in the sense that there are no nearby substitutes for the particular area or resource, the decision will depend on the fees for entry to the protected areas and regulations regarding the number of visitors. Where visitor numbers are unrestricted and entry fees low, tourism will tend to intensify; where numbers are restricted and entry fees higher, tourism will be more selective, confined to visitors who attach a higher value to the ecosystem or protected resource in question.

Tourists and the industry itself will reap all the benefits offered by the particular area; tourists, because they will be paying only a fraction of the value which they themselves attach to the enjoyment of the area being visited, would in economic terms be receiving a large "consumer excess"; as would the industry, because in making use of the protected area or resource, it receives more benefits than it needs in order to make a satisfactory profit. It may be said that when the government, which is the representative of the society and owner of natural resources, does not charge for entry or charges too little, it is giving away its products; it is also risking the deterioration of the area by allowing overloading if it sets low entry fees or does not use some other mechanism to limit the number of visitors

If one wishes to view ecotourism as an engine for economic development, it must be borne in mind that even if one acknowledges the fact that economic growth and environmental protection can be compatible within a plan for sustainable development, they must be recognized as conflicting objectives. The commercial objective of ecotourism in its widest conceptual formulation is sure to be at odds with its conservationist objective.

In approaching the matter of expansion or support of ecotourism it is appropriate to consider two alternative visions-partly interchangeable, partly complementary-which may be represented by the following propositions:

(1) Ecotourism should be expanded:
   - to generate high levels of foreign exchange, employment and national income;
   - to offer to the tourist different possibilities from those offered by other destinations; and
   - to finance activities for the conservation of the resources.

(2) Ecotourism should be seen as a fast growing activity capable of threatening the conservation of protected natural resources; it must therefore be restricted and regulated with a view to protecting the natural resources of the areas in which it is practiced.

Definitions

Ecotourism

– The following paragraphs present interesting definitions which are to be found in the literature. This is done to offer a frame of reference of sorts to readers of this report who are not yet fully aware of what ecotourism is.

One definition of ecotourism which has become popular judging from the frequency with which it has been reproduced in the specialized literature is that of Ceballos Lascurain (1987) which states, more or less, that ecotourism consists of trips to relatively undisturbed, unpolluted natural areas for the specific purpose of studying, observing or enjoying the surroundings and wild life as well as any manifestations of past or present culture to be found in these areas.

A definition which is more extensive and emphasizes a developmental perspective is that proposed by the Hon C.A. Maynard, Dominica's Minister of Tourism and current President of the Caribbean Tourism Organization at the First Caribbean Conference on Ecotourism, held in Belize in 1991. He suggested that ecotourism could be defined as a type of tourist development geared towards the development of natural historical, cultural and social structures in harmony with the physical environment, land use and cultural characteristics to ensure sustainability in the sense of preservation for future generations.

Jean S. Holder, currently Secretary General of the Caribbean Tourism Organization made reference, at the same conference, to those factors which must ultimately be a part of any definition of ecotourism and which consequently must be a part of the activity itself. The factors to which he referred are the following: responsibility of travel agents and travellers to appreciate the fact that certain things have value, obligation to the country, its people and its way of life; honesty in terms of the product being offered; consistency in the sense of offering an enjoyable vacation coupled with education about what the traveller is seeing and enjoying and its worth; involvement in the sense of interaction in a context of mutual benefit and respect.

Ruth Norris (1992) asks the question: what is ecotourism and how does it differ from nature tourism or adventure tourism? For her, neither nature tourism nor adventure tourism can be equated with ecotourism, not as long as they fail to foster greater protection of the environment. She points out that for at least two decades conservationists have been aware of the fact that the great expansion of nature tourism and adventure tourism is in itself a threat to natural areas. She concludes that to constitute "ecotourism", tourism must be linked to resource protection; she adds that if its purpose is to be of benefit to natural areas instead of being another mechanism for extracting utility from them, then the challenge to ecotourism is to guarantee meaningful benefits for local populations. An apt and possibly more technical definition is that proposed by the Corporación de Turismo de Venezuela (Tourism Corporation of Venezuela) which states that "ecotourism involves low density, low impact activities in natural areas of sufficient biological, cultural and geographic interest to attract tourists."

The criticism has been voiced that "eco" seems to exclude other options for alternative tourism such as cultural tourism, adventure tourism, archaeological tourism etc... A more generic expression which would place the accent on the environmental rationality of recreational and tourism activities is "environmentally correct alternative tourism".

Ecotourists

Various classifications for ecotourists have been proposed, based on levels of commitment to conservation or willingness to forego comforts out of a desire to discover areas or resources which are difficult to access. Below is the Lindberg (1991) classification which identifies four types of ecotourist.

Researchers and Specialists: Scientific researchers, participants in tours specially designed for education, waste collection and similar activities.

Committed Ecotourists: Persons who travel out of a specific interest in seeing protected areas and a desire to understand the natural and cultural history of the area.

Average Ecotourists: Persons who visit for example the Amazon, the gorilla reserve in Ruanda or other destinations mainly out of a wish to take a trip which is out of the ordinary.

Occasional Ecotourists: Persons whose contact with nature is fortuitous, arising out of a trip made for other reasons.

Laarman and Durst (1987) developed a simpler classification which distinguishes between seasoned ecotourists and dilettantes according to the level of the physical rigours to which the tourist is subjected or the extent of his interest in nature. This typology demonstrate the diversity of the situations existing in the nature tourism market, situations which must be considered for planning. Elizabeth Boo in her study of ecotourism in Latin America (1990) emphasizes the difficulty of defining the nature tourist given the large number of activities which may be associated with "nature". For the purposes of the study the tourists interviewed were classified into three groups: those for whom protected areas were the main motivation for travel, those for whom visits to protected areas were important and those who did not contemplate visits to protected areas or for whom such visits were of secondary importance in the decision to travel. 46% of those surveyed fell into the first two groups.

Analysis and Conclusions

The following paragraphs set out some considerations based on a free interpretation of the results of the survey and case studies, some of which are dealt with later.

The Practice and Concept of Ecotourism

It should be noted that the questionnaire was deliberately formulated in such a way as to provide no definition of ecotourism to which persons responsible for completing it could refer. The point of reference is therefore the focal point's own interpretation of the meaning of the term or the scope most often attributed to it, or some official definition of the term. The fourteen responses to the questionnaire demonstrate that in the States and territories involved, some tourist activity takes place which may be associated with the concept of ecotourism, more so to the concept implicit in the body of responses received than to the definition expressly adopted. Apart from a few exceptions there is no distinction made between analogous expressions such as alternative tourism, ecological tourism and others. In the three case studies, generally speaking, whenever a significant portion of tourism activity involves nature, in so far as it takes place in national parks, government and industry authorities consider what is done there to be ecotourism.

In general, the express formulation of the concept of ecotourism is of an activity centered on the observation and enjoyment of nature; some see it as specially linked to national parks and other types of protected areas which still offer unspoiled environments. In some responses ecotourism was seen as an "educational-recreational, small scale, controlled, directed" activity, or as an activity which should be accompanied by a "programme of environmental interpretation and/ or education". In other responses the concept was viewed in wider terms, embracing elements such as "study and preservation of the natural wealth of the country". Others include ideas such as enjoyment and study of "cultural expressions" or the requirement of an "understanding of the cultural history" of the site. Several responses emphasize the economic benefits to be derived by local populations which would serve as an incentive to conservation of protected areas or other aspects of nature as well as diverse cultural expressions. Finally, some responses included activities such as underwater sports and water sports as well as activities such as golf and horseback riding.

Despite greater or less emphasis on certain factors, there are many elements common to all or a large number of the definitions found in the literature. If one were to propose a definition which would bring together the elements most often included in survey responses, one would no doubt produce a definition very similar to those used or suggested by some of the leading organizations and outstanding writers in the field. One can however detect a contradiction if it may be thus described, between the conceptual level and the operational or real level, levels which may be likened to extreme positions on the question of the definition of the scope of ecotourism. Indeed, generally speaking, at the conceptual level, the level of definitions, ecotourism is viewed as a somewhat restricted activity, subordinated to the requirements of conservation, oriented towards education and culture, with benefits which should be limited to local populations. At the level of reality, on the other hand, the view of ecotourism emerging from the responses to the questions asked and from what has been observed, is one of an economic development strategy based on natural resources in which, even if the conservation factor is not ignored, it is not a conditionality and it may precede, follow or be contemporaneous with the exploitation of resources through tourism. This view is especially obvious whenever ecotourism is linked to mass utilization of particular natural resources. The distinction mentioned above between forms of ecotourism and their link to segments of the market with which they are associated is relevant here. Earlier references to the implied and express forms of ecotourism correspond to these levels.

The contradiction becomes more obvious in the case studies in which persons closely associated with the management of protected areas and with government units for the protection of the environment reveal their disquiet at the intensification of tourism in protected areas and at tourist overload in these areas and show skepticism regarding the likelihood of conserving unprotected areas where there exists the possibility of profitable expansion of traditional tourism. These persons are of the opinion that the tourism practices which have been developing in the cases they represent are not in keeping with the concept of ecotourism. It should be pointed out in any case that in Bonaire, Costa Rica and the United States Virgin Islands serious efforts are being made to protect national parks, reserves, sanctuaries etc in an attempt to rationalize tourist activity for conservation.

Significance and Impact of Tourism

The results of the survey demonstrate the difficulty, as revealed in responses to the questionnaire, of establishing objective linkages between the development of tourism and its contribution to the national economy and between tourism and ecotourism. The field research yielded no records of such relationships. Despite this, some observations arising from analysis of the survey results will be mentioned.

The answers provided by those surveyed concerning the relative contribution of tourism as a sector or sub-sector of the economy to gross domestic product, employment and foreign exchange earnings, revealed no homogenous patterns among States or territories grouped by characteristics: large continental countries; medium-sized countries; small islands. Bearing in mind the relatively uniform levels of development in the sector, one would expect that the contribution of tourism to the variables selected would be in inverse proportion to the size of the country-given the more diversified economies of the large countries of the region and the greater dependence on tourism in the smaller islands-but no such pattern emerged. There does however seem to be some correspondence in the behaviour of the three indicators chosen.

The differences between these figures could be indicative of the importance of tourism in each State or territory however it says nothing about their importance in international terms as tourist destinations. The number of rooms and the annual number of visitors are absolute figures and provide an indication of the relative importance of the country or territory as a tourist destination in comparison to alternate destinations.

The average hotel occupancy rate may be seen as indicative of traveller preference, probably attributable to relatively lower prices (hotels or packages) and not to the available attractions which, particularly in the case of island States and territories are scarcely distinguishable. Occupancy rates, combined with other elements, could be an indicator of competitiveness.

It is therefore both appropriate and important to emphasize the risks involved in attaining a highly competitive position by means of low development and operational costs which are the result of controlling authorities' tolerance of environmental degradation or of the lack of environmental regulations and standards to protect natural resources (pollution, tourist development detrimental to surroundings, destruction of coastal resources, tourist overload in protected areas etc.) Artificial competitiveness gives rise to environmental degradation and depressed salaries when faced with the true competitiveness which only becomes possible with improvement in the quality of the product and more efficient operation. This in turn results from rational environmental management and the incorporation of technical advances into tourism activity.

As regards the relationship between ecotourism and tourism, given the breadth of the implied concept of ecotourism discernable from the survey responses, a concept with strong links to traditional tourism, it is reasonable to think that one factor which will contribute to comparatively greater development of the activity is the development already achieved by traditional tourism. In other words, it is submitted that the present development of traditional tourism will determine the future development of ecotourism, in comparative terms. The greater the number of tourists arriving in a particular State or territory the greater the possibility of involving larger numbers of tourists in ecotouristic activities. One very important complementary factor is the availability and adequacy of protected areas reserved for such activity. This question will be dealt with below.

Ecotourism and Protected Areas

Importance of Protected Areas

Although strictly speaking, neither national and territorial statistics nor survey responses reveal the real importance of ecotourism in terms of the number of ecotourists or the ratio of ecotourists to total number of tourists, the development of ecotourism can still be linked to the number of protected natural areas. It is in fact noticeable that the greatest increases in the practice of ecotourism occur in those countries having the greatest number of protected areas. However, neither the size of the protected areas nor the proportion of such areas made available for ecotourism necessarily implies better use of ecotouristic resources or greater development of the activity. There are factors such as development of and access to protected areas which may determine the number of visitors.

According to the definition of ecotourism suggested by some survey responses and observed in personal interviews, ecotourism consists of visits to protected areas. As few responses mentioned the number of visitors, a comparative analysis in terms of the objective relationship between ecotourism and protected areas was not possible. However, the cases studied, Bonaire, St. John and Costa Rica, are important in that conscious efforts have been made to develop tourism through relatively wide extension-in proportion to total size of territory-of protected natural areas. A large proportion of the tourists who come here visit protected areas.

As was pointed out above, a second determining factor in the development of ecotourism is the extension of protected areas to the maximum possible extent, subject to appropriate management schemes within the context of promotion of such resources.

It should be noted that, from a conservationist point of view, the creation of protected areas is a useful mechanism for regulating the use of resources and protecting them in areas which are the focus of intense tourism activity, namely, marine and coastal zones where enforcement of environmental regulations is difficult.

Capacity of Protected Areas

Ecotourism, in its widest interpretation, can be and in fact is destructive except where precautions are taken to prevent this.

There are useful technical concepts for assessing the recreational potential of an area or resource. One of these is the tourist carrying capacity or tourist capacity of the area. The tourist carrying capacity of an area is the maximum number of visitors who can be accommodated over a particular period without adverse effects on resources or on services while at the same time providing a high level of visitor satisfaction. This concept is linked to that of tourist pressure which is the number of visitors an area can accommodate at any one time during a particular season, given the same constraints: minimum negative impact and maximum satisfaction. Another concept, not fundamentally different from the first, is that of acceptable visitor load which is the number of visitors sustainable over time. It must not be forgotten that these concepts are merely planning tools that inform and invite management decisions which, one logically expects, will be subject to a number of different considerations. It should on the other hand be recognized that tourist carrying capacity is relative and dynamic because it is determined by changing circumstances and depends upon variables which cannot always be objectively assessed. One has to bear in mind finally that the carrying capacity of an area must be fixed in accordance with objectives which depend on the manner in which the protected area is managed. This determines the use to which a given area may be put.

The conservation or degradation of an ecosystem or a particular resource depends upon the relationship between number of tourists per unit of time-visitor load-and the level of protection given to the ecosystem or resource. A certain measure of degradation can result from the combination of few tourists and a low protection level or many tourists and a high protection level. Thus the carrying capacity or acceptable visitor load of an area will vary with the level of protection provided through restricted entry and/or protection mechanisms. The question of capacity of protected areas-crucial to any expansion of nature tourism-is one which has been under examination for many years. This issue is dealt with in a recent publication of the Centro Agronómico de Agricultura Tropical de Investigación y Ensenanza (CATIE) which outlines a methodology for assessing the capacity of a particular area (Cifuentes, 1992). There are however few protected areas for which a definite carrying capacity has been fixed and even fewer which have managed to prevent overload by regulating visits.

In the administration of specific protected areas very diverse criteria have been applied to regulate visitor load through combinations of protection levels and visitor numbers. In Costa Rica, as a result of situations of perceived overload, studies have been undertaken to systematically ascertain the carrying capacity of the areas most frequently visited. In the interim, working from visitor load limits established through past experience, efforts are being made to exercise some control over visitor load by increasing protection-for example by prohibiting camping in certain parks-or by reducing the number of visitors to these parks through procedures which include agreements with the industry. In the case of protected areas under private management (non-governmental organizations), daily visitor limits have been set.

In Bonaire where studies have been carried out on the carrying capacity of the marine park in terms of the number of divers, setting the limit, for the level of protection provided, at approximately the number of divers now holidaying on the island, efforts have been made to control the number of these visitors. The aim is to increase protection, in particular by training operators and by regulating their activities. No studies on carrying capacity have been done in St. John but the park administration estimates that the present number of visitors cannot be increased unless new regulations are introduced. There is no direct control over the number of visitors to the park; conservation has taken the form of various protection measures, financing for activities taking place in the park and restrictions on the size of cruise ships permitted to anchor in the vicinity of certain beaches. The desire to protect certain areas has at times led to over-loading of others, this is the concept of "sacrificial areas".

Context and Status of Ecotourism

Institutional Factors

On the topic of institutions, States and territories directed their answers to survey questions at identifying organizations responsible for or interested in the tourism sector and environmental conservation; organizations supposedly responsible for ecotourism. However, the impression created by the wide ranging data requested and received is that these organizations rather than being actively involved at the moment in the study, promotion and regulation of ecotourism have a "potential" role to play in ecotourism which sooner or later will cause them to become involved in such activities. This does not mean that there are no public or private sector organizations currently handling these matters. The body of organizations identified is now carrying out some activities in relation to certain forms of ecotourism. These are, on the one hand, organizations responsible for the administration of protected areas which are in almost direct contact with large groups of tourists wishing to visit these areas and on the other, various national, non-governmental organizations and travel agencies which in some cases come together to form advisory bodies such as for example the Ecotourism Council of the United States Virgin Islands. One may however conclude that with the exception of matters concerning the use of protected areas for tourism, the treatment of ecotourism is still confined to the conceptual level.

Approach to Planning

Most of the States and territories which responded to the survey provided information on the diverse initiatives which seek to integrate environmental protection, tourism and ecotourism on various levels. This was also observed in the three case studies.

It was generally made clear that where attempts are made to include environmental conservation in the management of development, ecotourism is almost invariably a component of the initiative. There are few plans for management of protected areas or land use and few regional or local development projects which do not include ecotourism. Further, with increasing consideration of environmental matters in public administration at the operational level, ecotourism is perceived as an important tool for reconciling conservation and growth. This is a proposition that, at the conceptual level at least, gives rise to no conflict. It must however be emphasized that in many of these cases large scale tourism in protected areas is being equated with ecotourism, creating the impression that the conflict between large scale tourism in protected areas and conservation or alternative uses does not exist or that it is minimal or easily resolved.

Priority Requirements

Among the range of factors which could contribute to the development of ecotourism, the States and territories participating in the survey emphasized as first in the order of priorities the need for infrastructure, qualified staff and an institutional framework; also high on the list, though at a secondary level, are factors such as hotel facilities and legislation; and finally incentives, transport, communications and information. It is unclear, from the factors given priority, whether the survey subjects were thinking of ecotourism as currently practiced or as they hope to see it practiced in their States and territories; in other words, the responses do not make it clear whether the approach is that of large scale ecotourism focused on natural attractions, protected or otherwise or that of restricted ecotourism, geared towards protection of natural resources, in which local communities play a meaningful role. Either way the priorities set out seem to be more in keeping with the former.

Achievements and Failures of Ecotourism

It is clear from some responses that neither the achievements nor the failures associated with ecotourism are yet evident. Others emphasize certain perceptions of the benefits normally associated with ecotourism. Among the deficiencies referred to is a low level of institutional efficiency in the management of tourism. The responses point, finally, to the risks of causing degradation through expansion of tourism beyond the physical carrying capacity of the areas being visited.

In this respect, two factors are worthy of mention. In the first place, given the short history of the activity in the States and territories of the region, the benefits of ecotourism which are viewed as achievements may, in some cases, be more the expression of a hope than actual observation of real achievements. Still, the benefits referred to are, to a great extent, the benefits expected, these are referred to in the literature among real and positive experiences.

Secondly, even if no negative or positive effects of the practice of tourism were noted in some cases, the literature records the negative effects resulting from intensive and prolonged practice of ecotourism in certain areas. Ecotourism is here defined as visits to parks and other types of protected areas.

Guidelines for the Development of Ecotourism

The list of references to be found at the end of this document would suggest that a substantial body of literature has been developed, the operative scope of which could facilitate the creation of plans and strategies for developing ecotourism. For this reason and because of the nature of the study undertaken, this report will confine itself to some strategic proposals worthy of expression and attention. The following questions must first be asked in a deliberate attempt to stimulate a discussion which will serve to clarify the meaning to be given to the word ecotourism:

* Does ecotourism include large scale tourism in national parks, large scale diving activities in marine parks or in marine and coastal points of interest, as well as sun, sea and sand tourism?
* Is there a conflict between the growth of ecotourism and the conservation of the natural resources involved?
* Is ecotourism important as a development strategy or as a conservation strategy? Is the ecotourism phenomenon to be studied with a view to expansion or restriction?

Useful References (Documents)

Without detracting from the importance of the other items on the list referred to above, it would be useful to focus attention on certain documents which may be of direct assistance to State or territorial authorities in the region for the development of specific guidelines.

The first documents which government and industry authorities should consult when designing strategies for ecotourism development are the conclusions and recommendations which comprise the synthesis of the presentations and debates of the three Caribbean Conferences on Ecotourism sponsored, to date, by the Caribbean Tourism Organization (CTO) (1991, 1992 and 1993).

Second, mention must be made of the study by the World Wide Fund for Fund "Ecotourism Potential and Pitfalls", which focuses on Latin America and the Caribbean with five case studies, three of which concern countries of the Wider Caribbean Region: Belize, Costa Rica and Dominica. Its conclusions, recommendations and development strategies for nature tourism appear relevant and worthy of consideration in the shaping of national plans and strategies for using protected areas with a view to ecotouristic development.

A second document of great interest is that prepared by a group of experts from the International Union for the Conservation of Nature for the International Tourism Organization and the United Nations Environment Programme, entitled "Desarrollo de Parques Nacionales y Areas Protegidas para el Turismo" ("Development of National Parks and Protected Areas for Tourism"). This document sets out a number of concepts which must be considered to assess the tourist potential of protected areas and design development strategies. Among the aspects of the document which are of particular interest are a table showing the potential negative environmental effects of tourism on protected areas, a check list for assessing the tourism potential of specific protected areas, a guide for incorporating the tourism factor into protected areas management plans and guidelines for developing tourist facilities in national parks.

A document published by the East-West Centre of Hawaii entitled "La economía de las áreas protegidas-Una nueva mirada a beneficiosy costos" ("The Economics of Protected Areas-A New Look at Costs and Benefits"), is interesting in that it sets out in a systematic way the economic costs and benefits to be considered when making decisions affecting protected areas. With respect to entry fees and the issue of numbers as they relate to the financing of the management of protected areas, a document published by the World Resources Institute "Políticas para el manejo de áreas silvestres" ("Policies to Maximize the Ecological and Economic Benefits of Nature Tourism"), provides the necessary theoretical and practical foundations for developing a strategy for the financing of protected areas.On the question of management of protected areas "Políticas para el manejo de areas silvestres" ("Natural Areas Management Policies") by Thelan and Dalfeit, published in Costa Rica in 1978, has lost none of its relevance. "Nature Tourism-Management for the Environment" published by Island Press, brings together a number of important articles which are general and specific references covering, among other topics, certain ecotourism destinations, participation of local communities in ecotourism projects, commercialization of ecotourism products and recommendations for sustainable ecotourism. A document on methodology recently published by "Centro Agronómico Tropical de Investigaciones y Enseñanza" (CATIE) under the sponsorship of the WorldWide Fund for Nature is very useful for assessing the tourist carrying capacity of protected areas. The Corporación de Turismo de Venezuela (Venezuelan Tourism Corporation) has recently published a worthwhile document, wide-ranging in content, which deals systematically with tourism in general and ecotourism in particular in comprehensible diagrammatic style. It is of great interest as a general model of a basic document for promoting ecotourism internally among industry and government agents and for informing discussions on strategic guidelines.

Basic Premises

Before turning to specific factors to be considered when formulating strategies, one should take cognizance of some basic premises. The first to be borne in mind is that, whether planned or not, ecotourism is going to take hold in this region. The spontaneous explosion of alternative forms of tourism across the region, placing pressure on protected areas and on valuable unprotected ecosystems and resources, is a reality. Alternative tourism is here to stay in the region and it will continue to develop whether national and territorial authorities have anything to do with it or not. Given the differing definitions of the concept, ecotourism and its variants form part of a growing segment of the tourism market which for agents, is creating its own opportunities, challenges and obligations, none of which has anything to do with national promotion strategies. This does not mean that the product offered to visitors in the various States and territories of the region cannot be made more or less attractive so as to encourage, particularly in the medium term, smaller or larger numbers of ecotourists. The private sector of the industry will, in any case, determine local dynamics.

The second premise to be considered is that ecotourism will not by itself save the ecosystems, resources or specific environmental functions which require protection, neither will it necessarily contribute to pulling local communities out of their state of under-development; ecotourism may even become another factor serving to aggravate present processes of environmental degradation-new forces for negative environmental change may be unleashed through ill-conceived forms of ecotourism. Mechanisms must therefore be devised to maximize the expected benefits of these activities while minimizing the negative environmental impact of ecotourism. It is for this reason that regulations governing the use of protected areas and the management capacity within national protected areas systems are important, as are the mechanisms being developed to allow local communities to benefit from tourism. A third premise points to the need for open recognition of the fact that, in the final analysis, the private sector of the industry is the true catalyst of tourism.

There are two main areas to be considered: on the one hand, environmental conservation and protected areas development; on the other, promotion and development of environmentally sustainable tourism. In both areas, and without prejudice to the role of the public sector, the private sector, both business and non-profit (non-governmental organizations), must be actively involved.

The fourth premise emphasizes the role of government without detracting from the importance of the foregoing premise. It must be borne in mind that only government can represent the long term interests of the society. The free market is unfit to properly perform this function because of its own imperfections, the fact that environmental resources are public property, the externalities involved in consumption and production activities, imbalances in the functional and geographic distribution of wealth and income and the often negative implications for future generations of decisions made today. What is needed is an approach which embraces the tendency towards a decentralized, non-interventionist public sector which will delegate responsibility for cultural and natural heritage to social intermediaries and to a more dynamic, imaginative private sector, operating under clearly defined medium and long term rules which will facilitate empowerment and development.

Some Strategic Proposals

As was indicated at the beginning of this chapter, proposals will be few so as to minimize duplication of the abundant literature being produced in the field.

The first proposal deals with the management of protected areas. There is a need to regulate the use of protected areas now under increasing pressure with the development of that new segment of the industry which targets those interested in alternate forms of tourism. The environmental impact of ecotourism is basically a question of overload-the extent to which the number of visitors exceeds the receptive capacity of the target ecosystem. This leads to changes in the cycles of the ecosystem including the habitat of flora and fauna and eventually to the destruction of the ecosystem or of certain unique resources. Protected areas have to be assessed to determine which of them can be used for purposes of tourism and to what extent, and which cannot be used in this way.

A second proposal relates to the fees for access to protected areas. The authorities should place a value on protected resources in terms of visitor potential, harness visitor spending power through entry fees for protected areas and use these resources to finance the management of these areas. One may consider different rates for visitors of different origin (national or international), rates varying by season, "passports" for access to all the protected areas in the country over a particular period or other strategies. Rates or fees should not only cover direct administrative costs but should include an amount to cover the value of the resource involved, biodiversity, biotic resources, geological formations etc. This amount would be determined by the relative scarcity or the uniqueness of the resource in question.

A third proposal concerns the role of the private sector-profit or non-profit making-in the management of protected areas for the purpose of tourism. Non-governmental organizations can take full responsibility for managing protected areas. There have been many such very positive experiences in various States and territories of the Wider Caribbean Region (Costa Rica, Netherlands Antilles, Dominican Republic etc.). Further, even where a particular protected area is directly managed by some State entity, certain associated services, such as cafeterias, internal transport, beach facilities, camp sites, hotels etc. may be provided on a concession basis by the private business sector.

A fourth proposal points to the need to identify non-protected areas which can be developed into ecotourist attractions as either public or private protected areas, with a view towards improving the range of ecological choices within the national protected areas system as much for their intrinsic value as ecosystems-the species of flora and fauna found there, the geological formations present-as for their historical or cultural value, or with a view towards recovery of natural or man-made economic resources that have been subjected to serious degradation. In such cases, ecotourism could provide justification for singling out areas which are threatened or subjected to serious degradation so as to introduce special management practices, or it could provide the means to generate the financial resources needed.

A fifth proposal relates to training. The two groups of actors should be educated with respect to the phenomenon of ecotourism. Industry agents should be equipped with an understanding of nature, cultural heritage (biotic resources, biodiversity, geomorphology, anthropological and archaeological factors etc.), as well as of the rules which regulate national protected areas systems and of environmental standards in general. The administrative staff of protected areas on the other hand, as well as the staff of non-governmental environmental organizations should be given a knowledge of the tourist industry and of the tourism market. There is a need for biologists and other professionals involved in the field of ecology to be trained in tourism and thus equipped to handle specialized groups of visitors. At the same time, the normal training given to tour guides should include the areas mentioned above.

The sixth and final proposal deals with regulations for ecotourism.

This does not mean that ecotourism itself should be regulated. What must be regulated is the use of protected natural areas intended for ecotourism. Moreover, from an environmental point of view, the most appropriate approach is that which leads to he conclusion that the tourist industry must also regulate itself to avoid the negative environmental changes which can result from attempts to take advantage of natural and cultural attractions. Strictly speaking, these are not specific regulations for the tourist industry but general ones for all economic activity. Indeed, national regulation should include environmental audits of all existing tourism projects, environmental impact assessment of new projects and financing for the enforcement of existing environmental standards in each State or territory.

However, with regard to regulation of the tourist industry, there is one additional mechanism which must be given priority because it can lead to important positive impacts. These are cooperative agreements between government and industry, in particular the hotel sub-sector, with a view to reducing effluent, reducing or adequately disposing of solid waste, installing treatment plants and rationalizing coastal plans and operations (maintenance of beaches, marinas, etc.).

6

Contribution of the Tourism Sector to the Economy

It should be pointed out that the indicators presented here must be treated with caution as national accounting systems do not include accounting procedures which deal adequately with this sector; estimates of the contribution of the tourist sector to macroeconomic aggregates may be the result of different methods of calculation. Comparisons may therefore, in some cases, be subject to discussion. Further, with respect to employment, it may be that the survey itself may have given rise to confusion and it may not be at all possible to compare the responses.

Contribution to Gross Domestic Product

Twelve countries provided information on this question. In five countries this sector accounted for less than 10% of gross domestic product; in four others it contributed more than 10% but less than 15%; in the others, tourism was the source of more than 50% of gross domestic product.

Although one would expect that the contribution of tourism to gross domestic product would be in inverse proportion to the size of the particular country-given the more diversified economies of the larger countries of the region and the greater dependence on tourism in many of the smaller islands-this variable shows no clear pattern of behaviour, corresponding to types of States or territories, which would allow relative levels of contribution to gross domestic product to be linked to particular groups of States or territories. Thus for the larger countries-Colombia, Mexico and Venezuela-the contribution of tourism to gross domestic product was 1.5%, 3% and 13.1% respectively. Guyana, also a large country though less developed, reported 15%. Participating countries which could be classified as medium-sized-Costa Rica and the Dominican Republic-reported contributions from tourism activities of 7.5% and 11.5% respectively. The Eastern Caribbean islands recorded contributions ranging from 4.6% in St. Vincent and the Grenadines to 60% in Antigua and Barbuda, with 5% in Martinique, 12% in Barbados, 50% in the Turks and Caicos Islands and 55% in the Bahamas.

The percentage contribution of tourism to gross domestic product in each country may be seen as indicative of the importance of this sector in relation to other sectors of the national economy; very high contributions may be a sign of heavy economic dependence on tourism. In Antigua and Barbuda, the Bahamas and the Turks and Caicos Islands tourism bears an enormous burden. In Barbados, the Dominican Republic and Venezuela, where input is greater than 10%, tourism is a fairly important sector. It is relatively important in Costa Rica where it accounts for 7.5% of gross domestic product. For the economies of Martinique, St. Vincent and the Grenadines, Mexico and Colombia, by contrast, this sector is less important-judging from this variable-as it accounts for no more than 5% of gross domestic product.

This indicator does not however reveal the relative importance of tourism activity from an international point of view. Among the States and territories of the Wider Caribbean Region, Mexico, where the tourist sector accounts for only 3% of gross domestic product, is the most important tourist destination, after the United States; Antigua and Barbuda and the Turks and Caicos Islands on the other hand, although generating more than 50% of gross domestic product through tourism activity, are of little importance in terms of their share of the international tourism market. To arrive at a better appreciation of each State or territory's position in the context of regional or international tourism, one must determine the absolute contribution of the sector to gross domestic product in each country.

Contribution to Employment

Only seven cases responded to this question according to the terms specified in the survey-percentage contribution to employment. Three of them-the Bahamas, Barbados and the Turks and Caicos Islands-reported that tourism contributed more than 20% to employment. For St. Vincent and the Grenadines, Martinique and Costa Rica the contribution of the tourist sector was 10%, 4.2% and 2.5% respectively.

In Colombia and the Dominican Republic 130,000 and 50,000 jobs respectively, were directly created by tourism.

Apart from an apparent qualitative correspondence with the responses concerning contribution to gross domestic product, there was no information pointing to objective conclusions.

Contribution to Foreign Exchange Earnings

Eight of the States and territories responding to the questionnaire did not deal with this question, these were Antigua and Barbuda, Belize, Guyana, Martinique, Mexico, Surinam, Turks and Caicos Islands and Venezuela. The figures given by those States and territories which did respond confirmed the importance of the sector to foreign exchange earnings. Figures given for foreign exchange earnings ranged from 25% for Costa Rica to 75% for the Bahamas with St. Vincent and the Grenadines reporting 35%, the Dominican Republic 45% and Barbados 60%.

Finally, Colombia and the Dominican Republic recorded annual foreign exchange earnings from tourism of 440 million and 1200 million American dollars respectively.

Hotel Capacity and Number of Visitors

Information was requested on the number of rooms, occupancy levels, annual number of visitors and number of all-inclusive resorts. The relative importance of tourism for the States and territories which participated, as tourist destinations, in the survey.

Number of Rooms and Occupancy Levels

Responses fell into clear categories. At the highest level was Mexico with 150,000 rooms, followed, though not closely, by Colombia with a little over 43,000 rooms; next in line were Venezuela and the Dominican Republic with between 25,000 and 30,000 rooms, the Bahamas and Costa Rica with about 13,000 rooms each, Barbados and Martinique between 6,000 and 7,000, Belize almost 3,000 and Guyana, St. Vincent and the Grenadines and Turks and Caicos with a little over one thousand rooms each. Antigua and Surinam provided no information on this topic.

Hotel occupancy levels ranged between 40% and 69%. Guyana with 40% occupancy was well below the other participating cases. Barbados, Costa Rica and Turks and Caicos reported 50% occupancy; the Bahamas, Colombia, Martinique and Mexico fell between 54% and

56%, while Venezuela and the Dominican Republic recorded 68% and 69% respectively. The other cases provided no information on occupancy levels. Higher occupancy levels may be seen as indicative of traveller preference, attributable no doubt to lower hotel rates and possibly cheaper tourist packages. If this is so then occupancy levels may be considered an indicator of competitiveness on the tourism market.

All-Inclusive Resorts

The purpose behind the survey item-number of all-inclusive resorts-was to elicit information about a specific category of tourism generally considered to be the exact opposite of ecological tourism. However, as the responses to the specific survey question, of which there were eight, seemed to give different interpretations, they were of no assistance.

The informants in three cases-Barbados, Colombia and St. Vincent and the Grenadines-reported that there were no all-inclusive type hotels. Costa Rica has 192 tourist centres of which 10% were classifiable as all-inclusive. Mexico has 43 such resorts, Guyana 10, Antigua and Barbuda 6, the Bahamas 7 and Turks and Caicos only one.

Visitor Arrivals

The following figures for annual visitor arrivals were extracted from the responses received (figures are rounded):

* Antigua and Barbuda 194,000 86,000*
* Bahamas 3,600,000 1,600,000*
* Barbados 394,000 105,000*
* Belize 215,000 116,000*
* Colombia 856,000
* Costa Rica 580,000 377,000*
* Martinique 751,000 409,000*
* Dominican Republic 1,100,000
* St. Vincent & Grenadines 155,000 97,000*
* Turks & Caicos 56,000
* Venezuela 598,000 244,000*

It must be borne in mind that the relationship between the annual number of visitors and the number of rooms may vary. No pattern could be observed on which to base any type of analysis.

Ecotourism

This section of the survey is aimed at establishing whether or not ecotourism is practiced in the country or territory in question, what definition is given to this concept, whether there exist similar tourism activities identified by another name and what restrictions could have halted initiatives towards developing this type of activity in cases where it could have taken place. Concepts and definitions are present.

Almost all the responses received offered concepts and definitions. Generally speaking, the answers revealed that ecotourism and ecological tourism are synonyms. Only in the case of Costa Rica is there a distinction-ecotourism is seen as the commercialization of the concept of ecological tourism. In its response, the Dominican Republic makes a few minor distinctions between ecotourism, alternative tourism, ecological tourism and adventure tourism.

The definitions offered include various elements: among those worthy of mention are the following. Ecotourism is defined generally as an activity centered on the observation and the enjoyment of nature. Others see it as linked exclusively to national parks and other types of protected areas where there is still an untouched environment. It is defined as an "educational-recreational activity that is organized, controlled and small-scale", as an activity to be accompanied by an "environmental interpretation and/or education programme." Other responses expand the concept even further and incorporate into it elements such as "research into and preservation of the country's natural wealth". In addition, in defining the activity, the expressions "any cultural manifestation" and "understanding the cultural history", are also used. In some responses, emphasis is placed on the economic benefits to local populations, thereby providing greater incentives for preserving protected areas and other forms of natural manifestations and cultural expressions. Finally, some responses included sporting activities such as deep-sea diving and other water sports as well as golf and horseback riding.

The definitions proposed contain many common elements despite greater or lesser emphasis on certain aspects, many of which are already included in more generic definitions adopted by different organizations. Nevertheless, as far as definitions are concerned, there appears to be no major discrepancies between those proposed in the responses to the survey. However, in practice, the perception of ecotourism may vary significantly from one country or territory to another.

However, the question of factors likely to have hindered the development of "ecotourism" activities was not discussed in any of the responses received although in all cases, activities of this nature were being carried out. In one case, it was pointed out that conditions were not yet appropriate for ecotourism while, in another, all the factors highlighted in the questionnaire had been present at one time or another. These factors include the absence of adequate conditions, a lack of interest on the part of relevant sectors, lack of qualified personnel, insufficient knowledge of the area, lack of understanding of the benefits to be derived from this activity and finally the reduced number of areas with natural beauty which lend themselves to ecotourism and other types of tourism.

Protected Areas

Protected Terrestrial Areas

The total number of existing and planned protected areas, as well as their respective size. This information was given in the answers to the above-mentioned survey. The fourteen countries which responded to the survey dealt with this question, albeit somewhat superficially with regard to planned areas. In two cases-Barbados and St. Vincent and the Grenadines-it was reported that there were no land-based protected areas even though some had been proposed and, while in four other cases, there were no definite plans to create new ones.

Certain conclusions on ecotourism and its future may be drawn from information presented earlier, on its own, or in conjunction with information gathered from the survey. It should be stated, in absolute terms, that if the concept of ecotourism is restricted to activities such as excursions, sightseeing or other activities carried out in naturally protected areas, the greatest potential for the development of ecotourism would have to be in those countries with larger areas under protection. It has been shown that the countries with larger protected areas practice ecotourism on a larger scale: 21 areas of approximately 34,000 km^2 in Colombia, 6 areas of about 33,000 km2 in Mexico and 38 areas of more than 73,000 km2 in Venezuela. Belize, with 31 protected areas, reports that ecotourism is practiced in all of them. However, neither the size of the protected areas nor the proportion of these areas devoted to ecotourism implies better use of ecotourism, or greater development of this activity. In fact, in Costa Rica, one of the countries where nature-oriented tourism is most developed, ecotourism is practiced in 1,200 km2 in 13 of the 27 terrestrial protected areas mentioned in the survey, which covers a total area of nearly 12,000 km^2.

The main attraction, common to all the States and territories which responded to the survey, and present in the areas where ecotourism is practiced, is nature. However, there are other important attractions in the protected areas open to ecotourism such as cultural, historical, anthropological, archaeological, geological and scientific attractions. In one case, beaches were indicated as an important attraction.

Coastal Protected Areas

The data obtained from the survey on coastal protected areas is present. It should be pointed out that, in some cases, the protected areas defined as land-based include some coastal areas.

In three cases-those of Barbados, Martinique and St. Vincent and the Grenadines-there are no coastal protected areas; all other States and territories claim to have such areas, some of which are devoted to ecotourism. The largest areas were reported in Mexico and Venezuela-each having nearly 30,000 km^2-followed by Costa Rica with 5,600 km^2 and the Bahamas with nearly 2,900 km^2. The other States and territories have protected coastal areas of between 700 and 1,800 km^2. Only Barbados and Surinam are considering the creation of new coastal protected areas.

Nature is also the most important attraction in coastal protected areas. The responses are however more specific, especially in terms of the natural attractions which represent a great diversity of ecosystems, fauna and coastal formations. With regard to fauna, avifauna and marine fauna are most prominent, with certain species in abundance, mangroves, coral reefs, beaches, special landscapes and formations; archaeological, anthropological and cultural attractions.

With the exception of the cases of Mexico and Venezuela outlined earlier, the areas in question are small. It is hoped that with the evolution of a Protocol on specially protected areas and wildlife, signed in 1992 by all the States and territories of the Wider Caribbean, will lead to a significant growth in the total size of protected coastal areas.

Marine Protected Areas

Marine protected areas cover an even smaller surface area than coastal protected areas. It is possible that the boundaries between the one and the other is not quite clear; in any event, the distinction between the three types of protected areas that have been discussed is not formally established in any of the cases studied.

Venezuela reported the greatest expanse of marine protected areas with approximately 4,400 km^2; this is followed by Costa Rica with 3,100 km^2, Mexico with 2,300 km^2 and Colombia with a little under 700 km^2. At the other extreme, the Turks and Caicos Islands with 31, Antigua and Barbuda with 25, and Belize with 2 km^2, respectively.

The attractions mentioned are virtually the same as those specified for the coastal zones, except that there is great emphasis on sporting activities such as deep-sea diving and recreational fishing. Also highlighted were the whales in Colombia, and the marine prairies of Venezuela.

Non-protected Areas

There were very few responses to this question. One observation which could probably be generalized and applied to most of the countries and territories of the Wider Caribbean is that made by Belize which states that ecotourism-related activities take place in almost the entire country and that it would be very difficult to identify all the non-protected areas where this type of activity is carried out.

Frequency of Visitors and Areas most Visited

It was only necessary to answer this section of the survey if the section relating to protected and non-protected areas was not completed; the question was not always correctly interpreted.

Seven countries and territories provided no information on the frequency of visitors. Of those that did, only Costa Rica and the Dominican Republic provided some figures.

Costa Rica stated that 280 thousand local tourists and 318 thousand foreign tourists visited protected areas during 1992. The Dominican Republic estimated that some 389 thousand visits were made to areas of special interest such as islands with undeveloped beaches, cays and zones of high biodiversity and outstanding geological formations.

The other cases gave qualitative information on the frequency of visits. In Antigua and Barbuda, the areas most frequently visited were Devil's Bridge and some reefs. Guyana has a number of areas as designated tourist zones which are included in the packages offered to visitors and these are, consequently, the most frequently visited. Martinique points out that the attraction to which most visitors go is the ruins of St. Pierre, a city destroyed in 1902 by a volcanic eruption; the ruins were declared a part of the heritage of mankind. St. Vincent and the Grenadines noted that the areas most frequently visited were those most easily accessible (the Botanical Garden) or most promoted (waterfalls) or exceptionally appealing for excursions (cays). Surinam indicated that the areas most visited were those with natural attractions, indigenous to the country. On the other hand, Venezuela reported that the most frequently visited areas were those developed for ecotourism, the main attraction of which was wildlife, especially avifauna.

Institutions, Standards and Planning

The answers relating to these matters in the survey. None of the States and territories responding to the survey indicated economic policies affecting tourism or related activities, except for Guyana and St. Vincent and the Grenadines where reference was made to the existence of fiscal incentives for the expansion of tourism infrastructure, and Martinique where the economic policies of France apply to the territory.

Organizations Involved in Ecotourism

Generally speaking, the questions were aimed at identifying those organizations responsible for or with interest in the tourism sector and in environmental protection. It may be said that these organizations, in addition to being actively involved in the study, promotion and organization of ecotourism, have a "potential" vocation towards this activity which, sooner or later, will cause them to become more involved.

Nevertheless, a number of organizations are already developing activities relating to certain types of ecotourism. They are basically organizations responsible for administering protected areas and have an almost direct link to large contingents of tourists interested in visiting them and to various national non-governmental organizations and travel agencies.

Costa Rica has declared that there are several tourist agencies offering ecological tourism packages. Its National Parks Service is very involved in promoting ecotourism in some protected areas. In Mexico, several non-governmental organizations, as well as a governmental organization, the National Tourism Foundation, (FONATUR) are promoting ecotourism. In the Dominican Republic, the National Parks Administration created a Department of Ecotourism and there was at least one tourism agency specializing in ecotourism. In St. Vincent and the Grenadines, an advisory group on Ecotourism was established while in Suriname a company was formed to develop the tourist areas (METS) and it is believed that they are taking ecotourism aspects into consideration. In the Turks and Caicos Islands, there are some non-governmental organizations involved in ecotourism while in Venezuela, several of these organizations as well as government agencies in the tourism sector have begun to develop ecotourism.

Criteria for Regulating Tourism and the Environment

Colombia, Costa Rica, Martinique (French standards), Mexico and Venezuela are the countries which possess the most developed legislative framework in the area of environmental protection. In the other States and territories responding to the survey, there are different legal bodies dealing with the question of the environment: it was difficult to determine the scope of these bodies from the answers to the survey.

In none of these responses were criteria aimed at regulating tourism activities mentioned. The Dominican Republic was the only country to make reference to a management plan developed in 1990 but never implemented. Furthermore, it is the only country which did not mention the existence of any legal instrument that addresses the protection of the environment. Colombia indicated a draft study of policies and guidelines for the development of ecotourism.

Planning

With the exception of Belize, Barbados, Martinique and St. Vincent and the Grenadines, the countries and territories reported the existence of various types of initiatives for integrating environmental protection, tourism and ecotourism into development plans.

The following are the most significant aspects relating to planning. Worthy of mention are those countries where ecotourism is an important element in the creation and management of protected areas (Colombia), in regional management plans (Costa Rica), in environmental management plans for coastal areas appropriate for tourism (Mexico), in the incorporation of environmental protection into plans for tourism development, management, plans for parks, among other initiatives (Dominican Republic), into management plans for physical, insular and tourism development (Turks and Caicos) and in the Sustainable Development Plan for Tourism and Recreation in the Amazon (Venezuela).

The responses also contained references to plans for developing areas where ecotourism would be an important element. The following initiatives are worthy of mention: the development of a Marine Reserve for Birds and a Wildlife Sanctuary in Antigua and Barbuda; the national evolutionary conservation strategy of Barbados; the identification and study in Colombia of protected areas where ecotourism could be vital for regional development; a plan for the Guanacaste conservation zone in Costa Rica; designation of areas with conditions appropriate for ecotourism within the context of the Mexican government's environmental management plans; the development of certain areas in the Dominican Republic where private-sector ecotourism would be the main focus; studies on cays in St. Vincent and the Grenadines; the identification of certain protected areas for ecotourism (Suriname) and; plans for an integrally-planned environmental tourism centre in Venezuela.

Current Status of Ecotourism

The responses to the survey questions relating to priority requirements for the development or sustainability of ecotourism, to local facilities and/or experience in the area of training for ecotourism and to the achievements or shortcomings of ecotourism.

Priority Requirements

The survey identifies nine factors likely to contribute to the development or sustainability of ecotourism as well as the need to establish an order of priority among them. Those factors likely to be given the highest priority (Nos. 1, 2 and 3 in the hierarchy were selected and are present. The following are the factors that were given the highest priority by the countries and territories which responded to the survey. The number of times that the factor was selected is also indicated:

* Infrastructure 7
* Qualified personnel 6
* Institutions 5
* Hotel facilities 4
* Legislation 4
* Incentives 3
* Transport/communication 3
* Information 2

It may be observed that the factors "infrastructure", "qualified personnel" and "institutional structure" were most frequently chosen as priority factors for the development or sustainability of ecotourism. These were followed by the factors "hotel facilities" and "legislation", which were given equal weight; then by "incentives" and "transport and communication". Finally, the factor "information" was mentioned in only two cases.

Local Facilities and Experience in Each Country for Training in Ecotourism

Countries and territories were asked whether or not they possessed adequate infrastructure or experience to train persons in ecotourism, whether they foresaw future demand in this area and if they were planning to carry out training programmes in ecotourism. Five countries did not respond to this survey item; of those that did, the responses were varied. Antigua and Barbuda, Bahamas, Colombia, Mexico and St. Vincent and the Grenadines reported that they possessed neither the necessary facilities nor local experience locally to train their staff in ecotourism. Costa Rica and Venezuela, on the other hand, have the necessary experience and local facilities to provide training in ecotourism. All seven agreed, however, that there was a growing demand for training.

Turks and Caicos did not respond either to the question regarding facilities and experience for training nor to possible future demand for training.

In the case of the Bahamas, Colombia, Costa Rica, Mexico and Venezuela, there are plans for training in ecotourism. There are no such plans in Antigua and Barbuda or in St. Vincent and the Grenadines. Turks and Caicos recognizes that training is a necessity and that this need could be satisfied through in-house seminars.

Achievements and Failures of Ecotourism

No responses were received from Antigua and Barbuda, Bahamas, Belize, Guyana, Martinique or Surinam. Those countries that did respond to this question, however, generally did not refer to geography.

In three cases, Barbados, Colombia and Mexico, success was linked to fairly specific aspects, the most important of which is conservation. It was pointed out that ecotourism has given greater value to conservation activities has won greater respect for the natural and cultural environment, and has increased public awareness. The countries also indicated that ecotourism has encouraged activities aimed at protecting certain species. On the other hand, among the successes attributed to ecotourism are the diversification of the tourism industry, the popularization of conservationist values, economic benefits to local communities and certain programmes for assisting indigenous communities.

Costa Rica considers that the achievements that may be attributed to ecotourism are not yet evident in that country. Turks and Caicos, which considers its tourism to be 100% ecotourism, warns of the risks associated with that activity. St. Vincent and the Grenadines, as well as Venezuela, list among achievements, acceptance of or interest in this activity.

With regard to the failures associated with ecotourism, responses to the survey were quite varied. Barbados, as well as Turks and Caicos, pointed to the risk of degradation caused by visitor overload. Colombia has indicated out that these failures are linked to poor management of tourism on the part of institutions and a lack of adequate planning. Costa Rica and Mexico have reported no failures linked to this activity. St. Vincent and the Grenadines has cited instances in which the activity led to the displacement of a local community. Venezuela declared that its failures were linked to lack of resources available to the organization responsible for the management of national parks.

7

Balancing Water, Religion and Tourism on Redang Island, Malaysia

Introduction

The tropical island of Reading Island (Pulau Redang), located 45 km from Kuala Terengganu, Malaysia, is the largest (~ 40 km^2) of 9 islands in the Redang archipelago (5.7716°N, 103.0066°E) in the South China Sea. The Redang archipelago was designated as a Marine Park in 1994 to conserve the 500 species of corals and the thousands of fish and invertebrates living among them. A number of studies have investigated the marine biology around the island; some reports have focused on the Marine Park at Redang Island. The island is inhabited by an ephemeral population of 600–1500 villagers, comprised roughly of 250 Muslim families reliant on fishing.

Figure 1. The island of Pulau Redang off the east coast of western Malaysia in the South China Sea.

Juxtaposed with the pristine waters and untouched landscape is a growing tourism industry. The tourism industry totalled 19 resorts (1103 rooms) with more resorts under construction. The island receives up to 8000 tourists per day during the peak season. The tourism industry provides wealth and jobs to some of the villagers, but also puts a strain on the natural resources, in particular the fresh water supply.

Because Malaysia is a predominantly (60%) Muslim country—Islam is the official religion of Malaysia—we were interested in how Islam guides two aspects of this exploratory investigation: expanding tourism and water resources. In Muslim countries, tourism plans often do not facilitate local control and expression, but may still be guided by Islamic teachings. In fact, it has been argued that Islam is counter to consumerism and postmodernism. Local attitudes to expanding tourism may be either positive or negative. Positive attitudes result from notions that tourism creates community development, improves agricultural markets, generates income, and may bring good fortune; these attitudes could potentially lead to pro-tourism behaviour following the Theory of Reasoned Action. Local attitudes to tourism could be negative, especially because the tourism centres (i.e., the new hotels/resorts) are perceived as guests to the locals, but the hotels/resorts act as local hosts to outsiders and may misrepresent the locals to new guests. The hotels/resorts may act inappropriately in either or both roles as guest and host. Finally, benefits reaped by the hotels/resorts may not be well re-distributed back to the entire community.

Government interest in tourism to Malaysia in particular was limited until the 1970s because of concern with liberal attributes associated with Western permissiveness. But, Malaysia has generally been considered comparatively moderate. The Malaysian Tourism Development Plan (1975), which was prepared by a Hawaii-based company, sought the expansion of foreign exchange and the labour market. It allowed for special provisions for tourism in poor regions, as contained in the Investment Incentive Act of 1968. These provisions may be consistent with the welfare-oriented philosophy in the basic tenets of Islam. The Tourism Development Corporation Act (1972) continued the growth of the industry, but there were no explicit references to Islamic ideas or goals. Promotion did contain Islamic motifs such as mosques, architecture and Muslim festivals, but they also contained images that went against Islamic principles. More recently, however, there was minimal portrayal of Muslim images by Malaysian tourism destination organizations. It has been found that tourism development in Malaysia has given insufficient attention to local capacity building, reluctance to integrate local settlements, misplaced notion of professionalism, and insensitivity to cultural and ethnic differences. Although Islam prohibits prostitution, gambling, and the consumption of alcoholic beverages, it does not exert any significant influence on the operation of tourist-related activities, which are Western-inspired and run counter to the Islamic concept of tourism in stressing the sacred goal of submission to the ways of God. Tourism has been blamed for sexual permissiveness, flagrant indulgence in alcohol, gambling, drugs, pornography, voyeurism, particularly threatening local youths. In addition to the social-cultural impacts of tourism on Islam, so too are there environmental impacts, particularly with water, and associated Islamic implications. The Quran[Note7] and Hadith[Note8] have relatively elaborate strategies for water conservation and pollution-prevention that are widely accepted and complied with by Muslims when linked to state policies. Women play a central part in the provision, management and safeguarding of water resources. Water has an economic value, which is compatible with Islam. But, the distinction between 'public' and 'private' water may be unclear. Further, the issue of wastewater reuse is controversial when it provides relatively clean water in drought-prone regions yet potentially blemishes religiously significant practices with potentially 'impure' water.

The objectives here are to explore the water quality and quantity issues on the Redang Island. Of particular interest is the relationship between the local villagers and the emerging resorts. Because Islam guides the religious and day-to-day practices of the villagers, we are also interested in the relationship between Islam and water conservation practices.

Methods

We conducted semi-structured interviews about water sources, usage, quality, conservation and disposal with locals from the village and managers and staff from the resorts. Semi-structured interviews were an appropriate method for gathering information in an open-ended format, particularly useful in an exploratory study. All interviews with villagers and resort staff were conducted in Malay and translated by the Malaysian researchers; interviews with resort managers were done in English. Because Malaysia is a predominantly Islamic country where the Quran and Hadith guide not only religious practices, but day-to-day living habits as well, we investigated whether water use was in any way influenced by the Quran/Hadith, particularly among the villagers. Faruqui *et al* (2001) report that these Islamic texts place great importance on water and its conservation—the Arabic word for water occurs 63 times in the Quran, and water use and wastage guidelines are described in the Hadith.

In the village, we interviewed 15 women and 11 men, all but one of whom were metered for water consumption. Ages ranged from 27 to 53. Professions included business, carpenter, fisherman, police officer[Note9], resort employee, restaurant owner, shop owner, and waitress. In addition, we were able to talk with the head of the village, who is also the religious head (Imam), and with the 'second man' of the village, who is also the head of water distribution for the island. Respondents were selected from restaurants and a community centre, and from walking door-to-door in three different neighbourhoods. The village is located in the interior of the island, and the resorts are located along the coast. We visited the six largest resorts (of 19) where we interviewed supervisors ($n = 6$) in charge of water supply and quality (managers and engineers) and support staff ($n = 10$) (maintenance, handymen, gardeners and swimming pool cleaners). We also interviewed 10 tourists at the island's airport, on a boat and at a restaurant.

Limitations to our methods included general qualitative assessment biases due to the individual analyst and subject in a socially constructed environment, representative samples in space, time and depth, and interpretation of the results. We aimed to maximize the credibility, competence and perceived trustworthiness of the qualitative researchers and triangulated where possible to increase reliability. Establishing credibility, competence and trustworthiness of ourselves was relatively straightforward. We initially explained that we were researchers at universities from the UK who were interested in water and resort issues. The fact that we were associated with universities rather than government agencies immediately helped to build credibility and trust (mistrust was associated with government agencies), in addition to competence. We attempted to triangulate by comparing (a) interviewee response to the same questions posed by different researchers (e.g., questions posed by Malaysian versus UK researchers), and different interviewee responses to the same questions about a particular topic (e.g., upper management versus maintenance worker resort employees about water), (b) interviewee claims to specific behaviour and observed behaviour (e.g., mosque attendance), and (c) interviewees response and official published documentation.

However, we were unable to calculate a proportional reduction in loss (extension of Nunnally's rule of thumb for Cronbach's alpha in quantitative measurement), nor produce a rigorous calculation of judge number and agreement. Judge number and agreement is analogous to sample size and standard deviation (or standard error). In quantitative sampling, there is a central tendency to the population mean and reduction in standard deviation (or error) to that mean as the number of samples increases. It is therefore possible to estimate the number of samples required from an initial sample and standard deviation to obtain that standard deviation with statistical power. In qualitative sampling, we also aim to find the 'true' or mean value, but this value is qualitative rather than numerical. The 'true' value is determined based on judge (or interviewee) agreement or thematic similarity in answers to questions. Unlike measuring a physical property, like air temperature where a given temperature is recorded for a given measurement, a qualitative 'measurement' carries with it a degree of certainty whereby the respondent may or may not be 'sure' as to their answer. Bias on the part of the recorder is possible in both quantitative and qualitative research, but air temperature, for example, is what it is—it is never unsure as to what its value is. Proportional reduction in loss is therefore a statistical method for qualitative research to minimize the error in certainty with which a respondent feels confident about his or her answer. Because the research was exploratory, we did not implement this method but the method would be useful for further research.

Results

Village

The villagers received their water piped in from the mainland. A 151 m^3 (40 000 gal) tank supplied water to 238 households in the village. Each household paid on average $1.35 US (RM 5) per month for their metered water bill, which they all felt was a fair price. One household took their water from a nearby hill source and paid no bill. All households rated the water quality as good, though a few mentioned as a matter of course that the water always needs to be boiled. Primary water uses were cooking, cleaning and drinking.

In times of shortage the households took their water from the nearby hill. One household had its own well that was used in times of water shortage; the family shared the well water with neighbours and relatives. Nine people agreed (with few or no reservations) that they would be willing to use recycled water; however, four people were against recycled water use. Ten people indicated that in times of severe water shortage they would be willing to use seawater for ablution—the religious ritual of washing before prayer—but three were adamantly opposed.

When asked if the respondents had heard any lectures or advice on water conservation from the religious head (Imam), four people indicated that they had while nine said they had not. However, every respondent said that their use of water was influenced by the Quran and Hadith, but none could recall any specific passages or mentions from the teachings. All but one of the interviewees were interested in hearing any or additional lectures or advice on water conservation. Religious involvement (prayer, mosque attendance, read Quran/Hadith) ranged from regularly/always, sometimes and two days per week.

The villagers viewed the resorts from a largely socioeconomic, rather than environmental, standpoint. They were pleased that the resorts provided jobs for them, including women, and many of the villagers who worked at the resorts had been fishermen previously. Still, the villagers voiced disapproval of tourist behaviour and concern that their children were being exposed to that behaviour while working there. The villagers were generally unaware of the environmental impacts from the resorts and tourists primarily because of lack of access to the tourist areas. Although the resorts took water from the same sources used by the villagers, the relationship could be reciprocal—one resort worker said that when her water ran out at home she would bring back water from the resort.

Resorts

The Ministry of Tourism developed an Infrastructure Development Study for Tourism Islands, Peninsular Malaysia. One objective was to ensure water security for tourism. It was stipulated that the first option is to utilize local sources including exploration of common harvesting of natural resources such as rivers or ground water prior to importing water. Studies are required to avoid environmental damage when harvesting local sources. Only where the local source is deemed insufficient could water be imported. Desalination plants would only be considered for islands far out at sea where pipeline installation is difficult and there is also high current or future projected demand. Water conservation techniques should be taught and rainfall harvesting encouraged.

All of the resorts on Redang Island must pump their water from groundwater—none of them have been granted access to the mainland piped supply from which the villagers receive their water, with one exception. The largest resort managed a deal to secure access to the piped water—the resort helped set up the piped water access to the villagers and in return gained access as well; this resort used groundwater for 'decoration' (i.e., fountains). Another resort used groundwater for the pools and gardens, and used hill water for the kitchen and drinking. The most popular (highest annual visitor numbers) resort shipped in drinking water by barge every two days. The smaller resorts reported water use of ~ 190 m^3 (50 000 gal) per day. One manager stated that all of the resorts would be receiving mainland piped water by the end of the year, but no other resort manager would confirm that report.

Responses about water shortages and conservation practices were varied and inconsistent. Most of the managers or lead engineers reported that there were never any shortages and, hence, there was no need for conservation measures. Other reasons issued against conservation measures were that the resorts 'do not want to stress the tourists[Note10]', and because water was so cheap, there was 'no economic incentive.' Many resorts were unaware of the water conservation guidelines issued by the Marine Park. One resort lead engineer, when asked what they do with the water conservation guidelines, said, 'We slip those under the rug.'

During one interview with a resort manager we were told that there were no water shortages. Meanwhile, another one of our Malaysian researchers was interviewing the resort's swimming pool cleaner, who revealed a different story. This employee disclosed that there were generally two water shortages per year as an annual trend. The resort's response to these water shortages was to cut the water supply to the staff housing.

Responses about water quality were also varied and inconsistent. Two resorts denied any problems of saltwater encroachment; another resort explained that there were no water quality problems on the entire island, though another nearby island had problems. One manager told the UK researchers that there were no water quality problems, but he revealed in Malay to the Malaysian researchers that there were some problems with brown water. Another resort used reverse-osmosis to purify the groundwater, but the manager said that this method 'makes the water taste bad.' The resort that shipped in drinking water showed us their ten groundwater wells and the two that were contaminated. The resort lead engineer, on saltwater encroachment, stated, 'This is a huge problem. All of the resorts (on Redang Island) have this problem.' Signs are displayed in each of their rooms warning not to drink the water. Additionally, the researchers were given a tour of the rather extensive and expensive water treatment facilities on site. These facilities were the most sophisticated of the treatment mechanisms in place on the island that we surveyed. The simplest system from a smaller resort released untreated wastewater to the immediate rear of the resort (metres away from their groundwater well).

Figure 2. ***One of the groundwater wells contaminated by saltwater encroachment. The sea is located just beyond the end of the path.***

Discussion

In the village, access to information was initially a concern for us. The villagers tended to distrust the Malaysian outsiders as coming in to impose problematic policies. However, when the Malaysian researchers introduced the Western collaborators (both Muslim and non-Muslim), the villagers opened up readily (credibility, reliability, competence, and trustworthiness). The villagers wanted to explain the issues of the village to the UK researchers so that this information could be brought back to the West. Furthermore, because the UK researchers had contacts with Malaysian policy-makers (i.e., Malaysian Ministry of Energy, Water and Communication), the villagers hoped that their concerns would be passed on to the Ministry. Some of the villagers were particularly sensitive to two of our questions—on recycled water and on seawater for ablution. The strong opposition expressed was surprising, and perhaps indicative that they were unaware of the Islamic ruling on the use of seawater for ablution during sea voyages with limited freshwater supplies.

Our research group of five men was concerned that we would not be able to interview the village women (social context), who were generally the unspoken voice behind household management. Interview access to the women came readily, however. During an afternoon prayer, when the Malaysian researchers and one (Muslim) of the two UK researchers went to the mosque with all of the men in the village, the non-Muslim UK researcher was left alone in a restaurant. The women, who were also left behind, took an interest in the researcher and our research group was invited to dine with the women following the prayer. This resulted in not only our ability to interview the women, but also a greater number of female interviews than male interviews. We followed up the initial set of interviews with a female collaborator who easily gained access to female interviewees.

One of the women anomalously attended the mosque regularly with the men. The woman and her husband were un-characteristically relatively well-educated and up-to-date with current affairs. In fact, she explained to the researchers the water purification system in place in Singapore and expressed a desire for a similar system to be brought to her island. She also highlighted that she uses the Quran as the basis for educating her children on wise water use.

Perhaps the most interesting finding presented here was the disconnect in answers among resort managers and lower level staff employees, and between resorts, which is most certainly due to the context in which the interviews took place. With such a high degree of variance, it is difficult to determine the 'real story' behind the water issues and which narrative is the 'correct' one. Certainly, upper level resort employees have a responsibility to market the best interests of their employer. Lower level employees may be treated unfairly and thus motivated to use the interviews as a means of retaliation, or they may feel a sense of loyalty to their employers and thus motivated to support the best interests of the resort. This delicate balance may also be related to the villagers' give-and-take view of the resorts: the resorts provide jobs, but they also provide exposure of unwanted tourist behaviour to their children. Regardless of what the truth is behind the interviews, it is nonetheless interesting that the truth is obviously masked; there appears to be an underlying tension with respect to these issues.

The findings we report here are by no means statistically significant due to time and sampling design constraints, but are useful as an initial probe for further studies. Future research should be methodologically designed not only based on our initial results as a guide, but also with a systematic plan to reduce uncertainty in the findings and 'unravel the truth' on issues such as the discordant answers between upper management and lower level resort employees. Limitations detailed in the methods section should be actively addressed—reducing the subjectivity of the analyst and subject in a socially constructed environment, increasing the number of samples and representativeness, assessing change (answers, policies, demographics) over time, refining the questions to reduce the openness of interpretation of the results, and triangulating different sources of information and methods to clarify contrasting results. Further research should build upon the credibility, competence and perceived trustworthiness that we established with the villagers. Finally, introducing a more quantitative and statistical approach to this qualitative research would strengthen the results. Further, conventional environmental management strategies for islands that have had limited success may need to consider the cultural and religious backgrounds of the island inhabitants. For instance, a recent Islam-oriented environmental education program for fishing communities, government officials and religious leaders of a small island off the coast of Zanzibar has been developed in coordination by the World Wildlife Fund, Care International, and the Islamic Foundation for Ecology and Environmental Sciences. Inasmuch as these collaborative efforts inform conservation strategies, they can also harmonize with Malaysian conservationists and inform the West.

A November 2006 Nature issue focused on 'Islam and Science: Must the Muslim world stay science-poor?' Malaysia was argued to have been isolated from international science. The opening editorial called for cooperation and collaboration between Muslim states and the West. In this work, UK scientists successfully collaborated with Malaysian scientists, addressed environmental issues with an Islam/culturally-sensitive framework, and opened doors to future research opportunities.

As the tourism industry on Redang Island grows towards maturity, the industry will become increasingly institutionalized and dominated by outside interests. Two actors stand to lose in this development: the villagers and Islam. Further research with a rigorous assessment framework based on our initial results should assess the balance between religion, economic development and environmental sustainability for Redang Island, and what the future holds for the strengthening or weakening of those parts.

Sustainable Tourism Indicators for Mediterranean Established Destinations

The notion of sustainable development has expanded to cover all forms of development and economic activities including tourism. The interpretation of the concept of sustainable development in tourism remains vague and a number of different approaches have been proposed in an effort to define what constitutes sustainable development in tourism and what not. Coccossis (1996) recognizes four different interpretations of sustainable tourism. These four perspectives are the "*economic sustainability of tourism*", the "*ecologically sustainable tourism*", "*sustainable tourism development*" –where although the need for environmental quality is apparent, the focus is on the long-term viability of the industry-and "*tourism as a part of a strategy for sustainable development*". The first three interpretations address only parts of sustainable tourism. It is contradictory to the concept of sustainable development to consider sustainability in tourism isolated from the different dimensions the concept implies. In order to stay close to the vision of sustainable development a holistic and integrated approach has to be adopted; this is the standpoint of this research.

Sustainable Tourism and Already Developed Resorts

Managing existing destinations is a key element of this research. The need to redefine tourism development in existing destinations on a more sustainable basis although may seem contradictory is actually a necessity. Sustainable tourism is often perceived as the opposite of mass tourism, which is the dominant form in most of the resorts. Although, it may seem unreasonable to expect that resorts with an intensive form of tourism, large numbers of visitors and a total dependence of their economies on tourism will be transformed overnight to sustainability paradises, there is an acute need to shift their tourism development towards a more sustainable direction. Confronting and proposing solutions to the problems of already developed tourist areas is a key objective of sustainable tourism and not just creating new destinations even if these are considered sustainable. Moreover, mass tourism in many instances can be considered to have less impact than the new forms of tourism.

The Mediterranean Tourism

Mediterranean is considered to be the most popular destination worldwide with about 155 million of tourists in 1990. In this area, tourism is considered a very significant economic activity contributing foreign exchange and leading to further economic gains. As a result, mass tourism, which brings in immediate economic gains, at the expense of long-term viability in many occasions, has flourished and often has been extensively promoted by the national authorities. However, these characteristics along with the fragility of their ecosystems to receive and absorb the pressure posed by large numbers of tourists in relatively small areas and the lack of proper planning at an early stage are turning them vulnerable and forcing them to face the deterioration of their established markets.

Indicators for Sustainable Tourism

Indicators for sustainable tourism are a relatively new field of research and work interest. WTO since 1992 has been undertaking work on this field (WTO 1993, 1996). However, the indicators proposed, as well as the overall framework appear to be too tourism centric targeting on safeguarding tourism businesses. Although, this is a wishing component in sustainable development it should not be the only issue addressed. Moreover, it appears that the focus was on newly developed destinations, particularly in developing countries while, linkages between economic development and the environment are not clearly stated.

Sustainable tourism indicators alike the sustainability indicators are about integrating tourism to its environmental and socio-cultural context. Furthermore, sustainability indicators for already developed tourist destinations should be formulated in a way that the weak points where action must be taken and must examine the sector's relationship to the rest of the activities and the environment in an effort to achieve overall sustainability for the area.

One way of defining a set of indicators for sustainable tourism that perceive tourism in a more holistic approach, is to relate them to the principles of sustainable tourism, as these are discussed in the literature. This is the approach chosen to be followed in this paper.

Sustainable Tourism Principles and Proposed Indicators

Several sets of principles for sustainable tourism have been proposed in the literature in an effort to operationalize the term of sustainable tourism and facilitate its implementation. Bramwell & Henry (1996); Eber (1992); Gerken (1988); McIntyre (1993) as well as International Organizations (WTTC, WTO & Earth Council, 1996; WTO & UNEP, 1998) have proposed principles for sustainable tourism. Most of the sets refer to aspects such as involving local communities, sustainable use of the resources, planning for tourism, promoting information and research etc.

The set of principles proposed by Eber (1992) is chosen here to guideline the definition of indicators. The analysis and discussion provided in its original source for these principles might seem to be rather tourism-centric, focusing extensively in the tourism sector per se. In this paper the same principles are used to guideline the definition of indicators, but a broader interpretation is considered here to reflect the notion of sustainable development.

The principles of sustainable tourism are as follow:

1. Using resources sustainably.
2. Reducing over-consumption and waste.
3. Maintaining diversity.
4. Integrating tourism into planning.
5. Supporting local economies.
6. Involving local communities.
7. Consulting stakeholders and the public.
8. Training staff.
9. Marketing tourism responsibly.
10. Undertaking research.

Among several of the principles of sustainable tourism there is a strong relationship. This is not surprising given the complexity of tourism, the interrelation in the different components of sustainable development and the need for holistic approach. In the following discussion some principles are examined jointly since they are conceptually interrelated, and similar indicators can be used in measuring sustainability. Thus, the principles of "Integrating tourism into planning", and "Marketing tourism responsibly", are examined together. This is also the case in the principles", "Involving local communities" and

"Consulting stakeholders and the public". Indicators are defined for the local scale of application. The scale of application is significant since more detailed information could be considered as it gets lower while aggregations are mostly used in a broader scale of application. Moreover, different indicators are meaningful at different scales although some of them could be used in local as well as regional and/or national level. The local scale was chosen here in order to facilitate local communities and stakeholders to adopt sustainable practices. It is also believed that research in the local scale could help in clarifying theoretical as well as practical issues about sustainable development and facilitate in this way in its implementation.

The number of indicators vary from principle to principle according to the different dimensions this might have as well as the apparent lack of data or not. Data availability is a significant issue, especially in Mediterranean countries. For this reason, in some instances, more than one indicator may have been proposed which more or less refer to same parameter.

Using Resources Sustainably

As Hunter (1995) points out, *"for renewable resources, SD requires that the rate of utilization does not exceed the natural regenerative capacity"*. Resources can be interpreted as natural, cultural and social. This principle is part of what elsewhere is referred to as cultural or social sustainability. For natural resources, water and energy are the key concerns for sustainability since both are extensively used by the tourism industry in the host areas, most often at rates far exceeding use by local population. Additionally, in the

Mediterranean area these two resources are in scarcity and often are the object of conflicts due to competing demands for different uses. For renewable resources, recycling and/or regeneration rates are appropriate since they can be utilized to demonstrate some effort to manage consumption, as well as, emissions and littering. The indicator of water/energy consumption per tourist (or bed or night) is often suggested in the literature (WTO 1993, 1996) to measure key resource consumption. Although this measure could be utilized, particularly in situations where no other data are available and/or when strategies for consumption reduction have been implemented, such an index should be compared to:

a) some standard norms of consumption;

b) the relative redundancy of the resource in the region;

c) the amount of resources needed by other sectors of the economy (agriculture, industry) which are developed or could be developed in the area (opportunity cost).

d) the consumption before the implementation of reduction policies

Landscape is another natural resource, to be considered. Overexploitation by the industry leads to deterioration of the landscape and the tourist. With large numbers of tourists visiting a beach, a park or other attractive site it should be expected that there would be loss of attractiveness, and disturbance of natural habitat because of the congestion and overuse. The large scale of infrastructure development also can limit the open space and dramatically alter the character of the area, the traditional ecosystems, the quality of life for the residents and of the experience for the visitors.

In most of the Mediterranean destinations the quality of bathing water is a major resource which should be considered as well. Measures such as continuous monitoring of water pollution, existence of some prize award or even number of locals swimming on a beach can be used to indicate the sustainable use of this resource.

The list of indicators for resources at the local scale includes:

- Renewable resources (solar, wind, etc.) used in tourist accommodations as a percentage of total fuels used,
- Amount of water recycled as a percentage of total water that could be potentially recycled,
- Water/energy consumption per tourist (or bed or night),
- Square meters beach (park or other site) per tourist (average and peak),
- Square meters of open space per tourist,
- "Open" space as percentage to that built for tourism infrastructure,
- Existence of procedures for continuous monitoring of the swimming water,
- Number of samplings of swimming waters exceeding safe limits, as these are defined nationally or internationally,
- Quality of water expressed as concentration of various pollutants,

- Blue Flag award (or similar awards if existed),
- Number of locals swimming on the beach It is difficult to measure directly social and cultural sustainability. This is because most of the variables related to these are qualitative rather than quantitative. Another reason is that cultural changes are inevitable when people from different socio-cultural background come together in some degree of interaction. Growth in tourism is only one part of the development process. Although it appears that tourism accelerates cultural changes it is definitely not the only driving force of changes. Moreover, as Inskeep (1991) claims the changes are not necessarily negative or undesirable.

An indirect measure for socio-cultural sustainability can be the involvement of local communities in the decision-making and other processes, along with the right information to tourists about the place they are visiting. These issues are examined in following principles.

List of proposed indicators includes:

- Ratio of local population to peak season tourists,
- Ratio of local population to annual number of tourists,
- Marriages between tourists and locals as a percentage of all marriages,
- Number of bars/discos per local population,
- Divorces as a percentage of marriages,
- Females employed as a percentage of the labour force,
- Rate of growth of population,
- Unemployment rates in the off-season periods,
- Local unemployment compared to Regional or National unemployment.

Reducing Over-consumption and Waste

Reducing over-consumption and waste has a two-fold dimension; saving the resources used by tourism for the production/consumption of other goods and reducing the pressure on the environment resulting from the waste treatment and disposal. In this sense, the first component is somehow related to the first principle mentioned above.

Related to this principle is the existence and adequacy of the infrastructure and the methods used for the safe waste –solid and liquid- treatment and disposal. Adequacy relates to the capacity of the existing infrastructure to handle the waste generated and the right method of treatment. For waste and wastewater production, what is important to measure is the existence of sustainable patterns rather than the amount of waste produced per se. The low consumption patterns (increased efficiency, new technologies, responsible behaviour) –adopted by both the industry and tourists, as well as, recycling are indicators of responsible management and responsible tourists. They both lead to resources savings and a decrease in the cost –natural and in economic terms-of managing large amounts of waste. In case of existence of such methods the amount of waste per tourist can be used to indicate the effect.

The indicators proposed are as follows:

- % of materials which can be recycled and receive this kind of treatment,
- % of water recycled,
- Number of hotels, restaurants and other places offering tourist services which have enacted environmental sound systems for eliminating over-consumption of resources and waste generation as a percentage of all establishments,
- Readily available information for tourists and the industry in general for the adoption of low-consumption patterns,
- Solid/liquid waste generated per tourist,
- % generated solid waste treated with the land fill method,
- % generated solid waste in dump,
- % of wastewater receiving treatment.

Maintaining Diversity

Diversity is a multifaceted aspect and includes biodiversity, socio-cultural diversity as well as, diversity in terms of products and recreations offered to the tourists. The latter is discussed in the next section. Biodiversity is important but possible loss should be compared to that caused by other activities. Since some kind of development is decided there will be some loss in different fields, unless an area is left unspoiled and without intensive activities around. For developed resorts it is practically impossible to measure changes in biodiversity as a result of **tourism** since data on the conditions that existed before development are in most cases not available.

Maintaining diversity is mostly a consideration at the regional level. Biodiversity is apparent and common in a larger area, while the impacts on biodiversity are spread out on a broader spatial scale. However, the indicators could be used on a local scale too in order to have a measure of this parameter. Moreover, when the scale of application is not limited in the tourist area itself but on the broader area where local activity is taking place, is a wishing component that diversity indicators are included. Proposed indicators for the regional level:

- Number of special interest sites (natural, cultural) under protection Vs to those without any protection,
- Existence of legislation for species protection,
- Number of endangered/threatened species on the region,
- Monitoring of the number (e.g. ratio of species disappearance and/or Vs to the present numbers) and the patterns of species,
- Monitoring of the mobility patterns of the fauna.

Integrating Tourism into Planning and Marketing Tourism Responsibly

Effective planning along with its marketing dimension and the focus on diversification needed can be used to rejuvenate and give a more sustainable future on the tourism product offered, the environment and the development in general.

To determine indicators for planning we look on the three dimensions of planning in tourism, planning in the traditional sense, marketing and providing a diversified product for the tourists. Indicators for traditional planning include the existence of:

- Master plan for the development of the area/resort,
- Established procedures to monitor continuously the progress of tourism development,
- EIA procedures for analyzing the impact of new developments Marketing is actually part of the planning process whose goals and objectives can be established locally, regionally or nationally. The way an area is marketed can influence perceptions, expectations and attitudes of the tourists before and after they reach their destination. With a responsible marketing, resort could be able to attract responsible tourists who fit the goals and objectives established for the area.

Diversification is related to sector's sustainability, as well as economic, socio-cultural and ecological sustainability. Diversification should be examined in terms of:

a) Who brings the tourists,
b) The seasonally of tourism,
c) The product offered,

Mass tourism-the predominant form of tourism in most Mediterranean resorts-and its reliance on few tour-operators may lead to an oligopoly which can limit substantially the profits for the host area and is not easy to be controlled locally or nationally. The number of different ways of distribution of the tourist product and the existence of local network of distribution are two proposed indicators.

Seasonal diversification is an important aspect as well. The pressures paused on the environment because of the high tourist numbers in a limited time period and the seasonal and non-career character of the jobs offered, are important considerations. On the other hand, the "winter" pause could be considered as positive since locals could have some time to strengthen their family and social bonds while ecosystems could also take a period of "rest". The need for diversification of the tourism product in order to restructure development appears to be essential. The new consumer culture with the increasing awareness about environmental quality, make apparent the need for new alternatives to be promoted in areas which have developed a massive and undiversified product so far.

Proposed indicators:

- Tourists perception for the place they are visiting,
- Number of different products/activities supplied locally (historic-cultural tourism, sports based, conference, explorative tourism etc as well as recreational opportunities),
- Number of visitors and (and No of groups) in other than 3S places/activities comparing to total number of visitors,
- % of hotels (or beds) operating during winter,
- Ratio of activities available in off season period to activities offered at peak time,
- Percentage of tourists arriving with charter flights vs total arrivals,
- % of tourists having booked in three major T.O.,
- Number of tourists "moved" by independent tour operators vs those "moved" by large-scale mainstream T.O.,
- Percentage of tourists arriving with already booked accommodations vs total arrivals,

- Existence of legislation or zoning regulations determining the land use and the impregnated tourist areas,

Supporting Local Economies

In many areas in both developed and developing countries tourism has become the last 20 years one of the most significant economic activities. Employment growth and income generation are the two key economic benefits gained from tourism.

Tourism is a labour-intensive sector that has direct, indirect and induced benefits on local incomes. On the other hand, tourism is an activity that may necessitate large amounts of investment, which usually are not available locally and have to be procured from abroad or other parts of the country. As a result, it is possible to have excessive expropriation of profits from the business interests that invested and gradual loss of control over local economic activities. Employment and income generation for local people, compared to similar indicators for other economic sectors, is one indicator for this principle. However, when the proportion attributed to tourism is unevenly high, this could indicate a non-sustainable pattern of development.

It is common that large number of the businesses offering tourist services belong to non-locals. Also non-locals may take many of the jobs. Additionally, a large share of the expenditures made by tourists may never reach the host community.

Finally, a very significant contribution of tourism to the local economy is the increased demand for the local products, agricultural, crafts, products of small artisans etc. The only way of measuring this impact is through an input-output table that shows the interrelationships among the various sectors and the consumption patterns.

Proposed indicators:

- Employment in tourism as a percentage of total employment,
- Number of "locals" employed in tourism as a percentage of total employment in tourism,
- Revenues generated by tourism as a percentage of total revenues generated in the area,
- Business establishments offering tourist services and owned by locals as a percentage of all business establishments,
- Income multiplier for the tourism sector as estimated in an input-output table,

- Revenues exported as a percentage of total revenues in the business establishments owned by foreigners.

Involving local communities and Consulting stakeholders and the public

Involving local communities is examined along with the seventh principle "Consulting stakeholders and the public", as they are actually expressions of the need for communication, information and experience exchange. As McIntyre (1993) states, community involvement in tourism can reinforce positive impacts while mitigating negative ones, as in this way residents understand tourism, participate in its decision-making and receive benefits from it. Involvement of the local communities on the processes and the decision-making of tourism can better ensure locals' positive attitude to tourism as well as their commitment to developmental goals –where these later exist. As Bramwell and Henry (1996) points out consultation of all stakeholders is essential if they are to work alongside each other.

Local participation is also interrelated with educational elements, such as informing local communities for the processes and the impacts of tourism. Although, in already developed resorts it is likely that the host community will have some experience, it is important that they have the right information about the needs for the long-term impacts and the long-term viability of the industry.

Proposed indicators:

- Existence of educational/informational programs for the public,
- Number of local meetings to discuss issues before policies are implemented,
- Availability of procedures for public and stakeholders involved to suggest changes in policies,
- Public-private partnerships/investments.

Training Staff

Training and continuous education is important for the improvement of the tourism product offered. This later is important in its turn, for developed areas facing some stagnation or decline in their product.

There is a need for continuous training in every type of job related to tourism, from cooks to higher managers. Better quality, greater productivity, increased effectiveness, introduction of new technologies and environmental extensions should be some of the subjects to be worked on. The training element is better reflected at the regional level or even more at a national level. Indicators, such as availability of vocational courses offered on tourism services, are more meaningful when measured regionally. It is not expected that each resort will organize courses while it is expected that in a broader area courses will be available for people from around the region.

Therefore this principle is better examined in a regional scale. However, in order to have some kind of indication for the training element the indicators of a broader region could be used indicatively of the situation.

An indicator for the local scale is:

- Number of short-term courses realized locally concerning tourism However it is better reflected in a broader scale. Proposed indicators for this are:
- Attendance in short term courses per 1000 employees,
- % of employees that are graduates of tourist schools,
- Initiatives by the public sector and/or the industry for training,
- Availability of short-term courses per 1000 tourists,
- Diversity of courses offered,
- Graduates of tourist schools per 1000 tourists .

Undertaking Research

"Governments, industry, authorities, and tourism-related NGOs should promote and participate in the creation of open networks for research, dissemination of information and transfer of appropriate knowledge on tourism and environmentally sustainable tourism technologies" (W.T.O. & U.N.E.P., 1998) Tourism is similar to other economic sectors in that on-going research and monitoring using effective data collection and analysis techniques is essential to help solve problems, create new products, make efficient use of the resources, better implement sustainable development in practice. Several issues of tourism and sustainability research are common in more than one resort. Furthermore, there are many implications that cross the narrow local boundaries and expand in a broader area. Therefore, it is expected that research will likely take place in a regional scale –or even more in a national scale.

However, the following indicators could be used at the local level as well in order to reflect the local commitment to sustainable development principles.

Proposed indicators:

- Number of surveys made concerning tourist preferences and perceptions,
- Number of surveys made concerning locals perceptions for tourism,
- Number of research studies on the profitability of the industry/ number of research studies on the impacts of tourism,
- Conferences and other activities attracting interest in tourism research organized locally.

Conclusions

This research was an effort to propose indicators for sustainable tourism in already developed resorts in the Mediterranean Basin. Sustainable tourism is an integral part of overall sustainable development. In order to stay close to the vision and goals of sustainable development the methodology for the extraction of the indicators was based on the principles of sustainable tourism. As it is illustrated in the Bellagio Principles (1996) for sustainable development *"Assessment of progress towards sustainable development should be based on an explicit set of categories or an organizing framework that links vision and goals to indicators and assessment criteria".*

The indicators proposed here aim at offering a tool for evaluating the tourism development and the practices used so far in existing destinations linking tourism industry to the economic, environmental and socio-cultural context of a resort or a region. Although some characteristics of the Mediterranean tourist destinations were taken into consideration, it is apparent that some site specific indicators –related to the special characteristics and needs of each resort-may be added to the list.

Data availability is an important issue in most Mediterranean countries especially when talking about existing destinations, since in most cases, no early monitoring of some aspects and variables took place. Therefore, it is difficult to compare the pre-and after-tourism situation, simply because no data are collected for the existing conditions before the tourism development. Nevertheless, data availability induced in some way the definition of indicators without however restricting it. Moreover, in order to overwhelm this problem emphasis was placed on the sustainable management practices adopted so far It may still prove to be difficult to estimate some of them but as it stated in the

Hart Environmental Data (1999) "*if you define a list of indicators and find that the data is readily available for every one of them, you have not thought hard enough about sustainability. Try to define the best indicators and only settle for less as an interim step while developing data sources for the better indicators*"

The Outer Islands in the South Pacific Popular

The research reported in this paper describes the findings of an investigation into identifying the drivers of remote Pacific island tourism. The research was undertaken on Espiritu Santo, an outer island of Vanuatu and addresses a gap in the current literature on small island. In global terms, the Pacific region attracts approximately 5.4% of the world's international tourism arrivals. In spite of its small size, tourism is one of the mainstays of the region's economy and is a major employer in many of the countries in the region. Parnwell noted: "tourism represents a potentially powerful means by which economic activity might be spread to peripheral, economically underdeveloped areas". Projectedgrowth in intra-Pacific travel and increased interest in heritage and cultural tourism is essential for developing tourism growth. Problems associated with tourism development and marketing in small remote areas are well illustrated in the South Pacific where there are two effective orders of remoteness: 170 geographically remote island nations such as Nauru, Pitcairn Island, Tonga, Cook Islands occupy an outer periphery location relative to the major tourism generating nations, and remote or peripheral regions within remote island nations.

In the case of island nations such as Vanuatu these are termed 'outer' islands. Research into the development of sustainable tourism in remote communities, particularly those which are island based, has attracted the attention of a number of researchers including Craig-Smith & Fagence (1994), Craig-Smith (1996), Main (1989), Fagence (1997) and PATA (1991), Tisdell and McKee (1988). According to Fagence (1997) Nauru faces an uncertain future if new industries such as tourism are not developed and able to achieve long term sustainability. Further, remote communities generally face problems in developing sustainable industries. However, these are not insolvable as tourism has succeeded in larger islands such as Bali and Fiji, Hawaii and smaller island nations including the Maldives, Saipan.

Problems commonly encountered include distance, environmental impacts, lack of infrastructure, poor transport connections, unwelcome income distribution consequences, lack of political and administrative leadership and a lack of destination knowledge by potential visitors. In remote islands these issues can be seen in different contexts-a core–periphery problem where the political centre of power resides in larger islands and where the main city is the main centre of tourism development, particularly in the early stages, or in terms of push-pull motivational mechanisms that may be operating. The impact of both forces shapes development and can be seen in many tourism areas. For example, the main island of Efate receives more international visitors than the nation's outer islands, a reflection of the considerable public funds that are directed towards international tourism marketing.

In a study of Barbados, Dann (1977) found that 'pull' factors in the destination such as sunshine and sea, draw tourists to certain destinations or resort areas, while 'push' factors in the origin nation work to encourage or push the tourist to travel to a particular country. Push factors include income and nostalgia. In developing tourism in Vanuatu both forces can be observed. The emphasis on developing the main island of Efate at the expense of the outer islands such as Espiritu Santo, Tanna, Malekula, Pentecost, Ambae and Maewo result in the pull factors being strongest on Efate. Lack of development of the outer islands reduces their pull power and dilutes their ability to take advantage of push factors in major generating regions Although Vanuatu is considered a less developed country (LDC), tourism has been seen to have economic advantages as well as social, cultural and environmental benefits. Tourism in poorer countries provides financial reasons for preserving cultural, historical and natural resources or traditions, which might otherwise neglected or degraded. Some researchers disagree however, and consider that tourism, especially mass tourism, has led to problems including environmental issues, cultural and social degradation, unequal distribution of economic benefits and eventual spread of disease.

In initiating development in remote areas, some conditions need to be met and include: government recognition of the development of tourism, willingness by residents to accept that development may impact on their lifestyle, acceptance by both private and public sectors that they must contribute to tourism infrastructure, and lastly, effective marketing of remote localities. These are significant for small island states whose traditional primary product exports are declining and there are few options apart from tourism to generate export income.

Primary production such as bananas, cocoa beans, green coffee, coconuts and maize, has fallen in recent years with productivity falling by 27% in 1999, 11% in 2000 and 26% in 2001. Thus tourism is one of the few relatively reliable sources of foreign exchange. To date, tourism development in Vanuatu has been mainly centred on the main island, Efate, particularly in the capital Port Vila. This is a legacy from the past, as colonial administrators from the United Kingdom and France concentrated development in Port Vila rather than the outlying islands of Espiritu Santo, Pentecost and others. Consequently neglect of regional economic development in the outer islands has left a legacy of poor transport, education, health and tourism infrastructure.

The outer islands have much to offer, including unique cultures, abundant coral reefs, diving and fishing, as well as idyllic beaches, forests, and mountainous panoramas. Together with the tourism product currently available on Efate, the tourism potential of Espiritu Santo, Pentecost and other islands could provide a broader range of tourism experiences making the country more attractive as a destination. Vanuatu forms part of the Melanesian region, which comprises Papua New Guinea (PNG), New Caledonia, Solomon Islands and Fiji. Tourism has been developed in each of these countries. However, there is great disparity in the amount of tourism to each country and financial returns from tourism. In recent years, unrest in Papua New Guinea, Solomon Islands, New Caledonia and Fiji, has at times, caused steep declines in tourism arrivals and gross tourism receipts.

Espiritu Santo is known for its casual life style, beaches and culture, however, tourism facilities are under-promoted and there are only a few developed tourist attractions. There are World War II relics for diving and it is noted for the fact that James Michener wrote the well known novel 'Tales of the South Pacific' (1947) when Espiritu Santo was a major US military during the war and about 250,000 service personal were stationed on the island. Much of the infrastructure from this time still exists. Currently Espiritu Santo produces copra, coffee and cocoa and exports beef and has a small tourism industry. The number of visiting cruise ships has fallen and because they usually stay for only a day so they have limited impact on the local way of life. World War II wrecks are popular with divers, particularly the 'President Coolidge', an intact US warship sunk near the coast. 'Million Dollar Point' where considerable military equipment was dumped is also a popular diving location.

There appears to be little recognition by the national government of the aspirations of residents of outer islands to develop tourism and little effort to identify and develop the necessary infrastructure to support tourism. This lack of commitment hinders tourism and is surprising given the importance of special niche tours, or ecotourism in general, to this, and other Pacific Islands.

Research Methodology

In order to gather sufficient data to address the research question, namely to identify why the outer islands of the South Pacific are popular with some tourists and not others, primary quantitative data was collected by distributing questionnaires to visitors in the outer islands. Respondents were asked to rank a series of questions in order of importance from 1 (representing the most important point) to 9 (the least important point). Secondary data was derived from government sources, the tourism industry and general literature on Vanuatu and the outer islands. The researchers also consulted travel brochures, academic and government reports from the Research School of Pacific Studies at the Australian National University (ANU), Vanuatu Bureau of Statistics (VBS), Government of Vanuatu, the National Tourism Office of Vanuatu (NTOV) and the Pacific Asia Travel Association (PATA).

This paper reports on the findings of the questionnaire. Despite some previous research into Vanuatu's tourism industry, there was a gap in the knowledge about traveller needs in Vanuatu and the outer islands. There is also a knowledge gap on issues related to the tourism needs of a number of Pacific Island regions including Micronesia, Melanesia and Polynesia. One major gap is understanding visitor and local resident needs. A survey was conducted at Bauerfield International Airport, Port Vila, Vanuatu during a one-week period in 1999. Before undertaking the survey the instrument was piloted and modified where necessary. The survey was distributed by one of the authors to allow respondents to clarify points about the survey if required. The survey targeted two groups of tourists; those visiting only the main island and those visiting outer islands. A total of 185 valid responses were collected and represented 0.37% of all tourists visiting Vanuatu during 1999. Because of the small sample size and its timing, some significant visitor groups may have been under or over represented. The primary data collected came from two sub-sets of travellers returning to Australia viz.:

1. Respondents who did not travel to an outer island (164 respondents), and
2. Respondents who did travel to an outer island, (21 respondents).

The survey frame was designed to include all adults over 18 years of age who were visiting Vanuatu for leisure reasons. Only one person who was approached did not agree to participate. Questionnaire data was analysed by cross tabulation of the tested variables to determine travel trends to the outer islands of Vanuatu. Previous studies that utilised this methodology were reported by Suvilehto & Borg (2001) and Ryan (1995).

Research Findings

The response rates and rankings of respondents based on patterns of visitation within the country. The most important reason for not travelling to the outer island given was the high cost of airfares followed by factors that pointed to a lack of knowledge of the specific attractions located in the outer islands. The high cost of airfares was also a major concern for respondents who did travel to the outer islands. Respondents who travelled to an outer island ranked the need for cultural awareness by tourists as the most important consideration in their desire to travel to an outer island. When asked to give recommendations, respondents indicated that the outer islands should have additional advertising and marketing, and should have more exposure in the wholesale travel brochures. Travellers to the outer islands also indicated that there was a need for a better standard of accommodation than is currently available, a wider range of activities and they also expressed the need for local residents to have a greater awareness of visitor needs.

These findings have specific implications for developing more tourist 'friendly' tourism services particularly in the accommodation and attractions sectors in the outer islands of Vanuatu. The responses of the two groups indicate that there is a difference between the perceptions of the outer islands by respondents who did not go to an outer island and the recommendations of respondents who actually experienced the product. Whilst those who did not visit an outer island did not believe that the accommodation there should be of a higher standard, those who experienced the accommodation thought that it needed improvement.

Conclusion and Recommendations

This investigation was designed to identify factors that would assist peripheral areas develop their tourism sectors. There is an urgent need to increase tourism activity in these regions as income from traditional commodity based export industries are declining. The study found that respondents who only visited the main island of Efate were deterred from visiting outer islands because of high airfares and also a lack of knowledge of the experiences that were on offer.

Whereas the cost of airfares was quite significant to both groups, respondents who visited the outer islands also identified the need to build greater cultural awareness and to improve accommodation standards.

However, these findings should be seen as needing further refinement because of limitations of timing and sampling in this research. It is suggested that consideration be given to conduct further studies including longitudinal studies in order to overcome timing deficiencies such as seasonality effects and broadening the sampling frame to include tourists from other countries to gain a wider perspective about tourism needs in the region.

8

The Challenges to Sustainability in Island Tourism

Introduction

Islands are special places with a natural attraction for tourists and a special challenge to sustainability. The thousands of islands on the face of the earth include some of the finest and most sought after destinations, such as the Balearic Islands, the Hawaiian Islands, the Galapagos Islands, the Canary Islands, the French Polynesian Islands, and the Caribbean islands. The mystique associated with islands is dependent on a blend of different lifestyles, indigenous cultures, unique land formations, flora and fauna, and ocean and coastal resources. To keep that mystique alive and thriving, islands must implement sustainable tourism policies in all areas including environmental, economic and socio-cultural. This paper will examine the unique challenges that islands face as they attempt to build sustainability into their tourism development policies. It will also propose policies to assist in attaining and maintaining quality island tourism.

Types of Island Tourism Destinations

Islands vary in many ways, and understanding the various types clarifies for the decision-makers the policies that need to be used. One classification is islands' climate which can be cold, temperate or tropical. Even though tropical islands (Caribbean, Hawaii, French Polynesia) tend to have most allure for tourists, cold and temperate islands also have environmental or cultural features and lifestyles that attract tourism– for example the Shetland islands off the coast of Scotland. Baum 1997 describes the general attractivity of North Atlantic islands, including their remoteness, their small size, the slower pace of life, the chance to go back-in-time, the wilderness environment, the water-focused society and the sense of difference yet fam. Very cold islands such as Iceland and Greenland offer unique landscapes and flora and fauna and are alternate destinations often attracting scientists, photographers and other specialized travellers. Another island classification is the proximity to the related mainland and also its size. Islands that are more remote and distant face more challenging accessibility and transportation issues due to their isolation. Visitors will tend to stay longer in islands that are remote and larger, whereas those close to the mainland and smaller may experience more excursionist tourism. For example, Cousin Island in the Seychelles, hosts only day visitors that leave the island at the end of each day. The island's choice to host excursionists versus stay-over visitors requires a careful evaluation of the strengths and weaknesses of each type of tourism.

A third classification is whether an island is a single island or part of an archipelago. Multi-destination travel in island chains may be an added attraction for tourists, whereas the peace, or 'sun, sand, sea' experience of a single island vacation may be the choice for others. Cooperative marketing and complementary product development is important for archipelago islands. This will create a diverse touristic experience giving archipelagos an advantage over single islands, particularly if they are small.

A fourth classification is the governance of the island destination. Some islands have autonomous governments and others are part of the mainland government system. Those with autonomy have more control over the direction of sustainable development of the island. They are also more likely to reap the maximum economic benefits from tourism, without any revenue being leaked to the mainland through taxes and other means. Islands under the jurisdiction of the mainland need to ensure adequate representation in the government decision-making. Fifth, some island destinations have growing resident populations (which may be due in part to tourism) and other with weak economies are experiencing declining populations. In the latter case, there is a special need to ensure economic viability to prevent the out-migration of residents – especially young ones who look for opportunities elsewhere. Some islands, of course, have no human population and are simply nature-reserves, and others are privately owned with their own policies.

The last classification relates to the homogeneity of the population and the socio-cultural sustainability of island destinations. Islands with homogeneous, indigenous populations are particularly vulnerable to tourism development since they have different cultures with different values than the source markets. The close interaction that islands create between hosts and guests must be managed. Islands with more heterogeneous populations may be more resilient to socio-cultural impacts.

It is clear from the categories above that islands differ in many ways from the mainland and from each other. Each island has its uniqueness and that uniqueness needs to be nurtured and strengthened through sustainable tourism policies. The next section will examine the specific issues and problems that islands face in sustainable tourism development.

Sustainability Issues Facing Island Destinations

Many researchers have studied tourism in an island context. Some of these studies relate to specific islands (Malta, Briguglio and Briguglio, 2002, Seychelles, Shah 2002, French Polynesia, Salvat and Pailhe 2002, Boracay Island, Philippines, Trousdale, 1999, Canary Islands, Gil, 2003, Hawaiian Islands, Sheldon et al. 2005) and others address island tourism in a general, conceptual manner. All islands must address issues of economic impact, environmental consequences and those relating to the social, cultural and political fabric of the island all of which are affected by the density of tourism on the island. High tourist and resident densities in islands such as Malta are the source of many sustainability problems and carrying capacity needs to be considered.

Measures of tourism density are important for policy makers to assess possible growth scenarios. One measure of tourism density or saturation, which considers all three areas of impact is the Tourism Penetration Index (TPI). TPI includes three variables: 1) visitor spending per capita of population (economic measure), 2) average daily visitors per 1000 population (social measure), and 3) hotel rooms per square kilometre of land (environmental measure) (McElroy and Albuquerque, 1998). McElroy and Albuquerque used this to cluster Caribbean islands into different clusters depending on whether their TPI is low, intermediate or high value. McElroy notes that for islands with low TPI's the most important challenges are establishing profitability and international recognition, for those with intermediate TPI controlling growth is the most important, and for those islands with the highest TPI the greatest challenge is to sustain vacation quality. The next sections will address the economic, environmental and socio-cultural challenges faced by islands in their quest to sustainability.

Economic Issues

A challenge to the economic health of an island is the often limited economic resource base. Islands may have few resources or viable industries other than tourism to provide revenue and employment for the local population. The value of agricultural and mining commodities on the international markets is declining and fishing is less reliable as fish populations are being depleted, and global warming is changing the nature of coastlines and fish movements. Tourism can be an economic catalyst for small island development. In fact, Croes (2004) suggests tourism as a tool for small islands to enlarge their economies and overcome the disadvantages of smallness. The extra market demand produces economies of scale and increases efficiency and decreases costs of production. Tourism also increases competition, encourages new start-up businesses, democratizes market structure, and deters rent-seeking behaviours and corruption. He also argues that this competition can provide greater consumer choice, trade openness and increase the quality of life for residents.

Despite this, the revenue form tourism must remain in the island economy as much as possible. Policies of import substitution to ensure minimum economic leakages, and 'buy local' policies to maximize linkages are essential. Taxation policies, entrepreneurial subsidies, and investment incentives are all useful to strengthen the economy. If development strategies are such that the incoming wealth is leaving the island economy, tourism needs to be re-designed. Islands under the governance of the mainland need to ensure a fair share of tax revenue due. Islands under their own governance will gain most economically.

Seasonality in island tourism is another challenge to the economic sustainability of the island and the well-being of the island people. Fluctuations in visitor arrivals must be understood and mitigated through product and market diversification so that employment stabilizes and tourism infrastructures and superstructures are well utilized. Escalating land prices represent another economic concern in islands forcing local residents out of the housing market. This promotes out migration, leading to a possible dissolution of the culture, and second home ownership by foreigners. These trends if unmitigated can generate a serious chain of problems for the island economy.

Environmental Issues

Environmental issues of sustainability on islands are multi-faceted, since islands have diverse land formations, coastal areas, and wildlife species. Tourism often contributes to the environmental degradation in small, island states which are host to fragile eco-systems rich in biodiversity. The isolation of the island environment created the biodiversity, and by opening to tourism, some of that sheltered biodiversity is endangered. Islands' prime tourist environmental resource is often the coastal regions (beaches, sand dunes, coral reefs) that are easily damaged, heavily used, and requiring of careful visitor management. The large amount of waste (solid and liquid) created by tourism is a problem since space for its disposal on islands is limited.

Socio-Cultural Issues

Islands face complex socio-cultural issues, particularly those with indigenous populations. Tourism on islands, particularly small ones, brings hosts and guests into closer contact than on mainland destinations, creating a more vulnerable situation for social disruption. Crime, commoditization of culture, and loss of traditional lifestyles, moral standards and family life impact islands more than mainland destinations. Studies of resident sentiment and response to tourism in the islands of Malta and Hawaii (2003, Sheldon et al 2005) show the importance of this component. Community integration is key to successful and sustainable tourism development, meaning that all islanders affected by tourism must be involved in the planning process. Stakeholders on islands are not only in closer proximity but also have long histories of conflict making it even more important to involve them in the decision-making process.

Approaches to Overcome the Challenges to Island Tourism

The experience of many island destinations over the years has provided a rich source of policies that can assist with sustainability on all levels. The next section presents examples of some of these policies.

Long-term, Stakeholder-involved Planning

Long term planning, developed with comprehensive community and stakeholder input is becoming and important foundation for tourism on islands. Plans also need to be values-based plans and reflect the indigenous culture and traditions. Long range planning must consider the balance of supply and demand of tourism, both quantitatively and qualitatively. A study of tourism in the Canary Islands showed that when these two growth patterns were out of balance the industry is not healthy. Once the plans have been put in place, methodologies to measure and monitor impacts of tourism are essential. This requires the assignment of government agencies to the task of ongoing monitoring of effects. The need for stakeholder-driven planning and indicator development is essential. In Hawaii for example, a process that covered almost two years brought together stakeholders to define their vision, goals and indicators for sustainable tourism. Community involvement to guide tourism planning, development, management, research and evaluation of community-based tourism projects has been implemented in Taquile Island in Peru. On this island, decision-making powers, local control and ownership, and type of employment patterns were measure of community involvement in the planning process.

Empowerment of the Island Community and Culture

Empowerment of the island community and culture is a necessary part of planning. Frameworks to protect and conserve the social and cultural structure are important also. A building of cultural pride through story-telling and memory of traditions, and a sense of identity are paramount. This may involve the re-enlivenment of festivals, arts, language, folk lore and policies to encouraging local people to engage in entrepreneurial activities. Efforts towards sustainable tourism in French Polynesian islands found the meaningful integration of culture into the tourist experience difficult to accomplish. Achieving a balance of respect for the culture and providing tourists with the opportunity to learn about and appreciate the culture is the core of the challenge

Tourist and resident education are a critical part of island sustainability. To empower the residents education and training programs are needed for meaningful careers in the industry. This may involve distance education since islands do not always have comprehensive tertiary education programs in tourism. Residents also need to learn about the impact tourism is having on their community, through the sharing of statistics and facts. The receptivity and openness to change and innovation is also needed. Education for tourists is also important. They need to learn about the unique cultural and environmental features of the island and appropriate behaviours.

Environmental Management

Given the challenges to the island's ecosystems, environmental management is crucial for island sustainability. The paucity of land causes land usage issues, and the trade-off of land for tourism versus agriculture and other industries, or preservation and conservation needs to be addressed. The environmental resources are a main visitor attraction and tourist interfaces with those resources need to be planned and cared for. Conlin, 2002 in a study of Tasmania tourism, gives nine different types of parks or reserves that can be created (national park, state reserve, nature reserve, game reserve, conservation area, nature recreational area, regional reserve, historic site and private sanctuary). This may include designation of zones that are off-limits to tourists, and those that are only visitable with guides and interpreters. Islands with unique wildlife must also take steps to sustain those populations.

Tourism can actually assist as an anti-poaching mechanism and an engine for conservation management when residents realize the economic value of the wildlife as in the Seychelles. Policies to keep the land and ocean unpolluted are also necessary. Waste management and recycling programs are essential, particularly on small islands. Also the use, through incentive programs if necessary, for alternative fuel sources will make the destination more sustainable. The shortage of land for landfills may need waste to be sent to the mainland for some islands. Recycling programs for all types of waste are essential, and the use of alternative energy sources (wind, solar, geothermal) is an important consideration since tourists use much higher per capita user of energy than locals and rarely can islands survive on fossil fuels. Water shortages also are common on islands, limiting the amount of tourism development. Environmental management includes recovery from natural disasters to which islands are so vulnerable. Disasters such as tidal waves, volcanic eruptions, cyclones, drought and rise in sea level are all natural hazards that islands face. Funds for conservation and disaster management are needed and can be gained through taxation, visitor fees or other mechanisms.

Visitor Management

Visitor impact is so much greater on islands, requiring tools of visitor management to ensure island sustainability. Control of numbers of tourist arrivals is possible through the methods of transportation. Once the tourists arrive on the island they need information and guidance on possible attractions, tours and events. One method of visitor management is the zoning of land for different uses, and the creation of national parks and conservation areas to conserve historic sites, biological and geological diversity, preserve water quality, and to encourage education. The management of visitors on coral reefs is another issue of environmental management faced by many islands such as Hawaii and the French Polynesian islands.

Clear signage, information and interpretive information assist the tourists in finding and understanding the attractions. Guides, rangers, wardens and other staff can guide tourists through delicate environments. The recognition that visitors seek education and knowledge of species and land formations requires good interpretative systems. The private sector such as tour operators need guidelines for places that are off-limits or have restricted access. The Galapagos archipelago with its unique biodiversity had to use visitor management techniques due to the large volume of visitors (including scientists, writers, photographers) wanting to see the nature reserves. They attempted to control tour operators by asking them to adhere to cruise itineraries fixed by the national parks however that has not been totally successful. Standards and certification for employee performance particularly in the tour-guiding arena will help with the interpretation and sustainability of the island.

Knowledge and Information Systems

Knowledge and information systems can help islands market their tourism product and also manage their tourist resources. Web-based marketing by the public sector and by private suppliers helps islands locate and target the market segments they want, and reduces the reliance on tour operators. Destination management systems with comprehensive product databases and other information to assist and educate the potential tourist are an important competitive tools in the matching of tourist and island experience. Because islands are smaller, it may be easier to install location specific technologies and databases and data communication systems. These could include mobile visitor information systems, geographic information systems (GIS) mapping systems, global positioning systems (GPS), and intelligent transportation systems. GIS system scombine data and spatial information to help planners conduct spatial analysis of touristic areas. They have been used for example in the Cayman Islands to assess the impact of tourism on fragile reefs and in China for disaster monitoring using remote sensing data. Location specific information can be displayed on hand-held devices to assist travellers in their knowledge of the destination and its attractions. They also can keep visitors on appropriate routes through warning messages, and can direct visitors' attention to an item or species of interest.

The placement of GPS devices on wildlife may increase visitors' chances of viewing the species. The use of GPS devices on tourists can help to rescue them from dangerous situations in the ocean, the mountains or other wilderness areas. Information technology can support the planning and stakeholder involvement processes on islands. For example, expert systems which simulate the knowledge-base of an expert can be used to facilitate decision making for sustainable tourism. Groupware can be applied to build stakeholder consensus, and the Internet is a valuable resource to gain community input from residents in remote communities.

Accessibility and Transportation

Accessibility and transportation to island communities is an important area of policy for islands. Different transportation modes both to the island and on the island are usually necessary, and can be used as a control mechanism for how many tourists visit the island. The security, safety and costs of such transportation are also important considerations. The balance of public and private transport use by tourists is a policy variable. Once tourists use their own transportation (hire car, motorbicycle), the control of their activities on the island is drastically reduced. Some islands prohibit motorized vehicles in certain areas, others suggest the use of electrical vehicles that are quieter and less pollutive. Air transportation to islands is most common, however it leaves islands vulnerable to stoppage of flights due to strikes, terrorism etc., and vulnerable to high fares if there is little competition on the route. It also requires the use of land for airports. The low-cost carriers that serve many European island destinations today is fuelling growth in second homes since owners can travel very cheaply to their island property. With out this cheap form of transportation, the development of a second home tourism market is in jeopardy.

The ocean is a natural option for transportation – both functional and recreational. Yachts, boats and ferries of different types are useful to transport the visitors from island to island. In the Hawaiian Islands a high-speed ferry between the islands is being added to provide additional capacity to the inter-island flights. Large cruise ships, and their interest in island ports-of-call, make expansion of island tourism a distinct possibility. The large 2,500 berth cruise ships are potential sources of extra visitors, however they bring with them needs and impacts that may not always be in the best interests of the sustainability of the island. Accessibility to the island also includes data, voice and fax communications and credit card use. These are necessary for a destination to function well.

Marketing and Market Diversification

Marketing and market diversification is important for islands. Markets may be domestic or international, but the match between island facilities and resources and the tourist is the most important consideration. Domestic markets are likely to create less socio-cultural disturbance and may therefore be preferred. When defining market segments, islands often try to identify niches to generate the highest expenditure for the island, as was done in the Canary Islands. Hawaii's Strategic Plan 2005-2010 has a similar focus on the quality visitor and focuses on expenditures and length of stay in its marketing plans. Product innovation to match those segments and the extension of the life cycle for island tourism products are important components of island tourism marketing. The development of niche markets based on the islands resources is an important market strategy. For example in Tasmania, Australia, they focused on agricultural based tourist activities such as farm-stays, agricultural museums, wineries, and other activities based on crops such as lavender and raspberries (Conlin, 2002). Some islands with very popular and delicate attractions may choose to practice de-marketing of sites that are over visited. The type of infrastructure and superstructure that the island invests in will also determine the type of tourists that come. For example, the building of only luxury hotels in French Polynesia attracted only high-income visitors. Many islands are famous for the "sun, sand and sea" image and may want to diversify their product to attract a different type of tourist, for 'sun, sea and sand' can be found in many islands.

Summary

This paper has identified some of the challenges facing islands in sustaining their tourism industry. It has also recommended some policies and approaches to assist in this area. Each island is unique and has unique attributes. The challenge to sustainable management is to keep those unique elements that are part of the mystique that attracts tourists. Shifts toward homogeneity of tourism experiences without giving the visitor an experience of 'sense of place' will not be sustainable in the long run either for the host community or for the tourism markets.

Understanding Tourist Beaches as Eco-social Landscapes

Now coral reefs are not merely pretty,...of much greater consequence is their vital importance of protecting our shores, this may not be generally realised. We had a nice example of this in Barbados recently when a certain hotel, in order to improve its beach facilities, bulldozed a certain piece of inshore reef to make a "white hole" for bathing. Although the area removed was perhaps only 20 x 30 yards, the consequent change in wave action resulted not only in the removal of the sandy beach previously existing but also the knocking down of the sea wall of the hotel itself. So here we have a very close ecological connection between tourism and the natural environment.

While tourism development can have significant affects on environments, much of the critical scholarship on tourism and its affects on local places has focused upon social impacts. Scholars such as sociologists Chris Rojek and John Urry (1997) have approached tourism as a specifically cultural process, while others, such as anthropologist Ian Munt (1994a; 1994b) have written ethnographies of "the toured". The political economy of wealth flows from developing world destinations to developed world capital and its local effects was insightfully described by Stephen Britton. While such work is vital to understanding tourism development as a social practice, the human-environment tradition in geography mandates a synthesis of social *and ecological* processes as they interact in place and across space.

The importance of environments to tourism has been acknowledged in the tourism literature. As noted by researchers working in the tropical Pacific, and in the Caribbean, the environmental effects of tourism can be especially significant on small islands. Though Edington and Edington recognized the need for better understandings of ecological processes that closely interact with tourism in 1986, Hall and Page have recently lamented the continuing poverty of such understandings.

Antigua, a small island in the West Indies provides a good illustration of how tourism might affect environments and environments affect tourism, and how we might understand and manage those interactions more effectively for all concerned. With nearly one-half million visitors spending approximately $250 million each year, tourism is vital to Antigua's formal economy. The industry employs over half of the Antiguan labour force, generates a per capita GDP of US$7,500, and is responsible for sixty percent of the island's gross domestic product issues directly from the (ABDT 1996; ABMF 1996; EU-ACP 1996; Courier 1997, 36; Gortier 1997, 32). Antiguan tourism is focused upon its beaches to an extreme degree. Over 95 percent of all hotel rooms are in beach resorts. Antigua has little night life, few heritage tourism sites, and minimal shopping venues outside its duty-free mall at the base of a relatively new cruise ship quay. Antigua is know for and promoted as a place for quiet and/or romantic beach vacations. Peter Ramrattan, the head of Antigua's Hotel and Tourism Association characterized the island's tourist clientele as the "newly wed and the nearly dead" (1997). Though now adding "The heart of the Caribbean" to the Antiguan brand, the slogan "365 powdery white sand beaches… one for every day of the year" has been used for decades (AHTA 1996, 31).

The social construction of beaches as tourism places has been well explored generally in Corbin (1994), Lencek and Bosker (1998), and Shields (1990). The relationship between Antigua's coastal environment and the governance of tourism development has been complex and highly problematic. I have described these conflictual social processes specific to Antigua's beaches elsewhere and refer the reader to discussions for further background. While those social processes are central to the dialectic amongst Antiguan coasts and their users, the physical condition of the coast has recently become equally worthy of consideration. In 1996, it became clear that Antigua's beaches were eroding (AHTA 1997, 3; CCA 1991; COSALC 1996; UPR 1994); the environmental basis of Antigua's national tourism economy was disappearing into the Caribbean.

As in many developing world economies, tourism development in Antigua is a project dominated by the national government and foreign investors. In Antigua the government is also charged with, and is the only agent capable of caring for common lands and resources such as its beaches. Also typical of landscapes caught up in the extensification and intensification of economic activity (i.e. development), the Antiguan government has not responded effectively to environmental degradation and so beach erosion now threatens the well being of Antigua and its people.

The goal of this paper is *not* to analyze the problem of beach erosion; we have outlined the socio-ecology of erosion carefully elsewhere. Rather, my interest here is to elaborate a conceptual framework that tourism planners could use generally in their address of human-environment relations. This is not a wholly original project. Concern over environmental degradation at the behest of economic development has spawned many venerable projects aimed at preserving or conserving valued environments. In order to learn from what has gone before, we review three different attempts at developing tools for planning development that have been especially relevant in tourism management in the developing world: these are sustainable development, indicators of environmental health, and what Harris and Nelson refer to as "whole economy analysis" (1993). In that discussion we identify some of the aims and strengths of each, and some of the problematic assumptions that weaken their ability to integrate environmental with social processes.

Antigua serves as a robust illustration for such a review. In the third section I develop a tourism planning paradigm that encompasses formal, informal, and ecological economies, as well as the interaction between those economies. In the fourth section I apply that planning framework to Antigua's situation today and use it to make concrete recommendations that might more effectively address their beach erosion problem.

Alternative Paradigms for Managing Tourism Environments

There are several alternative paradigms tourism planners may turn to as they seek to mediate the environmental impacts of tourism development. Sustainable development, environmental indicators, and "whole economies" have all been recommended. While each of these planning frameworks seek to integrate economy with ecology, each have inherent problems in their application to tourism-environment relations generally and in Antigua in particular. These problems are important because they suggest areas that any new paradigm must improve upon.

Sustainable Development

Sustainable development, first formalized by the Brundtland Commission in *Our Common Future* (1987) describes one of the most institutionalized and far ranging attempts to mitigate the ill effects of economic development upon environments. Sustainable development arose from the conservation movement's encounter with free market economics. Because mainstream economics recognizes only matters valued in markets, it does not encompass many concerns dear to conservationists and a host of others. Matters valued outside of markets, whether it be child-caring in and for a household, human appreciation of natural beauty, water filtered and made more useful by a wetland, or nitrogen fixed in soil by clover: all are considered external to economy. The Brundtland Commission prescribed the internalization of economic externalities. Though appealing, the prescription is problematic, as it would require nothing less than "a restructuring of national politics, economic, bureaucracy, ... and a new system of international trade and finance".

Adams observes that the concepts of sustainable development *have been* helpful in "laying out principles for peasant agriculture, or expounding the benefits of appropriate technology and the importance of indigenous value systems and technical knowledge" (ibid, 57). For tourism development, sustainability has been useful for ecotourism and forms that Poon has categorized as "new tourism" (1993). Such tourism uses "wilderness" or "authentic" cultural landscapes as their primary product. However, because its scope and scale is necessarily small, "new tourism" cannot serve as a development pole for a national economy. It is mass tourism that has served as a growth pole for the national economies of many small island states, and it is mass tourism that must concern the planners in places like Antigua where the. tourism industry has already matured. Preservationism is equally problematic. In Antigua not only is there little beach wilderness left to preserve, but where they persist they often do not conform to tourism ideals of a beach paradise and must be significantly changed, sand and palms imported, wetlands drained, gardens and accommodations built.

Environmental Indicators and Planning for Sustainability

Some have suggested that the solution to environmental impacts lies in better monitoring through environmental indicators. As Hughes observes, the idiom of sustainable development has turned to the certainty promised by scientific quantification in understanding environmental relations; yet indicators are often poor windows into complex biospheric processes (2002, 458). Many political ecologists have problematized one-dimensional indicators. In a critique of using "indicators" to manage reef health in tourism areas, Butler notes that visitor declines are among the most common indicators of non-sustainability, and that in "many cases such indicators come too late for satisfactory remedial action, even if that had been possible" (1993, 39). As Hall and Page assert, index driven technical fixes often maintain the appearance of normalcy while environmental degradation continues (1999, 52).

The number of tourist visits, for example, may be poor indicator of environmental sustainability. In Antigua, technical fixes such as beach nourishment address the symptom of beach erosion, but not the cause. Tourists see no problem, but more careful surveys indicate that beaches are eroding and that the coralgal community that both provides sediment inputs and moderates wave energies is in decline. Simultaneously, those very fixes are further degrading the coralgal communities that once produced beach berms so valued in the tourism industry. Antigua's case demonstrates the inefficacy of environmental indicators. Though beach erosion and coral decline have been documented, those indicators have not successfully directed scientific management in an address of the underlying problems. To address the problem in a sustainable way, one must also understand why the coralgal community is dying, one must understand holistically why the reefs are dying, and what ill affect tourism has on the production of the beaches it values so much.

Whole Economies?

Where sustainable development fails by dichotomizing humans from nature, relying upon rational management, technical fixes, and insufficient environmental indicators, the authors of "whole economy" frameworks attempt to bridge the divide between the "conditions of production" (nature and not-for-market human production) and production for exchange. The efficacy of the paradigm is illustrated by Harris and Nelson (1993) who apply a "whole economy" approach specifically to planning for tourism development in Pangandaran, Indonesia. The authors describe an "ABC Resource Survey Method" which encompasses abiotic elements (A); biotic elements (B); and cultural elements (C). Though the method sounds hopefully holistic, the A and B portion of their "whole economy" unfortunately are treated as inert spatial "resources" to be mapped and valued for their appeal to human "appreciation for nature" (ibid, 184). Unlike traditional economics, such substantivist economic frameworks do seek to encompass *all* human production—from businesses, governments, collectives, voluntary activities, mutual aid, and households. However, whole economies are anthropocentric, and do not include *non-human* production. Thus, the human-nature dichotomy, with its attendant problems for understanding human-environment relations remains.

Problems with Management

These alternative techno and econo-centric paradigms share a fundamental and problematic model of environments as mechanistic and passive. No dialectic between human and other biospheric systems is allowed or imagined possible. However, environments are not immune to human use. They respond and change to human activity as they do to all disturbances. In Antigua, developers have treated beaches as passive or dead objects which are motivated by physical forces. Beach erosion, therefore, has been categorized as an engineering problem whose solution lays in moving sand from artificial jetties, reef bottoms, and Antigua's sister island, Barbuda, and deposited in front of resorts. However, in the long term, this techno-centric management has only exacerbated the problem of beach erosion. In order to understand beach erosion it is important to understand beaches. Briefly, throughout the insular tropics, most beach sand is biogenic, i.e. it is produced by living organisms. Such beaches are primarily composed of the accumulated bodies of calcium carbonate fixing corals and micro-algae (hereafter referred to as *coralgal* communities), and free floating foraminifera living in the reef environment. Wave action breaks those calciferous bodies and moves them across the sea floor, often depositing them on shore where they form beach berms. In addition to supplying sand to beaches, these living communities create sea floor roughness that works to moderate erosive wave energies. Coralgal communities thus produce and maintain beaches.

Dredging sand from off-shore reefs for beach nourishment is problematic to this process on several counts. Dredging physically destroys portions of these living sand sources. In addition, dredging mobilizes fine sediments that can require years to sequester. Those fine sediments hurt coralgal communities in several ways. They cause turbidity that decreases photosynthesis and growth both among the tiny palm tree shaped Halimeda alga and the zooanthellae alga that live symbiotically in coral polyps. When the fine sediments do settle, they can mantle micro-alga and corals, neither of which have the ability to uncover themselves. Finally, when fine sands are deposited upon beaches they are easily re-mobilized by wave action and move back over the coralgal community. Nourishment can increase turbidity and degrade coralgal communities for years.

Beaches are the by-product of a living community, a community that, like all life, is directed toward, and interested in its own perpetuation. When its life-activity is disrupted, its vitality diminishes. Beaches and the living non-human communities that produce them cannot be treated as passive physical elements. They can be managed, but they must be managed in a way that recognizes their self-interestedness in their own persistence.

New Conceptual Tools

Planning for sustainable development could be made more effective by changing two conceptual fields, both of which arise from assumptions that humans and non-humans are essentially different. As Costanza, Wainger, and Bockstael (1995) observe, research into *systems* tends to dichotomize our worlds into economic or ecological models. Ecological models tend to include humans only as exogenous disturbances and economic models rend to reduce ecology to a set of constraints. In that rubric, "the studies are completed using different terms and units of measurement, and the studies neglect to account for the interaction between the processes and populations" (ibid, 45). A category is needed that is capable of encompassing all production, all value. Wealth, broadly conceived as all matters valued by living beings can provide such a category. I refer to work by Pierre Bourdieu to formalize wealth as a category that is both useful in making sustainable planning policy and encompasses formal, informal, and non-human production.

Secondly, ecological systems are not well described as passive or as mechanically manageable. Through a more careful examination of beach erosion in Antigua the value of conceptualizing non-human communities as active and self-interested can be made apparent. Towards that end, I refer to evolutionary biologist Mae-Won Ho's (1993) development of "coherence" as a pragmatic way to understand biospheric dialectics.

Wealth

To re-conceptualize wealth in a way that seeks similarities between humans and other life, it is helpful to categorize wealth by what it does, rather than what it is. Such a categorization leads to two propositions: first, broadly defined, wealth is anything that has value to some valuing entity; and second, wealth is inessential matter its value is relative and its form is changed by living beings into other forms. Though one cannot ask non-humans what they value, valuing can be observed empirically by watching for choice. Coral polyps, for example, differentially anchor to surfaces that are more sunny than those that are less so. In that practice they demonstrate choice, and therefore valuing. Corals value sunlight because the *zooanthellae* algae that live behind a thin transparent membrane covering the hard calciferous surface of the polyps' shell produce carbohydrates through photosynthesis. Corals depend upon those carbohydrates as a necessary source of food. In their life-activity, the *zooanthellae* transform sunlight, water, and nutrients (some of which are the by-product of the corals' life-activity) into food. Corals with their *zooanthellae* symbiants, and micro-alga like *Halimeda*, transform matters they value, sunlight, water, dissolved nutrients, into matters that they value even more, carbohydrates and other metabolites. Reflecting human exceptionalist assumptions of his time, Marx defines this activity as the labour process: "purposeful activity aimed at the production of use-values. It is an appropriation of what exists in nature for the requirements of man" (1976, 290). If one is willing to grant non-humans the ability to value their own production, the word "man" could accurately be replaced with "life" with interesting implications for Marxist theory.

In 1847, James Joule did characterize this transformative process. He observed that in life-activity, as something is quantitatively consumed, it is simultaneously qualitatively transformed. As life is distinct in its self-organization, life is also marked by its intentional transformation of energy into matter and information, into energy and matter, and matter into energy and information. All fit into the category of wealth, which is understood functionally as matters useful to life in its drive to extend itself in time and space.

Bourdieu formalized this same transformative process in human/social activity. In his research into social exchange and its interaction with *knowledge*, Bourdieu endeavored "to grasp capital and profit in all their forms and to establish the laws whereby the different types of capital (or power, which amounts to the same thing) change one into the other" (1986, 243). Bourdieu demonstrated that people "trans-substantiate," i.e. transform or exchange, one capital into or for another (ibid). Our categories of power, knowledge and money are explicitly *inessential* in that they have no intrinsic, immutable, or universal quality. Bourdieu explained that through our life-activity people produce and transform wealths as needed (Bourdieu 1984, 1986; also Shilling 1993, 127). We accumulate knowledge, associations, power, and money which help us to be appropriate and effective in various situations. He asserted that we then invest available wealths of one sort into other forms of wealth as needed. Raymond Williams (1980) has forcefully argued that the by-products of life activity also have agency in the biosphere and may act to degrade or destroy wealths. After Gallagher (1989) I adopt the term "illth" to refer to matters which destroy or diminish various forms of wealth.

Coherence as a New Spatial Metaphor

As "embodied selves," we are complex wealth transforming and wealth managing mechanisms. Through and in our physical being, we organize stores and flows of power, knowledge, and money. We transform one into the other as needed according to our abilities. In this life activity we are very much like a plant transforming sunlight, nutrients into material wealth in accordance with genetic and environmental information. Humans do what life does. All life organizes flows and accumulates stores of wealth. Through their activity living beings transforms each of these inessential categories of wealth into the other.

This basic process of wealth acquisition, transformation and use-value production suggests a spatiality that does not conform to dominant spatial metaphors people use to understand living beings or their life activity. Though not the sort of thing most people think about in their daily lives, a debate regarding the nature of our existence—are we object as Parmenides argued, or in accord with Heraclitus are we process, or as Nagarjuna suggests, are we neither or both—extends at least to the fourth century BCE. Though proponents argue for mutual exclusivity, both seem to be true at once. One's hand is clearly a solid object in space capable of moving other objects. Yet, its substance is in flux. Very few of the atoms that originally constituted one's hand are still there. New material is constantly flowing into place as the old leaves. Forty years ago, biologist Clifford Grobstein observed this quality of life as an explicitly spatial phenomenon.

Despite this *constant turnover of energy and materials*, there is a net increase in the mass of the complexes at higher levels of structure. Even more remarkable than this is that *continuity of properties* is preserved in the large molecule complexes.

Life is characterized by consistent form, constituted by flows, organized into ever greater complexity. 28 Social scientist Michel Foucault describes the spatiality of entities in a similar fashion, suggesting that "the living being wraps itself in its own existence … and constitutes itself as a new space" (1970, 278). The space life creates of itself is an "interior one of anatomical coherences and physiological compatibilities, and the exterior one of the elements in which it resides and of which it forms its own body" (ibid, 274). Life is marked by its ability and insistence upon organizing flows of matter and energy into coherent forms in accord with information stored within individuals and taken from their environments. Coherence is a helpful concept in grasping processes that are at once transient and permanent.

Scientists of non-human life have also found coherence useful in describing life. Though he did not specifically use the term "coherence" in his characterization of life, Grobstein wrote that life is "characterized by replication, metabolic turnover, and exquisite regulation of energy flow constitutes a spreading centre of order in a less ordered universe" (1964, 1). In her analysis of life as an energetic/spatial process, evolutionary biologist Mae-Won Ho asserts that living beings are "organized heterogeneities, or dynamic structures on all scales" (Ho 1993, 21), and that "*An individual is simply a field of coherent activity*" (ibid, 178).

A contemporary of Foucault, French social philosopher Henri Lefebvre also noted this tension between continuity of form and fluidity of environmental wealths and illths:

> The living organism may be defined as an apparatus which, by a variety of means, captures energies active in its vicinity. It absorbs heat, performs respiration, nourishes itself, and so on. … Around the living organism, both those energies which it captures and those which threaten it are *mobile:* they are 'currents' or 'flows.' By contrast, in order to capture available energies the organism must have at its disposal apparatuses which are *stable* (1991, 176).

We create security in stabilizing those flows, our access to them, and their access to us. Life is unique in this, it is distinguished by it. *Unlike* an inanimate dynamic form such as a standing wave, living beings are not constituted solely by external forces; they act to bring those flows to and through themselves. Life reaches out into the world. Serres (1982) suggested that we think of organisms as seeking homeorrhesis (constant flow), rather than by homeostasis (constant state).

Applying New Tools to Planning

This ontological metaphor of coherence translates directly into planning for sustainable development. People concerned with the sustainable use and development of tropical island beaches, for example, are obliged to follow the flows that create and maintain those highly valued sandy strands to reefs and coralgal communities. More importantly, in order to attain sustainable use of beaches and coasts, one should ask what inputs do coralgal communities value and which abhor, which flows are wealthy and which are damaging.

While resilient to indigenous disturbances, such as hurricanes, coralgal communities can be seriously damaged by flows of terrestrial sediments and nutrients. Both flows interfere with coralgal photosynthesis—the conversion of sunlight into food and biomass. Sediment flows can mantle small and immobile corals and micro-alga. Excessive nutrients allow large leafy macro-alga to grow rapidly and shade the coralgal community from the sun.

Because Antiguan reefs are in decline, it is reasonable to search for flows that are wealthy, but are now missing, and/or for flows that are damaging and have become more present. Field work and historic environmental information indicate that tourism related "development" on Antigua's coasts has produced both, less wealth and more illth. Resort development in Antigua has followed the path of least resistance, first developing the already picture perfect pocket beaches on the remote Atlantic coast. Once the few pocket beaches on the Atlantic coast were occupied, developers began to build on the more populated Caribbean coast. Though Antigua's Caribbean coast beaches are generally long and conform well to "tropical beach" archetypes (white sand beaches fronted by warm, gentle seas and backed by swaying palms), beyond their fringing palms, they are also typically backed by basin mangroves – a landscape feature inconsistent with tourist expectations. Through sand mining, the blockage of tidal channels, and intentional filling and or dredging, these mangroves have been widely degraded if not destroyed. Maps 1 and 2 illustrate the extent of damage. As a result the flows between coralgal communities have been disrupted, altered, and/or terminated.

Previously, mangal communities mediated and transformed these reef damaging flows of sediment and nutrients into wealths, flows that reef communities find useful (Alevizon 1994). Several mangrove species have dense concentrations of aventicious (above ground) root stalks that effectively slow water flow, trapping sediment born in run-off. Salt ponds also work to sequester and transform the nutrients carried in surface run-off. Through various processes the soils are able to absorb significant amounts of nutrients such as phosphorous, nitrogen, organic carbons, and metals commonly present in sewage and waste water. Through their life activity, mangroves also sequester and transform nutrient flows into *biomass*, stems and leaves. The leaves that drop from the mangroves anchor a food chain which sustains the larval fish of numerous species. Many of these fish move to reefs as they mature. There, they graze upon macro-alga which would otherwise shade the coralgal community. Tourism related alterations along the coasts of Antigua have undermined the living communities and wealth exchanges that produced and maintained Antigua's beaches.

The primary question for those interested in truly sustainable development of tropical sun, sand, and sea tourism then becomes "how can human projects co-exist with the non-human projects whose products and by-products are also valued by humans?" At minimum, non-human communities are important from the perspective of human self-interest. A less ego or anthropocentric perspective might acknowledge that non-human beings are self-interested and value their production and lives as they work continuously and with purpose to maintain themselves and those with whom they are in mutualistic inter-relationships. Such an acknowledgement further implies that non-human beings are morally considerable, and that humans interested in "sustaining" their socio-economies might adopt the culture of co-evolution which for millennia has guided life toward long-term richness and security rather than short-term monetization and resulting impoverishment. It is vital that planners have a framework that helps them understand the inter-play of wealth and illth among all living communities involved in eco-social projects.

Despite the economic benefits of tourism, Antiguans have grown increasingly resistant to continued resort development. They understand that approximately 90 percent of all resort rooms are owned by non-Antiguans, and that profits made on the island therefore flow to distant continents as Antiguan environments are impoverished. The wealth that is produced by Antiguans and on Antigua belongs there. And many Antiguans are unwilling to submit to the exploitation implicit in the taking of the wealth that they produce—for the benefit of non-Antiguans. They understand that wealth flows produced by global tourism are transforming their land into money which then flows away, threatening Antigua's future security. The management of Antigua's coasts have become central to national politics since the late 1990s and played a part in Prime Minister Lester Bird's recent electoral defeat.

Recommendations

These understandings of the processes that effect beach production in Antigua suggest several appropriate policies and practices. I offer two groups of recommendations here. The first focuses upon the socio-ecology the Antigua's coasts and its revitalization. The second group focuses more upon the international political economy of Antigua. By addressing both sorts of concerns I address the concerns of political ecologists to successfully mediate between large scale power structures and local ecologies through the island community. I also address sustainability in a way that encompasses both local ecologies and the political economies of development in Antigua.

Integrated Local Socio-ecologies

Re-establishing the basin mangroves that work with reefs to maintain beaches is perhaps the highest priority. However, it is not clear that these former mangrove basins can recover quickly. A recent survey of wetland reclamation projects suggests highly variable results and notes that the desiccation of salt marsh soils frequently leads to significant acidification as the soils are exposed to air. This acidification may be problematic in attempts to rehabilitate coastal wetlands in Antigua and elsewhere. Given this uncertainty, a small pilot project, perhaps at Ffryes Point salt pond would be advisable.

In some cases, relatively simple and low cost measures might provide significant benefit. The topography of the two very large basin mangrove areas at The Flashes and Jolly Hill (near Five Islands Harbour and LigumVitae Bay in Map 2) has been profoundly changed through dredge and fill operations. Restoration would be expensive if not impossible. However, for many of the other basins, restoration might be relatively inexpensive. The salt ponds at Ffryes Point, Valley Church, Club Antigua, and McKinnon's suffer first and foremost from being cut off from tidal circulation. Channels could be re-established at a relatively low cost by installing effective culverts under the obstructing roadways. The large pond at Darkwood has been mined for sand and the stream channelized. Infilling the channel near its opening to the sea to enhance ponding would immediately begin to trap sediment and enable mangrove growth. Some transplantation would assist in the re-establishment of the forest. The very large pond at Deep Bay was dredged and all vegetation scraped clear in order to create a "reflecting pond". The result is an unattractive and biotically poor, but still inter-tidal pond. Because the pond is immediately adjacent to the nine story Royal Antiguan resort, it could well serve as a tourist attraction if biotic communities were re-established in a mangrove park. Raised walk ways could give guests access to a reconstructed "natural" area. Due to dredging, much of the pool is now too deep for mangroves. The pool could be made shallower with the spoil from ongoing dredge projects at Deep Bay, the cruise ship harbour at the capital city nearby. Darkwood Pond might also benefit from some infilling to replace the sand that was originally mined from the basin for beach nourishment. Depositing dredge spoil in these pond areas has the added benefit of solving the problems of spoil disposal.

Re-establishing basin mangroves would benefit nearby reefs. All reefs benefit from measures that decrease nutrient and sediment mobilization and deposition on reefs. More care in coastal construction and replanting denuded soil would benefit reefs and therefore beaches and the resorts that depend upon them. Because the nutrients in sewage are so problematic to coralgal communities, all sewage should be treated.

While some resorts have been careful to maintain treatment facilities, others have not. Uniform treatment must be enforced. If the salt ponds can be re-established, they can effectively assist in treatment. Inter-tidal salt ponds have a considerable capacity to transform problematic sewage into living biomass in the form of trees, leaf litter, and the fish that feed upon the litter and live among the roots. Through vigorous basin mangroves, if managed properly, resorts could transform their sewage into more stable beaches – saving the costs of both sewage treatment and of sand importation.

Political Economy

My second set of recommendations involves monetary wealth flows. First, it is vital that ownership of tourist capital migrate to local hands so that it can be invested locally, rather than siphoned away. Antigua, like all places, is capable of producing only so much wealth without mining its various stocks and productive capacities. If conditions of life are to remain at least at their current levels, no more wealth can be exported than can be reproduced. The geographies of those flows must become more closed, and the spatial withdrawal of local wealths minimized. Government ownership has proven problematic in Antigua, both from the standpoint of the liberalizing IMF and due to improper personal involvement in the government's finances. Local ownership remains possible through smaller scale resort developments. Smaller, locally owned resorts might prove particularly effective as Caribbean tourism evolves.

Currently, Caribbean tourism is dominated by up-market, mass tourism and large operators able to capitalize upon economies of scale. However, as Cuba becomes increasingly accessible to American mass tourist, other Caribbean islands with higher operating costs will need to re-position themselves in the market. Antigua has already begun to vigorously construct itself as a honeymoon location with its "heart of the Caribbean" campaign. People go to Antigua for a quiet time with family and loved-ones, not for night-life. Because it seems likely that large, homogenous Antiguan resorts will be least able to compete with new, cheap Cuban resorts, small, up-scale boutique resorts might be far better positioned to withstand Cuban competition. Small resorts are much more within the capabilities of local Antiguan capital – both financial and human. Smaller projects require much more modest financing, an attribute that might discourage some of the shady dealings of the past. They are also more within the capabilities of the Antiguan business class, many of whom have received training in hotel management through the sponsorship of the Curtin Bluff resort and through the Antiguan Hotel Training Centre. Though a move towards smaller resorts is counter to the Bird administrations' successful drive to gain legitimacy through job creation, there are indications that resort jobs are becoming less valuable to Antiguans.

As tourism has matured on successive islands each has become a regional destination for labour immigration. In Antigua the number of official guest workers in the tourism sector increased by 52 percent between 1993 and 1996. There are troubling indications that both registered and undocumented workers are undermining unions and the relatively high wages they have long maintained. Local labour leaders are beginning to question the wisdom of continuing job expansion if it no longer benefits Antiguans.

Finally, a shift in management practice and policy is essential. The Bird administrations, concerned with electoral politics and job creation, focused upon short-term returns at the expense of long-term coherence. Many Antiguans are well aware of this, and some have begun to challenge ongoing tourism development. In 2001, for example, a large group of Antiguans blocked three shipping container-loads of supplies outside the Carlisle Bay resort. The group was protesting the Resort's attempts to put a new road through a mangrove to by-pass Old Road, a nearby town. Antiguan police eventually responded by firing tear gas and rubber bullets at the protesters.

The conflict continued into 2002 as the initial road foundations were removed, then new footings poured. The fresh violation instigated an arson at the resort, which was in turn followed by illegal police searches of several of the protest leaders' homes (*EAG'er* 2001). The construction project was in fact in violation of regulations that protect Antigua's coasts.

Antiguan courts may still provide a mechanism for enforcement, though that process is slow. The laws to protect Antigua's coasts are on the books, the institutions for their enactment require strengthening. A revitalized Development Control Authority and an Integrated Coastal Management Plan as outlined by Bunce (1997) are two potentially productive alternatives. Finally, the weight of Lester Bird's transgressions swept him from office in 2004. It is too early to tell what if any changes Antigua's new Prime Minister Baldwin Spencer will bring to tourism development and coastal protecti0on policies.

Conclusion

Without much imagination one can understand reefs, beaches, and salt ponds as biogenically produced infrastructure (the physical forms life produces to institutionalize flows). They are analogous to human highways, power lines, and neighbourhoods. None of these landscape elements would exist without these living communities; they are physical institutions built by and for non-human communities. The flows of sand to the beach and the quiet inter-tidal environment formed by those sand flows are wealths for mangals. Mangroves stop illthy flows to reefs and transform some of those flows into living wealthy flows to reefs.

The proposition that humans are able to dominate their wider worlds over the long-term is spurious, at best. The consequences of failed attempts at dominance are nowhere more apparent than on small islands. If the project fails, there is no place else to go. The ill effects of sand mining operations on Barbuda provide a poignant example. As the largest source of sand exportation in the Caribbean, mining has destroyed the only fresh water aquifer on the island. Now Barbudans are dependant upon expensive and tenuous water imports and/or desalinization. As their water wealth was transformed into money, they have become less secure, and less coherent.

Bacon's realization that we can (and always have) put nature to work for us is powerful, but it is a half truth. Living beings and their communities do produce wealth, often in abundance. However, they can withstand only a certain level of wealth appropriation. Taking too much of those flows and productive stocks initiates a negative feedback spiral, which dampens wealth production in ecologies and tourism economies along Antigua's coasts. Antiguan history demonstrates this. Under the extremely exploitative conditions of slavery, planters took more wealth from Black bodies than they could produce. As a result life expectancy on the island never rose above 20 years. Through the power resident in collective bargaining, Antiguans successfully negotiated wages in excess of the survival levels predicted by Ricardo. They have retained a portion of the "surplus" they produced. The living communities along Antigua's coasts are little different. They also must retain both their productive stocks and a portion of their product in order to persist.

Our ability to engineer living coastal landscapes is questionable at best. Those ecologies are far more complex and interrelated than we have imagined. As Frank Elgar observed, "The ecosystem is not more complex than we think, it is more complex than we *can* think". It is clear that development related coastal alteration has installed a precarious regime based in expensive sand importation, a practice that further undermines indigenous sand production. The long-term security, stability, and coherence of Antiguans, human and otherwise, lies not in unsustainable dominance-over nature, but in *collaboration-with* coastal ecologies, as Bruno Latour suggests in his *Politics of Nature* (2004). In this sense coastal management a political project. It is about aligning differing interests into coherent, synergistic projects that benefit as wide a constituency as possible. Antiguans *can* form coalition with coastal communities and still pursue sun, sand, and sea tourism. They need only to respect the claims to the wealth produced by their non-human neighbours, just as the North Atlantic community came to recognize Black Antiguans' claims to their own labour. It is time for a new Emancipation. Antigua could lead the world.

9

Tourism Development in Indonesia

Indonesia is located on over 13,000 islands and has over 17 percent of the earth's species. Roughly and conservatively, Indonesia houses about 11 percent of flowering plant species, 12 percent of the world's mammals, 17 percent of all birds, and at least 37 percent the world's fish.Since its independence, the government of Indonesia has exploited the natural resources of country to fuel "development". Minerals and oil are heavily extracted; forest have been cleared and cut down.

The development—which emphasizes very much on economic growth—has neglected almost all aspects other than economic growth. Until the late 1980s, the focus of the development had been on import substitution, and after that on developing export oriented industries. Hence, development in Indonesia means nothing more than industrialization. Moreover, industrialization in Indonesia has been focused on manufacturing.

As stated in its long-term plan of development, Indonesia started its development by boosting the agriculture to be self-sufficient in food, and at the same time, establishing the foundations for industrialization. After completing the phase of developing its secondary (manufacturing) industry, the country moved forward to tertiary (service) industry. Relying on this concept on the early 1990s, Indonesia promoted the development of service industries. The most prominent sector in this industry is tourism.

Tourism has played an important role in some provinces in Indonesia. The province of Bali, for example, enjoyed revenues from tourism even before the Government of Indonesia gave its attention to this sector. In order to promote the tourism industry, the president established a Ministry of Tourism, Post and Telecommunication in 1988, and set a "Visit Indonesia Year 1990" program.

National Policy on Tourism

National policy on development of tourism is based on a long-term plan of development. During the last 32 years, a centralized development policy, including the tourism, was adopted. As a result, many provinces of Indonesia were not optimally and equally developed. The growth of tourism had been lower than that of neighbouring countries in ASEAN, a surprising fact when taking into account the richness of Indonesia's "tourist attractions". Recent development shows increasing efforts by the central government to work together with the local government to identify, develop and promote potential tourist destinations other than Bali. Along with the increasing awareness of nature protections, which will attract special tourists to visit Indonesia, the government has also introduced regulations on environment which are related to the sector of tourism, such as:

1. The Decree of the Minister of the Environment, No. Kep-32A/MENLH/7/1995 regarding Proper Clean River Program (Prokasih);
2. The Decree of the Minister of the Environment, No: Kep-52/MENLH/10/1995 on Standard Quality of Liquid Wastes for Hotel Operations;
3. The Decree of the Head of Environment Control Institution (BAPEDAL), No: Kep-32/BAPEDAL/05/1997 regarding Clean River Program, to require hotels to install liquid waste management unit;
4. MOU between the Ministry of the Environment and Indonesian Association of Hotels and Restaurants, No: 02/MENLH/12/1995 concerning the Training and Monitoring of Environmental-friendly Hotels and Restaurants
5. Programs on Evaluating the Achievements of Business Entities in implementation of Clean River Program.

Implementations of those regulations include the effort to apply environmentally friendly standards for the operations of hotels in Indonesia. The government has planned to include hotels in point 5 above, which include the evaluation of environmental management with the use of rating through coloured labels starting in 1998, as follows:

- Gold labels are given to hotels which have achieved the level of zero emission;

- Green labels are provided to hotels which have adopted clean technology or minimizing environmental impacts;
- Blue labels are produced for hotels which are abiding the current regulations on environmental control;
- Red label is for a hotel which has tried to adopt, but failed to meet the requirements of the regulations on environment;
- Black labels are for hotels that do not try to abide the regulations on environment, and even damaging the environment.

One effort of the government to prevent pollution is by providing incentives through the Program of Soft Loan for Environment from Overseas Economic Corporation Funds on Pollution Abatement Equipment. This program is designed to encourage the installation of pollution management units in some businesses of which the operations are potentially damaging the environment. The soft loan with a period of 3 to 20 years is expected to answer the problems of high cost of investments in waste processing units faced by domestic investors.

More on Tourism Policies and Their Benefits to the Indonesian Economy

After several years, private tourism sectors as well as the government, realized that the development of tourism in this country is not only beneficial but has also its negative impact, such as: environmental degradation, economic gap between those related to the tourism business and those who are not, cultural degradation, etc. Massive development of high rise hotels, roads and infrastructures, along with changing use of the land, etc. for the purpose of tourism, have resulted the serious degradation of the environment. Some of these impacts will be described in the case studies. As tourism developed, profit-seeking investors have come. Their fresh capital enabled them to own most of the resources, and eventually expel the local community from their own land. This left them with choices of either stay as farmers in less-fertile and smaller size of lands, or taking other jobs such as small merchants, providing services to the tourism activities, etc

As will be described in the case of Bali, the pressures of capital have affected not only Bali's economy, but also its culture. Under the pressure of Indonesian NGOs, informal leaders, religious leaders and other concerned people, the government of Indonesia has started to change its policies on tourism. The government has put its best efforts in promoting people-centered tourism and ecologically friendly tourism.

Unlike the previous ones, the new policies provide more opportunities for the local people to participate in the tourism development. Under the "tourism build prosperity and peace" theme, the Government of Indonesia empowers small and medium scale entrepreneurs and cooperatives in tourism sector, encourages private—especially the small and medium ones, deregulates licensing process for eliminating high-cost economy, and implements community based tourism.

Environmentally friendly tourism, or eco-tourism, has been adopted in the last five years. It, as a mater of fact, has not been a mainstream in the tourism development. Only some areas—consist of national parks, rivers, and forests—are designated to be used for eco-tourism. In developing eco-tourism. It is understood that eco-tourism should make requirements of nature and environmental protection the basis for touristic activities. Thus, it ensures its ecological sustainability.

Tourism in Bali Island

Compared to the total area of Indonesia, Bali represents only 0.29%. Based on 1997's data, the total population of Bali is about 3.3 million, with a population density of almost 585 person/sq.km. However, Bali ranks as the first in terms of popularity among tourist-destination areas in Indonesia. Tourism in Bali had started since 1926 with the exploitation of the unique Balinese cultural and natural beauty by the Dutch colonial government. The government of Indonesia started in 1960 with the building of the Bali Beach Hotel in Sanur and the Ngurah Rai international airport.

Bali is internationally known for its dances, temples, and beaches, which have long been recognized as main tourist attractions. In 1996 Bali attracted a total number of around 3 million tourists, or about 30% of the total number of foreign tourists coming to Indonesia. The trend shows an escalating number over several years. The increase is supported by the infrastructures and facilities.: more than 25,000 hotel rooms of various qualities, international airport which can accommodate large airplanes, ports and more than about 500 thousands Balinese involved in tourism activities.

Despite the deterioration of Indonesian politics and economy, Bali is still perceived as a very safe and nice place to visit. Bali enjoys the ever increasing number of visitors whom each stays the average of 9 days, with an average spending of about USD 80 per day. Bali is indeed the only tourist destination in Indonesia that is still recommended by the government of Japan, USA, Australia and other European countries. Other areas in Indonesia still suffer significant drop due to the recession and partly to travel bans set by foreign countries. On the contrary, Balinese merchants, brokers, etc. have gained profit from the condition. Tourism industry in Bali still enables Balinese to sustain their consumptive lifestyle.The development of tourism industry has played an important role in Bali's economy due to its limited natural resources. An important indicator of the growth in revenue is the income per capita which has been increasing since 1994 of Rp. 2,22 million, Rp. 2,56 million (1995), and Rp. 2,95 million (1996), with several tourist destination areas as the highest per capita income.

An indirect impact from the growth is the relatively high population growth rate in these areas compared to other areas. The urbanization as well as migrant workers from other provinces have caused high growth rate of population which affect natural environment, social, economic and cultural life of the Balinese.

The tourism development plan of Bali is based on two regulations i.e. (1) The Decree of the Governor of Bali No. 528/1993 regarding Tourism Area; (2) The Decree of the Local Government No. 4/1996 regarding Spatial Planning for the Province of Bali.

The objectives of the above regulations are: (1) To provide guidance for the optimum use of space at tourist destination areas, especially in less developed areas; (2) To reduce the negative impacts of tourism activities on the sustainability of the environment. The strategies on the above are based on the Balinese philosophy of Tri Hita Karana that includes:

- Strategy of managing sanctuaries;
- Development of agricultural areas and regional infrastructures;
- Development of urban and other priority areas.

Social and Cultural

Aside from its benefits, the growth of tourism in Bali has some negative impacts, particularly in the social and the cultural dimensions. The Balinese culture has changed due to commercial influences, people alienation from their own land, market orientation of artworks. Among them are:

Tourism has created income opportunities. Unfortunately,-young generations have failed to exercise religious and/or ethical values to generate income; Cases of young people involved in various types of prostitution are common in several popular tourist destination areas. There are street souvenir vendors who sell their merchandise in such ways that annoy the customers, while some others put very high price on the low quality merchandise. These will create the negative image of Bali as a safe and enjoyable tourist destination.

Expecting more money, some local people who do not have-necessary skills take shortcuts to wealth which, in most cases, are not morally acceptable.

There are also cases where the local community has been-alienated from their own village. The flow of investments on hotels along the beach has driven local community out of their lands and even beaches. Beaches are essential to the Balinese, for their religious believe to the Sang Hyang Widi Wasa. Land, sea, and mountain are perceived as one unity. As some beaches are converted into private areas, Balinese are alienated from their own values and can no longer perform their rituals.

Other main tourist attractions are dances, paintings and-sculptures. These art forms have generated a lot of income from the rise of tourist visit to Bali. However, the products of these art forms have been adjusted according to the taste of the market. This resulted in popular market products rather than high quality of art itself. Sculptures, dances, and other art products are originally—for Balinese—for ritual and religious purposes. However, thanks to the market pressure, they are turned into commercial commodities.

Economic Perspective

The Tourism industry — including transportation, hotel, hospitality, and travelling services — is the biggest industry in Bali that provides quality employment opportunities for the Balinese, and is still one of the fastest growing sectors in the Island. Employment opportunities have been provided by small businesses especially in the home industry, supporting the tourism activities. Many of them are located in the urban areas. Considering the economic crises suffered by the country, it is projected that the growth of the industry in Bali will not exceed that of 1997/98.

Tourism industry is expected to contribute a major portion of GDP in foreign exchange, which is very much needed at this moment, and to provide 2.6 million, 2.8 million, and 3.4 million employment opportunities in 1996, 1997, and 1998 respectively. The figures above have shown the important role of tourism in Bali's economy. Most of Balinese are economically depend on the tourism directly or indirectly.

During the political riots in several major cities of Indonesia, considered as the safest place to stay, hotels in Bali were fully booked. The government of Bali also benefited from this situation, specifically from income tax and local retributions.

Tourism industry has played an important factor to boost exports. Foreign tourists spend their foreign exchange directly by buying products of the visited country. About 14% of the total value of Indonesian export are generated from tourism. The transactions are directly between tourists and merchants.

Another important impact of the tourism in Bali is that it generates a multiplying effect. The growth of tourism will enable other sectors such as construction and manufacturing to grow as well. In 1997, there were 61 new investments in tourist destination developments in Bali alone.

Environment Perspective

The increasing activities in tourism have resulted in some negative impacts on the environment, e.g.:

- Ground water: The significant increase of water consumption for daily activities as well as for recreational purposes, such as swimming pools. Many hotels in Bali are forced to provide their own sources of clean water because the limited access to the local water companies (30% of the current needs). These hotels have turned into ground water extraction, amounting to about 46% of their needs, to supply their needs for clean water. The extensive use of ground water may decrease the ground water reserve in the long run, and induce the absorption of seawater (intrusion) even further.
- Liquid wastes: Based on review done by the government on some hotels in Bali, about 63 % have installed a liquid waste management unit, while the rest still use the absorption methods. A conventional system on liquid waste management (absorption) has grown businesses for providing the service of hauling human wastes. Their service seems to solve the problem of liquid waste of the hotels. However, the lack of regulation on waste management, has excused the private haulers to pour liquid wastes directly into the sea and rivers. Thus creating a

higher potential damage to the environment. The regulations also failed to set parameters on some factors, such as content of oil/fat, NO3-N, Phosphors, Faecal Colii, etc. in the ambient water.

- Solid wastes: Most hotel operators in Bali are using private hauler in maintaining their solid wastes. These private haulers are responsible to collect, transport and dispose the wastes. Wastes from the hotel kitchen are often used to create compost and feed for pigs. Some hotels have also worked together with private sectors to recycle some wastes like papers, glass bottles, etc. There are also cases, however, of some irresponsible private haulers disposing the solid wastes in places other than the designed area, as seen in some parts of the coastal areas.
- Noise and fuel emission: As there is a sharp increase of tourists coming to Bali, direct impacts including noise resulted from airplanes to and out of the province. Inland transportation within the province has resulted in pollution. There are also cases where some dwellings around hotel areas are affected by fuel gas emission that comes from incinerators and electric generators.
- Eradication of Landscape and ecosystem: Lands conversion for tourism are common in Bali. A rocky hill which is rich of natural flora and fauna was "developed" into golf field; some others are cut to build boulevards and bungalows. This conversion leads to the extinction of Bali's natural flora and fauna, such as the famous indigenous bird called Jalak Bali.

For the last six years the production of wastes and garbage, as well as depletion of environment and its flora and fauna, from tourism related activities tend to increase up to 25% per annum. These, if not properly maintained, may pollute the environment especially in popular tourist areas and its surroundings. To handle such potential problems, Bali needs to improve its policies and control system regarding the environment management.

Tourism Development in Lombok Island

Existing Conditions of Tourism Sector

The Island of Lombok is located next to Bali. Lombok is currently considered as a very potential tourist destination area after Bali. It is part of the province of West Nusa Tenggara Barat. With a total population of 2.6 millions for the whole province, of which about 6 % is employed in tourism sectors, tourism activities has contributed an amount about US$ 106 millions, or about 25% of the local GDP. In 1997 a total number of about 200 thousands tourists originating from America, Europe, Asean, and Asia Pacific visited Lombok.

As also in Bali, tourism activities in Lombok Island have created opportunities to generate income. Aside from hotels and restaurants, there are several art or souvenir shops introducing specific art products from West Nusa Tenggara which is quite different from that of the Balinese: hand-woven Ikat, clay works, pandan weavings, primitive wood sculptures, etc. With its unspoiled land and diversity of religious and cultural values, West Nusa Tenggara offers a unique natural as well as cultural attraction.

Policy and Strategy of Local Government

As a tourism destination next to Bali, the local government has encouraged the involvement of private sector, community, and cooperative in developing tourism. This effort included the development of infrastructures to support the tourism, and, especially, the improvement of the quality and capability of the local work force.

With properly planned actions, the government of NTB expected the growth of tourism to increase 15% per annum. This means about 500,000 employment, and about USD 115 millions generated annually at the end of 1998, from about 309,000 tourist. In an effort to develop tourism, the government of West Nusa Tenggara has established a joint venture company with the private sector called the Lombok Tourism Development Corporation (LTDC). The plan of this cooperation is to develop tourism facilities in a total area of 1,250 ha which consists of hotels, golf course, business centre, and other tourism facilities.

However, learning from tourism in Bali, the government will prevent negative impact from tourism activities. They have anticipated that problems like wastes, over investment, land acquisition, illegal buildings, environmental degradation, privatization of beaches which created less access for fishermen and public, as well as social and cultural impacts that may appear as the tourism developed.

Social Perspective

Lombok has natural beauty that can be developed as tourism resort. As the island located near Bali-a major tourist destination, Lombok has the advantage to be the second tourist destination to catch the overflow of tourists from Bali. The provincial government of NTB understand very well the strategic position of Lombok and it includes tourism as a leading sector in the provincial development. Tourism in Lombok has provided 6.09% of total employment opportunity in that area. However, the number is much lower than the available graduates of tourism schools, as well as the expectations of the government to provide employment for local community around tourist destination areas. The development of tourism has also shifted employment opportunities from agricultural to tourism related activities.

Efforts, which have been done by the government, include facilitating training to improve the quality of local handicrafts in order to enable them to compete and to reach a much larger market share. The consideration of empowering the surrounding community is particularly important, because of the current gap between quality of local human resources compared to those from other parts of Indonesia. If left unanswered, this will lead to economic, and thus, social gap between the local community and migrants. However, negative impact of the development of tourism is not hard to see. More and more people have moved, either voluntarily or not, for the reason of developing tourist resorts such as the case of Ms.Inaq Ameneh of Gili Trawangan.

Economic Perspective

The natural resources of Lombok island has attracted a lot of investors—domestic as well as foreign ones—in establishing tourism related industries: hotels, resorts, travel agents, restaurants, etc. Based on data collected, there are domestic investments amounting to Rp. 362 billion and foreign investments amounting to USD 2.57 million in hotels, restaurants, etc. It is also expected that these investments could lead to other activities beneficial to the local community surrounding them. The multiplying effect of the growing tourism sector has been expected to happen in Lombok.

Environment Perspective

The local government of West Nusa Tenggara has taken some preventive measures based on the negative experience of Bali, such as the degradation of quality and quantity of natural resources, as well as the impacts on the local community. However, with a current economic condition of the area (i.e. population of almost 4 million, income per capita of Rp. 1.8 million—less than 55% of its neighbouring Bali—and limited amount of local revenue of the government), it seems that the government of West Nusa Tenggara is facing a difficult choice between maintaining the quality of the land and a fast way to increase economic conditions of the region. Stringent regulations on investments will create the impression of West Nusa Tenggara as an unattractive investment area, especially in a worsening condition of Indonesia in foreign investor's view. One example is the opening of a gold mine in Sumbawa. A foreign joint venture called Newmont has recently established its open mining area there. With an increase of expatriates in the project, it is expected to boost local economic activities (including tourism) as well as employment opportunities for the local community. The available jobs for local community is mostly for the unskilled ones, although in quite a big number. The open mining system, however, is considered as degrading the quality of land.

Proposed Solutions for Sustainable Tourism

In Indonesia, ecotourism has not been a mainstream. Although, some efforts in promoting it are flourishing. The efforts, considering the current Indonesian situation is harder now. The country suffers bad publication due to the prevalences of riots, loots and ethnic conflicts. According to Hermawan Kertajaya, the President of Asia Pacific Marketing Federation, Cohort 1-Indonesia: as a product in tourism business, Indonesia needs repositioning to promote its positive brand equity and good image. The positioning of Indonesia has to be directed to the objectives to achieve 'New Era' of Indonesia which is the process of transformation from corruption, collusion, and nepotism to the era of clean, transparent, and professionalism. This issue should be born in tourism actor's mind and activities. This is a priority beside the needs to develop of many tourism facilities and infrastructures. In parallel with the effort to reposition Indonesia's image, it also needs to pay more attention to all potential risks which may arise, and will cause negative impacts on the important elements such as social, economy, and environment. The development of tourism should also be directed to achieve sustainable tourism.

In social perspectives, the need is to minimize the negative influences of tourism activities in social life of local people who live near or at the tourism area in order to preserve culture and tradition for the future. In economy, more attention should be paid to the need, ability, skills and characters of local people, so that they can be actively involved and can get the benefit from the tourism. The development should increase their quality of life, and not otherwise. Tourism in Indonesia is the activity of selling the beauty of nature and the unique culture of

Indonesia. To achieve the sustainable tourism, Indonesia needs to protect the environment from tourism activities. This must be in our behaviour – both of Indonesians and tourists.

As Indonesia currently faces an urgent need of foreign exchange, while local products have not reached competitive advantage, tourism is playing an important role. Tourism is very much depend on infrastructures as well as safety of the destination. Unstable economic and political condition that Indonesia is experiencing is not a favourable condition for Indonesia to compete over tourists visiting the region. Unless a lot of money are allocated to promote Indonesia, it is very difficult for Indonesia to regain its popularity. Ambitious plans and projections would be very unrealistic with a very limited amount of funds available. At time of very low foreign tourists such as this, it is important for Indonesia – the government and private sectors in tourism – to evaluate all negative damages of tourism in the past and develop measures and activities to increase the quality of all aspects of things to offer to support tourism. These include the services as well as the products to be sold of which natural beauty plays a very important role.

Tourism Development: A Geographical Perspective

Tourism is the world's largest industry. As a sector of the economy, tourism is used by many countries to advocate economic development. It is used as a development strategy due to its economic effects such as generating foreign exchange, creating employment and stimulating local economies. It is suggested here that tourism has evolved, and has continuously progressed along the trajectory path of development theory. On the other hand, the processes that produce these forms of development are susceptible to features generated by the surrounding environment. This includes prominent economic, cultural and political aspects.

Definitions of Tourism

Tourism has pluralistic meanings. Mieczkowski (1981) and Hall and Page (1999) contend that scholars are troubled by the multitude meanings and concepts of tourism. Thus, there is no standard meaning of tourism whereby researchers can have a point of reference. Consequently researchers are spending more time debating typologies and classification rather than exploring the actual content of tourism, leisure or recreation. For example, Pigram (1985) argues that tourism is a component of recreation, while Murphy (1985) counter-argues that. Nonetheless Dan and Cohen (1991) note that there are also scholars who adapt a more ecclectic stance, instead of being tied down by a specific theoretical approach.

In this manner researchers adapt their choice of concepts and meanings according to the demands of their work. Smith (1988) argues that researchers, international and national tourism associations, business entities and government agencies give different definitions based on their own perception and interest. Policy-led and industry sponsored research work, for example, may ensure an inclination towards industry priorities, while scholars will define tourism from within their own intellectual domain. Jafari defines tourism based on an anthropological point of view. "Tourism is the study of man away from his usual habitat, of the industry, which responds to his needs, and of the impacts that both he and the industry have on the host's socio-cultural, economic, and physical environments". On the other hand Murphy (1985, cited by Smith, 1988) defines tourism as "the sum of … the travel of non-residents (tourists, including excursionists) to destination areas, as long as their sojourn does not become a permanent residence.

It is a combination of recreation and business". Nonetheless, Shaw and Williams (1994) argue that the World Tourism Organisation's (WTO) definition of tourism or tourist is the most commonly used by literature on tourism. "Any person residing within a country, irrespective of nationality, travelling to a place within this country other than his usual place of residence for a period of not less than 24 hours or one night for a purpose other than the exercise of a remunerated activity in the place visited. The motives for such travel may be (1) leisure (recreation, holidays, health, studies, religion, sports); (2) business, family, mission, meeting" (WTO, 1981). Smith (1988, 1995) contends that the WTO's definition gives guidelines on statistical data collection and thus it gives the most agreed point of reference. These guidelines give scholars, governments and institutions a means to not only measure the growth of tourism within their own constructed borders but also a means to compare them on a global level.

Tourism and Development

Smith (1988) and Britton (1991) argue that much tourism work lacks a theoretical framework, due to the fact that many of the contributors are trained in peripheral fields, and thus are not exposed to the dynamic complex of social and cultural processes, which inundate tourism phenomena. Previous tourism related studies in the literature, which has a significant amount of work revolving around the impacts of tourism, witnessed concepts and theories that were borrowed or adopted mainly from other branches of social sciences, including geography, though, many researchers failed to recognise their origin. For example, concepts and framework from Geography often serve as foundations for the study of tourism, where the dynamic process that underlie a tourism destination could be understood using approaches such as spatial analysis. On the other hand, Pearce (1979) identifies six major areas of specialisation from the perspective of geographical interest in the study of tourism: the spatial aspects of supply, the spatial aspects of demand, patterns of movement and flows, the impact of tourism, the geography of resorts, and models of tourist space. Erstwhile, Oppermann (1993) and Pearce (1995) suggest that existing geographically-related theories in tourism have grown along two main paradigms: the diffusionist model and the dependency model. Both contain the construction of places and spaces at their heart. However, the former addresses tourism as a regional agent of development, and as such, tourism development is diffused from core to peripheral areas. The latter on the other hand, carries the notion of a subjugated peripheral area by its core counterpart. In the context of countries deemed peripheral, such as the world's less developed countries, there is little detailed research undertaken on tourism.

Modernisation Theory

In the context of modernisation theory, tourism has been advocated as a development strategy to generate foreign exchange, to increase the balance of payment, increase GDP, attract development capital, increase the transfer of technology, increase employment and promote modern western values of life. Van Doorn contends that the processes of tourism development could only be elucidated within the context of the development stage of a country. In this sense, Rostow's (1967) argument that there are five stages of economic development was imperative when tourism development was discussed. Elsewhere, Thurot (1973) has suggested that there are three stages of development in relation to the evolution of the airlines routes. However, Miossec (1976) proposes five stages of development, from the original pioneer resort to a fully developed hierarchy and specialised saturation stage when conceptualising tourist space dynamics. Modernisation in tourism development also stipulates for the consumption of 'experience' as an end product. Tourists improved their social structural status when they manage to travel and consume these experiences and hence fulfil their ego needs Butler (1980) further improvised the evolution of tourism development through his product cycle-based evolution of tourist destination. Butler proposes six stages of development: involvement, exploration, development, consolidation, stagnation and decline or rejuvenation. More recently, Agarwal (2002) has used Butler's work as a template when she contends that many British seaside resorts, which were in the stagnating or declining stage, have rejuvenated when for example theme parks were introduced at these resorts. Agarwal argues that endogenous or exogenous forces also play a significant role in a process of destination development. In the context of number of stages involved in tourism development study of destination, Oppermann and Chon (1997) argue that there is no unanimous number.

Meanwhile, Myrdal (1957) uses regional economic development theory in tourism studies, to look at the filtering of economic benefits through regional, national and local economies. In parallel, Pearce (1989) argues that tourism has been used as a tool of distributive justice. Similarly, the establishment of the tourist boards for England, Wales, Scotland and Northern Ireland during the late 1960s, which was initially linked to regional economic policy, underpinned the Labour government's orientation towards welfare, which has resulted in a much stronger public intervention. Significant powers of strategic planning were also bestowed on local government at county level in England and Wales, and at regional level in Scotland.

Apart from influencing local authorities, whose new powers in strategic planning were recognised as an important tool in the managing of tourism, the English Tourist Board (ETB) also adopts the thesis of "growth poles to tourism growth points". For example, a grant under Section 4 of the Tourism Act stipulate that the ETB could adapt a confinement of eligible projects to areas within England that were formally designated as development areas. Similarly, Baidal (2003) explores the decentralisation of the state's power in Spain during the late 1970s (post-Franco's authoritarian administration) that paved the way towards regional development policies on tourism. Under the Franco's regime, the foundations for tourism development revolved around macroeconomic objectives that treated tourism as a generator of foreign exchange to rehabilitate the balance of payments, which had been in deficit. But by the 1990s policies on tourism were based on the configuration of a framework of collaboration between regional and local authorities and the central administration (Ibid). Baidal contends that the adoption of the EEC's structural policy principles, and becoming the net recipient of financial resources from the European Union's budget, provided the impetus for the creation of new tourism products that entailed the organisation of new emerging spaces. Consequently, the manifestation of microeconomic objectives in favour of past macroeconomic objectives resulted in qualitative changes and expansive tendency in tourism demand that gave rise to a new model of tourism in Spain. From a different perspective, Oppermann (1992), through the use of international forms of tourism, explores the use of tourism as a tool for regional development in Malaysia. He found that 'active' travellers who travelled and stayed in many destinations contributed more to regional development while 'passive' travellers tended to reinforce existing spatial disparities. His research also dwells on the issues of dualism in developing countries, where he argues that tourism is least important in Malaysia's peripheral regions while at the same time its political and economical centres have more than the average share in tourism industry.

However, writers such as de Kadt (1979) and Komilis (1994) began to question the use of tourism as a development tool. De Kadt, for example, questions the benefits posed by tourism where the multiplier effects are lower and leakages are higher than had been previously presumed. On the other hand, Komilis specifically argues about the effectiveness of using tourism in regional economic development in peripheral areas. Such issues are underpinned by the relationship between central and peripheral countries.

Dependency Theory

Tourism development in peripheral countries is strongly influenced by events in the core countries. The flow of mass tourists from central to peripheral countries, and the running of hotels and resorts, are subject to various control mechanisms found in the former. The roles of tour operators in core countries, one of the most influential tourism suppliers due to their huge financial resources and industrial leverage, for instance, can exert a strong impact on the occupancy rate of hotels and spatial distribution of tourist flow in receiving countries, many of which resemble peripheral areas. Furthermore, many of the hotels, particularly those of an international class, are owned or managed by Transnational Corporations. However, Din (1990) contends that not all international standard accommodation chains in developing countries belong to developed countries and hence are not controlled by external force. He exemplifies this notion by noting that locals own several of the luxury hotels in Penang, a tourist destination area in Malaysia. At a different level, these relationships posit the notion of underdevelopment of developing countries because of the exploitation by developed countries. "Thus, according to dependency theory, tourism is an industry like any other, which is used by the developed countries to perpetuate the dependency of the developing countries. Instead of reducing the existing socio-economic regional disparities within the developing countries, tourism reinforces them through its enclavic structure and its orientation along traditional structures".

In parallel, Walpole and Goodwin (2000) contend that this peripheral relationship also exists in a local context. Their study of ecotourism in the protected Komodo National Park in Indonesia, illustrates that economic distributional inequalities favoured external operators and urban residents rather than the villagers. Outsiders control most of the accommodation and boating facilities.

Neo-liberalism

Meanwhile, a chain of global events, including the oil crisis and economic depression that occurred from the mid 1970s to the mid 1980s, has led to an increase in neo-liberalism in tourism development in many developing countries. Desforges (2000) contends that the national government in Peru 'rolled back' its active role when President Alberto Fujimori imposed a drastic cut in state spending on the tourism industry. The state tourist board's budget went down to zero until it could clearly define and justify its role, and the Ministry of Industry, Tourism and Integration and Commerce's number of employees reduced from 2700 to 300, while state owned hotels were privatised and fees were imposed at the state's tourism school.

Such deregulation, privatisation and liberalisation acts, which were partly inspired by the World Bank and IMF through SALPs, have reduced state influence and at the same time the acts permitted the increased role and importance of the private sector in the tourism industry. Brenner and Theodore (2002) contend that neo-liberalisation has entailed a reorganisation of institutional, political and geographical settings. Nonetheless the decline of the political-economic power of a nation-state in the advent of a crisis of profit in global economy foretells post-*Fordism.* Fordism is characterised by economies of scale, mass replication, small number of dominant producers, product standardisation, inflexibility and mass marketing to an undifferentiated clientele while its post period is underpinned by more specialised and small scale production.

Alternative Development

The last remaining form of tourism development is alternative tourism. The concept started to surface in the literature some two decades ago. Mowforth and Munt (2003) argue that there is no standard uniform agreed meaning among scholars pertaining to this form of tourism. Butler (1990) suggest that alternative tourism has been associated already with wide ranges of different notions and concepts, and therefore it is impossible to define it explicitly. Nonetheless, the approach has remained focused on the concept of sustainability (ibid), a concept that can be traced back to the conservation movement in the west during the late 19th century. However, in the context of tourism specifics, concepts of alternative tourism encompass a range of tourism strategies that include 'soft', 'responsible', 'green', 'appropriate', 'controlled', 'people friendly', small scale' and 'cottage' characteristics. The 'green movement', which is associated with the wider concept of the 'green consumer', for example, puts forth the promotion of environmental issues in tourism. Krippendorf (1986), furthermore, argues for the notion of 'a soft and human tourism', which discourages intolerable social and ecological damage. Environmentally conscious tourists, many of whom are part of the 'inner-directed' lifestyle group whose leisure pursuits are motivated by new experiences, creativity, human relations and personal growth, lead to the demand for environmentally sound holiday. Gordon adds that it is the tourists' influence that forces politicians and tourism businesses alike to consider the environment a genuine concern. Such conditions culminated in ecotourism, a new form of tourism development:

"Travelling to relatively undisturbed or uncontaminated natural areas with the specific objective of studying, admiring, and enjoying the scenery and its wild plants and animals, as well as any existing cultural manifestations (both past and present) found in these areas...". While Shaw and Williams (1994) noted a new trend in which tourism businesses such as tour companies have started to reassess their image by offering 'ecological holidays' to potential clients, Mowforth and Munt suggest that "...the term 'sustainability' can be and has been hijacked by many to give moral rectitude and 'green' credentials to tourist activities". Similarly, Ioannides (2001) treat the phenomenon cautiously. Ioannides argues that British-based International Federation of Tour Operators (IFTO) embrace of sustainable tourism is more to do with profit, particularly in an era where tourists are becoming discerning and sophisticated. However, Shaw and Williams argue that "while many tourists will only pay lip-service to 'green holidays', as equally will sections of the tourism systems; but this may not ultimately detract from the importance of green tourism". To this Poon (1994) surmises that in the era of 'new tourism', package tours are fast becoming a thing of the past and tourism has become segmentalised. In the same vein, Ateljevic and Doorne (2000) argue that small-scale tourism businesses are becoming more important due to the demand of a new hybrid of tourists. The advent of this lifestyle entrepreneur has been a positive stimulus in the growth of small tourism related businesses or tourism entrepreneurship. Ateljevic and Doorne argue that unlike the conventional entrepreneurship of production and consumption, the lifestyle entrepreneur has an underpinning factor in that "business represents an opportunity to indulge in in-depth place experience, which integrates both lifestyle and identity". In this sense, lifestyle, rather than economic gain is the main motive behind business operations such as the Black Water Rafting, an enterprise that deals with river 'sledging' activity in New Zealand. Hence 'lifestyle' is one of the diverse reasons on why people indulge in tourism related businesses other then financial rewards. Ateljevic and Doorne go further by denoting that these entrepreneurs had social and cultural obligations, which more than often delimit the growth of their businesses. They are content with their ways of life.

However, Shaw and Williams (2004) offer caution against such a notion. According to the authors, how these businesses are run varies according to the place and type of touristic activities. Based on a study of the surf tourism industry in Cornwall, they argue that although surf entrepreneurs are influenced by desires for freedom and being their own boss, and have interest in the environment, there is clear evidence that they, nonetheless also, have plans for business development and expansion, and are therefore profit oriented. Meanwhile, sustainable tourism has taken the phrase alternative tourism, a generic term, to distinguish it from the conventional mass tourism. Weaver's notion of alternative forms of tourism, which among others have criteria that denote small-scale accommodation development, lower market volume and low import sector. Using Dominica as a case study, Weaver (1991) argues that tourism which started as a 'circumstantial' alternative tourism destination, conform to characteristics such as low visitation and impacts levels. Such a situation mirrors Butler's (1980) early stage of exploration and involvement. Dominica adopts a philosophical approach towards alternative tourism, using the Kastarlak Report (a United Nations' sponsored report on Dominica) as a blueprint to move forwards. This suggests among other things, specialised markets, such as environmentalists, as suitable for the country's tourism industry.

Alternative tourism as represented by many small companies emerges in the era of post-modernism to take advantage of the changing consumer trend, which demands more on special interest tours. From a wider perspective, there is a shift from Fordism, to a more flexible and small but specialised scale of modes of production and consumption. However, scholars like Lickorish challenge this notion. Ritzer contends that even in specialised niche market like *Starbucks*, there tends to be a replication of mass production and consumption. Replication of a chain of Starbucks in other towns and countries mirrors the mass production of this branded product. While many researchers have favoured alternative tourism development in place of mass form of tourism, work written by scholars on alternative development has wide range of issues.

Some researchers like, Long and Wall (1995), Din (1997) and Dahles (2001) have explored the tourism entrepreneurship of indigenous population. Din (1997), for example, further argues that the lack of empowerment that has caused locals to be marginalized in Langkawi, Malaysia. Conversely the better equipped locals and outsiders are in the better position to reap the benefit. This gives rise to a question of empowerment in alternative tourism development. In term of empowerment and the participation of the local community in sustainable tourism planning, there is some literature produced by researchers such as Murphy (1985), Gunn (1994) and Slinger (2000). Slinger, for example, shows that the indigenous Caribs have managed to revive their traditional crafts and culture which, earlier on, been subjected to a process of cultural erosion, encouraged by the government to participate in ecotourism activities. Furthermore, the Caribs have recognised the necessity of protecting the environment is important, particularly when they need raw materials from the forest to produce their handicrafts.

By using the empowerment issue in tourism development researchers such as Kinnaird and Hall (1994) and Apostolopoulos *et al*, (2001) have also further diverged into the new field of gender and tourism. Hitherto the history of tourism, which can be attributed by its birth from industrialisation and its transformation by post-industrialisation, has been mostly described from a 'masculine perspective'. Kothari (2002) contends that this view has been at the expense of other dimensions such as feminism. This is imperative given that tourism also takes into account the changing role of gender, such as the 'softening' of tourism attractions, activities, experiences and tastes. The stereotyping of this sexual imagery is further being enhanced by marketing brochures selling tourist destinations and products that use women as the pulling factor. While the male is associated with power and ownership the women are portrayed as passive and being owned. At the same time, this has produced a notion that tourism leads to prostitution. A by-product of mass tourism, this particular form of activities is associated with male tourists who aim to travel to exotic places to indulge in sexual encounters with prostitutes either as a primary or a secondary agenda. Many scholars relate this phenomenon to developing countries. Hall (1994) on the other hand, argues that these activities also persist in developed countries even though it is more exploitative in the former. Conversely, sex-tourism has also evolved into the exploitation of male hosts by female tourists and also the emergence of the so-called gay tourist circuit. Gender relations in the tourism industry also transgress into the labour field. Bagguley (1990), for example, explores the relation of gender in tourism employment where a majority of part-time workers in the hotel industry are women. Nonetheless, Mowforth and Munt (2003) argue that although this new form of tourism has extensively influenced tourism activities in both developed and developing countries, it is arguably a western phenomenon. These authors argue that poor developing countries are still experiencing the effect of conventional mass tourists due to a major increase of such tourist groups from increasingly affluent middle class societies such as in Southeast Asia. However this trend is part of the evolutionary process that is happening in the region.

Having said that, alternative tourism development unlike its predecessors provides not only a novel feature through its bottom-up process of advocating development but also incorporates a holistic notion of development process through its inclusion of indigenous or local participation in its framework.

Conclusion

This paper documented factors that underpinned tourism development theory, which are derived from the dominant theories of development; Modernisation, Dependency, Neo-liberalism and Alternative development. It also showed that development was progressive, as experienced in many countries. Development theory provides the suitable conceptual framework and platform to elucidate the processes in tourism development. It shows these processes are not solely the result of unilateral actions. Instead, the nature of tourism development is a highly contested one, which among others, is susceptible to influence from the surrounding milieu, invoked by factors such as politics, economics, culture and the environment. Such processes are made more complex by the fact that the tourism industry is composed of diverse inter-related fields, and as such are broad in scope and depth. In sum, this paper provides the analytical framework whence strands in tourism development can be explored. It documents the links between development theory and the processes of tourism development, which are characterised by a complex nature of relationships between the four dominant paradigms of development theory and the nature of tourism development. This poses the question of the role of tourism in fulfilling the objectives of economic development.

Bali Tourism in the 21st Century

Mobilizing the Potential and Avoiding the Pitfalls

Almost a year ago the Bali Tourism Board and the World Tourism Organization held an international seminar on Recovery and Repositioning of Bali Tourism. The meeting highlighted the urgency for action. Thus far progress has been little and slow. We at L'Ultimo Paradiso feel that this a priority challenge in Bali and wide spread consultation and debates needs to take place towards mobilizing actions for recovery and repositioning. L Ultimo Paradiso asked Dr. Mahendra Shah, President of Holistic Wellness Zen Resort Bali to share his vision of Bali tourism in the 21st century.

World Tourism and Globalization

One a half million years ago, Homo Erectus started to walk upright and thus began the first of human journeys to all corners of the world. These foot journeys, then taking many years to travel less then a thousand kilometres, were driven by the need to find food and more congenial living environments as well as the human curiosity to discover and experience the unknown.

The transport and electronic revolution of the last one hundred years has made the world one in that it is today possible to traverse a thousand kilometres in under an hour and more then that to be in contact with anyone and anywhere at the touch of a button in a second.

These communications developments have a substantive potential to contribute to worldwide sustainable development in the 21st century era of globalization. Here the challenge is to ensure that globalization in an increasingly interdependent world contributes to worldwide social responsibility, environmental sustainability and economic efficiency. While globalization thus far has been driven by economics, primarily international trade, it is essential that the human dimensions and environmental issues be fully integrated since without this the very foundation of the Earth's life supporting capacity and a peaceful, sustaining and progressive world will be put at risk. International travel and tourism is an important sector in the above context. It can contribute to reducing poverty and disparities, overcoming social prejudices, understanding conflicts and supporting resolution, enhancing actions for environmental protection not only at the local level but also in the context of global environmental change such as climate change which is a result of polluting "modern" lifestyles, often in distant places.

The promotion and development of sustainable tourism deserves the highest national and international political commitment and practical actions as it has a substantive potential to contribute to the peace aspirations and development goals of the United Nations Millennium Declaration for the 21st Century. The international tourism market is increasingly focusing not only on beautiful and serene locations with a wide variety of recreational and sports activities but also on places for relaxation and rejuvenation during a short holiday break especially as potential tourists often have stressful lives with long hours and intensive work schedules often resulting ill health.

Bali Tourism Recovery

The recovery and repositioning of Bali tourism should take account of sectors and services where it has a competitive advantage and how this can be maintained as well further facilitate the development of new sectors and services where Bali has the potential and the assets to do so. Bali, a small island with a population of less then 3 million, has been repeatedly recognized in the last four years as the Best Holiday and Spa destination in the world. At the same time these four years have seen a severe social and economic downturn in Bali tourism, primarily a direct consequence of the continuing travel warnings, especially in the major developed countries.

The loss of life and economic damage in 2002 and 2004 bombings were tragic and substantive. However the threats of terrorism are world wide, including New York, London and Mumbai. But there are no travel warnings to these destinations. So one might ask why Bali is singled out for continuing travel warnings and bans. The situation is already resulting in loss of employment and livelihoods and decline of small scale industry, particularly related to the arts and crafts. All this is affecting the poor and the situation can only get worse unless there is recovery in the number of tourists coming to Bali.

Bali today needs a champion that can highlight its plight. None of the developed nations can be relied upon as they issued and continue with the travel warnings. Perhaps India, with its emerging stature in the world, could rise to this challenge especially as it has long historical links with Bali. A high level political voice from India, "We urge holiday-makers to go to Bali as it is as safe a place as any in the world of today and we are committed to partner Bali's recovery", would not only reinforce India's traditional position as a voice of the world's poor and the discriminated as so often emphasized by India in the developing country Group of 77 forums. Furthermore this might even arouse the conscious and concern of the politicians and decision-makers in the major developed countries regarding the injustice and unfairness of their continuing travel warnings to Bali. At the same time a concerted national and international policy action effort in Indonesia is critical to ensure Bali's recovery. This is an ideal opportunity to develop an innovative and integrated medium and long term strategy to reposition Bali in the world tourism markets.

Bali Tourism Repositioning

First and foremost Bali needs a core marketing message to highlight its unique holiday destination attributes in the world tourism markets. India tourism is marketed under the label "Incredible India" and Malaysia as "Truly Asia". Bali is renowned the world over by its cultural heritage, ceremonial traditions, art and architecture, the warm hospitality and genuine service, the natural beauty and ecological diversity of a varied and serene land and marine environment, the host of relaxing and recreational holiday activities including the long traditions of holistic wellness and spa. The bliss and beauty of life and living in Bali is well captured by "Bali is my life", recently adopted by the Stakeholder Bali Tourism Board as a core message to position Bali in the World tourism markets.

Marketing Bali Tourism

Following the lack of progress towards recovery of Bali tourism since 2002, there is an urgency to develop a strategic and comprehensive national and international marketing plan comprising, for example:

* Content focused TV advertising including joint marketing with other tourist destinations in Asia and also relevant airlines.
* Official umbrella participation in major travel shows such as WTM London, ITB Berlin, ATF and regional shows in Asia.
* Strengthening the traditional markets in Oceania, Europe and North America and developing new markets for Bali tourism in the Middle East and Asia.
* Bali information dissemination and briefings by Indonesian Embassies in selected countries.
* Joint targeted campaigns emphasizing Bali's attributes – with WTO(World Tourism Organization), UNESCO (culture, art and architecture), UNEP (Environment and Landscapes), UNICEF (children and women), etc.
* Need for initiation of direct flights to Bali from Europe, Middle East, India etc and development of all inclusive air travel holiday packages.
* Developing activity focused holiday packages such as, marine based diving, snorkeling, fishing and sailing, culture, art and architecture, biodiversity and ecological tours, spa and integrated holistic wellness retreats, honeymoon and family reunion holidays, business and corporate meetings, especially targeted to markets in Hong Kong, Sydney, Singapore, Kula Lumpur, Tokyo etc
* International conferences and workshops, especially the UN system.

An international marketing strategy cannot be implemented without the provision of adequate financial and human resources. An integrated public-private partnership in Indonesia as well as international funding in support of recovery and repositioning of Bali tourism should be mobilized, formulated and implemented.

Bali Cultural Tourism

There are not many places left in the world where culture and traditions, morals and values, spirituality and community solidarity and arts and architecture have been preserved from generation to generation and are regularly practiced to this day. Bali is such a place and its unique human wealth and diversity are admired the world over and Balinese hospitality and friendly service stand out in the world of tourism.

While the Balinese openly welcome tourists to experience the culture wealth and traditions, at the same time it is important to ensure that the local community life and solidarity are not affected by many of the negative and worrisome developments in so many other tourist destinations. The latter relates to rise of binge drinking, drug culture, prostitution, street crime and theft etc, all of which are still alien in the case of Bali. Additionally in many other places the breakdown of family and community relationships, loss of local dialects, languages, and traditional costumes and clothing have become the norm. The rise of pop and electronic music, the TV and cinema that tends to more and more depict violence as the basis of entertainment has in many places substantively resulted in decline of small live performances, plays and traditional shows.

Bali has a long tradition of natural health care that makes a substantial difference, especially among the poor who cannot afford the pill culture of modern medicine. These traditional methods are important to document and share with increasing worldwide call for natural and holistic health care.

Bali has successfully preserved its traditional music, live theatre and ceremonies and the arts and these elements should be given due consideration in planning the kind of tourism that is relevant and desirable.

The fact that unlike most places in the world, Bali has succeeded in preserving its culture and traditions and thus far avoided the above issues is admired and much appreciated by tourists. There is a growing demand for culture based tourism and Bali is well positioned to meet this market niche. Ubud stands out as one of the most cultured and an artistic place in the world and Bali needs to create more "Ubuds" across the island.

Bali Wellness Tourism

Bali has a long tradition of natural health care, be it the secrets of a Jamu drink or beauty enhancement with Mandi Lulur. The daily prayers and offerings as well as the ceremonies and rituals such as rice field prayers all encompass a way of life that is based community solidarity and caring as well as respect and living sustainable with nature.

The lifestyle changes and pressures of work in the office, all in an urban environment of concrete and glass with little nature and greenery around, is resulting in much stress and ill health for many people around the world. Tourists today demand not only beautiful resorts and serene environments with a host of holiday activities but they also increasingly search for places where they can have wellness treatments and learn yoga and meditation. Around the world people are discovering the potential of holistic and natural health care and this is also a niche market where Bali can be well positioned.

The world wide interest in ayurveda, yoga, pranayama, meditation, Thai massage, Shiatsu and Balinese spa and beauty treatments could be capitalized on by integrating the best of such natural wellness systems. It is however important that a professional approach be taken as authentic and expert treatments are essential to create a sustaining positioning of Bali as a holistic wellness tourism destination.

Bali Marine Tourism

As an island with a wide diversity of coastal and marine ecology, Bali has great potential for development of diving, snorkeling, surfing, fishing and sailing The cliff diving at Mejangen Island, the mud diving at Puri Jati, scuba diving in east and west Bali and dolphin sunrise sails in North Bali are all well known sites with unique ecology and marine life. The problem of marine pollution in some areas is already serious, with agricultural runoff and dumping of household waste all along the coastline, resulting in severe pollution, loss of corals, breeding sites and threatening marine species unique to Bali. There is an urgent need for assessment of the coastal and marine areas to identify sites where tourism should be promoted as well sites which should be designated as protected areas.

Bali has to compete with other diving sites in the Philippines, Maldives, Thailand etc and it important that a master plan for marine tourism development be formulated, focusing on distinguishing the features that makes Bali unique, for example, an ideal location for beginner divers, surfers and other marine sports enthusiasts.

Bali Eco-tourism

The rice fields and the tropical clove and coffee plantations in Bali are well merged with the natural landscapes of forest and vegetation with masses of flora. The micro climates such as in Bedugul, Ubud, North and West Bali etc provide for a wide range of Eco-tourism development. Tourists often describe rice trekking and forest bird and plant biodiversity walks in the serene environment of Bali as something very special. Agriculture in Bali is small-scale. It is the foundation of many cultural and ceremonial traditions. Tourism development needs to heed the need to protect agriculture as well as the areas of natural forest and vegetation that makes Bali attractive as an island where nature and agriculture can coexist. Sustainable agriculture needs to be promoted and supported, especially as a significant share of the population in rural areas derive their livelihoods from it. There is a real risk that if agriculture dies, many traditions and culture will decline too.

Bali Tourism Development

A dilemma in tourism development relates to what should be the right mix of small, medium and large hotel resorts and what regulations should be enforced regarding the type of architecture, use of local materials and participation of local community. In many places around the world multinational hotel chains have been widely established and in most case these hotels tend to be the same in all locations.

Small and medium sized hotels also generally generate more employment and livelihood opportunities through arts and craft industry. In contrast large corporate hotels have to focus on share holder profits. There is an increasing demand for small boutique luxury hotels built with local architecture and materials and blending into the local environment and communities. Tourists very often prefer to stay in such resorts and are prepared to pay a premium price for the personalized service and privacy. The above considerations should be incorporated in planning the right mix of small, medium and large hotel development, well imbedded in the local environment and with the participation of and fair benefits to the local community. This aspect of socially responsible tourism is also of interest to many tourists.

Bali Sustainable Tourism

Bali has much to offer the world's tourists and the tourists from around the world have much to contribute to enhancing and developing this blissful and unique tourism destination.

A survey of the guest comments at a number of hotels and resorts surprisingly identified similar issues that tourists most admired about Bali. These included the genuine smiles and warm hospitality, the culture, human values and ceremonies, the daily floral offerings and prayers, art, crafts and architecture, the rice fields amidst floral tropical landscapes, the blue seas and sandy white beaches, the diversity of marine and terrestrial biodiversity, the blending of the traditional and modern architecture, the beauty of intricate small household gardens and temples and the personalized art and craft shops all over Bali..

While an international partnership and goodwill is paramount for the recovery and repositioning of Bali tourism, it is also an opportunity to develop and implement an integrated and focused medium and long term tourism development strategy that ensures the competitiveness and uniqueness of Bali in the world of tourism.

Challenges and Issues for Tourism in the South Pacific Island States: The Case of the Fiji Islands

Tourism has come to play a significant role in the economies of South Pacific island states in terms of generating employment, income and foreign exchange earnings. Wilkinson (1989) concludes that tourism is 'inevitable' in those island states that lack viable economic alternatives to growth because of their isolation, size, lack of resources and high cost structure, among other inhibiting factors.

For those island states that have some economic alternatives for growth, tourism is a welcome diversification that provides additional opportunities for employment, foreign exchange earnings and higher standards of living. Milne (1992), who studied five South Pacific island states (Tonga, Vanuatu, Kiribati, Niue, and Cook Islands), found that these island states had embraced tourism for reasons other than economic growth and sustainability. The states depict MIRAB economic structures: that is, they are characterized by outward migration (MI), a dependence on high-level remittances (R) and aid (A) payments to cover deficits, and a reliance on bureaucracy (B) for job creation. While these economies are able to sustain themselves on MIRAB structures, they 'treat tourism as an economic bonus'. Almost all South Pacific island states depict varying degrees of MIRAB characteristics, and common to each country is government bureaucracy for job creation. For politically unstable economies like Fiji, which has experienced three coups since 1987, outward migration and bureaucracy for job creation are more prevalent characteristics.

What is not debatable is that all South Pacific island states have embraced tourism with varying degrees of importance, and the tourism sector features prominently in the development and strategic plans of these island states. Most countries have a National Tourism Organization (NTO), with a separate government ministry or department to facilitate the development of tourism. The South Pacific Tourism Organization (SPTO), a regional tourism organization founded in 1983, further reflects the importance of tourism to the South Pacific economies. The primary objective of SPTO, which is principally funded by European Union, is to: foster regional cooperation in the development of tourism and to undertake regional initiatives in the fields of tourism marketing and promotion, research and development, and human resources development and training. (SPTO, Annual Report, 1999, p 4)

While the island states recognize the importance and the positive impacts of tourism on their development agenda, they are also mindful of the negative impacts that uncontrolled growth of tourism can have on the local community, culture and heritage, and the environment. Milne (1992) finds that, while island states appreciate the positive impact of tourism, they are also aware that it brings the 'potential for environment and socio-cultural disruption and they are therefore reticent to adopt policies that create too much dependency on the industry'.

Historically, island tourism has been dominated by foreign enterprises with limited local participation and control. Fears and concerns of uncontrolled development and lack of local control and participation in the industry are commonly raised by the states in their development plans and in both regional and international forums. It has become increasingly clear that there is a greater need to involve the community at tourism planning levels. King, McVey and Simmons (2000) applied the World Tourism Organization (WTO) model of the 'societal marketing approach to national planning' in Niue and Vanuatu: the model addresses the importance of local community input in the national planning process. The key components of the WTO model are: close dialogue between marketing issues and socio-cultural inputs and a commitment to ensure that community needs and aspirations are central to the planning process; an marketing inputs should embrace the stakeholders, including the local community as well as tourists.

The critical aspect of the model is that market analyses (demand-side elements such as evaluation of market preferences) are taken only after local needs and aspirations have been identified and assessed (that is, supply-side elements such as physical product and socio-cultural and infrastructural assessments) and after the resource implications of alternative development options have been considered. Such a model, incorporating community values and aspirations as a central component of planning, if proved successful, may be a useful tool for planners in all island states. Most of the challenges that face the island economies are inherent in globalization and development processes.

Addressing these issues requires committed, resourceful and vigilant public-sector management working in close cooperation with all stakeholders to maximize the benefits and minimize the adverse impacts of the development process. However, in the last two decades or so tourism development in the Pacific island states has faced a new challenge: that of political instability and its ramifications for growth and development. Political instability in one island nation can have ripple effects across the region given the island states' relatively close physical proximity, regional groupings and linkages through transportation, trade and tourism. Burns (1995) notes that one of the problems the Pacific island states face is the 'sensitivity of tourism to political instability'. He cites examples of New Caledonia and Papua New Guinea, where political unrest and poor political relations adversely affected tourism in the 1980s. The author also discusses the impact of the coups in Fiji in 1987 and the resultant political instability on Fiji's tourism. This will be discussed in greater detail later in this chapter. The second contentious issue increasingly faced by island states is that of land tenure and property rights associated with the use of land. Sofield (1996) highlights a dispute between Anuha Island Resort (tenants) and the landowners in the Solomon Islands, about a conflict between the resort owner's legal right to use the land and the landowner's customary expectations that ultimately led to the closure of the resort. The prolonged battle between the foreign management and customary landowners and the fall-out from the dispute adversely affected foreign investment in the Solomon Islands for several years.

International visitors may be oblivious to the underlying problems in island states, and South Pacific island destinations may very well live up to their image of an 'earthly paradise'. However, island nations increasingly face significant developmental problems and challenges. As the President of Kiribati said, The sooner we stop using the word Paradise the better; the Pacific islands as a Paradise is the imagination of tourist people and the media … Islands are full of problems. I live on one of those islands, and it's only a Paradise when you don't have to live there long. It is good to come and see the natives and so on, but I am not sure you would want to spend the whole life staying in the Paradise. There are a lot of real problems here. Against this backdrop, the rest of this paper examines and analyses challenges and issues facing the most developed Pacific island state, the Fiji Islands. In addition to outlining the historical development of Fiji's tourism industry, the paper addresses issues of land tenure and property rights and their impact on the tourism industry, analyses the impact of the 1987 and 2000 coups in Fiji on the tourism industry and the role played by the private–public partnership in minimizing that impact, and draws conclusions that may be useful for the future development of the tourism industry in Fiji and in other South Pacific island states.

Methodology

Relevant literature is reviewed to discuss and analyse the above issues. Secondary sources of data and information relating to Fiji tourism sector are then used to examine the problems and issues identified. The paper is structured as follows. First there is a review of Fiji's tourism sector and tourism policy. Second, there is a discussion of the coups of 1987 and 2000. Third, strengths, weaknesses, opportunities and threats for the tourism industry are assessed. Fourth, property rights and their impact on tourism are examined. The fifth section assesses the impact of the coups on tourism and the role played by private–public partnership in assisting the industry to recover, and, finally, conclusions are offered.

The Fiji Tourism Industry

There are 322 islands in the Fiji Islands, occupying about 750,000 square kilometres in the Southwest Pacific Ocean and accounting for 18,376 square kilometres (about 7,000 square miles) of land area. The Fiji Islands are located approximately 3,000 kilometres northwest of Sydney, 2,000 kilometres north of Auckland and 5,000 kilometres southwest of Honolulu. According to Fijian legend the great Chief Lutunasobasoba led his people across the seas to new land of Fiji at least 3,000 years ago. Most authorities agree that the origins of the South Pacific people can be traced back to Southeast Asia, with migrations across the Pacific through Indonesia. Fiji was first 'discovered' by the Dutch explorer Abel Tasman in 1643, followed by English explorers including Captain James Cook, who sailed through the Fiji Islands in 1774. However, most credit for the discovery and recording of the Fiji Islands goes to Captain William Bligh, who sailed through Fiji in 1789.

The first outside contact that Fijians experienced were with shipwrecked sailors and runaway convicts from Australian penal settlements in the early part of nineteenth century. European sandalwood traders, whalers and missionaries had arrived by the mid-nineteenth century. Fiji was ceded to Great Britain in 1874, and became a British colony. From 1879 to 1916, the British brought labourers from the Indian sub-continent to Fiji to work on sugar plantations under the indenture system. After the abolition of the indenture system, 60% of the people who had come from India remained in Fiji primarily as independent smallholder sugar-cane farmers, and, over the years, this community has become a significant economic and political force in the country. According to the 1996 census, Fiji had a population of 772,655, with indigenous Fijians accounting for 51%, Indo-Fijians 44% and other ethnic backgrounds 5%. Sixty per cent of the people live in rural areas, and 93% live in the two major islands of Viti Levu (75%) and Vanua Levu (18%), with the other 7% spread over 100 smaller islands.

Sugar has been the major industry in Fiji for over 100 years in terms of foreign exchange earnings, employment, contribution to Gross Domestic Product (GDP) and its linkages to other sectors of the economy, particularly the banking and retail sectors. The importance of tourism was recognized mainly after independence in 1970, and in 1998 tourism surpassed sugar as the largest foreign exchange earner. However, foreign exchange leakage in the tourism sector is estimated to be around 70%, and therefore in terms of net foreign exchange earnings the sugar industry remains the largest contributor. Other important sectors of the economy today include forestry, fisheries, mining and agriculture (other than sugar). A small but significant manufacturing sector has also developed. Garment manufacturing and exports, fish processing and exports, and other manufacturing and processing industries provide a relatively well diversified base for the Fiji economy compared to other Pacific island states. A well developed wholesale and retail sector is strongly integrated with the tourism industry. All in all, sugar and tourism are traditionally the mainstays of the Fiji economy and continue to play dominant roles. Fisheries, forestry, mining, garment manufacturing and service sectors also make notable contributions.

Tourism industry: background The comprehensive analyses of tourism development in Fiji undertaken by Britton (1983) focuses on the growth of tourism in a neo-colonial economy shaped by the dominance of foreign capital and the profit-seeking interests associated with it. The author writes: The distribution of the benefits of tourism is determined by the organization and structure of the industry. This structure reflecting the capitalist and often the monopolistic nature of enterprises ...

directly shapes the industry's internal and external linkages and determines the role the tourism market and tourist destinations play within the international system. These in turn decide the regional, sectorial and class distribution of benefits derived from tourism. Central to such analysis is that the growth and development of tourism served the profit-seeking interests of foreign capital at the expense of the development needs and aspirations of the local communities, in particular their economic, socio-cultural and the ecological concerns. Britton concedes however that foreign capital, with its access to finance, marketing agencies and transportation and by virtue of having substantial capital resources and managerial expertise, did contribute to tourism development in Fiji as shown by the tourism industry's increasing contribution to GDP, employment and foreign exchange. The distribution of benefits, however, may have been lopsided, as will be discussed later. Britton's analysis is important and useful, for it puts the development of Fiji in its proper historical context. Moreover, it gives a historical perspective of the present complex economic and political relationships, and explains the evolution of economic institutions and structures and the overall development of Fiji as a product of the colonial legacy.

The importance of tourism in Fiji's economy has grown steadily, particularly since Fiji gained its political independence from the UK in 1970. In addition to its growth the industry is beset with a number of problems related to land ownership, ethnic conflicts and resulting political disturbances, as manifested in the coups of 1987 and 2000. Moreover, lack of good governance and inefficient public-sector management have cost the economy millions of dollars and have adversely affected the social (health, education, welfare) and economic sectors, and public-sector investment in infrastructure to support the productive sectors of the economy.

Growth of the Tourism Industry in Fiji

The origins of tourism in Fiji can be traced back to the 1890s when Fiji was recognized and was used as the 'crossroads' of the Pacific for steamship lines. The steamships used Suva, the capital city, as the port of call, and a colonial administrator of the period saw the potential for tourism in this transportation activity. He published the first travel guide to Fiji in 1893. Subsequently, to fill the need for accommodation in Suva for visitors from the steamships, in May 1914 the Grand Pacific Hotel was completed. GPH, as this colonial hotel came to be known, symbolizes the beginnings of tourism in Fiji. Sadly, it is currently in a dilapidated state. The Suva Tourist Board, Fiji's first tourist planning and coordination office, was established in 1923. In 1925 it became the Fiji Publicity Board and Tourism Bureau, and this in turn later became the current Fiji Visitors' Bureau. The Board's attempt to establish a viable tourism industry was hindered not only by a lack of funds but also by a lack of support for the industry from the colonial government:

Colonial administration was never convinced of tourism's significance, let alone its long-term viability and profitability, as in the case of sugar. There was thus no direct assistance by colonial administration and local hoteliers had to bear the cost of development and maintenance as well as marketing Fiji as a destination. A significant impetus for tourist development came after the Second World War, when Nadi National Airport (built for wartime transportation needs) opened Fiji to the major tourism markets of Australia and New Zealand. At the same time the country became the gateway to South Pacific tourism. In addition, there were various policy initiatives, including the Hotel Aid Bill of 1958 and an amendment of this Bill in 1960 known as the Hotel Aid Ordinance, which provided tax allowances for tourism capital expenditure and so laid the foundation for modern tourism development in Fiji.

In 1969, one year before independence, Fiji's tourism industry attracted 66,458 visitors to Fiji, generated F$20.6 million in gross foreign exchange earnings or 31% of the total export earnings, and created 4,000 jobs in the tourism industry. In 1999 Fiji hosted 409,955 visitors and the tourism industry contributed 16.7% to the GDP, providing employment directly and indirectly to 40,000 people. The gross tourism earnings in 1999 amounted to F$559 million, making tourism the largest gross foreign exchange earner after sugar. Foreign exchange generated by the sector accounted for 47% of the gross export earnings. However, as noted earlier, for every foreign exchange tourism dollar earned about seventy cents leave or leak out of the country.

Tourism Product

Fiji also has benefited from the image of the South Pacific, created by 18th and 19th century sailors and writers, as a discovered paradise. Douglas and Douglas write: It was in the South Pacific, on the island of Tahiti specially, that the modern version of the myth of an earthly Paradise was born, created not by islanders, who had their own quite different belief systems, but by weary navigators from a world distant to give expression to peculiarly European fantasies.... Paradise had been disclosed, and the term, or a variation of it, became in time the most overworked expression in the lexicon of travel, particularly Pacific Travel. From the early days Fiji was promoted as the ideal South Seas tropical island with unique cultural and other attractions. The destination offered experience unavailable in urbanized Western lifestyles. It is worth noting that tourism destinations, particularly in their early stages of development, have to some extent to facilitate and promote mass tourism in order to create the critical mass of visitors that will make the industry viable. This is essential both for hotel facilities (occupancy rates) and airlines (number of seats filled) serving the destinations. Destinations in the early stages of development help to promote mass tourism out of necessity and, perhaps more importantly, in response to the demands of international capitalism. Fiji was no exception. Plange notes that in the case of Fiji 'mass tourism product is dominated by expatriate investments with emphasis on the culture and friendliness of Fiji's people as a draw card, and naturally the tropical climate; long white sand beaches and extensive coral reefs as the natural facilities for leisure and recreation'. McDonnell and Darcy (1998) identify three types of tourism facilities and services in Fiji: With the opening of Nadi International Airport in 1941, resorts and hotels became established around the airport area, and now Nadi town is seen as the 'tourism town of Fiji'. Nadi also has come to be known as the 'transit' tourism town, since it is the gateway to resorts in outer islands and the coral coast.

In order to provide visitors with the 'Fijian experience', *bure* (a traditional-style Fijian house) type accommodations were established on offshore islands with various water sports on offer such as snorkelling, fishing, water skiing, sailing and scuba diving, and a central area for eating. From the late 1960s, a series of similar *bure* style accommodation centres (based around the theme of the 'Fijian Experience') 'of varying degrees of comfort got established on the coral coast – from Nadi to Suva along the stretch of coastline on the Queens Highway' on the western side of Viti Levu.

These facilities were on the mainland rather than island-based. McDonnell and Darcy further note that the tourism product in Fiji remained largely unchanged from 1982 to 1995, with few additional hotels and resorts appearing. Moreover, the lack of development of tourism precincts resulted in Fiji losing half of its share of the Australian market to Bali during that period. However, the importance of tourism development areas or tourism precincts (clusters of tourism facilities) to attract a more diversified range of visitors is now recognized by the government of Fiji: In Fiji many of individual hotels, resort properties, and indeed the whole islands, produce an excellent product and have a loyal and growing market in specialist segments. But there is no doubt that Fiji is missing out on the major parts of the market which wants the more comprehensive and active facilities of resort centres. Fiji's tourism product and appeal can be summarized as based on sun, sea, sand and an exotic social and cultural environment, with an emphasis on the friendliness of the Fijian people. In recent times the promotion of cultural and ecotourism has been given greater attention. Moreover, an acquaintance of the author who is familiar with the tourism industry in Fiji has pointed out that 'sex and drug' tourism are on the rise and are attracting certain categories of tourists to Fiji. Though the government and other stakeholders in the tourism industry are aware of this trend, it remains an undiscussed phenomenon in the country. The problem has also escaped the attention of academics and researchers. Objective research is needed to ascertain the extent and gravity of the problem before the government and other stakeholders can be persuaded to pay attention to it.

Tourism Policy

As indicated earlier, Fiji's colonial administration, convinced that the tourism industry had no long-term viability or profitability, left the industry to develop on its own. McDonnell and Darcy (1998) conclude that the lack of the development of tourism precincts in Fiji led to the loss of half of the potential Australian visitors to Bali in 1982–95 and that this shortcoming may be related to the government's lack of involvement in developing tourist infrastructure and superstructure. The authors point out that the 'Bali Tourism Development Corporation directed concentrated tourism precinct development and the government tightly controlled foreign investment and immigration'. On the other hand, the Fiji government's role historically has been one of support, largely through its funding of marketing campaigns by the Fiji Visitors' Bureau and incentive packages for tourism development. In its most recent 'Strategic Development Plan, 2003–2005', the government reiterates its long-standing tourism policy: Government will continue to play a facilitative role in tourism development through the provision of infrastructure, fiscal incentives, appropriate policies and legislation. Whilst the Ministry is responsible for overseeing the overall development of the sector, the Fiji Visitors' Bureau is responsible for promotion and marketing activities. Although the government of Fiji neither encouraged nor influenced investment in tourism precincts, it should be pointed out that it did invest heavily (through a World Bank loan) on the new (reconstructed) Nadi–Suva highway in the 1970s that opened up new tourism areas along the coral coast and provided tourists with greater and easier access to existing resorts along the new highway. Chand (1989) argued that, though reconstruction of the Suva–Nadi highway was not economically viable, the government of Fiji was politically committed to its construction to meet 'the needs of capitalistic development in Fiji – in particular the needs of the tourist industry development ...'. Provision of electricity, piped water and telecommunications further assisted the development of tourism along the coral coast on the western side of Viti Levu. It is also important to note that the local communities in these areas benefited from these improved services, and from employment opportunities that might not have arisen without the tourism development.

In contrast, the eastern side of Viti Levu was until recently neglected in terms of tar-sealed roads, electricity, piped water and telecommunications, due to its lack of tourism potential compared to the western side of the island. Certain parts of eastern Viti Levu still lack infrastructure and basic facilities that are now taken for granted by many on the western side. Similarly, many parts of Vanua Levu, the second largest island, do not have tar-sealed roads, electricity, piped water and telecommunications, and again this underinvestment in infrastructure and services can be largely attributed to a lack of tourism potential.

Thus the local communities in tourism-attracting areas benefited considerably from tourism development with the improved infrastructure, electricity, piped water, telecommunications and employment opportunities that accompany it. In contrast, those in areas without such potential for tourism development remained disadvantaged. This no doubt underscores Britton's (1983) point that the dominance of foreign capital and its predominantly profit-seeking goal ultimately determine the regional development of the tourism industry and the distribution of tourism benefits (because foreign investors lobby and influence government policies to develop infrastructure and essential services selectively in those areas where they will benefit the interests of foreign capital).

As will be discussed later, the generous government incentives outlined attract investment in the tourism sector, since the fundamental problems that influence investments have not yet been adequately addressed. Before discussing pertinent problems and challenges, it is important to examine briefly the coups of 1987 and 2000 to put that discussion into perspective.

The Coups of 1987 and 2000

There are many parallels, at least superficially, between the coups of 1987 and 2000. In 1987 the Indo-Fijian dominated Labour Party, campaigning on liberal-democratic policies, won the elections and formed the government with smaller Fijian parties. While the Prime Minister was a Fijian, the majority of Cabinet members were Indo-Fijians. Sitiveni Rabuka, the third ranking army officer, carried out the coup on 14 May 1987, and a military-backed government was formed. The first constitution (1970) of independent Fiji was abrogated and a new racially weighted constitution (1990) was promulgated, in which voting was based only on ethnic lines and political supremacy was guaranteed to indigenous Fijians by virtue of a guaranteed majority of seats. The 1990 constitution was described as worse than the South African constitution of apartheid era. Domestic and international pressure, combined with a lack of investment, led to a widespread consultative process and a Constitution Review Committee was charged with formulating recommendations for a constitution that would be acceptable to all communities in Fiji as well as to the international community. The Constitution Committee Report led to the formulation of the 1997 constitution and this was endorsed by all political parties, the existing parliament, non-governmental organizations and the traditional Fijian institution, the Great Council of Chiefs. It was internationally hailed as the solution to Fiji's problems. Elections were held under the new constitution in January 1999 and again the Labour Party won (winning 37 out of 71 seats). It formed the Government of National Unity with other parties as required under the 1997 constitution. Mahendra Chaudhry, the leader of the Labour Party and an Indo-Fijian, became Prime Minister and the majority of Cabinet ministers were Fijians. During the one year for which the Labour Party led coalition government was in power, a small but vocal minority of Fijian nationalists launched a campaign to destabilize the government. Their tactics included creating fears among indigenous Fijians that their rights were being diluted and that their land would be alienated under the present government policies.

This was not possible because land and other Fijian rights were well protected under the constitution. On 19 May 2000 a group of armed (military) men led by a failed businessman, George Speight, stormed the parliament and took the government hostage in the name of indigenous Fijian rights. The events from 1987 to 2000.

20 May: A group of Bavadra supporters who have gathered in protest at Suva's Albert Park are attacked by coup supporters. Sporadic violence spreads to the greater Suva area and Nausori.

23 September: The Coalition and Alliance Parties agree to form a caretaker government following the Deuba Accords initiated by Ganilau.

1 October: At 4pm Rabuka stages his second coup, citing dissatisfaction with the Deuba Accords.

1 October: Rabuka issues two decrees formally abrogating the 1970 constitution and sacks Ganilau.

6 October: At midnight Rabuka formally declares Fiji a Republic, ending its ties with the Commonwealth.

5 December: Rabuka dismisses his Taukei (Fijian Nationalist) government and announces a 21-member, mostly Alliance Cabinet. Ganilau is appointed president and Mara is Prime Minister. 1988.

3 November: Dr. Bavadra dies, aged 55. 1990.

24 July: Ganilau promulgates the new constitution giving ethnic Fijians political supremacy. 1991.

11 July: Rabuka resigns from the military to join the interim government as Deputy Prime Minister. 1992.

28 June: Fiji goes to the polls. Rabuka becomes Prime Minister after the chiefs-sponsored Soqosoqo ni Vakavulewa ni Taukei (SVT) party has captured most seats. 30 November: The government budget falls after eight SVT members, led by Josefata Kamikamica, vote against it. Fresh elections are called. 1994.

18 January: Ratu Mara succeeds the late Ratu Peniana Ganilau as President.

28 February: The SVT is returned to power in the general elections with 31 seats. The dissident group led by Kamikamica forms the Fijian Association Party and wins three seats. The National Federation Party (NFP) wins 20 seats. 1996.

6 September: The Constitutional Review Commission completes a review of the 1990 constitution. Rabuka and NFP leader, Jai Ram

Reddy had led the way for the review to give Indians fairer political representation. 1997.

4 April: The joint parliamentary select committee looking into the Reeves Report agrees on a multi-party executive government with 71 seats – 31 for ethnic Fijians, 27 for Indians, two for generals and one for Rotumans. Ten seats are allocated for cross voting. 1999.

May: Elections are held under the new constitution. The Labour/ Party of National Unity/Fijian Association coalition sweeps to power. Labour wins 37 of the 71 seats. The NFP, previously the major Indian Party, fails to win any seat. Rabuka's SVT wins just eight seats.

19 May: Chaudhry is sworn in as Fiji's first Indian Prime Minister after President Mara persuades the Fijian parties to support him. 2000.

21 April: About 500 ethnic Fijians march through Lautoka in protest against the government. They are led by the ultra-nationalist politician Apisai Tora who had earlier revived the Taukei.

Movement, a Fijian pressure group. (Note that the former Minister of National Planning in the coalition government disputes the figure of 500. He claims that he himself counted the protestors and that the number was 15! The author has directly communicated with the former Minister regarding these figures).

28 April: Over 4,000 Fijians stage a second protest march in Suva. (Again, the former Minister claims that the number of protesters was around 700, not 4,000).

19 May: A third march by protesting Fijians attracts 10,000 people. While it is taking place a group of armed men led by failed business executive George Speight storm the parliament and capture Chaudhry and his MPs. The drama takes place on the first anniversary of the Chaudhry government. (The figure of 10,000 is again on the high side, according to the former Minister).

The purpose of the paper is not to analyse the events that led to the coups and the reasons and justifications for them, but rather to analyse the impact of the coups on the tourism industry in Fiji. In particular, given the social, economic and political situation, what challenges and opportunities does the tourism sector face in 2002 and beyond? It is therefore useful to examine the strengths, weaknesses, threats and opportunities of Fiji's tourism sector in the aftermath of the coups.

The SWOT Analysis

Narayan (2000) identified the strengths, weaknesses, opportunities and threats to the Fiji tourism sector after the coup of 2000. Probably the most significant strength of Fiji's tourism industry is the foreign domination that Britton (1983) ironically described as responsible for the underdevelopment of the neo-colonial Fijian economy. Well established and world-renowned companies in Fiji's accommodation and tour-operating sectors, with their expertise and intricate marketing networks in source markets, have shown resilience in times of crises (coups) and will continue to play a critical role in tourism industry growth in Fiji. Given that only a few airlines service Fiji's tourist source markets, the presence of a national airline, Air Pacific, which is dedicated to the interests of Fiji even in times of crisis, is also a major strength.

The weaknesses identified by Narayan can be over-come, the opportunities can be taken advantage of and the threats can be minimized if the conditions and prerequisites for growth of a robust economy are first achieved. Political instability intricately linked to the issue of property rights and lease agreements is probably the most critical factor affecting investor confidence in Fiji. The coups of 1987 and 2000 have been at least partly linked to the issue of land problems in Fiji today. If Fiji is to achieve political stability and racial harmony, and subsequently investor confidence, one of the greatest challenges facing the islands is to resolve the issue of property rights.

Crisis in Tourism: Property Rights

To examine the complex issue of property rights in Fiji, it is important to understand the land tenure system. Customary landowners own 83% of land in Fiji and this native land is leased and administered by Native Land Trust Board (NLTB) on the behalf of landowners who are members of various *mataqali* (local landowning units). About 8% of the land is freehold and so can be bought and sold freely in the marketplace. The remainder is state-owned. Landowners or individual members of *mataqali* cannot sell or individually lease out native or communally owned land. Leases can be traded with the consent of the NLTB and can go up to 99 years, depending on the nature of the project. The NLTB, as custodian of all native land, has the legal authority to lease land and negotiate fair premiums and rent for landowners among other conditions (depending on the nature of the project), such as ensuring that investors give preference to members of the landowning units for employment and training opportunities.

The majority of the native land leased out (in fact, a small proportion of the total 83%) is under sugar farms operated mainly by Indo-Fijian farmers, the descendents of indentured labourers brought to Fiji by the British to work on sugar plantations. The cane farms have been the foundation on which the Indo-Fijian tenants farmers have been able to build a community based on social, religious and cultural cohesion. As the community became firmly established on the cane growing areas of Fiji in the early days of the colonial period, it became a political force, with needs, demands and aspirations.

Before the coups of May 2000, the tenant leases were expiring and in most cases were not to be renewed, given that the landowners wanted to cultivate the land themselves. However, the non-renewing of leases was not unrelated to the Fijian nationalist agenda of breaking up the Indo-Fijian community and subsequently destroying their political base. Today, resolving the renewal of land leases is a hot political issue and it affects all other sectors of the economy in which land is an issue. The problem is equally important to the tourism sector given that, after sugar, tourism is one of the largest sectors making use of land and the demand for land will increase as the tourism sector expands. In 1989, 43% of all hotel rooms were on native land and, as noted, the demand for native land will increase. This is becoming increasingly important in light of the uncertain future of the sugar industry and the government's consequent recognition that future economic growth is likely to come from tourism. The government's current emphasis on the promotion of ecotourism and marine tourism will further increase demand for land and sea resources. The Fiji government's policy of private-sector led tourism development on the one hand and the impossibility of freely buying and selling land in the marketplace on the other have undoubtedly increased risk and uncertainty, which have acted as disincentives for investment of private capital. Recent examples also demonstrate that the NLTB has not been effective in resolving disputes and protecting both the hotel owners' and customary landowners' rights. Prasad and Tisdell point out that 'tourism development and the issues of property rights cannot be ignored in any policy development for the industry'. A report cited by the authors highlights the problem: the group raised concern at the increase in hotel cases where indigenous Fijian landowners opt to take unlawful acts such as roadblocks to express their grievances as it relates to the application of their land and fishing rights.

In 1997 Ratu Mosese Volavola, then General Manager of the NLTB, highlighted the major land issues from the NLTB's perspective.

Unlawful acts by Fijian landowners adversely affect new investment and re-investment and the media publicity surrounding such acts creates a perception that the problem is pervasive and discourages investment, including foreign investment, not only in tourism but in all other sectors.

However, the genuine concerns of the landowners cannot and should not be ignored: problems need to be identified and solutions found. It is important to note that the problems relating to land ownership and the tenant's right to use the land go beyond formal lease agreements, which need to be fully understood both by the landowners and the tenants. Customary landowners, as we saw in case of Anuha Island Resort in the Solomon Islands, expect much more than premium and the rent income they will get from the leased land. There is a certain degree of hospitality expected from tenants; and landowners' demands are expected to be met, sometimes *ad infinitum*.

Harrison (1997) highlights a dispute between landowners and tenants in the case of Fiji that illustrates the above point. The Mana Island Resort was built by an Australian on leased land located on Mana Island. Subsequently, a Japanese citizen bought the lease and further developed and operated the hotel that catered to the high end of the market; but the landowners built two backpackers' hostels adjacent to the resort and insisted that their guests should use the resort facilities and also could cross the resort area to access the beach.

This dispute led the Japanese developer to erect 'an imposing, hardly decorative, 8 feet wire fence complete with watchmen and security boxes' between the two properties. Harrison emphasizes: … the major issue at least for Fijians operating the backpackers' hotels was the alleged right of Fijian landowners to control access to land they had leased to a third party.

Hospitality for them meant that guests had access to their land, and leasing arrangement to the Japanese was not seen … to have removed that right. Land issues continue to dominate the political landscape of Fiji and were responsible, at least in part, for the coups of 1987 and the coup of 2000 that shook investor confidence in Fiji, not to mention their overall effect on the social, economic and political fabric of this multicultural country.

Since the coups of 1987, Fiji has increasingly embraced globalization, with an emphasis on private-sector oriented growth strategies. This is reflected in all the Strategic Development Plans of the last decade.

Growth: Policies and Strategies for Fiji in the Medium Term, 1993; Development

Strategy for Fiji, 1997; and the most recent *Strategic Development Plan 2003–2005*). When a government adopts market-led growth strategies it is imperative that institutions be reformed to support such strategies. For instance, the Fiji government has pursued privatization and public-sector reforms over the past decade so that institutions are able to respond to the needs and demands of the marketplace. However, no such attempt has been made to reform the NLTB and the land tenure system to make it more responsive to market signals while at the same time protecting the interests of landowners and tenants. The Labour Party led coalition government's attempt to introduce a Land Use Commission, which would have been a step towards some form of reform, met with strong opposition from the nationalist Fijian political parties and the NLTB. The concept of the Land Use Commission was highly politicized by the opposition political parties and Fijian nationalists, who in particular aroused fears in indigenous Fijians that their customary land would be alienated under such a Commission. According to most observers, the politically sensitive issue of reforming land tenure system gave the Fijian nationalists enough ammunition to rally support to agitate against the coalition government.

The communal nature of land ownership in Fiji and the impossibility of freely trading land in the marketplace, combined with the role of the NLTB as the custodian of the landowners, pose complex problems that render any market solution to the land issues almost impossible. According to a Bank of Hawaii report on Fiji,... the operation of Fiji's land market does pose certain unfamiliar complexities for foreigners. Despite attempts to streamline the NLTB, the land regulatory mechanism is sometimes criticized as inefficient, particularly when land transfers and land use are concerned. Communal ownership creates certain incentives problems as well. Ultimately, contemplating Fiji's alternative development path under private property rights in land is fruitless: the communal regime should be expected to remain a permanent fixture of Fiji's economy. It is imperative for long-term political stability and growth that acceptable solutions to the land problems are found. Given the political nature of the NLTB, the solutions suggested by its General Manager may minimize short-term problems and resolve some disputes, but they do not provide a long-term resolution that will build investor confidence, provide fair returns to landowners and give security to tenants. Moreover, there are often conflicts between the NLTB, the legal owner of the native land, and the individual landowners, as noted by Prasad and Tisdell:... the orthodox legal model of land tenure in which NLTB is a legal owner has increasingly being questioned by landowners themselves. This is one reason why there have been occasional illegal takeovers of resorts and hotels by landowners. For example in 1996 on the island of Viti Levu, there were two cases where landowners illegally took over resorts and closed them. This was so, despite the legal guarantee of land lease to the resort owners. The conflict clearly involves the issue of who is the real owner of the land? Is it NLTB or the individual Mataqali members themselves? The NLTB legally is the owner but consults the landowning units who feel that they are the owners. The conflict, according to the authors, arises from a system of *Vakavanua*, in which the individual landowners can lease land to Fijians and non-Fijians and collect rent themselves. Though the system is illegal, it is practised widely in Fiji.

In addition to the conflict between the landowners and the NLTB, another critical source of conflict is the formula used to distribute lease income between the NLTB and the landowning units and within the landowning units themselves. Given the hierarchical structure of the landowning units (*mataqali*), the majority of *mataqali* members, who fall at the bottom the structure, receive almost next to nothing in lease/ rental income. Robertson and Tamanisau point out that: Many problems highlighted publicly in the mid-1980s focused on the disproportionate levels of rents, which went to the Chiefs rather than their own people. Money thus gained by many Chiefs has been used for personal aggrandizement and not for the benefit of their own people, the often-claimed purpose of their traditional role. The formula for the distribution of rental income within the *mataqali* has not changed and still remains a critical issue. A formula for a fairer distribution of lease income within the *mataqali* must be central to any solution to the land use problem in Fiji.

Impact of the Coups on Tourism and the Role of the Tourism Action Group

The political instability that resulted from the coups has both short-term and long-term implications for tourism. The immediate effect no doubt is on visitor arrivals, but the long-term impact may be very profound in terms of future growth and development of the industry. The discussion in this section is based on Teye's (1988) Impact Model, which is used to explain the impact of the coups and the resultant political instability on tourism. According to the model, the coups and the political instability affect development of tourism in three broad areas: the effectiveness of the National Tourism Organization (NTO); the flow of international tourists (demand for the tourism product); and the development of tourism resources and attractions (supply of tourism products), as well as the delivery of tourism services. *Impact on the NTO: Fiji Visitors' Bureau* Teye points out that tourism development in developing countries is largely a public-sector initiative, and that successful implementation of tourism plans and programmes is dependent on an effective and strong NTO. Applying his model to Ghana, he concludes that military coups and military governments in Ghana produced a weak, unstable and ineffective NTO. Contrary to the case in Ghana, the coups in Fiji produced a greater government commitment to the NTO – the Fiji Visitors' Bureau (FVB) – that probably made it stronger and more effective.

The rapid response from the Fiji government in assisting the tourism sector through the marketing campaign of the FVB explains the financially stronger FVB in the aftermath of the coups. Other sectors of the economy that may have been equally affected by the political turmoil did not attract the government's attention and financial commitment. For instance, three weeks after the first 1987 coup, the press reported the need to 'protect tourism' and the 'Governor General announced an extra F$500,000' emergency grant to the FVB 'to assist in marketing and crisis management'. Moreover, four weeks after the coup, the Governor General agreed to address the 1987 Tourism Convention, which went ahead as planned despite the coup. He outlined a nine-point plan for reconstruction of the industry, reflecting the importance of tourism to economic recovery (Burns, 1995, p 265). Since then the budget for the FVB has steadily increased under a Fijian-dominated administration from 1987 to 1999. The FVB's marketing budget for 1991 was F$2.5 million, and this steadily increased to F$11 million in 1999. The Bureau has consistently been able to convince the government over the years of the need to increase its budget, justifying the increases as necessary to sustain the increasing visitor numbers and foreign exchange earnings and to protect employment. It has also been perceived that the tourism sector benefits the Fijians more than any other sector of the economy, and it has therefore been actively supported by the post-coup Fijian administrations.

Moreover, the FVB and tourism industry, using World Tourism Organization (WTO) criteria for per-visitor expenditures could easily justify the case that the marketing of tourism is underfunded. However, no objective study has been undertaken to evaluate the return on marketing for the public funds allocated to the FVB. The proportion of increase in visitors' arrivals attributed to the FVB's marketing efforts is unknown. The effectiveness of Fiji's NTO is rather debatable, but it is widely thought in industry and government to be generally effective. In addition, the Bureau's operating budgets have been slowly declining since 1995, which may indicate that its overall efficiency has increased over the years.

However, the demarcation and classification of operating and marketing budgets can be blurred, and a reclassification of certain expenditures from operating to marketing expenses may indicate an increase in efficiency when none exists. Another underlying reason for the government's quick response in assisting the tourism sector's recovery is related to the notion that declining visitor arrivals is a reflection of political instability. Arresting the decline of visitor arrivals as quickly as possible and achieving the pre-coup levels of visitor arrivals is indicative of the return to normality and political stability that the post-coup administrations use to justify their existence and legitimacy. Third, given that the tourism industry is dominated by foreign enterprises, their managers are more than willing to cooperate with post-coup administrations to protect their companies' interests and investments. The tourism sector, and in particular visitor arrivals, is used by the post-coup administrations as a barometer for the degree of political stability in the country.

Since the 1987 coups, the tourism industry in Fiji has been increasingly identified as the 'Fijian Industry' given that the industry is using Fijian land and sea resources, and Fijians are the front-line employees. Moreover, the Fiji tourism product is built around the indigenous Fijian traditions and cultures, and is promoted as constituting a unique 'Fijian Experience'. The success of the tourism industry is perceived by Fijian administrations as synonymous with the economic success of the Fijians, even though the industry is foreign-dominated with around 70% foreign exchange leakage. Fijians, who have historically failed in scores of commercial ventures despite generous financial assistance from the government, increasingly see the tourism sector as the one that could 'challenge' the sectors dominated by Indo-Fijians, particularly the sugar industry. The tourism sector, therefore, is seen by Fijians in some ways as a symbol of their success in commerce – an image they feel they need if they are to take control of their destiny.

Given these nationalistic sentiments, it is undoubtedly important to protect and support the tourism industry, particularly in times of crises, such as the coups. The coups, according to their perpetrators, were carried out in the cause of Fijian nationalism and interests. It is therefore in the political interest of the post-coup Fijian administrations (which have largely comprised people who were involved in or who supported the coups) to support the tourism sector in the aftermath of the crises.

When the Labour Party led coalition government reduced the FVB's budget from F$11 million to F$7 million in 2000, it was seen (at least by some opposition political parties and Fijian nationalists) as one more instance of the Labour Party's policy of discriminating against a sector that supported Fijians. After the coup of May 2000, the military-backed Fijian administration restored $4 million to the FVB. In 2001, the FVB's budget was maintained at $11.0 million for 'intensive marketing campaigns to pull the industry out of the decline it suffered in the immediate period after May 19'. No forms of assistance were extended to the other sectors of the economy.

The budget for 2002 will continue to be maintained at $11.0 million (2002 Budget Address). The point to note is that the government's commitment to Fiji Visitors' Bureau has increased since the coups of 1987. It has also been generally recognized by the government and the tourism industry that the FVB has been effective in marketing Fiji because of increasing visitor arrivals and foreign exchange earnings. Moreover, as noted before, the tourism sector was recognized by the military-backed Fijian administrations established after the coups as supporting the economic well-being of the Fijian people and it was therefore realized that funding the FVB in times of crisis was essential to gain and maintain the political support of Fijians. The post-coup administrations' readiness and commitment to support the industry financially does not, therefore, come as a surprise.

Impact on the Flow of International Visitors

The immediate impact of the coups was on visitor arrivals that subsequently affected the airline flights and schedules to and from the major source markets. After the coup in May 1987, visitor arrivals in June fell to 5,000 compared to 18,000 in June 1986, a decline of 72.2%. In 1987 visitor arrivals fell by 26.4% from the 1986 level.

Though the arrivals improved in subsequent years, they only reached the pre-coup level of visitors after more than two years. In 1987 the

FVB projected visitor arrivals of 313,000 by 1991, but this figure was not achieved until 1994, with 318,874 arrivals. In terms of visitor arrivals, then, Fiji's growth curve was put back at least three years. Similar impacts on visitor arrivals were noted in the aftermath of May 2000 coup. Arrivals for June 1999 totalled 38,445 and they declined to 12,066 in June 2000, the month after the coup. The monthly visitor arrivals declined drastically in the months following the coup. Although visitor arrivals began to recover in the third quarter of 2000, it was not until December of 2001, with visitor arrivals of 31,871, that they came close to the pre-coup December 1999 figure of 31,926. This was some 19 months after the coup. On an annual basis, visitor arrivals declined by 28.3% in 2000 compared to the 1999 level. The projected figure for visitor arrivals for 2000 before the coup was 428,000. On the basis of the projected arrivals for 2000, the decline in visitor arrivals in 2000 was 31.3%.

In 2001, visitor arrivals recovered to 348,014, an increase of 18.3% over 2000 but still a 15.4% decline over 1999 arrivals and an 18.7% decline over 2000 projected arrivals. The current projection for 2002 is 369,000, well below 1999 actual arrivals and the 2000 projected arrivals (prior to the coups). It is clear that in terms of visitor arrivals the tourism industry has lost at least another three years because of the 2000 coup: it seems that visitor arrivals will recover to the 1999 level only in 2003.

All in all, because of the coups the tourism industry in Fiji has lost at least six years of growth in visitor arrivals. Given the growth in world tourism in the 1990s, there is little doubt that, had the coups not taken place, Fiji would have surpassed the 500,000 visitors target by 2000, the target set in 1987 by FVB. Given the current projections, it may well be that 500,000 visitor arrivals will be achieved by 2006. This loss in opportunity affects other sub-sectors of the tourism industry and the economy as a whole (there is, for example, an impact on the development and delivery of the tourism product).

This is discussed below. The severity of the impact of the coups on visitor arrivals (other things being equal) depends on the effectiveness of the NTO, the government's commitment to the recovery of the sector and the role played by all stakeholders in the industry. In the aftermath of the coups the Tourism Action Group (TAG), a public–private partnership, played an important role in arresting the decline of visitor arrivals in Fiji.

Tourism Action Group (TAG)

TAG was 'born' at the Fiji Tourism Convention in June 1987. As noted above, the Convention, an annual gathering of private and public stakeholders in the industry, went ahead as planned despite the coup in May 1987, and the occasion was used to deliberate on recovery plans for the industry. The Convention reached a consensus that a crisis management team should be formed in the Fiji Visitors' Bureau comprising industry representatives. This team would be called the Tourism Action Group. The sole objective of TAG was to arrest the decline of visitor arrivals to Fiji as effectively and as quickly as possible. Its four key goals were: the removal of travel warnings and union bans in Australia and New Zealand; a doubling of the National Tourism Organization marketing budget; familiarization visits from the main markets for trade representatives; and marketing of special airfares and packages to those markets. TAG was disbanded eleven weeks after its establishment, when there was evidence of recovery as a result of its strategies. Given the experience and usefulness of this approach in the tourism industry's recovery efforts, the TAG model was quickly adopted to counter the negative impact of the 2000 coup.

Within a few weeks of the May 2000 coup, the Tourism Action Group was revived under the auspices of FVB 'to try and counter the negative publicity of the crisis with our source markets and to formulate a recovery plan for tourism'. One of its key objectives was to return the tourism industry, particularly visitor arrivals, to pre-coup levels speedily and effectively, and to minimize the losses. The TAG team comprised key stakeholders in the industry, including the Fiji Hotel Association, the Society of Fiji Travel Associates, the airlines, and the Fiji Visitors' Bureau. After making presentations to the military government on its objectives and strategies to assist in the industry recovery, TAG secured F$5 million for a promotional campaign which included: seeking the services of a public relations and media management consulting firm to assist in the management of the recovery programme; lobbying the governments and unions in Fiji's key markets against sanctions and travel warnings on Fiji; coordination of advertising and promotional activities in proven media outlets in Fiji's key markets of Australia and New Zealand, and North America, Europe and Japan; and devising special recovery fare packages. TAG's action plan after the 2000 coup of 2000. In short, TAG's efforts were largely successful. As can be seen from the monthly figures, the recovery began in the third quarter of 2000, some four months after the coup and continued throughout 2001 on a monthly basis. The relatively quick recovery, despite the prolonged nature of the crisis (the government was kept hostage for 56 days), is attributable largely to the strategies and efforts of TAG.

The experience of TAG shows that, when industry stakeholders come together– government with the funds and industry with expertise – the impacts of political crises on visitor arrivals can be minimized and the tourism industry can recover relatively rapidly.

Impact on Tourism Product Development and Delivery

Frequent coups and subsequent changes in government disrupt the continuity of policies that are critical for sustained economic development. Coups and the resultant political instability adversely affect investor confidence, leading either to postponement or cancellation of investment projects. Development plans that were being implemented either receive little attention from the new administration or are overtaken by more pressing priorities. The pro-nationalist agenda of the coup perpetrators and military-backed governments, combined with the fact that landowners were taking over resort properties and utilities, further reduced investor confidence in Fiji. In short, political instability in the aftermath of the coups created an environment that was very hostile to investors and business in general.

At the time of the 2000 coup, a Tourism Development Plan covering 2000–2004 had been completed, and a National Development Plan, which included the tourism sector, was nearing completion. As a result of the coup, these plans received little or no priority, first because the conditions and assumptions on which they had been formulated were changed,

TAG Action Plan Following the May 2000 Coup.

19 May 2000: Attempted coup and seizure of the parliament by George Speight and his followers.

29 May 2000: Crisis meeting of FVB, Air Pacific and industry representatives to discuss the crisis. The decision is taken at this meeting to form the Tourism Action Group (TAG) and appoint Damend Gounder as Chairman. The first course of action for TAG is to seek international expertise on media management through the appointment of an international PR company.

7 June 2000: Appointment of Hill & Knowlton, an international public relations consulting firm based in Australia to provide PR consultation for TAG.

9 June 2000: Presentation to the Interim Military Government (IMG), formally seeking its assistance and support.

June/July 2000: Monitoring of overseas media by Hill & Knowlton and lobbying with key union leaders in Australia and New Zealand to reconsider trade cargo embargoes on Fiji. Circulation of accurate weekly news updates from TAG via FVB on the current situation to overseas media organizations along with positive experience statements from tourists who had stayed in Fiji during the crisis. TAG meetings with Fiji wholesalers to determine a recovery campaign in all the key source markets and to seek financial support from wholesalers for cooperative recovery marketing.

August 2000: End of consultancy services by Hill & Knowlton. Continued lobbying of embassies by TAG to revise travel restrictions for the western region of the Fiji Islands, which had remained calm and peaceful throughout the crisis. Signing of the Muanikau Accord between George Speight and the Military Commander, Frank Bainimarama, setting the stage for the release of political hostages.

September 2000: Release of political hostages from the parliament complex. Surrender of firearms by the rebels. All coup supporters leave the parliament complex after an occupation of over five months. Capture and arrest of George Speight and armed rebel supporters by the Fiji Military Forces. Appointment of an Interim Government for Fiji by the President, Ratu Josefa Iloilo. Interim Government Prime Minister is Laisenia Qarase. Modification of travel warnings by the Foreign Offices of the UK, the USA, Australia and New Zealand. Travel restrictions eased for the western region of the Fiji Islands. TAG meeting with the Interim Minister for Tourism and Transport to secure funding support to TAG and FVB in 2001. First phase of the TAG Recovery Campaign is launched in Australia and New Zealand with special recovery airfares and land content packages.

October 2000: TAG continues lobbying through embassies to downgrade travel warnings on Fiji and to urge overseas unions to remove trade embargoes.

November 2000: Announcement of FVB 2001 Marketing Budget of FJ$11 million. A total assistance package of FJ$16 million is announced by the Interim Minister of Finance as part of the Interim Government's assistance in the revival of the local tourism industry. TAG launches the second phase of its Recovery Campaign, with emphasis on efforts in Fiji's long-haul markets of Japan, North America, and Europe. Travel warnings on travel to Fiji were downgraded by the Foreign Offices of Australia, New Zealand, and North America.

December 2000: Second phase of TAG Recovery Campaign is in full swing. Provisional results from the first phase indicate a good success rate in terms of visitor arrivals. TAG makes a presentation to the Fiji Tourism Forum with a summary report on its activities and the recommendation that TAG be disbanded. TAG Boxing Day Specials are launched in Australia and New Zealand to stimulate travel during this low season.

January 2001: TAG Committee votes to keep TAG active through monthly meetings with a focus on assisting the Fiji Visitors' Bureau in its destination marketing efforts. Tourism product development and delivery are dependent on visitor numbers, visitors' motivations, visitors' spending habits, and in general on their needs and expectations. It is estimated above Fiji has lost six productive years in terms of visitor arrivals. It is reasonable to assume that there is a direct relationship between tourism product development and delivery and the growth of visitor arrivals. It is likely that tourism product development and delivery in Fiji have also been set back by around six years because of the coups.

At the time of the 2000 coup, F$600 million worth of new investment projects, most of them in the tourism sector, had been approved by the Fiji Trade and Investment Bureau and were ready for implementation. The coup placed these projects in jeopardy. Seventy million dollars worth of the projects had progressed to the point of securing land and commencing construction. The high rate of approved investments was no doubt due to rising investor confidence following the democratic election of the government in 1999 under a constitution that was accepted both domestically and internationally. Democratically elected governments signal political stability, one of the prerequisites for investor confidence. The approved investment of F$600 million at the time of May 2000 coup was testimony to the fact that investors were bullish as never before about the future prospects of the Fiji economy. In addition, it is worth noting that, since the coups of 1987, private, public and government investment has tended to fall as a percentage of GDP. The trend. From 1970, when Fiji gained independence, to 1987, when the first military coups occurred, private-sector investment as a percentage of GDP averaged 12.6% annually and total (private, public and government) investment averaged 22.2%. In the aftermath of the 1987 coups, between 1988 and 1999, private-sector investment a percentage of GDP averaged only 4.9% annually and total investment only 12.5%. After the 1987 coups, numerous fiscal incentives (such as the tax-free factory and zone scheme, by which enterprises that exported at least 80% of their output qualified for a tax holiday of 13 years, including duty-free importation of raw materials, plant and machinery), a Short Life Investment Package (SLIP) for the tourism sector, and various other sectorial incentives failed to attract sufficient investment in Fiji.

The coup of 2000 has further jeopardized investment in the tourism sector and in other sectors of the economy. It takes a long time for investors to regain confidence and to start re-investing after periods of political instability. At such low levels of investment as those experienced in Fiji, it is likely that the capital stock is depreciating faster than the new investment, and so the net result is likely to be 'disinvestment' – that is, the stock capital stock of the economy is steadily declining. This has serious implications for the productive capacity of the Fiji economy and is hardly a scenario that will attract adequate new investment. Political stability, respect for rule of law and good governance remain the critical fundamental prerequisites for capital inflows, and investment in Fiji's tourism sector is no exception.

The cost of the coups to the tourism sector has been great, and not only in the economic sense. Hafiz Khan, the President of Fiji Hotel Association, alluded to the deeper cost of the coup when he said that 'the icon of Fiji being a safe destination with happy friendly people has been lost'.

Conclusion

South Pacific island states have embraced tourism as a development option and recognize its potential for the generation of employment, income and foreign exchange. The industry's importance for island states is reflected in the fact that most of them have a National Tourist Office and separate ministries or departments to promote and facilitate tourism. The importance of tourism to the region is further reflected in the establishment of the South Pacific Tourism Organization to promote tourism for the region as a whole. South Pacific island tourism has been built largely on the romantic image of the islands created by early explorers and writers, who praised the pristine and unspoiled environment, the exotic cultures, the friendly people, and the sand, sun and sea. This image is increasingly in danger of being shattered as South Pacific island states face real problems and challenges which, if not resolved, may seriously affect the long-term viability of their tourism industry. South Pacific states are aware that some problems are inherent in the process of globalization (which they have embraced to varying degrees) – such as the impact on environment, tradition, culture and the local community in general.

Island states need to make deliberate decisions and trade-offs so that they can enjoy the fruits of growth and development and at the same time preserve the local traditions and customs that are important to them. Effective and efficient public-sector management, with the involvement of all stakeholders, would maximize the benefits and minimize the adverse impacts of the growth of tourism. Policies that enhance good governance are of critical importance in this regard.

Political disturbances and political instability are major issues facing the South Pacific region. Over the last two decades political instability in Papua New Guinea, New Caledonia, Fiji and the Solomon Islands has not only adversely affected tourism and overall development in those countries, but the ripple effect of instability has affected other states in the region as well. In the case of the Fiji Islands, political coups have seriously damaged tourism.

Their economic costs have been great, and Fiji may have very well lost six productive years of growth in its tourism sector. The non-economic cost of political instability no doubt is immense, and the notion that Fiji is an earthly paradise with friendly people and exotic culture is in danger of being lost forever. Critical challenges face the future sustainable growth of tourism in Fiji that can be best understood by examining the historical factors and events, and the vested interests associated with them.

Historically, the development of tourism in Fiji has been shaped by the dominance of foreign capital, and today foreign investors continue to play significant and influential roles in the development of the industry. The ability of the industry to recover relatively quickly in the aftermath of the 1987 and 2000 coups is largely attributed to the presence of foreign companies, whose financial resources and marketing networks enabled a rapid response to the adverse impacts of the coups and assisted the recovery. The willingness of the tourism industry leaders to cooperate with the post-coup administrations is manifest in the formation of the private–public partnership, the Tourism Action

Group in the aftermath of 1987 coups and again immediately after the 2000 coup. The TAG model was effective in mobilizing resources to arrest the decline of visitor arrivals. This partnership model can provide a useful forum for addressing critical issues such as land problems and disputes, drug and sex tourism, and other factors that relate to sustainable tourism development. It is interesting that the tourism industry is emerging as a symbol of the economic success of the Fijians and the Fijian nationalism associated with it. The industry is also increasingly perceived as benefiting the Fijians more than any other group, and therefore promoting and protecting the industry, particularly in times of crises, fit well with Fijian nationalist sentiments. The coups of 1987 and 2000 were justified by Fijian militants and nationalists as protecting Fijian interests against Indo-Fijian domination. It is therefore satisfying for Fijian nationalists and post-coup Fijian administrations to claim that the economic recovery has been led by the tourism industry and has had little to do with the contribution of the Indo-Fijians.

These nationalist sentiments are reflected in the post-coup Fijian administrations' policies and their commitment to the tourism sector recovery immediately following the coups. This is particularly significant in light of the fact that no such support was extended to other sectors of the economy. In addition to giving the FVB extra funds to assist in recovery efforts following the coups, the marketing budget of the Bureau has steadily increased since the coups of 1987. Contrary to Teye's (1989) conclusion that coups and resultant political instability create weak NTOs, in the case of Fiji the FVB has come out financially stronger and is also recognized by the government and the private sector as effective. While the coups and the resultant political instability created a financially stronger and effective NTO in Fiji, they have had a substantial detrimental long-term impact on the growth of visitor arrivals.

The combined impact of the coups has undoubtedly resulted in the likely loss of at least six years of growth in visitor arrivals. This setback has adversely affected investment in the tourism sector and tourism product development and delivery. Both private-sector and total investment have declined substantially as a percentage of GDP since the coups of 1987 – to the extent that the new investment may hardly be replacing depreciation of the capital stock, resulting in a steady decline of the capital stock of the economy. This has serious implications for the productive capacity of the economy and creates an unpromising climate for capital in flows.

One year after the first general election in 1999 under the 1997 constitution, investor confidence was on the rise and investors seemed bullish about the future prospects of the Fiji economy, as indicated by the relatively large amount of approved investment at the time of the 2000 coup. Political stability, respect for the rule of law and good governance based on the principles of democracy remain the fundamental prerequisites for investor confidence, particularly in small island economies like Fiji with limited resources, a small domestic market, low production capacities, and a high cost structure, among other inhibiting factors. A critical challenge for the people of Fiji in the coming years is to create a socio-political and economic environment that is conducive to attracting quality investment, not only in the tourism sector but in all other sectors of the economy.

The tourism sector in Fiji is dominated by foreign investors, who are in a powerful position to influence government policies towards provision of the infrastructure and services that accord with their profit-seeking interests rather than towards a more balanced regional development that will benefit a greater number of local communities. In the 1970s the government's priority was to provide modern infrastructure and services to the western side of Viti Levu, which was seen by tourism developers as having greater potential for tourism development than the eastern side of Viti Levu and most regions of Vanua Levu. However, tourism development did benefit the local residents of western Viti Levu by providing them with access to developed infrastructure and services that might not have been possible otherwise and that are still lacking on the other side of the island. It is evident that tourism development in Fiji has been influenced by tourism developers and operators to maximize their returns on investment. Their strong influence on government's policies, combined with the lack of an active role by government in directing tourism investment and development, has resulted in unbalanced regional development of the tourism industry. In addition to this unbalanced development, the government's failure to direct tourism development through such measures as the establishment of tourism development zones and precincts has also resulted in *ad hoc* tourism developments, with tourism facilities isolated from each other. The absence of a cluster of tourism facilities (as in tourism precincts) may have compromised the competitiveness of Fiji a destination in the South Pacific region. Since the coups of 1987, the Fiji government has adopted market-led growth policies through deregulation and export-orientation. Accordingly, while gradual public-sector reforms have been implemented, no such reforms have been made XC to the NLTB, which administers the native land and the land tenure system, X to make it more responsive to market signals. The lack of such reforms has X adversely affected the overall growth of the Fiji economy, including the tourism C sector. It has also been claimed that land issues and problems have in part contributed to political instability in Fiji. Moreover, the communal nature of land ownership and the traditional expectations associated with it have been shown to be incompatible with modern contractual lease obligations and have been the main source of land disputes in the tourism industry (which undoubtedly have had an adverse impact on the long-term growth of the industry). Paradoxically, the slow growth of the tourism industry due to political instability and the land problems may have benefited Fiji by putting less strain on the environment, marine and land ecosystems, and on socio-cultural fabric of local communities. A free market for land and the strong private sector in the tourism industry, combined with the government's lack of direct involvement in directing tourism development, would have resulted in more rapid tourism growth with its consequence of greater stress on those important resources and values.

The Fiji tourism industry is at a crossroads. Fiji can articulate a vision for long-term sustainable growth of the industry, first, by finding a solution to the land problems and disputes; second, by government playing an active role in influencing and directing tourism development to enhance the competitiveness of the product and ensure more balanced regional development; and third, by protecting the environment and ecosystems and minimizing adverse impacts on local communities. The WTO planning model could be a useful model for sustainable tourism development that meets the needs and aspirations of local communities as well as those of international visitors.

Finally, addressing problems with an *ad hoc* and piece-meal approach may bring short- term respite, but the long-term growth of Fiji's tourism industry, and indeed of its economy as a whole, requires lasting solutions to the apparently conflicting socio-economic and political demands of the two major ethnic groups: the indigenous Fijians and the Indo-Fijians

10

Ecotourism in Southeast Asia

Introduction

Tourism is often promoted as the world's fastest growing industry and ecotourism is quoted as the fastest growing component of this. The tourism potential to natural areas is vast. Reflecting the explosive growth in global ecotourism there has been a large number of ecotourism organisations and centres established.

Organisations include The Ecotourism Society (TES), a surrogate global ecotourism association which is based in the United States of America and The Ecotourism Association of Australia (EAA). Centres include The Institute of Ecotourism, Srinakharinwirot University, Bangkok, Thailand; the World Travel and Tourism Research Centre (WRTTERC) in Oxford, England; the International Centre for Ecotourism Research (ICER) Gold Coast, Australia; and the Centre for Ecotourism, at the University of Pretoria South Africa. Tourism, and in particular ecotourism, is growing rapidly in Indonesia, Malaysia and Thailand. Now many other South East Asian nations such as Brunei, Cambodia, Myanmar and Vietnam are poised to benefit from the emerging popularity of ecotourism.

Ecotourism has been defined as tourism and recreation that is both nature-based and sustainable (Lindberg and McKercher 1997). It is a subset of natural area tourism and may combine elements of both nature based tourism and adventure travel. However, it is also characterised by a number of other features-notably its educative element and conservation supporting practice. There are five key principles which are fundamental to ecotourism. They are that ecotourism is nature-based, ecologically sustainable, environmentally educative, locally beneficial and generates tourist satisfaction. The first three characteristics are considered to be essential for a product to be considered 'ecotourism' while the last two characteristics are viewed as being desirable for all forms of tourism.

Ecotourism has the potential to be a major market segment to be targeted for the expansion and promotion of nature based tourism resources within the countries of South East Asia. It has come to signify an attractive investment proposition especially in countries at a growing stage of development. Within developing countries it is estimated to earn US$12 billion from an overall US$55 billion in tourism earnings.

Therefore ecotourism, can provide the economic basis for the conservation and protection of natural areas. Moreover, since many of the natural attractions are located away from urban areas it has the potential for regional revitalisation. An indication of the commitment to ecologically sustainable tourism within the region is shown by the fact that over 500 South East Asian companies exhibited at the 18th annual Association of South East Asian Nation's (ASEAN) forum on tourism held on the Philippine Island of Cebu in January 1998. At the conference the three ASEAN travel associations, the Tourism Association, the Federation of Travel Associations and the Hotel and Restaurant Association, met to discuss plans to improve the quality and sustainability of tourism within the region.

In addition, some South East Asian countries are to be commended for the legislation introduced in order to ensure the protection of the environment and organisations such as the Pacific Asia Travel Association (PATA) were amongst the first to develop an environmental ethic. The principles of sustainable tourism are to a large extent expressed in PATA's charter and include strategies for tourism development which benefits both the host country and population. Thus ecotourism is based on the premise espoused by PATA that environmentally responsible policies fully respect the natural and cultural identity of tourism resources. However, the development of ecotourism has not occurred without difficulties. Frequent problems associated with the advancement of ecotourism within these countries include the lack of infrastructure development, the need for, and adequacy of, personnel training, the implementation of plans, and political instability. This paper now addresses the impacts of ecotourism operations within selected ASEAN countries, focusing on Thailand, and poses the question 'is South East Asian ecotourism environmentally appropriate?'

Ecotourism is South East Asia

Issues of ecotourism development in a range of ASEAN countries including Indonesia, Malaysia, Brunei and Vietnam is now illustrated through a series of selected vignettes.

Indonesia

Tourism is of great importance to the Indonesian economy and has been accorded progressively higher priority in the Repelites or five year plans. It is postulated that Indonesia brought ecoawareness to the South East Asian region with the 1991 PATA conference 'Enrich the Environment' being hosted in Bali. Traditionally tourism within Indonesia has been highly concentrated focusing on Bali and Jakarta. Now the country is promoting ecotourism as a major income earner with the government's current policy being to expand tourism from the nation's traditional, developed sites into remote and sometimes sensitive areas.

For example, Komodo National Park in eastern Indonesia, the nation's oldest park and home of the world's largest monitor lizard, the Komodo Dragon, is keenly touting for tourists. The island is becoming increasingly popular as an ecotourism destination and the number of visitors has risen from around 3,400 per year in the late 1970s to over 12,000 per year in the early 1990s.

Unfortunately there is a tendency for investors to capitalise on the ecotourism market regardless of whether or not it is being practiced responsibly. This is illustrated by comparisons of tourism developments in Kuta Bali and Kuta Lombok. Both islands foster ecotourism but have not found an adequate balance amongst the elements of environmental, economic and social sustainability. Wall's (1996) summation of ecotourism development in the two destinations presents an interesting contrast. He concludes that tourism development has taken place rapidly, but haphazardly in Kuta, Bali in the absence of firm planning guidelines. As a result, the environment appears to be suffering many adverse consequences. In contrast the more detailed planning in Kuta, Lombok has encouraged greater environmental protection. However, he warns that there will be difficult challenges in providing an adequate water supply in the relatively remote and dry area if substantial development occurs along the southern coast of the island. Thus Indonesia is facing increased demand for ecotourism and appears to be keen to meet this demand, whatever the cost.

Malaysia

Another country which is progressively marketing ecotourism is Malaysia. As hosts of the XVI Commonwealth Games later this year Malaysia has launched a year-long global tourism promotion aimed at raising awareness of the country's new sport and leisure facilities. However, most of its attractions are nature based and ecotourism is being heavily promoted. Malaysia's tropical rainforests are amongst the oldest and most diverse ecosystems in the world. Current tourist visitation and consequent adverse environmental and social impacts are not a problem, but this is a situation which will have to be monitored especially with the government's aspiration that by the year 2000 there should be one tourist per head of population.

The Seventh Malaysian Plan is designed to boost the country's tourism industry by popularising the country's considerable natural attractions. The plan promotes ecotourism which is particularly targeted for intensive development. Eligible projects include the construction of new accommodation and recreational facilities. This strategy focuses on eight tourist destinations most of which are in natural areas. They include Langkawi, Penang, Pangkor, Taman Negara, Malacca, Sarawak and Mount Kinabalu. The plan emphasises capitalising on existing attractions and promoting the surrounding tropical hinterlands. One example occurs in Batang Ai, Sarawak. Here the development of ecotourism has created employment opportunities for the local villagers as well as helping to reduce the hunting pressure on exotic wildlife.

Tourism Malaysia is heavily promoting Sarawak and Sabah as nature and adventure tourism destinations. Recent research at Bako National Park, an established ecotourism destination in Sarawak, clearly identifies some of the negative and positive impacts of ecotourism (Chin, Moore & Dowling In Preparation). A survey of 210 visitors indicates that the more common adverse environmental impacts observed includes litter, erosion and damage to vegetation. Specific issues are litter along the beach, soil erosion and vegetation damage along walk trails, the provocation of wildlife, and a lack of enforcement of park regulations. Most visitors strongly support the management strategies of educating visitors more about conservation; providing additional directional signs and maps; limiting overall number of visitors; limiting areas of forest use; and limiting the number of people in a group. Activities participated in by most respondents include photography, hiking, sightseeing and observation of wildlife. This study indicates that adverse ecotourism impacts are apparent at Bako National Park, and visitors generally notice their occurrence. The study has important implications not only for Bako's park managers, but also for managers of other national parks in Sarawak because it represents one of the first efforts to address conservation management based on the outcomes of nature tourism.

Robert Basiuk, the managing director of the Kuching-based Borneo Adventure, feels that ecotour operators should focus on providing good guides. He suggests that there is a need to raise the minimum standard to ensure that such tours are operated in a manner commensurate with the principles of ecotourism. He suggests that the protection of the natural environment is important if products are to be promoted for the long term. A similar view is shared by David Gill from the National Park and Wildlife Office of Miri's Forest Department. He believes that Sarawak should make it the highest priority to conserve what it has, in particular the rainforest which is its greatest asset.

Sabah is also being promoted as an ecotourism destination with the recent completion of a number of new accommodation facilities. For example, last year Shangri-La opened a second, five star hotel in Sabah, located on the edge of the rainforest 40 minutes drive from the capital, Kota Kinabalu. The 330 room hotel has an 18 hole golf course and its own 64 hectare wildlife reserve Sabah's in bound operation also offers soft adventure activities such as natural history tours, including trips to the Sandakan orangutan sanctuary in the northeast of the island.

However, despite the growth of ecotourism in Malaysia concerns for its future have been voiced by Geoffrey Davison, a conservationist with the World Wide Fund for Nature, Malaysia. He states that Malaysia has about 20 ecotourism sites all of which are so over-used that new sites will have to be developed otherwise ecotourism will become unsustainable. He describes the attention given to ecotourism as slight and patchy and suggests that only a few operators have a credible ecotourism record. Operators have been slow to develop new ecotourism products mainly due to economic constraints and lack of expertise. In addition profit margins derived from ecotours in the country are slim. To minimise costs some operators have not invested in the research and development of new products.

Brunei

Tourism in Brunei is still in its infancy and it has not yet reached the level of development found in Sarawak and Sabah. However, ecotourism offers the country the promise of sustainable tourism development through its relatively low impact use of natural resources. Brunei's newly established tourism unit is currently positioning the country as the gateway to Borneo as a whole because it is considered too small to sell itself as a holiday destination in its own right. Brunei is beginning to work with its neighbouring states of Sabah and Sarawak to jointly promote Borneo and it is the only destination on the island with direct flights from Europe. The case for fostering ecotourism development in Brunei is suggested as being "particularly attractive and compelling". He states that it fits in well with the national policy of keeping the country's land covered by about 80 percent forest. These forests are gazetted for conservation purposes but have much potential for ecotourism which could also generate economic benefits for the indigenous people. These include establishing markets for their jungle produce and handicrafts and providing services as transport operators, porters and guides.

In Brunei the development of ecotourism has been spearheaded by the Forestry Department and various blocks have been converted for recreation. The Batu Apoi Forest Reserve has been converted into a national park. A number of 50 metre high observation towers have been built which are linked by some of the longest aerial walkways in the world. In Brunei Bay and in the Belait District additional walkways have been built over mangrove swamps. Observation platforms have been erected in Batang Duri and the S. Liang Arboretum Forest Reserve and wooden chalets have been built at the beach park in Pantai Sri Kenangan, Tutong. The parks are small and are unable to provide a wide range of ecotourism activities thus giving credence to the argument for the establishment of large integrated nature reserves with multi-faceted facilities for visitors. However, it must be noted that to replace forest production by nature based ecotourism will not necessarily guarantee sustainability of the natural, cultural and economic environments.

Vietnam

The Socialist Republic of Vietnam has significant potential for tourism development and it is rich in natural and cultural tourism assets. Its new economic policy of 'doi moi' or 'openness' is facilitating considerable tourism development and it is anticipated that the country will attract about 1.5 million international visitors by the year 2000.

In 1991 a tourism development master plan for the Vietnam was published by the World Tourism Organisation (WTO) in collaboration with a United Nations Development Plan. The government has recognised the importance of the development of tourism by making it a priority industry for national development. This has involved preparing a new master plan focussing on infrastructure requirements, education and the marketing of tourism. Vietnam has certain advantages as an international tourism destination through its central geographical location in South East Asia combined with its ability to cater for tourists all year round. One of the new tourism concepts proposed is 'Vietnam by train'. This will disperse tourism over many regions of the country with minimal environmental impact and low infrastructure costs. In the future it is also proposed to build rail links with China and Cambodia.

Tourism development is being concentrated in and around four main economic zones. Northern Vietnam is to developed as the staging area for excursions to Ha Long Bay, with its famous scenery, beaches and ocean for cruising. The southern part of the central zone has greater potential for ecotourism. There is an abundance of natural resources favouring coastal resort development and consequent nature based activities in the terrestrial (mountain climbing and rafting) and marine (boating and recreational fishing) environments. The preservation of the environment is identified as a key issue for this area. For example, there is a need to prevent forest destruction, the pollution of the Perfume River (which flows through Hue) and the Han River (which flows through Danang) and in general the pollution of water, air and the coastline. Southern Vietnam will particularly foster ecotourism based on the central node of Ho Chi Minh City. It appears that the Vietnamese government is committed to develop tourism along sustainable guidelines. However, the achievement of this development will be difficult in light of the urgent need for Vietnam to earn foreign exchange and because of its limited resources and knowledge. The issue of sustainability therefore hinges on the political will of the government and the ability of the tourism sector to learn from other countries in the region which have developed sustainable types of tourism.

Thailand

Thailand is promoting itself as an international destination and the gateway to other Indo China countries, such as neighbouring Vietnam, Myanmar, Cambodia, Malaysia and Singapore. The government is hoping that its current 'Amazing Thailand' campaign will attract approximately

18 million visitors over the next two years. As part of the promotion cultural performances are being held across the country during 1998 and 1999. Today Thailand is at the forefront of ecotourism development within the South East Asian region with the release of its national ecotourism strategy (TAT 1995). Further enunciation of their interest is demonstrated in the holding of a large number of ecotourism conferences within the past three years. These include two international ecotourism conferences hosted by The Institute of Ecotourism Srinakharinwirot University Bangkok held in February 1995 and July 1996 and the New Zealand-Thailand Ecotourism Forum held in Bangkok July 1997. As part of the 'ecopush' the Tourism Authority of Thailand (TAT) is assisting in the design of new hotels to minimise environmental impact. Other measures already undertaken include electrifying Bangkok's tuk-tuks and installing water purification plants to clear Pattaya's beaches. The push for ecotourism development in Thailand now has the country being marketed as three distinct destination regions-mountains in the north, culture in the centre and beaches in the south. Ecotourism issues in each of the three zones is now presented followed by a specific focus on Phuket.

Northern

Lisu Lodge in northern Thailand is approximately one hour's drive from Chiang Mai. It has been upheld as an exemplar in ecotourism building design, environmental interpretation and community involvement (Muqbil 1994). Established by John Davies the lodge plays a central role in the creation of low-density, high-quality ecotours with minimal environmental impact. It promotes exotic experiences for ecotourists while providing the Lisu hill tribe people with an economic alternative to fanning as well as a renewed interest and pride in their culture. Park entrance fees have the potential to contribute directly to management expenses, but are currently channelled into the Thai government's general revenues. Doi Inthanon, a national park, world renowned for its 'birding' or 'du nok' now has a two tiered fee system, where foreigners pay a higher amount US$ 1.00 compared to $0.20 per person approximately). Recent research in the park indicates that 80% of tourists state they are willing to pay more for conservation.

Birding is a popular form of ecotourism but it has the potential to cause adverse environmental impacts. The possibility of the harassment of wildlife is a negative outcome of ecotourism development. For example, some birders attract birds by whistling or playing a tape recorded song, which brings them out into the open to confront the 'intruder'. However, when used too often, this strategy may cause birds undue stress. Other environmental issues include trampling, litter and air pollution. Attempts are being made to mitigate these, for example, through the construction of a board-walk around the summit of Dol Inthanon and through increased tourist awareness of litter and pollution. One of the key elements of ecotourism is that it should be locally beneficial. Within Doi Inthanon there are 600 villages located in the park and the residents earn their living by growing rice and cash crops and through collecting plants and fuel wood for personal use or sale. If hill tribes can benefit economically from ecotourism they may support habitat protection initiatives and depend less on unsustainable uses of park resources. However, according to Jean Michaud from Montreal University after a village has been overexposed the tour guides move onto newer, more 'authentic' territories. In a similar vein it has been suggested that ecotourism may exacerbate social and cultural impacts by intensifying the degree of contact between hosts and tourists.

Central

Today 13% of the land base of Thailand is environmentally protected. However, efficient management of the protected areas is constrained by low budgets. Attempts to alleviate this have been made by the construction of resorts within natural areas to create funds. This has not always been successful as demonstrated by occurrences at Khao Yai National Park. In the late 1980s TAT constructed a resort and golf course inside the park. The finding of dead deer in the park which had eaten golf balls, and incidents of elephants killed by falling off steep cliffs after new roads in the park obstructed their normal feeding routes, finally led to the closing down of these projects.

One of the benefits of ecotourism is that it acts as an exemplar for tourism through the promotion of sustainable development principles, especially in the area of the 'greening' of tourism. The Thai Hotel Association is urging its members to 'turn green'. It has conducted a seminar series on the economic benefits of being 'environmentally friendly' and it has implemented a 'Green Leaf' program. The Electricity Generating Authority of Thailand has offered interest free finance to re-equip buildings with energy saving equipment. The Tourism Authority of Thailand also helps in the design of new hotels to minimise adverse environmental impacts.

The Marriott Royal Garden Riverside Bangkok and the Royal

Garden Resort Hua Hin are exemplars within the field of green practices. The former has an eco code of ethics and in addition fosters environmentally friendly practices outside the immediate hotel environment. Its 'Preserve the Kingdom' environmental awareness campaign raises public awareness of some of Thailand's endangered species.

Southern

Another model in the field of ecotourism in Thailand is Sea Canoe. It is the only internationally acclaimed eco development laboratory applying innovative economic and management principles to conservation-based, locally owned rural development. Sea Canoe International began operating canoe expeditions in Phuket after years of operating open sea expeditions on the Pacific Ocean's coastlines. It has a strong environmental protection policy and the company "talks environmentalism to three publics-customers, staff and the host community". The company attributes its success to its commitment to the environment and its requirement of maintaining low tourist volumes. Another key element is Sea Canoe's desire to creatively seek out ecotourism experiences and hence business opportunities.

Siam Safari's Eco-Nature Tours was the first specialist ecotour company to be formed in Phuket. It was founded by Lerd Sun Khomkrit in 1989 and it organises 1-4 day safaris in Southern Thailand. The one-day Phuket Island Eco-Nature Safari by four-wheel drive Land Rover takes visitors off the beaten track, giving four to six people at a time a variety of insights into traditional rural life on the island. The two-day Tropical Rainforest Explorer tour encompasses Khao Sok National Park, 150 kilometres northeast of Phuket on the mainland. The trek in the rainforest with knowledgeable guides offers an opportunity to observe an environment with some of the greatest diversity of life forms on the planet.

In 1996 TAT invested a large sum of money towards developing facilities at Khao Sok National Park. Despite the interest in Khao Sok National Park by the TAT concerns have been voiced over the lack of apparent control or involvement from the National Parks Division and conservation groups. There are few plans for initiating scientific research or environmental or conservation programs in the park. To date there has been very little research carried out on the flora and fauna of Khao Sok, similarly in other protected areas in Thailand. However, if we do not know and understand the resource we cannot hope to manage it effectively. In addition if the intricacies and fragile life systems of the park are not understood by scientists then it stands to reason that the ecotourist will not either. To overcome this it has been suggested that ecotourism provides a ready made vehicle for the Royal Forest Department's National Parks Division and the TAT to work together to protect the environment, increase the scientific knowledge of the area, and to work with the local community.

Phuket

The tourist destination of Phuket is a microcosm of the issues affecting tourism and the environment in Thailand. It has a history of a litany of tourism induced environmental problems but also includes some sound examples of tourism-environment symbiosis. For example, in 1992 the Laguna Beach Resort located in Phuket was awarded the International Hotel Association's Environmental Award due to its transformation of a polluted tin mine into an ecosystem of indigenous vegetation which utilizes recycled water, organic waste and treated sewage.

The International Hotel & Resorts Association 1996 Green Hotelier of the year was awarded to Peter McAlpine then manager at the Phuket Yacht Club Hotel & Beach Resort. McAlpine's efforts reached beyond the walls of the resort to the wider area of Phuket, a once pristine island threatened by overdevelopment, mismanagement and a rapid increase in tourism. His first step was to raise the environmental awareness of the Phuket Yacht Club's 245 employees, organising staff beach cleanups and tree plantings. Gradually, energy and waste reduction programs were implemented. He organised environmental workshops at the hotel and in surrounding villages. With the help of two other hoteliers, he held a Bike-A-Thon a cycling fundraiser.

Hotels in Phuket have now agreed to accept a set of minimum standards for environmental protection. To embrace the flow of ideas McAlpine hopes to implement a formal structure for ecotourism in Thailand through a system of regional councils. A further initiative is to educate primary school teachers in Phuket on environmentally friendly practices through workshops with follow up seminars . Largely due to McAlpine's efforts Phuket has agreed to accept a set of minimum standards for environmental protection and a resource management act to protect new environmental initiatives is on the government's agenda .

A major survey of the tourism-environment relationship in Phuket has been undertaken in the western bays. This study indicates that increased tourism development causes adverse environmental impacts often leading to a complete alteration of the natural environment. However, the increase in tourism pressure continues. For example UK long haul specialist Silk Cut Travel has expanded its programme to the Far East with the launch of its 1998 'Hotels of Character' . Over the past two years client feedback has confirmed that the real appeal of the programme is for the character in the hotels featured combined with locational individuality, management and atmosphere. In Thailand, the operator has re-introduced its resort of Krabi, which it dropped two years ago, and has added hotels in the resorts of Phuket and Koh Samui. Phi Phi Island and northern Thailand itineraries featuring Chiang Mai, Chiang Rai and the Golden Triangle remain in the programme.

An important feature of the tourism industry in Thailand is its close association with ecosystems which have proven to be of only marginal value for other forms of economic activity. These include the mountain regions of the north as well as the coastal areas of the south. Parnwell's 1993 study of Ko Samui provides an illustration of some of the environmental pressures which have been associated with the relatively unplanned and uncontrolled growth of tourism. Although very small in size the island is estimated to host a projected 1.1 million visitors annually within two years. Ko Samui has been vigorously promoted as a major tourism destination by both private sector firms and the Tourism Authority of Thailand. As a consequence the environment is under increasing pressure from the tourism boom and the coast line has been changed dramatically. The coral reefs and their associated marine life have come under considerable pressure from scuba-diving and souvenir-hunting. This has caused considerable damage to the reefs. So has the large volume of untreated effluent which is discharged into the sea from the island. It is not tourism in itself that is destructive, but rather it is a consequence of the lack of tourism planning and management.

Discussion

The above examples indicate that Thailand's record of fostering environmentally sensitive tourism development is increasing. However, in addition to the problems cited earlier, others have been noted by Gill and Satyanarayan (1995). They state that with barely 15 to 20 percent of forest area remaining in Thailand the increasing demands on them made by ecotourism are now causing intrusions into the last few patches of 'unopened' territories. They conclude that Thailand may be treading into dangerous territory as watershed areas become exposed and polluted, natural forests are destroyed, and the remaining biodiversity of the country is lost. For example, on Ko Taen the local community has established a conservation club to 'conserve the unity of the people and to control the island's tourism to be real ecotourism'. The theme of the 7th PATA Adventure Travel and Ecotourism Conference and Mart held in Balikpapan, East Kalimantan, Indonesia from 15-18 January 1995 was Nature and Adventure Tourism: Megatrend or Niche. A key outcome was that in order for ecotourism to remain environmentally and socially responsible in future, it will be necessary to limit tour group size and frequency. Therefore, ecotourism will always remain a 'niche' market. Another major issue is the problem of 'ecopirates', that is, companies which copy existing responsible tourism products, but in a non-responsible manner. Such copies typically offer lower prices, inferior experiences, and detrimental environmental and social impacts.

The advancement of ecotourism in South East Asia has obviously had positive and negative impacts on the natural and cultural environments. From a positive perspective ecotourism fosters a better appreciation of natural environments and their intrinsic and economic worth for protection and conservation. It also provides greater exposure both for the public and governing institutions to nature and conservation and it also has the potential to motivate the designation of natural areas for conservation and protection. On the other hand pressures originating from ecotourism can and do result in degeneration of the very ecosystems on which they depend. Impacts can be particularly severe when there is visitor intrusion where there had been none previously. Another important, and often overlooked, factor is that local communities involved in the industry may not have sufficient knowledge to organise a conservation program involving visitor management techniques. Hence they may prioritise visitor satisfaction over the needs of the natural resource.

In the case of the South East Asian countries extra pressure will be brought to bear to hasten development in order to build up foreign exchange earnings particularly in the light of the current economic crises. Tourism to these countries has never been cheaper hence it is envisaged that there will be a large influx of Australian, American and European travellers. Demand could well outweigh supply and hence put unsustainable pressure on the environment.

The fostering of cruise ship tourism within the region is viewed as one way of bringing in foreign exchange earnings without the necessity of having the infrastructure in place and with minimal environmental impact. Robost growth is forecast for the cruise industry between now and the year 2000, with the Asia Pacific region rapidly gaining market share. It is the vision of the Singapore government that it become a cruise hub. From here can be generated an exciting multi-destinational ecotourism development program taking in many of the countries of South East Asia. Since the region has so much to offer naturally, historically and culturally.

Conclusion

Earlier this decade it was clear that tourism in Thailand had developed at the expense of its environment and the question was asked "is Thailand's tourism boom environmentally sustainable?". The question has as much validity today and can be widen to include the whole SE Asian region. Environmental issues in Thailand are still a pressing concern, but despite important gains such as the 1992 Environmental Act, the incapacity of provincial governmental bodies to enforce legislation against polluters and illegal builders in big resorts like Phuket Island and Pattaya is still evident.

The extent of ecotourism impacts depends on their efficient detection and identification (either through baseline monitoring of the natural resource or through indicators) and subsequent management actions. Impact identification requires some form of baseline data or indicators to determine acceptable limits of the impacts/changes to the natural environment. Resolving these impacts requires the formulation of management strategies that are able to maintain them at a level that is acceptable for both nature conservation and nature based recreation.

Tourism and the natural environment can form a symbiotic relationship. This can be achieved by developing purpose built tourist resort complexes; investment in and careful design of tourism infrastructure; and the hardening of sites to carry more tourists whilst conserving the natural environment. Thus there is a strong case for promoting 'sustainable' forms of tourism such 'ecotourism', as a way of fostering harmony between people and nature through tourism. Unfortunately, such principles would appear to be at variance with the economic arguments in favour of mass tourism

Finally, it is suggested that ecotourism development in South East Asia should not be pursued as the panacea for the economic woes caused by the 'Asian Crisis', but rather viewed as a tool for fostering the sustainable advancement of local communities, in a manner which is commensurate with sound environmental practice, cultural preservation and economic wellbeing.

In this way the development of ecotourism in South East Asia will advance tourism that is appropriate for the region when based on the principles of community participation and environmental sustainability, a philosophy advocated and pursued by the Thailand Environmental Institute (TEI 1996).

The Beauty and Danger of Ecotourism

Forward by BCN's Director Bernd Cordes

One of the benefits of working for BCN is that we sometimes have the opportunity to go to places we otherwise would never get a chance to visit. And, because of our relationships with our NGO partners and the community members, we have access to information, conversations and insights into local conditions that we would otherwise not get. That's what happened to Diane Russell, a former BCN Senior Program Officer who was based in Fiji. In 1998, she visited a BCN-funded conservation project in Makira, Solomon Islands. One part of the project there is to develop a sustainable, community-based ecotourism venture. So, she took the trip, but with a dual purpose. She went as a tourist, along for the guided ride through the forest and bringing her daughter with her. But it wasn't all play. She also went as a program officer partly responsible for the conservation and enterprise development work being done at the site. As she walked the trails and visited the villages, Diane kept notes as a tourist and as a partner in conservation, noting the good measure of success the business has had (e.g., Conde Nast travel magazine deemed this a stellar ecotourism destination and experience in the South Pacific), as well as its share of difficulties. Below are her notes, observations and experiences, which should be of interest to others doing similar work.

Trekking the Highlands of Makira Island, Solomon Islands

Ecotourism is often viewed as an ideal solution to the conservation and development dilemma: how to balance human use of biological resources with the protection of critical habitats and species. The concept is particularly attractive in the pacific islands where tourism is a dominant industry and local communities control their land. But what is the reality? What are the risks to habitats and to the local communities involved? Does ecotourism bring tangible benefits to a community? Is it truly compatible with conservation goals?

We examine these questions through the lens of my experience on a guided trek through the highlands of Makira, Solomon Islands in April 1998. Makira's Bauro communities, Conservation International (CI) and the Solomon Islands Development Trust, (SIDT), working together as the Conservation in Development (CID) Program organize this trek. The program is dedicated to conservation of the biodiversity of this unique island and the well being of the communities. In addition to the ecotour, the program also helps to manage a ngali nut *(Canarium indicum)* oil enterprise, and sponsors health, community-based monitoring and environmental education activities.

The Makira trek brings together a superb natural environment, cultural enhancement, appropriate cash benefits, and strong links to conservation. At present, it is a beautiful experience. But I encountered danger at every turn. The difficulties of setting up a sustainable enterprise in a remote location such as Makira cannot be underestimated. And community-based conservation is a process of negotiation and learning that often shreds the patience of local staff and leadership.

Background

Makira Island, also known as San Cristobal Island, is 3090 sq. km: 139 km long by 40 km wide. Mountains run like a spine down the island's centre: the highest point reaches 1040 m, then falls steeply to the sea along its southern shore. Many rivers penetrate the island in roughly parallel lines every two to five kilometres. Makira has more inland swamps—and saltwater crocodiles—than any other island in the Solomon Islands. Its coast is the only part of the Solomons where the rare olive, or Pacific Ridley, turtle is known to visit and nest. Because Makira Island was isolated for long stretches of time during periods of high sea level, a wide variety of unique plants and animals evolved. For example, 12 of its 70 resident species of birds are endemic, as are two tree species, both figs *(Ficus cristobalensis* and *Ficus illiberalis)*. This uniqueness highlights the importance of preserving Makira's forest habitat.

In 1992, the Central Bank of Solomon Islands estimated that all reserves of lowland forest would be cut down within eight to ten years. This unsustainable rate of extraction stems on the government side mainly from the desperate need to garner foreign exchange and perceived lack of alternatives. The reasons for landowner agreement to logging concessions include the desire for cash and status on the part of "big men." Many Makira communities have already succumbed to the relatively large amounts of cash that the logging companies offer people in order to cut high-grade timber on their land. To resist these threats, the CID program established Makira's first conservation area, which consists of approximately 63,000 hectares of largely undisturbed indigenous vegetation, representing the second largest protected area in the South Pacific. Since the early 1990s, the program has been working with the Bauro communities to define the area and to identify enterprises whose viability is linked to the need to conserve the area's biodiversity.

In 1995, the CID consortium of CI, SIDT and the Maruia Society received a $US347, 574 grant from the Biodiversity Conservation Network (BCN) to support these activities, particularly to assist in the enterprise and monitoring work.

Community

Makira has four main language groups. The ecotour involves people from the coast up to the highlands of central Makira, all of whom are Bauro speakers. The Bauro have been considered to be the most isolated and conservative of the Makira groups. In 1995, a CID survey found that the communities were cash poor and, though "isolated," experienced environmental problems due to more intensive use of resources. Seventy percent of households surveyed reported no cash income during the past month, and only six out of 320 households interviewed had access to salaried income. Few families (16%) had trade licenses and these involved petty trade only. The estimated 4-6% rate of population growth and use of destructive hunting and fishing techniques contribute to declining fertility of garden lands, and disappearance of river fish and some bird species.

Highlights of the Trek

On April 12, 1998, my seven-year old daughter and I joined a group of six people on a trek across the riverbeds and up the steep hills of the central Bauro highlands. Our young guides met us at the end of the road that leads from the airport — the only road on Makira. Porters took the heavy packs and started off, so that they would be there when we got to our first stop. The guides immediately put us at ease by chatting and telling us what we would expect. Their training and experience with tourists was evident. After a stop at the village of Mato, we climbed up and down two steep hills to get to a lovely bend in the western tributary of the Ravo river known as the Ravorighi, or "small

Ravo." A trail from the river led to a leaf house with a raised platform that served as our home for the night. The land for this rest house, in the area called Na'ara, is owned by ecotour manager John Waihuru's family. John and his family came down to meet us, to cook food and give us information about what we would be doing in the days to come.

The following day, after climbing up and down another steep hill, we reached the entry of Hunama village. As fatigued and hungry as the group was, we became highly alert — astonished by our greeting. Upon entry into the village, which had been decorated in flowers and leaves, we were taken to a shaded reviewing stand to drink water and eat fruit. There we had our first serenade by the Hunama pan pipers, led by Dominic, one of our guides. Later, Dominic told us that he borrowed some panpipe melodies from popular and religious songs, but other melodies came from the songs of birds in the forest. We were delighted to hear about this link between the music and the forest.

Our layover day in Hunama was full of laughter, drama, music and feasting. The community had crafted a creative program designed to entertain and teach us about their culture and lifeways. We learned how, in a warrior's education, boys attempt to match their elders in the art of throwing spears. Two lively custom skits concerned the relations between humans and spirits. The village children enjoyed the show as much as the visitors did: they screamed in anticipation and hilarity at the antics of their neighbours and relatives. In contrast to the boisterous acts of the men, the women's groups singing Christian songs were shy and sweet. The visitors also introduced themselves one by one, sang a song or told a table.

We watched demonstrations of traditional arts and crafts, including carving, food preparation, fire making and basket weaving. Villagers laid out the crafts and we purchased several items. A nice touch to the whole stay in Hunama was the presentation of handmade bowls to each of the visitors to use throughout their stay. These carved bowls were identified by the name of the sculptor, and John Waihuru, who hopes to encourage and improve the local artists, marked those chosen in a book. He asked us for detailed comments on the design and construction of the bowls. Months later, when John came to my home in Fiji, he was pleased to see these crafts displayed. As night fell, we gathered in the village commons again. A few kerosene lamps were lit. Beyond the circle of the lamps, the stars blazed with intensity rarely experienced by town dwellers. Seven-year old Eva gazed at a Milky Way she had never before seen so clearly. John Waihuru announced that we would have an evening of music, dance and sharing. He wanted to focus the discussion on conservation and the experiences of the visitors to the community.

But first the dance. Eva found a girl about her age and the two of them danced and ran through the crowd all evening. This freedom of village life — to be part of the festivities that have a role for all ages, to have the run of the village with a pack of children — has all but disappeared in the "developed" world. Virtually the whole village and all the visitors soon surrounded the circle of men and boys forming the panpipe band. The dancing turned carefree and experimental, mixing some pop and local styles.

Between the dances, our talk ranged over many topics. The Hunama people were above all concerned to understand more about conservation and the visitors' experiences. They were anxious to correct any problems and to improve the quality of the tour. Because Eva was the first non-local child to visit the area, they wanted to know if the food was adequate for her. Was the climate all right? What was it like in our place? Why do people want to come to Makira — to Hunama?

We pondered the relation between conservation and health. For one, the altitude of the intact forest in the Hunama area helps prevent the spread of mosquitoes. Hunama was delightfully free of those pests, and the highland dwellers do not contract malaria as frequently as their coastal cousins do. Second, the forest provides medicines. Our guides had pointed out some medicinal plants to us during the trek. The water source flowing from the forested hilltops provides clean water, thus keeping the people relatively free of parasites and other illness. Finally, the abundance of food crops could be attributed to the health of the forest because long garden cycles allow for regeneration of the soil. On day four, we went up the hill and across to Maraone. The visitors' first experience of Maraone began long before they actually saw the village. Where the terrain became extremely rugged, the community had built steps and banisters to guide the visitors. I felt that perhaps they knew I was coming! John Waihuru was surprised and pleased at the work that went into building this infrastructure — a spontaneous innovation on the part of the community.

During our two days in Maraone, we were treated to demonstrations of custom skills, and wonderful skits that had us whooping with laughter. The view from the village, across the conservation area, was stunning. While shy, the people wanted to talk about our experience in their village, and to share stories. Maraone is the home village of some Bauro clans, a bit slower paced and more conservative than Hunama. The beauty of the place revealed itself in the details: the design of our gift beads and headdresses, the delicious ngali nut pudding, the village decorations, and the church service we were invited to attend.

Hauta was our final stop before returning to the coast. To assure a good journey, John and the guides decided to take us up across the ridge rather than down and up the ravines we had traversed to get to Maraone. We trekked through mossy forest with views of the southern "weather coast" of the island. We observed a flying fox, huge spiders perched on their webs across the path, an array of birds, flowers, caterpillars and butterflies. The talk with John and the guides was as fascinating as the forest. I was amazed to find that, unlike my experience of African forests, there are no serious hazards in the forests of Makira: no dangerous snakes, insects or plants. Fire ants, which leave a burn when they land on the skin, are the worst hazards and they are relatively recent arrivals to the highlands. It began to seem like Makira was a Garden of Eden.

In this Eden, however, I learned that there were similar social problems to those I had encountered in Africa. These problems centered on jealousy that can inhibit initiative, and the corollary of finding ways to control the greed of a few individuals that can damage the social fabric. As cash enters a society, and cash values are placed on land, labour and natural products, more aggressive people can take advantage of others to claim land, establish large plantations or overhunt valuable species. In Solomon Islands, the laws governing access to timber and minerals encourage the division of communities, as those who support companies to get access can receive large cash rewards.

Hauta, the small village that harbours John Waihuru and his late wife's vision of a primary school and clinic to serve the Highland communities, perches on a gently sloping hill. Only three families now live in Hauta: John's, Paul Wori, the headmaster of the school, and Ephrem Waraba, a "refugee" from Bagohane. The panpipes greeted us again on arrival, led by the indomitable Dominic, who quickly switched from guide clothes to loincloth. Logging and mining tempt people with large cash payments that may seem on the surface to outweigh the benefits of ecotourism.

John and I sat down to discuss the enterprise. The transparent distribution of benefits is highly important. John records every transaction and together with other community leaders decides upon wage rates and who should get training. The allocation of payments to individuals can involve over 400 transactions for each tour. John's level of involvement in the enterprise is obviously not sustainable and he is training others to take on the financial records. But for the moment, John's active participation is critical to the functioning of the enterprise. He said that even after the money is allocated, people still come to wake him up before the light to ask about money issues. The fifth and final day of the ecotour saw us trekking down from Hauta to the coast. We spent the night right near the beach at Togori rest house, which had been decorated with flowers and paper mobiles. The ecotour was over but the memories remained vivid. All those who went on the tour felt that it was unique — almost magical. This ecotour experience seemed to be ideally suited to the level of economic development of the peoples of the highlands, and had the potential to encourage conservation. In 1997, the community sent away a Malaysian logging company. Village Resource Management Planning, to begin this year, will help people to decide how best to manage their human, biological and financial resources to deal with the intensification trends.

John Waihuru has been thinking deeply about conservation in the highlands:

"In my area, it is a bit complicated because I'm trying to do conservation on customary lands. There is a link with many tribes. If I say 'I want to conserve this area', I have to get agreement first from many different landowners. Conservation is not just one specific thing. It has to do with many things: water, land and air. When you talk about the land, it is complicated. Take a small piece of land like an island. One river starts from the north to the south. All rivers link up with this river. You might get one tribe that wants to conserve the river but on the other hand the other tribe might damage the river. You might want to try to conserve an endemic bird but it flies. Others might disagree. We still have a lot to do."

Beauty

The beautiful aspects of this experience can teach others how to go about setting up a community-based ecotour:

* *A Vision for the Future: Local Ownership*-The program team has a vision and plan for local control over all aspects of the enterprise. This vision is reflected in every decision and activity.

For example, local people without external assistance can maintain the infrastructure of the trek.

* *Planning and Wide Participation*-The planning that went into the tour, from the first germ of an idea, through training, testing and refining each segment, is responsible for the current success. Risks and benefits were carefully weighed, and wide participation encouraged. The community has taken the lead and not let the enterprise overwhelm them.
* *Cultural Pride*-Ecotourism has sparked a revival in local traditional knowledge, particularly by youth who now see the value of this knowledge. The pride in culture is a catalyst for conservation because of the emphasis on low-impact technology and use of forest products.
* *Appropriate Product Development and Training*-The community decided to strictly control the number of treks and tourists on each trek. The guides were given training appropriate to the type of trek and tourist. The enterprise created an important role for young people who might otherwise want to migrate.
* *Conservation Focus*-The program team has kept the focus on conservation. To help John Waihuru understand conservation and enterprise in a broader context, the program got a grant for him to visit New Zealand. His visit to conservation areas, particularly a Maori area, deeply impressed him and gave him a vision of the links between enterprise and conservation that he is transferring to the community.

Danger

This ecotour faces dangers shared by similar ventures. When these dangers are anticipated, strategies can be developed to counter them.

* Market Uncertainties-Any community-based enterprise faces challenges of selling its product unless it links up immediately with a secure market outlet. In the case of the Makira ecotour, there has been relative success in getting tourists to the site due to the diligence of the project team. But the situation is delicate in three respects. One is that the *number* of tourists coming through needs to be limited and timed to the community's needs. Second, the *type* of tourist has to be at least somewhat controlled. The expectations of tourists have to be managed so that they are comfortable with what is being

offered. Finally, the non-local tour operators need to be knowledgeable about both tourism and local community needs.

Strategies Used: Diversify tour operators, use a local in bound operator with knowledge of the area, and bring operators to the community to take the tour.

* ***Misunderstandings and Conflicts-***The case of Bagohane illustrates how local misunderstandings can cut off one part of the community from participation in the enterprise. More severe conflicts are well known in community-based enterprises, particularly those using common-property resources.

Strategies Used: Continual discussion, inclusion of all parties, wide sharing of benefits.

* *Burnout-*We saw how John Waihuru faces enormous pressures in managing the ecotour at the local level — in part because of the emphasis on participation and benefit sharing. Even the guides and porters can be overloaded, literally and figuratively.

Strategies Used: Organize local committees to streamline reporting and benefit sharing, train others to do some of the work.

* *Competition-*Other communities on Makira or other islands will certainly be attracted to the benefits from this type of enterprise. "Copy-catting" can lead to divisiveness, dilution of the quality of the product, health and safety hazards for tourists.

Strategy Used: Tourists who are not part of the ecotour are strongly discouraged on Makira, particularly in going to the highlands; the program has sought ways to complement the trek with a visit to community-based lodges elsewhere in the Solomons.

* *Inadequate Benefits to Counter Threats-*Logging and mining tempt people with large cash payments that may seem on the surface to outweigh the benefits of ecotourism. National policies foster these choices.
* *Strategy Proposed:* Village resource management planning for landowners. CID staff is also passing on information about the real benefits and risks of logging and mining.

Conclusion

Strong leadership, careful planning and a relatively undisturbed and homogenous community contribute to the beauty of the Makira ecotour. Keeping the focus on conservation is critical. But even in the best of circumstances, ecotourism is only a partial solution to the conservation and development dilemma. It is not a magic bullet. A conservation area needs a suite of viable enterprises, supported by strong institutions at the community and national levels. Communities should not be expected to face the dangers to their resources and their livelihoods alone. They need appropriate policies, markets for their products, and links to like-minded people.

For the visitors, the ecotour brings awareness of linkages between community and biodiversity. At its most profound, it is a rite of passage to a more ecologically oriented worldview. Each visitor comes away not only with an experience in a specific community, but a vision to transform global culture. In this way, ecotourism can be a powerful tool for building a more sustainable world.

Community-based Transboundary Ecotourism in the Heart of Borneo

The Kelabit Highlands of Sarawak, Malaysia, and the Kerayan (also called Krayan) Highlands of Kalimantan, Indonesia, are highland plateaus separated by the Apad Wat mountain range in the interior of the island of Borneo. This area is now known around the world as the Heart of Borneo, which references the high-profile transboundary conservation initiative led by the World Wide Fund for Nature (WWF). These highlands offer a combination of experiences that appeal to ecotourists. Due to the altitude of just over 1000 m, the temperature year-round is cool and comfortable, thus more appealing as a trekking destination than areas in Borneo's hot and humid lowlands. Also, the remote, mountainous, and relatively 'unspoilt' (compared with other places in Borneo) forests here are the island's last places to do long-distance village-to-village trekking. The Kelabit and Kerayan Highlands contain a number of small villages and longhouse communities that have not yet been commercialised, allowing tourists seeking remote places and exotic people to experience a more genuine cultural encounter than is possible in other places in Borneo that are promoted as tourism destinations. These tend to be heavily commercialised and, to a certain extent, 'staged'. Based on numerous discussions with tourists who visit the highlands of Borneo, it became obvious that tourists do not come here wanting to stay in hotels or resorts; they prefer to avoid artificial or contrived lodgings made especially for tourists and come with the desire to stay with local families and to trek in the jungle with local guides.

The Kelabit and Kerayan Highlands are home to several closely related ethnic groups (including Kelabit, Lun Dayeh/Lun Bawang, Berian, Lengilu, Saban, and Penan) that speak related languages and have many cross-boundary kinship ties. Shared cultural features include similar wet-rice cultivation techniques and handicrafts (such as beadwork and weaving of baskets and mats), as well as a common history of megalith-making activities. These megaliths (erected or carved stones or large rock piles) and other cultural monuments dot the landscape surrounding the rural villages and demonstrate the cultural contiguity of these plateaus, which are a 2-3 day hike apart. These close cultural ties between the Kelabit and Kerayan Highlands, in addition to forests that have not yet been logged or converted to large-scale agriculture development, create an ideal situation for the development of community-based transboundary ecotourism initiatives that have the potential to be both a long-term source of revenue for rural communities and a land-use option that is compatible with local, regional, national, and international goals of conservation of biodiversity and natural resources. However, there are several factors that can make implementation of this type of tourism difficult to achieve on the ground. These will be discussed later in this article, but the most obvious one is that ecotourism development is one of the several goals for development proposed by the governments for this area, and it is not necessarily compatible with other governmental proposals.

This article examines the current state of transboundary ecotourism development in the Kelabit and Kerayan Highlands, with emphasis on the Kelabit Highlands of Sarawak. It situates the promotion of ecotourism here within the rhetoric of state and national conservation and development goals, and also identifies several of the main challenges faced by the local communities in the further development of community-based transboundary ecotourism. Research for this case study was conducted primarily in the Kelabit Highlands, and it included interviews with most of the guides and homestay owners in the Kelabit Highlands 1 and with 14 tourism professionals (tour operators, members of the Sarawak Tourism Board, and employees at visitors' centres) in the main cities of Sarawak, and participation in inter-community dialogues regarding transboundary ecotourism. In addition, it analyses promotional materials (both in print and on the Internet) on ecotourism in these areas, comments in the visitors' books of lodges in the Kelabit Highlands, and tourists' websites and travel blogs. Co-written by four local guides and homestay owners in Sarawak and Kalimantan and a graduate student from the USA who has conducted 3 years of ethnographic research in the Kelabit Highlands, this case study represents a stage of introspection by people actively engaged in current ecotourism activities and seeks to chart a course forward that takes into account the specific ecological, social, cultural, and political context of this region. The process of conducting this research project helped to pinpoint some of the specific challenges of transboundary ecotourism in this area, and will form the basis for a more comprehensive ecotourism management plan for local communities on both sides of the border.

Gathering, collating, and analysing the findings of this research with local community members revealed that the main issues that need to be addressed include: (1) protection of forests and cultural sites as foci for ecotourism; (2) improved communication between villages, guides, and lodges; (3) increased promotion of transboundary trekking options; (4) village-level preparation for more tourists and more equitable distribution of income generated from ecotourism; (5) careful improvements in tourism infrastructure; (6) the negotiation of legal complications arising from international border crossings by tourists and guides; and (7) the maintenance of local control over ecotourism management and the trajectory of future tourism development. Analysis of these issues in this transboundary area will not only help maximise local benefits from ecotourism in interior Borneo but also address many themes central to the academic literature on ecotourism in other parts of the world.

Background: Ecotourism in Malaysia

Tourism, and particularly ecotourism in developing countries rich with natural and cultural capital, is often touted as a sustainable source of revenue for indigenous and rural communities, and tourism often helps to bring developing countries and even local communities into the global economy. Although it is widely recognised now that while tourism has the potential to stimulate economic growth in marginal and underdeveloped areas, it can also serve to exacerbate inequalities within and between communities, and between local communities and the larger social, economic, political context in which these communities are embedded. Many scholars, human rights advocates, and tourism practitioners have argued that in order to address these issues of inequalities created or reinforced by tourism in rural areas, it is important that local communities are active stakeholders in tourism ventures and that such ventures are not imposed on them by outsiders who seek personal gain. However, this can be difficult and problematic on the ground, particularly when multiple communities are involved. The local communities in the Kelabit and Kerayan Highlands, both of their own initiative and with the assistance of international organisations such as WWF and the International Tropical Timber Organization (ITTO), have implemented several strategies for maintaining local control of tourism and promoting and improving community-based transboundary ecotourism.

In Malaysia, the Ministry of Tourism and Culture, established in 1987, became the Ministry of Culture, Arts, and Tourism in 1989. Now, tourism activities fall under the national jurisdiction of the Ministry of Tourism, and in the state of Sarawak, under the jurisdiction of the state Ministry of Urban Development and Tourism. In recent years, the Malaysian government has been steadily increasing its promotion of tourism, even globally advertising the year 2007 as Visit Malaysia Year. Malaysia is a popular tourist destination, and in particular, an ecotourism destination. Chin, Moore, Wallington, and Dowling notes that in the Malaysian state of Sarawak, 'tourist receipts have increased from RM 140.6 million in 1989 to RM 522.3 million in 1997'. According to Mohamed (2002), revenues from ecotourism in Malaysia were RM 655 million, of a total of RM 14 billion generated from all types of tourism. However, Davison (1995) notes that it is difficult to obtain reliable information on the number of ecotourists to Malaysia.

Tourism in Malaysia has been seen by Malaysians as a double-edged sword. On the one hand are the positive benefits of tourism such as increased employment, infrastructure development for rural areas, the enrichment of local culture through contact with outsiders, and the revitalisation of local cultural traditions, while on the other hand are deleterious effects such as the encroachment of new (Western) values on local communities, pollution and ecological damage, haphazard development, exacerbation of inter-and intra-community tensions, economic inflation, and in some cases, even prostitution and drugs (Din, 1997). These same benefits and concerns are echoed in case studies around the world, but are particularly salient in Malaysia, which aims to be a 'fully developed country' by 2020 (as articulated in Wawasan 2020, or Vision 2020, a common reference in Malaysian development circles). Din explained what he called this 'scapegoating' of tourism: 'tourism has either been disproportionally credited with all the good effects, or has received more than its fair share of the blame for the bad effects. A balanced discussion of the subject is rarely found, if at all, in Malaysia'. Since then, there have been several focused case studies of ecotourism in national parks in Malaysia that do offer more balanced and nuanced discussions. These studies describe benefits to local communities through employment and increased protection of natural resources. They also note specific problems caused by overuse by visitors, including subsequent ecological damage and economic leakages that direct the cash flow from ecotourism away from local economies.

In the early 1990s, national discussions on tourism in Malaysia began to reflect consideration for cultural issues, such as the commercialisation of culture and the equitable distribution of benefits from tourism, as well as the linkage of sustainable development to environmental conservation in the form of new ecotourism enterprises, especially in Sarawak and Sabah. The link between ecological and cultural tourism is particularly strong in Malaysia, and these alternative forms of tourism have been touted by governmental agencies, non-governmental organisations, tour operators, and local communities as a way to simultaneously promote conservation and non-consumptive use of natural resources, showcase unique indigenous cultures, and generate income for less-developed rural areas. The marriage of these goals is common to ecotourism endeavours around the world, but it represented an important shift in tourism goals by the Malaysian government, which previously did not thoroughly examine the effects of tourism on local communities.

Malaysia has officially adopted the World Conservation Union (IUCN)'s definition of ecotourism, and in 1997 created the National Ecotourism Plan, which outlined a set of 25 guidelines for categorising sites and ecotourism opportunities, defining carrying capacity and limits of acceptable change for each site, creating and improving national parks and forest reserves, promoting accreditation of ecotourism products and other activities necessary for ensuring compatibility between conservation and sustainable development through ecotourism. However, Abidin (1999) says that these guidelines are not specific enough, and that criteria and indicators for measuring carrying capacity, limits of acceptable change, and sustainability are lacking in this national plan, as are mechanisms for evaluating and monitoring future tourism and conservation programmes. He says: 'There are also no criteria and indicators developed for sustainable tourism management and biological diversity conservation in the protected areas of Malaysia'. Malaysia, while enthusiastically jumping on the ecotourism bandwagon, has its share of challenges and problems in ensuring such compatibility between conservation and sustainable development. An enlightening study by Lim (1999) revealed that travel agencies promoting ecotourism packages in Malaysia:

* are mostly new with 4-6 years experience;
* travel guides into ecotourism sites lack proper training and education; many have generic licenses but operate within ecotourism spots;
* only 11.9% of the agencies gave information regarding buying banned items when visiting ecotourism sites in Malaysia. And the same percentage contributed their income towards conservation activities;
* less than 46% have close relationships with the local communities;
* over 30% have little relation with the government; another 30.8% admitted they have no relation with the government;
* 10 out of 15 agencies do not really understand the principles and concepts of ecotourism;
* Almost 80% of the activities tend to be fun-filled or adventurous but lacking in terms of getting to know the nature.

The results of this study show that Malaysia clearly can improve its ecotourism practices rather than just promoting its natural areas as ecotourism destinations.

At the Borneo Ecotourism Conference in April of 2005, Mr. Rambli Ahmad, the Manager of Planning and Development of the Sarawak Tourism Board, stated that although ecotourism had benefited the people of Sarawak, 'an adverse consequence of this business was that most of the longhouses were trying to meet the needs of foreign tourists rather than preserving their culture'. Communities around the world have faced similar challenges when tourism (including ecotourism and cultural tourism) has been introduced, particularly that of the commodification or objectification of material culture and the staging of performative culture that can lead more to the falsification or exaggeration of culture than the preservation of it. According to Din (1997), the objective is to balance the needs of the guests and the hosts, and to allow the local communities to define their priorities. He says: 'For Malaysians, it is important that tourism will not jeopardize the societal goals that the host community defines'. In the case of the Kelabit and Kerayan Highlands, most community members agree that their main goals are conservation and development through their own local initiatives, and they see ecotourism as an important means of achieving these goals simultaneously. Community members have taken important steps to improve the quality of the ecotourism experience for visitors, to monitor and protect the natural and cultural resources in their villages, to expand the direct benefits of ecotourism to more community members, and to maintain control over the pace and course of ecotourism development.

Genuine community-driven ecotourism development requires that local communities determine the type and trajectory of tourism development, not merely react to the needs and desires of foreign tourists and accept top-down implementation of tourism projects by outside agencies. Due to the remoteness of this area, so far there has been little threat of the imposition of tourism on these communities, so it has remained in the hands of the community members. This could change in the near future, however, as the highlands become accessible by logging roads and more infrastructure development is sponsored by the government and the private sector. Concern for local autonomy has guided both local ecotourism initiatives and NGO-assisted programmes for ecotourism development in the highlands of Borneo. At the same time, communities and assisting organisations recognise the need to work with multiple stakeholders in ecotourism development. Participants elaborated on this sentiment during the Borneo Ecotourism Conference in 2005, as the conference fostered new partnerships between governmental agencies, private businesses, and local communities in ecotourism development. Both the federal government of Malaysia and the state government of Sarawak have made numerous public statements supporting the development of ecotourism, as both an income-generating activity for rural communities and as an important component of state and federal sustainable forestry policies. For example, the Deputy Chief Minister of Sarawak, Datuk Patinggi Tan Sri Dr. George Chan, said that:

The foresight of our Chief Minister has been instrumental in moving the tourism industry here to where it is today even though funds for such developments were often hard to come by due initially to the small number of tourist arrivals which did not justify the amount spent of such facilities. However, we persevere and spending wisely we have managed to bring Sarawak into the world map of eco tourism which is envisaged as a sustainable industry for the state for a long time to come.

The Eighth Malaysia Plan (2001-2005) includes an entire section on tourism development, with a focus on nature-based tourism or ecotourism; this rhetoric supporting ecotourism development is reiterated in the Ninth Malaysia Plan (2006-2010), particularly as a means to generate income for rural communities, while simultaneously demonstrating the commitment of the government to conserve natural resources in the geographical and metaphorical Heart of Borneo.

The Heart of Borneo Conservation Initiative

Led by WWF, the Heart of Borneo is a large-scale, tri-national transboundary initiative that aims to tie ecological conservation with sustainable development in the geographical middle (or 'heart') of the island of Borneo. Following an April 2005 meeting in Brunei, the governments of Indonesia, Malaysia, and Brunei publicly committed to a cooperative conservation initiative at the Convention on Biological Diversity (CBD) meeting in Curitiba, Brazil, in March 2006, and the official Heart of Borneo Declaration was signed by representatives of these countries on 7 February 2007. The area covered by the Heart of Borneo initiative is approximately 220,000 km^2 or 2.5 million hectares, and includes the upper montane forests in highlands and watersheds that cross international boundaries (World Wide Fund for Nature [WWF] Denmark,.

The interior of Borneo is recognised internationally by scientists, researchers, and conservation organisations as being globally important, and ecologically and culturally unique. It is a repository of numerous endemic and endangered species, a source of watersheds for the entire island, and home to a number of indigenous communities who have managed this landscape sustainably for untold generations. Local livelihoods, centred on income from organic rice production and ecotourism, are dependent on intact forests and watersheds. However, government agencies and private sector companies in both Malaysia and Indonesia are planning different scenarios for this area: expansion of protected areas, continued logging, large-scale agricultural development, increased smallholder agriculture, infrastructure and ecotourism development, and creation of income opportunities for local communities. These different scenarios would have enormous impacts on the future of ecotourism in the interior highland areas of Borneo, in ways that are generally self-explanatory. The future here is uncertain, which makes long-term planning difficult for local communities, but they are pursuing ecotourism development at the moment, with the support of various government agencies. Much of the Kerayan Highlands of Indonesian Borneo is already within the boundaries of the Kayan Mentarang National Park (KMNP), encompassing over 1.3 million hectares along the border with Sarawak (WWF Denmark, 2006). On 24 March 2006, a new national park was officially gazetted in Sarawak near the border with Kalimantan. Pulong Tau National Park (PTNP), which translates to 'Our Forest' in the Kelabit language, was first requested by members of the Kelabit community in the late 1970s as a means to protect the headwaters of several major rivers in Sarawak, including the Baram, Tutoh, and Limbang Rivers. Originally, this park included 164,500 hectares, but over the years, the area was decreased incrementally to its current size of 59,817 hectares. Key landscape features were removed from the park, and all but about 2 km of the transboundary areas were also removed.

There is currently a proposal by the ITTO and the Government of Malaysia to extend the border of PTNP in Sarawak to join with KMNP in Kalimantan, thus creating a large transboundary conservation area. This ITTO project, entitled 'Transboundary Biodiversity Conservation: The Pulong Tau National Park, Sarawak State, Malaysia', is now in its second phase. During the first phase, Sarawak Forest Department employees conducted baseline ecological studies within the park, as well as socioeconomic and cultural studies on the communities in the Kelabit Highlands, areas within and bordering the proposed extension area (International Tropical Timber Organization [ITTO] and Government of Malaysia, 2003). These baseline studies were intended to inform the long-term management plan of PTNP. The second phase of the project includes implementation of the projects proposed in the first phase, the most significant of which is the actual extension of the boundaries of PTNP to create a genuine transboundary conservation area with KMNP.

A large component of the sustainable development goals of this ITTO project is to establish an infrastructure for renewable income for local communities through ecotourism, while at the same time promoting ecoregional conservation of biodiversity and watersheds. The budget for Phase II of the ITTO project (ITTO and Government of Malaysia, 2007) includes USD 4000 for informational material on PTNP, USD 15,000 to improve and maintain jungle trails to Mount Murud, a popular trek for tourists, USD 6000 for tourist guide training and tourism information materials, and USD 2000 to propose Kelabit megalithic areas as a UNESCO World Heritage Site. It also budgets for a total of USD 29,000 for 'cross-border socioeconomic activities among local communities', of which USD 3000 is specifically earmarked for 'cross-border ecotourism: resource development, joint promotion materials, and tourist guides training/visits'. The ecotourism potential of this area is mentioned throughout this document, and it states clearly that: 'Through transboundary cooperation, the people across the borders can work to bring their economies closer, by improving roads, promoting cross-border trade and joint ecotourism for mutual benefits'.

Ecotourism is often proposed as an economic investment in conservation; however, positive examples of ecotourism in the academic literature are still rare. Many academic articles argue that the goals of ecotourism can conflict with the goals of conservation and preservation of cultural traditions, as well as local livelihoods, and that conservation laws can conflict with local livelihoods derived from ecotourism. A central concern with relying on ecotourism as a way to conserve natural resources is that tourism itself can bring about ecological degradation. But despite these critiques of ecotourism ventures in some areas, it is still a viable and desirable alternative in many places, so long as it is carefully planned and monitored. Malaysia is a signatory to the CBD, whose fifth Conference of the Parties (COP-5) decided that: 'tourism does present a significant potential for realising benefits in terms of the conservation of biological diversity and the sustainable use of its components'. However, it also noted that: 'Historical observation indicates that self-regulation of the tourism industry for sustainable use of biological resources has only rarely been successful'. Visitor impact assessment is vital to maintaining the health of ecosystems that are ecotourism destinations. This is particularly important in ecosystems as fragile as those found within the highland plateaus of the Heart of Borneo, and a central concern for promoting the development of ecotourism (or any type of tourism) here is minimising the negative social, cultural, and ecological effects.

The most recent ITTO document says that 'with careful planning and monitoring, it is unlikely that ecotourism development will affect the sustainability of the park (PTNP)'. But what is needed in the highlands is on-the-ground monitoring of the impacts of all types of development coming to these areas. Monitoring of, and mitigation for, ecotourism presents less of a challenge in the Kelabit and Kerayan Highlands than for other types of large-scale development that are also being proposed for this area, so it is difficult to consider this in isolation from other possible futures for this complex cultural and geographic landscape. The political landscape of this area is also complex; in addition to myriad governmental agencies and private corporations making plans for this area, there are also numerous actors involved in ecotourism efforts in the highlands of Sarawak and Kalimantan. In addition to state and national ministries and governmental agencies in Malaysia and Indonesia, a number of international conservation, development, and finance NGOs and agencies are directly and tangentially involved in the Heart of Borneo initiative: WWF, The Nature Conservancy (TNC), Conservation International (CI), the IUCN, Global Environmental Facility (GEF), Wildlife Conservation Society (WCS), ITTO, United States Agency for International Development (USAID), United Nations Development Programme (UNDP), United Nations Educational, Scientific, and Cultural Organization (UNESCO), the World Bank (WB), International Monetary Fund (IMF), Asian Development Bank (ADB), International Finance Corporation (IFC), and Association for East Asian Nations (ASEAN). Many of these organisations have attended meetings regarding the Heart of Borneo initiative, and/or have contributed financial or verbal support, but WWF is the most involved on the ground, particularly in Kalimantan. Involvement by NGOs is more limited in Sarawak, and in the Kelabit Highlands, only ITTO (working with the Sarawak Forest Department and Sarawak Forest Corporation) has been directly involved in conservation efforts.

Alongside, and to some extent in conjunction with these national and international organisations, there are several local organisations that are actively engaged in ecotourism in the Kelabit and Kerayan Highlands, including the Tourism Bureau of the Kelabit Highlands, the Bario-Ba' Kelalan Nature Guide Association, Lembaya Swadaya Masyarakat Tanah Tam ('Our Land' Indonesian NGO), and the FORMADAT (Alliance of the Indigenous People of the Highlands in the Heart of Borneo). The focus of this article is on the efforts of these community-level organisations to promote, monitor, and improve transboundary ecotourism.

11

Climate Change Threatens Island Tourism

The climate change literature and debate so far has largely focused on mitigation actions by the main contributors to greenhouse gas (GHG) emissions and global warming—developed market economies, as well as large industrializing economies like China, India, and Brazil. Small Island Developing States (SIDS) are not large contributors to the problem of climate change, but constitute the most impacted group of countries. While the key issue for SIDS is adaptation, these countries are also highly dependent on the tourism and travel industries, which are considered to be major emitters—and so are vulnerable to the effects of international climate mitigation policies in these sectors.

Adaptation Challenges and Costs

Scientists consider SIDS to be climate change "hotspots," highly vulnerable to the impacts of global warming—sea level rise, temperature rise, rainfall changes, coral bleaching, and increased storm frequency. For example, sea level rise will exacerbate inundation, erosion, and other coastal hazards, threaten vital infrastructure, settlements, and facilities, and thus compromise the socioeconomic well-being of island communities and states.

Warming seas threaten the coral reefs and the livelihoods of commercial and artisanal fisheries. This, by extension, has the potential to result in widespread unemployment of fishermen and tourism-related service providers (e.g., scuba tourism), the incomes of which depend upon the existence of healthy coral reefs. In addition, if climate change does result in changing rainfall distribution patterns, then many SIDS will be forced to find new and innovative ways to establish a consistent and reliable water supply. Moreover, the absence of a consistent water supply can also lead to a severe decline in agricultural production (subsistence and commercial), thus threatening food security within these island states along with the competitiveness of the tourism sector.

Adaptation costs can be devastating. This predicament is exacerbated by the fact that many SIDS are dependent upon monocrop agricultural production and export, as well as tourism, for foreign exchange earnings, employment, and contribution to GDP. They are also highly dependent on the importation of food and energy for domestic consumption and for the tourism sector.

Tourism, a Double-edged Sword

The travel and tourism sector is the key economic sector for SIDS in terms of earnings and jobs. Tourism earnings account for a significant share of the foreign exchange earnings in most SIDS. In the Caribbean, travel and tourism accounts for 14.8 percent of GDP, 12.9 percent of employment, and 14.6 percent of total exports. Oceania has a similar economic profile with GDP shares of travel and tourism at 11.7 percent, employment shares at 12.4 percent, and export shares at 16.9 percent of GDP. For both regions, however, ten-year forecasts (2018) by the World Travel and Tourism Council suggest declining contributions from travel and tourism to GDP and employment, but not to exports.

SIDS, which generally are long-haul destinations from key source markets like North America and Europe, have raised concerns regarding the potential adverse impact of prospective climate regulation of the air travel and shipping sectors and consumer preferences shifting in favour of short-haul destinations. Some governments and companies have also adopted environment-friendly charges, levies, and technologies, some of which have caused the cost of travel and transportation to increase. Such cost increases will likely have adverse effects on travel and tourism to SIDS. On the other hand, the cost of inaction on climate change could be even more dismal. According to a recent study:

1. The cost of inaction would amount to 22 percent of gross domestic product (GDP) for the Caribbean as a whole by 2100;
2. The costs of inaction will reach an astonishing 75 percent or more of GDP by 2100 in Dominica, Grenada, Haiti, St. Kitts & Nevis, and Turks & Caicos;
3. The Caribbean's largest island, Cuba, faces a nearly 13 percent

economic hit by mid-century, and a 27 percent loss by 2100, unless there is swift action to address climate change;

4. Losses from inaction would be less severe but still significant in Puerto Rico, reaching nearly 3 percent by 2050 and 6 percent by the end of the century; and
5. Colombia, with its long Caribbean coastline, faces permanent flooding of 1,900 square miles in low-lying coastal areas, affecting 1.4 million people.

Thus, the intersection of a number of factors makes for a critical scenario for SIDS in the evolving context of climate change and trade in international services, especially tourism.

Policy Responses

At the international level, developing countries, and particularly SIDS, recognize their state of vulnerability to climate change and therefore urge a focus on adaptation and support from those parties responsible for climate change, which need to take a lead on mitigation. At the same time, SIDS are also advancing a proactive agenda looking at adaptation and mitigation in tandem, urging the development, dissemination, and transfer of efficient energy technologies that can assist developing countries in mitigating the effects of climate change. Overall, developed and developing nations tend to respond to the threat of climate change in a way that is consistent with international consensus (as expressed through the UNFCCC), where nations take measures to protect the earth's ecological system through policies and instruments that reflect their common but differentiated responsibility. SIDS also acknowledge their responsibility to collect data on the effects and implications of climate change and sea level rise, to improve public understanding of the issue, to promote more efficient energy use, and to formulate their own comprehensive adjustment and mitigation policies to be able to cope with and respond to climate change.

Further, SIDS cooperate at the regional level to respond to the climate change challenge, and work with the international aviation and cruise line industries. For example, the Caribbean Community Climate Change Centre serves to provide research and information to the Caribbean Community. At the industry level, the International Air Transportation Association (IATA) has adopted a four-pronged approach to reducing greenhouse gas emissions, focusing on technological advancements, improved operations and infrastructure, and economic incentives. The cruise ship industry has also started taking its own steps to improve sustainability. SIDS also work with NGOs that seek to promote sustainable tourism, in order to improve their climate profiles. WWF, for example, recognizes that tourism and conservation are compatible and seeks to give tourists useful hints on how they can enjoy their vacation in an environment-friendly way.

Only a handful of measures to address climate change also seek to safeguard the interests of the tourism industry. However, some multilateral environmental agreements (MEAs) have the potential to serve the interest of the tourism industry, particularly in SIDS. These include MEAs that focus on conservation, such as the Convention on International Trade in Endangered Species, which helps preserve valuable tourist attractions and the basis for ecotourism.

From Vulnerability to Resilience

In order to move from a position of vulnerability and dependence to one of resilience, policy tools within the international trade arena can be used to boost the capacity of SIDS. The services sector, and in particular tourism, represent a genuine opportunity for SIDS to expand their economic activity while earning foreign currency.

In addition, SIDS can seek to liberalize trade in energy efficient goods in a bid to decrease their collective carbon footprint. This policy could include both tax incentives and zero-tariff measures for the import of environment-friendly products. The trade arena could also facilitate the transfer of technologies that contribute to the development of capacity among service providers. This can indeed be particularly useful as practitioners from SIDS within the tourism industry (and other industries as well) sometimes find the cost of technological devices to be prohibitive.

Technology transfer can also be important for environment-friendly technologies for local industries, and meteorological technology to inform tourists and industry officials of impending bad weather, especially severe natural hazards, enabling officials to take preemptive action to ensure the safety of citizens and tourists.

Perhaps one of the most direct and legally binding approaches that a group of nations can adopt is to sign a trade agreement that addresses issues closely related to climate change. An example can be found in the Economic Partnership Agreement (EPA) between the Caribbean Community and the Dominican Republic (CARIFORUM) and the EU.

The EPA represents a comprehensive trading arrangement between an archipelago of SIDS and a group of developed nations. In addition to expressing the overall objective of trade for sustainable development, the agreement contains a chapter on the environment. Additionally, the EPA contains provisions pertaining to environmental cooperation through technical assistance, trade in natural resources, and public education campaigns to foster trade in environmental goods and services.

Globalisation and Tourism: Deadly Mix for Indigenous Peoples

Indigenous peoples are paying a high price for tourism, says Raymond de Chavez. In their drive for profits, transnational corporations which dominate the international tourist industry have, with the complicity of governments (particularly those of the Third World), devastated the lives and lifestyles of indigenous peoples. The process of globalisation will only exacerbate their plight.

Globalisation and tourism have become a deadly mix for indigenous peoples. Tourism's impact on indigenous peoples' way of life and on their control of and access to their resources and environment has become more pronounced with globalisation of the world economy.

For several decades now, tourism has been a major source of revenue for countries, specifically in the Third World. Its growth has been nothing short of phenomenal. In the 1950s, 25 million people travelled to a foreign destination. In the 1960s, this grew to 70 million. By 1997, 617 million tourists had been reported by the Madrid-based World Tourism Organisation to have travelled to foreign countries.

The World Tourism Organisation has even predicted that by the 21st century, tourist arrivals would have reached billions annually. It foresees that by the year 2010, 1 billion tourists would have travelled abroad and by 2020, this would have increased to 1.6 billion. In terms of revenues, this would easily translate to billions of dollars yearly. In the 1960s, for example, tourism earned 'only' US$6.8 billion. In 1997, revenues jumped to US$448 billion. By the year 2000, the WTO predicts tourism earnings to reach $621 billion and by 2010, a whopping $1.5 trillion.

Tourism is also touted as a major source of employment worldwide. According to the World Travel and Tourism Council (WTTC), an aggrupation of more than 80 chief executives of the travel and tourism industry, tourism employs directly or indirectly more than 260 million. This translates to one out of nine jobs in the world economy generated by the industry. By the coming decade, the workforce is expected to increase by 100 million more jobs, 70% of these in the Asia-Pacific region.

The WTTC in fact now considers tourism as the world's biggest industry and a 'key 21st century economic and employment driver'. Its growth for the past decades has been a constant 9% annually, in spite of the economic slowdown. While acknowledging a decline in tourism activities due to the Asian financial crisis, the WTTC recommended in February 1998 that governments give continued priority to tourism to assist Asian economic recovery.

Tourism as Export Strategy

It is no wonder therefore that cash-starved Third World countries view tourism as a shortcut to rapid development. Its potential to earn billions of dollars easily has resulted in it being viewed as a panacea for debt-ridden countries. But more than this, tourism has become part and parcel of multilateral financial institutions' package for financial bail-outs for countries in distress. Tourism is now being pursued as a serious development strategy for the Third World.

The International Monetary Fund (IMF) has included tourism as part of its Structural Adjustment Programmes (SAPs). The SAPs, which are preconditions for the approval of financial assistance, require the indebted country to:

* be integrated into the global economy;
* deregulate and liberalise its economy;
* shift from an agriculture-based to a manufacturing and service industry-based economy; and
* liberalise its financial sector.

In essence, these preconditions link the Third World country to the world economy. The SAP opens up the local economy to foreign investments and multinational corporations, while eliminating subsidies and protection to local industries. Under IMF-World Bank prescriptions, tourism is classified as an export strategy. With its capacity to earn billions of dollars, tourism is being promoted by the IMF-WB as a means for Third World countries to repay their debts to them. Third World governments have therefore tried to fulfil their commitments to these SAPs by large-scale investments in tourism-related ventures. In conjunction with financial multilateral institutions and travel and tourism transnational corporations (TNCs), they have launched infrastructure projects such as roads, hotels and tourist-promotion programmes. Worldwide, public and private investments have reached $800 billion annually, accounting for 12% of total worldwide investments.

But these IMF-WB conditionalities have proven to be insufficient to integrate and open up Third World economies. The World Trade Organisation has taken further steps to fully liberalise the world economy. The most important international agreement with direct bearing on tourism is the General Agreement on Trade in Services (GATS). Signed in Morocco in April 1994, this agreement '... sets up a legal and operational framework for the gradual elimination of barriers to international trade in services'. GATS is an offshoot of the Uruguay Round talks of the General Agreement on Tariffs and Trade (GATT), the World Trade Organisation's precursor.

In short, GATS makes it easier for big tourist and travel TNCs to invest in the local tourism industries of Third World countries. Among others, it removes restrictions on foreign corporations' abilities to transfer staff from one country to another; and enables them to use trademarks, create and operate branch offices abroad, and more importantly, to repatriate their earnings to their mother companies abroad.

Under GATS, protection to the local tourism industry would be construed as unfair practice and would thus have to be eliminated. TNCs now enjoy the same benefits as local travel and tourism agencies. This opens the local industry to competition from giant TNCs, which virtually means effectively transferring its control to them.

Other international agreements integrating the tourism industry into the global economy include the Agreement on Trade-Related Investment Measures (TRIMs), which removes the requirement for foreign companies to utilise local input. The proposed Multilateral Agreement on Investment (MAI) also 'secure for foreign investors, unfettered rights to invest in all sectors of the host country's economy and to obtain for them the same treatment as investors from the host nation'. This proposal has, however, been shelved recently as a result of intense lobbying by non-governmental organisations, indigenous peoples' organisations included.

Threat to Indigenous Peoples

But what does globalisation and tourism mean for the indigenous peoples? It is already an established fact that tourism had brought pernicious and long-term damaging effects on indigenous peoples even prior to globalisation. The present economic order further exacerbates and hastens these impacts.

For one, indigenous communities, which have otherwise been left untouched by traditional tourism activities, have now been targeted for tourism ventures, most specifically, ecotourism. A relatively new variant, ecotourism is described as environment-friendly, sustainable and nature-based. It came about as a response to the growing environmental awareness worldwide these past decades.

Eager to cash in on this trend, the industry promoted ecotourism as an alternative activity, ostensibly to promote tourism while protecting the environment. This activity 'involves visiting relatively undisturbed natural areas with the aim of studying, admiring and enjoying the scenery, wild plants and animals, as well as any existing cultural aspects'. It includes spelunking, mountain climbing, scuba diving, bird watching, and whale watching, among others. This tourism sub-sector has been met with remarkable success. Today, it has become the fastest growing sub-sector, growing at a rate of 10%-15% annually. Ecotourism now accounts for 25% of all leisure trips abroad.

It is important to note that ecotourism destinations are more often than not in the Third World. Tourism here has been increasing annually by 6% as compared to 3.5% in developed countries. After all, it is in these areas that relatively undisturbed and preserved natural environments and exotic areas are located. But it is also in these countries that the majority of the distinct indigenous cultures can be found.

To a large extent, therefore, indigenous communities have become targets of ecotourism in this globalised economy.

In Africa, tourism's effects on indigenous peoples have been profound: widescale eviction from their lands, economic dislocation, breakdown of traditional values, and environmental degradation. Although ecotourism is a relatively new phenomenon internationally, it has long been existing in Africa.

In the 1950s, the colonial governments of Tanzania and Kenya under the British legalised the hunting and culling of wild animals by 'white settlers', thus paving the way for mass tourism. They set up zones for the exclusive use of hunters and prevented access to local inhabitants. Lodges and campsites were established near the preserves, making them major revenue earners. Some 70% of the protected areas and wildlife preserves, however, straddled lands of the Masai tribe.

Basically pastoralists, the Masai used these lands for their economic activities and traditional practices. The ban thus dislocated them economically. Forced out of their traditional grounds, they were left with little or no support from the government. And even after independence, the government failed to provide them with social services such as education and employment.

The Masai's traditional economic activity-pastoralism-has been attacked as primitive and destructive. Yet it has been noted that 'pastoralism and conservation of nature go hand in hand'. Alienated from their main economic activity and disadvantaged from job opportunities by a lack of education, the Masai were subjected to poverty.

Even the Masai's traditional socio-political institutions have suffered as a consequence of tourism. Lands outside the preserves where the Masai have been resettled are considered communal. In these areas, residents are registered, and land and resources are to be distributed equally by a management committee.

However, corrupt officials have registered even non-residents who have monopolised prime lands near the preserves. Land disputes have thus arisen. Elders, traditional mediators of conflicts, have become powerless against non-residents who are often backed by powerful persons. Destruction of properties by wildlife has also been reported but the government has not given any compensation to affected residents. This has caused disruption in the relationship between the tribes and the animals, which are given priority because of tourism. As a consequence, the 'Masai... are coming to abhor the very wild animals they have successfully coexisted with for centuries'. Tourism has not spared the environment and biodiversity. The rise in tourist arrivals in these preserves-more so with globalisation-has increased deforestation, pollution and disruption in the ecological balance. In the Masai Mara National Park in Kenya and in the Ngorongoro Conservation Area in Tanzania, forests adjacent to lodges and camping grounds have been cut down due to the demand for firewood.

The massive influx of tourists and their vehicles has also caused destruction of grass cover, affecting plant and animal species in the area. Hotels have dumped their sewage in Masai settlement areas while campsites have polluted adjacent rivers.

Masai culture has further been threatened and commercialised. Negative Western values have influenced the Masai youth, leading to a loss of traditional values, prostitution, and the spread of AIDS. Postcards portraying tribes in their traditional costumes abound in these preserves. It is in the interest of ecotourism to 'preserve' indigenous communities and their practices since exotic tribes with exotic practices serve as the main selling point to foreign tourists. 'There is rarely an acknowledgement-much less support-of indigenous people's struggle for cultural survival, self-determination, freedom of cultural expression, rights to ancestral lands, and control over land use and resource management.' In the Philippines, where tourism has long been considered as a major dollar-earner, ecotourism has also become a priority. Blessed with a rich biodiversity, the Philippines has developed ecotourism as a strategy to entice more foreign tourists and increase its share in world tourism revenue. Its Department of Tourism (DOT)'s Master Plan aims to develop 'sustainable' tourism while making the Philippines a leading tourist destination in Asia.

In support of this thrust is the National Integrated Protected Areas System Act (NIPAS) of 1992, which classifies certain areas as protected zones. The DOT has identified 17 protected areas all over the country as suitable for ecotourism. It is important to note that the majority of these areas are territories of indigenous peoples. In the Cordillera in the northern Philippines, tourism continues to affect adversely many of its 1.3 million indigenous population. Sagada in Mountain Province, home to the indigenous Kankanaeys, is known internationally for its cool climate, rice terraces, and caves, among others. Its people have maintained their indigenous way of life, subsistence economy and sustainable relationship with nature for centuries.

In recent years, tourism arrivals have grown tremendously, caused in part by ecotourism promotion packages advertising Sagada as a pristine community where one can commune with nature. Hotels and inns mushroomed, changing the town's landscape and straining its water resources. Pollution caused by littering and improper waste disposal has now become a major problem for the community. Apart from environmental degradation, the influx of tourists has disrupted the Kankanaeys' traditions and practices. The solemnity and sacredness of rituals, such as those relating to the agricultural cycle and passage of life, have been affected due to the presence of curious tourists. Caves, traditionally their burial grounds, have been vandalised by graffiti, and some of the bones of their ancestors stolen.

Western influences have also taken their toll on the local community.

These include the production, distribution and use of prohibited drugs such as marijuana and hashish. Taboos have been constantly broken by foreign tourists. Tourists, for example, have bathed in the nude in waterfalls, which is frowned upon by the local community. In 1995, the world-famous Ifugao Rice Terraces in Banawe, Ifugao province, was declared by the UN Educational, Scientific and Cultural Organisation (UNESCO) as a World Heritage Site. This was part of the Philippine government's campaign to sell Ifugao as a major tourist destination in the world.

The influx of tourists over the decades has similarly affected the Ifugaos, the indigenous inhabitants of the province. Foremost is the disruption of traditional economic practices of the community. The builders of the world-renowned rice terraces, the Ifugaos for centuries have subsisted on crops planted in their terraces. With the entry of tourists and hotels, the lure of money from tourist-related businesses such as selling of woodcarvings, became more attractive than subsistence farming. This has left many terraces untended and in danger of deterioration.

Commercial production of woodcarvings has also affected nearby forests. Trees have been cut down to support commercial woodcarving activities that cater to foreign as well as domestic tourist demand. This has led to the drying up of water sources much needed for irrigation. Joan Carling of the Cordillera Peoples Alliance aptly summed up the effects of tourism on the indigenous peoples in the Cordillera when she wrote: 'The tourism industry has facilitated the further disintegration of the peoples' indigenous way of life. Cash production for the tourism industry has led to commercialism and individualism in contrast to the indigenous ways of simple living and mutual cooperation. Likewise, the commercialisation of their culture has led to undignified ways of seeking a livelihood such as allowing themselves to be photographed as souvenirs or to do their indigenous dance for a fee. This practice was never part of their culture.

The pervasive effects of globalised tourism can also be seen in the way it has affected other indigenous peoples all over the world. In the Cook Islands in the Pacific, a 204-room hotel was built on land sacred to the local people. The construction has caused environmental damage amounting to US$1 million.

In the Russian Federation's Providenskij and Tchukogskij regions, home to the indigenous Tchukchi peoples, the development of tourism in the past years has affected their source of livelihood. Known areas of walrus concentration such as those in Rugor's Bay and the isle of Arykamchechen have become ecotourism destinations. Sightseeing tour groups ride on motorboats to walruses' breeding grounds. But a rise in such tours has affected the walrus population. Visitor arrivals have caused stress among the walruses, causing a decline in their population. This has in turn affected the quality and quantity of walrus catch, traditionally the Tchukchi peoples' source of livelihood.

Tourism's High Cost

Indigenous peoples are paying a high price for tourism. In their desire to cash in on the billion-dollar profits from this industry, governments, specifically in the Third World, and transnational corporations have disregarded the interests of indigenous peoples.

The effects have been devastating. Indigenous peoples have been evicted from their traditional lands, their control and access to their natural resources compromised. They have suffered social degradation brought about by foreign influences and the commercialisation of their culture. Even the rich biodiversity of their natural resources has suffered from pollution and environmental damage, unable to support the growing number of tourist arrivals. What few benefits indigenous peoples derive from tourism are far outweighed by the damage it has caused them. They have been made to bear the brunt of an industry over which they have neither say nor control.

With globalisation, these threats have been exacerbated. International agreements that open up access to the local tourism industry by big travel and tourism TNCs will only speed up exploitation of the natural resources, culture and way of life of indigenous peoples. Ecotourism, which has been touted as the fastest growing form of tourism in the Third World, has not proven to be sustainable at all. Rather, it has targeted indigenous communities as areas of destination and exploitation in the guise of being environment-friendly. Unless indigenous peoples have a direct participation in the planning, implementation, and regulation of tourism activities that affect them, and unless benefit-sharing mechanisms are put in place, tourism can never redound to their interest. Indigenous peoples will continue to be mere cogs in the wheel of this billion-dollar industry.

Achieve Tourism Sustainability in Mediterranean Islands

Globally, tourism activity increases at a rate of 3% to 4.5% annually and it is expected that tourism's growth will raise revenues of about €1,500 billion per annum until 2010. Being the dominant industry at a global level (in terms of expenses and employees),, tourism is currently considered to be an integral part of modern life, as well as an undeniable driver of economic development.

In the European Union, Mediterranean islands present the 2.2% of the internal European product and they attract the 30% of worldwide tourism (expected to be increased by 50% for the years to come). Several different kinds of tourism are present in these islands as «destinations of luxury» (Santorini or Sardinia), or as «fun destinations» (Mykonos or Ios). However, the increasing intensity of some forms of tourism and the overexploitation of the natural resources can threaten tourism's own existence at a local or island scale. Mass tourism, dominant in the majority of cases, is the prime contender which can lead to a degradation of natural landscapes, a lack of water provisions, coastal zone pollution, and the construction of massive transport and building infrastructures.

Islands are also exposed to pressures encountered from climatic changes: even they if are not emitters of CO_2, suffer from climatic change impacts more than mainland's areas. Their particular social, cultural, political and economical features, as well as the handicaps that islands present in their structure and development (such as small dimensions and geographic isolation, limited resources, insufficient productivity, competences and infrastructure, and ecological fragility), lead to an intensification of their vulnerability . In the energy field, islands suffer from insufficiency of electricity transport interconnections (more than 50% of EU islands are not interconnected) as well as a high cost of energy feeding. On the other hand, islands are rich in abundant natural energy sources and they constitute the ideal regions for the demonstration of innovative energy projects.

Within this context, the concept of sustainable tourism was born. For the majority of scientists this concept concerns an economic, social and environmental tourism development which aims at the continuous improvement of tourists' everyday life. Other authors strongly argue that the sustainability of tourism's development rely on the creation of particular characteristics of a tourism product which are in line with present and future tourists' needs. This kind of development is an additional opportunity for the local communities to benefit from the products of their own local identity, local natural resources included.

Among these natural resources, scientific literature and practical case studies suggest that the role of renewable energy should not be underestimated for tourism destinations. On the contrary, the use of this energy in hotel infrastructure as well as in the construction of thematic parks is particularly welcome. In our analysis we will assess the compatibility between renewable energy sources and sustainable tourism development. Using some Mediterranean islands as case-studies, we will further suggest that renewable energy technologies (RETs) can be used as a leverage for this kind of tourism development.

Our methodology unfolds in two steps: firstly, we are discussing some cases of RETs integration in Mediterranean islands and secondly, we are discussing the results of our analysis. These results will reveal conditions under which compatibility between RETs and sustainable tourism development is possible. Such a compatibility was discussed in the past, but only as far as the integration of environmental technologies in the hotel sector is concerned. Results will also argue that RETs can further promote the "sustainability" of a tourism destination. The Mediterranean cases which will be examined, concern the islands of Sicily, Sardinia, Cyprus, Corsica, Crete, Milos, Skopelos and Gavdos. The geographic locations of the islands are illustrated at the maps.

Integration of RETs in Mediterranean Islands

3 From 1946, Sicily is an autonomous region of Italy and the biggest Mediterranean island (a surface of 25,799km^2 and a local population of 5,100,000), situated in the southern part of Italy. Its economy is based mainly on agriculture, fishing, industries and tourism. During 1970s the island has suffered from the immigration of a large part of its population towards United States and Europe and therefore today's Sicilian economy is not largely facilitated from local investments and entrepreneurship. Therefore, the island suffers an unemployment rate of 20% and a lack of specialized professionals. From an energy point of view, 70% of electricity feeding is coming from fossil fuels and the 30% from renewable energies (mainly from hydroelectric plants). Nevertheless, the potential of renewable energies remains high, mainly for geothermy and thanks to the volcano Etna which is the largest volcano in Europe. This is why, in this island, full of areas characterized as UNESCO's natural heritages, an innovative energy system has been undertaken and is worthwhile to be discussed:

A system of electricity produced from waves is tested in the Messina Strait since water density (and therefore energy production potential) is 800 times bigger that the one of wind, and energy coming from waves can be perfectly predicted (contrary to wind energy). For the moment, results are very encouraging and the system is considered to be even more profitable than the wind energy installations. The pilot-project is used as a "demonstrative project" and attracts the worldwide attention and visits of scholars.

Sardinia is an island of 24,090km^2 and of 1,655,677 residents, which has gained the status of an «autonomous region» from Italy, since 1948. Its geological features are very important, since Sardinia's geology is formed from some of the most ancient rocks in Europe. The climate is typically Mediterranean with mild temperatures. In 1994, the Magdalena archipelago with its 180km^2 of coast, was classed as a sea park. As far as the island's economy is concerned, the primary sector holds the 33% of the total economy, the secondary sector the 19% and the tertiary sector the 48%. The tertiary sector (mainly tourism activities) occupies the 60% of local man force. Tourism activities in Sardinia are responsible for the 7% of the National Internal Product, and therefore a variety of hotel complexes have been constructed in the southern part of the island in order to host approximately 10 millions of tourists per year; 80% of them in July and August. Although it has a diversity of economic activities, Sardinia suffers from a high rate of unemployment (approx 12%), mainly in the young population (approximately 22%) which leads to its immigration especially from the areas located in the centre of the island.

As far as the energy feeding of the island is concerned, and even if the majority of the island is fed from imported oil, a renewable energy plan was elaborated according the specific energy needs and energy resources of each area separately. Therefore, it was after a study financed from European Union that the use of heating pumps has been decided for local residences, the biomass combustion for the heating of schools, offices and local residences, the solar energy for the tourism activities, illuminations, and greenhouses, the small wind generators for the energy feeding of local enterprises, farms, and camping infrastructures and the biofuels for transports. It is to be noted that the small wind generators attract the interest of local investors, since the investment cost is not high and the visual impacts are of an acceptable degree.

Furthermore, a synergy between thermal and hydroelectric plants is already in place. In fact, water is partly used in order to regulate the electricity charge in the network and in order to maintain the maximum efficiency of thermal plants. During the night, when electricity demand is low, the supplementary electricity production, generated from thermal plants is used for pumping the water back into the reservoir. Nevertheless, even if RETs are to conquer a large part of the local energy balance in Sardinia, the question of the further local awareness concerning these technologies remains important, mainly as far as their benefits for the local economy are concerned. Towards this direction, information campaigns have been organised (both from State and private investors) concerning –for the moment-the expansion of solar thermal systems.

Cyprus is an island near Turkey, Syria and Lebanon which hosts today 820,000 people and covers and area of 9,251km^2. The island suffers from geopolitical problems, as in 1974 there was a Turkish armed invasion in its territories, resulting at the occupation of a strategically important part of the island. Through accession to the European Union in 2004, the Cypriot Republic benefits from the financial and legislative European support towards a sustainable energy management. Its intense geomorphologic elements, climate, local natural sources and local acceptance towards the introduction of new energy forms vary depending on the region. This is exactly why different energy local plans have been elaborated and different energy technologies have been proposed. In areas for example with fragile ecosystems and historical monuments, some «mild» interventions were chosen which would not create optical perturbances. In areas of luxury tourism attraction the idea of the use of solar vehicles in the golf terrains were launched, whereas in remote areas the combustion from biomass was promoted for the domestic use.

Corsica is a French island, with an area of 8,680km^2 which hosts 279,000 residents. The island holds a long and perturbed history. It also presents an altitude of 2,706 meters and 1000 km of coast. Rich in renewable energy sources as well as in protected natural areas, the island is often threatened from fires and as a consequence is seriously threatened from climatic changes. From a demographic point of view, the island has an unemployment rate of 10.6% (in 2002), but a well organized local governance (360 communities). Corsica has multiple airports and diversifies productive sectors, as follows: primary sector 5.3%, secondary sector 15.3% and tertiary sector 79.4%. The local entrepreneurial activity is very intense, often on a family and on a multiactivity basis. All these activities though don't prevent from turning several Corsican areas empty of population. In this island of dispersed energy needs, a variety of renewable energy projects have been implemented.

Some of these projects clearly contribute to the achievement of a sustainable tourism development, two examples follow: In 1998, a German company implemented the second wind energy park (wind energy park of Calenzana) on the island. The time that was necessary from the decision to the implementation was rather long (1998 – 2003), but today 10 wind generators of a total installed capacity of 6MW exist in the island and support the electricity peak loads (often observed during the tourism periods). It is to be noted here, that the total investment (more than 5M€) was not subsidized from the French government, and that due to the geomorphologic characteristics of the islands the transport of the material on site was rather difficult. Furthermore, an exhaustive dialogue has been launched between the company and the local society before the construction of the project due to prior bad experiences with the first wind park installed in the island, and to the immature French legislative framework; this, even if the land where the wind park was installed belongs to the local municipality. Today except from covering local needs with electricity, the wind park serves as a demonstration project to European students who attend the summer schools organized from the RET's faculty of the Corte University.

Another case which demonstrates the special attention being drawn at the preservation of Corsica's natural and cultural sources is to be noted here: In 1967, the company Electricite de la France (EDF) has constructed a hydroelectric plant of 32MW (hydroelectric plant of Calacuccia) with a generated electricity of 120GWh a year, and of an overall cost of 160M€. The planning of the whole project was based mainly on technical criteria, and mainly on the hydraulic potential of the area, on the distance of water's falling, as well as on the possibility to regulate energy outcome according local needs. During this planning though, a special attention has been awarded so as the project would be perfectly integrated in the exceptional surrounding environment of the island (through artificial colours and through a dam and cables attentively sculpted in the mountain). No malfunctioning problem has been reported since operation began. As a matter of fact and even if at the time of its construction the project has met a variety of political and social reactions and oppositions, nowadays, the hydroelectric plant is operating under an efficient environmental monitoring during operation (updating of databases, development of impact studies for the water quality, biodiversity's protection and technical system's improvement). Hence, the plant contributes successfully to the feeding of energy demands whereas its dam permits sport tourism (sports activities in the river). The project is very often visited by students by several European Universities.

Crete is the second largest island of the Mediterranean Sea with a surface of 8,335 km^2 and a population of 650,000 in 2005. It's a mountainous island, full of olive plantations and vineyards, with an altitude of 2,452m. The tertiary sector of the island occupies the 80% of job posts, and secondary and tertiary sectors have been very much benefited from tourism activity. Tourism arrivals have been increased in a percentage of 53% between the years 1986 and 1991 (whereas a responding percentage in the rest of Greece was of 25%) and the 13.3% of visitors in Greece during 2006 were located in Crete. Intense tourism activity is due to the rich natural and historical monuments (Cretan influence in the civilization of the Mediterranean Sea and the ancient Greece was essential). The island's location as well as the location of all Hellenic islands presented in this study, are presented in the following Hellenic map: In the island, different forms of tourism are developing in perfect coexistence (leisure, religious, cultural, medical, ecological tourism, etc.), and therefore the island is very well equipped with transport infrastructures (two international airports) and facilities. A tendency of these infrastructures' enrichment is occurring in present times with bioclimatic elements to be integrated in hotels, attracting engineers and (mainly local) investors' interest. That's why one of the biggest solar thermal system in Europe is situated in this island, on a 275 bed capacity hotel. The surface of the solar collector is 2,358m^2 and covers the 70% of the hotel's total demand in hot water. Apart from this system, since 1999 some more hotels of Crete host solar collectors which enable the covering of almost 10% of their needs, meaning an everyday load of 450-500kWH.

Considering that Greece has a benefit of almost 3,000 hours of sun per year and the possibility of solar energy production is estimated in 1,900KWH/m^2 per year and considering that the construction sector in Greece consumes 36% of the total energy and produces 40% of the greenhouse gas emissions, solar energy is expected to lead at the improvement of living standards of local inhabitants and an increase of tourism's quality. In Crete, renewable energy projects play also the role of tourism thematic parks. For example the metallic windmills of Lassithy were built during 1930's in order to supply the surrounding villages with energy. At that period of time, these windmills seemed completely strange to the surrounding environment and local negative reactions emerged. Nowadays, however, they reflect the local tradition of the site, since, in general, wind generators are considered as the continuity of one of the fundamental symbols of the islander Hellenic cultural identity: the wind mills. Indeed, municipal authorities of the area seized the importance and the potential of this "historical" site and began to restore the mills, in order to transform them into a successful attraction. This example shows clearly the great opportunities arisen from the creation of thematic parks dealing with the issue of energy.

Milos is a Hellenic island of 160,1km^2 and of 4,771 people, situated in the complex of Cyclades. A rocky island in its majority, presents an altitude of 748m and a volcanic geology. A variety of ancient masterpieces has been discovered in the island's territories, the most famous among them being the statue of Aphrodite of Milos. The island's residents are occupied with tourism, commerce, fishing, agriculture and industry activities. Rich in mines and in geothermy, the island has often been proposed for the implementation of pilot-projects on hydrogen and geothermy. Nevertheless, because of an accident taking place back in '80's where toxic gazes have escaped during an effort of exploiting a geothermy plant, local residents remain always sceptical towards the operation of innovative energy projects in their territories. The yearly organisation in the island though of two of the biggest Hellenic conferences on renewable energy (the one being on RETs and the other on bioclimatic architecture) attract scientific tourism; this form of tourism is expected to lead to the extension of the tourism period in the island, as well as at the attraction of investments on renewable energy sources. Scopelos is a Hellenic island, situated in the Aegean Sea, belonging in the complex of Sporades with a surface of 90Km^2 and a population of 4,696 people. It's considered to be the island the most "green" of the Mediterranean see, while the capital of the island was declared from a Hellenic presidential degree as a "traditional area of a gorgeous beauty". In the island, the majority of the productive activities operate on the basis of the multiactivity and of "short family circuits". Nowadays, the residents of the island seem to be more and more ecologically sensitive and informed for the importance of renewable energies and their applications. They even think to create a synergy between all productive sectors by further exploiting local products and by using RETs in the dispersed energy needs occurring. Nevertheless, beyond this sensitivity which is certainly an essential pre-condition to engage new strategies, research in Skopelos highlighted a further need for information on renewable energy sources. This necessity occurred because of the residents' isolation and because of negative past experiences with renewable energy technologies in other islands (like in the Milos' island). Gavdos is a very small Hellenic island of 27 km^2, inhabited already from the 16th century, situated in the southern part of Crete. Nowadays, only 98 local residents live in this infertile and rocky island of a changing climate. Tourism infrastructures are almost non-existent, thought during summer the island is frequented from young campers. This results to some dispersed energy needs during the summer period and this is why a photovoltaic system of 20KW and some "electricity generators" are the sole sources of electricity feeding. Nevertheless, researchers have already proposed for this island the further use of photovoltaic modules which could feed increased electricity needs during the tourism peaks and orient the supplementary electricity production towards other applications (such as water desalination) during winter.

Results-Discussion

We have seen in our analysis that Mediterranean islands are rich in natural resources, cultural heritage and political interest. As a consequence of these features, Mediterranean islands attract intense tourism activity but at the same time suffer from the mass-tourism's negative effects, which together with the climate change constitute a threat for their own existence and development. On the other hand, Mediterranean islands present common social characteristics, such as the isolation of the islander communities, the high degree of unemployment, the immigration of young people mainly from the inner parts of the islands, the lack of specialized work force, different degrees of population's density in different areas, strong local political forces, and the conservative people's mentality. In addition, common economic characteristics are apparent as well, the principal ones being: the unequal distribution of productive activities throughout the islands, a distribution in the productive sectors usually in analogies approximately 6%, 15%, 80% in the overall economy (for the primary, the secondary and the tertiary sector respectively), the load of local employment on tourism activity (mainly during July and August), a deficit in local investments and entrepreneurship, and a local entrepreneurial activity which is often based on a family and on a multiactivity basis.

Environmental specificities should be pointed out as well: apart from commonly shared ecological sensibility among local residents,

Mediterranean islands often carry fragile ecosystems which are characterized as "sea parks" or "worldwide cultural and natural heritages". With fragile infrastructures and inefficiency of water reserves, and surrounded by sea with limited or no access to the mainland in times of bad weather, these "natural beauties" are exposed and threatened from human pressures. In the energy sector, some common problems are noticed as well: high prices of energy feeding, inadequacy of electricity transport infrastructure and a majority of energy feeding coming from thermal plants (oil) are the principal ones.

Therefore, being regional areas-especially vulnerable and largely contributing to National Internal Products-Mediterranean islander territories should influence the European energy policy. In order that islands develop this "political power of influence", they should create comparative advantages and added values. The restricted time available calls for action, methodology, effectiveness and collaboration of all policy makers and local actors. Cases studied have proved that integrated strategies which will link the governmental and the local administrative element with local entrepreneurship and research are possible and should be promoted with a view to achieve a sustainable tourism development. Especially for the Mediterranean islands, strategies should aim at preserving nature and heritage, developing society in a sustainable way, building energy capacity and energy autonomy and achieving economical growth.

Already mentioned "threats" could turn to be "opportunities" through autonomous and sustainable energy infrastructures. Special island geomorphological characteristics for example, permit the implantation of wind parks and hydroelectric stations. Abundant energy resources permit the construction of biomass and geothermy plants, as well as the installation of photovoltaic and thermal solar systems. RETs seem also capable not only to cover dispersed and peak energy demands on several application – see case of Crete-but also to facilitate the appearance of several special types of tourism (educational, scientific, sports tourism, or thematic parks)-cases of Corsica and Milos-. Moreover, when no energy needs exist, electricity produced through RETs could turn into water desalination for local needs –see case of Gavdos-or even being stocked for future use. Building knowledge on RETs seems also possible in the Mediterranean islands, especially in an era where people become more and more informed on these technologies. In any case, we have seen that implemented and well functioning RETs could serve as prototypes and demonstration pilot-projects and that local tourism infrastructures which are equipped with bioclimatic features do strengthen local entrepreneurship. In conclusion, RETs were judged by scholars as the ideal source of energy feeding for islands especially when combined with systems of electricity stocking. We have seen through this study that RETs seem to be the ideal solution as well, for the achievement of qualitative objectives in the field of tourism. Some prerequisites, thought, seem to be necessary to permit RET to develop alongside sustainable tourism:

First of all, local governance should be powerful and stable in decision-making and not necessarily *a priori* predicated on the central and national decision making process. The degree of coupling between local (island) and national decision making should be variable in different places and RET opportunities; however independent of the level of local-national coupling, a process of good governance in decision-making at an island scale can be considered to be a pre-requisite.

Secondly, a high degree of local acceptance of innovative technologies and local participation processes should be assured. The experiences in Corsica and Milos have shown that it takes time for a project to mature in local society's mind. Therefore, investors should formulate projects with an adequate time-line to inform and consult local societies before they implement the project, and RETs should be implemented by priority in areas where people are familiarised with these technologies. In this context, a continuous increase in local awareness is needed.

Thirdly, attention should be given in RETs implementation according the size of the island and the different resources from region to region. Renewable energy plans should be based on specific energy needs and natural resources of each area separately like in Cyprus and Sardinia. Local planning issues, local business initiatives and willingness, specific objectives and priorities of local policy, as well as specific existing pressures and the flexibility of local element, should also be taken into consideration. Moreover, RETs should also be used according to tourism's type existing in the area. The case of Cyprus has shown that the use of solar systems for luxury tourism, the wind parks or biomass combustion for ecotourism approaches, or the advanced energy technologies for scientific tourism and geothermy for greenhouse applications (agro tourism) could be recommended.

Further attention is also needed during the installation and operation of RETs. For the implementation of a "demanding" RET (such as a geothermy or a biogas plant) a step-by-step approach is needed, in order to avoid mistakes that might prove fatal in the future-like in the case of Milos-. A gained confidence among the local population not only contributes to the success of the project but also favours its promotion in other islands as well. Environmental impact studies are also needed before the implementation of the project for environmental protection and the most harmonious integration of the project into the surrounding environment. As a following step, the monitoring of the project's environmental behaviour, and the maintainance of databases for recording and for the dissemination of positive results are recommended. Attention should also be drawn in the technical aspects which could raise the degree of technical efficiency and reduce operating cost. Technical synergies such as the combination of hydroelectric plants and thermoelectric ones should be researched for eventual electricity stocking. In the above mentioned efforts the use of European financing and the support of national governments are vital components to support progress towards implementing renewable energy in islands.

Conclusion

19 The majority of Mediterranean islands seem to face similar problems, have similar vulnerabilities, and follow a similar trajectory for confronting the challenges of present and future. Taking into account the short duration of tourism's period (three or four times a year) and the increasing rate of tourism arrivals, problems connected with energy and water sufficiency are likely to become even more serious. This paper demonstrates that renewable energy sources, abundant in worldwide islands, can be implemented in a way which addresses the challenges and vulnerabilities of the future, in full compliance with the obligations at a national level and from European Guidelines and Directives. Consequently, it seems that the potential for RET to transform islands to "qualitative tourism" sites exists. This study has also concluded that transfer of success stories is necessary. Of course a "best practice" which seems to be the ideal for an island, is not necessarily the ideal one for another. Different parameters, such as different geomorphologic, cultural and social particularities impose a specific approach and strategy. This process is complex, but through a consideration of a range of Mediterranean islands, a number of prerequisites have been identified which guide the procedures that should be followed, the conditions which should be respected and actions which should be put in place to provide islands with a more sustainable future.

12

Island Tourism Development

Introduction

When facing choices for economic development, island destinations share a number of common characteristics. These include:

* Small population
* Limited resources
* Insufficient capital to finance investment
* Little or no manufacturing
* High transportation costs
* Geographic isolation from markets.

Faced with these difficulties, there are few alternatives that island economies can pursue in terms of development. Most are dependent on one or several of the following:

* Agricultural exports
* Light manufacturing
* Export processing
* Fishing or other marine industry.

Tourism

The role that tourism plays in the economic development of small island economies is not unique to Hawaii or Okinawa. It is taking place in nearly every Pacific island destination at the present time. While the volume of tourism arrivals and the scale of tourism development may vary, each island destination is looking to tourism as its primary or at least one of the most important means to achieve economic development, and all destinations face common problems.

Importance of Sustainable Development

Sustainable development is a term often used to apply to tourism destinations and especially to small islands with limited resources. Sustainable tourism development emphasizes the need to achieve an appropriate balance between the economic, environmental, and socio-cultural aspects of tourism development and management. Due to their small size, island tourism destinations face a special challenge in achieving economic benefits for its people, determining the best use of its natural and environmental resources, and ensuring that development is appropriate to the socio-cultural characteristics of its resident or host community. Each of these aspects are summarized in this session and explored in greater detail in other sessions.

Economic Constraints

For many island destinations tourism is viewed as a means of economic diversification. In many destinations, agriculture or fishing was the major economic activity but increased globalization of the economy has put them at a disadvantage as the importance of export crops such as sugar cane production or fishery activity have declined. However, tourism is not an easy solution.

Because of the geographic isolation and limited resources of island destinations, they are most vulnerable to tourism-related economic costs that larger, continent-based destinations do not have. Transportation is a key factor in terms of access of people and goods and in most cases poses a major obstacle for island destinations to achieve a successful tourism industry. The high economic costs of importing goods and services for tourists results in a high leakage factor from the gross tourism receipts or general revenues from tourism. To the extent that goods such as food produce consumed by tourists and services required to support tourism must be imported, payments must flow out of the destination and profits must also be shared with outside investors. The extent of this leakage is quite high, and many island economies have tourism leakages of over 50% meaning half of the income from tourism flows out of the destination to pay for essential goods and services.

Environmental Constraints

Many island destinations are economically underdeveloped but have natural resources suitable for tourism. However, the conservation of the fragile ecosystems of these islands requires careful consumption of resources (water, energy) and factors such as waste treatment. Islands also have limited fresh water resources and are more sensitive to sea level rises resulting from climate change. In terms of waste disposal, because of their size, islands also face environmental difficulties not found in larger continent-based destinations. If tourism is not well planned, developed and managed, it can result in negative environmental impacts such as: Water pollution-including pollution of coastal waters, rivers, and lakes resulting from improper waste management of sewage or solid waste system from hotels or other tourism facilities. In particular, coastal and marine environments are vulnerable to ecological damage caused by erosion and runoff which can endanger coral reefs Air, noise and traffic pollution-resulting from tourism activities and tourist vehicles and road congestion

Unattractive landscapes (visual pollution) – resulting from poor design of hotels and other tourism facilities, inadequate landscaping, obstruction of scenic views by tourism development Damage to historic and cultural sites – resulting from inappropriate development and overuse and misuse by tourists Ecological disruption of natural areas and wildlife – resulting from inappropriate development and overuse and misuse by tourists.

Socio-cultural Constraints

Although the economic benefits to the host or resident community may be substantial, the development of tourism facilities and services should also improve the quality of life for residents. A major benefit has been the development of community infrastructure such as improved roads, water and other services for residents as a result of tourism development. When properly developed, tourism can also serve as a means to stimulate the practice and preservation of local cultures, folklore, traditions, arts and crafts, and cuisine while preserving historical, archaeological and religious monuments and sites. However, at the same time, too rapid development or overdevelopment can often be detrimental to the host or resident community.

Destination Life Cycle

In understanding where an island destination is today in terms of tourism development, it might be helpful to review the concept of a destination life cycle. *(Refer to charts at the end of this section)* Historically, tourism destinations have tended to undergo an economic life cycle of four stages which may cover 50 to 75 years. This life cycle can apply to both the destination and to a specific resort. Each destination can be said to be at a different stage of the life cycle and faces different problems.

Exploration Stage

* Tourism facilities lacking
* Limited air transportation accessibility
* Destination relatively unknown.

Development Stage

* International class facilities available
* Better air accessibility
* Visitors increase, visible impact on local economy
* Government/residents welcome tourism
* Development is spontaneous and uncoordinated.

Maturity Stage

* Large number of tourists
* Loss of local decision-making power and control
* Hotels, airlines, tourism services dominated by international corporations
* Residents may develop hostile attitude toward tourism
* Competition for resources between residents and tourists.

Decline Stage

* Destination has well-established image but no longer popular
* Planning controls come too late
* Over-commercialized
* No sign of self-renewal.

While the destination life cycle may apply differently for each area, it can serve as a useful framework for policy makers to understand the development process for tourism and each destination's competitive position. Where the various destinations are on the life cycle scale is also of interest. Most island destinations are in the exploration or development stages, while others such as Hawaii are well into the maturity stage and some may even say it is in a decline stage. Certainly, Waikiki, which is Hawaii's primary tourist destination, is now over 100 years old and much of it was unplanned and coordinated. Whether it can continue to rejuvenate itself and prevent decline is a major challenge.

Challenge to Island Destinations

While it is not surprising that so many island groups have chosen tourism as their principal means of economic development, most have encountered a number of difficulties. As each island destination has experienced more extensive tourism development, the common problems include:

* Increasing the number and type of tourism attractions
* Maintaining adequate air transportation routes and reasonable air fares
* Providing an appropriate level of accommodations and services
* Establishing adequate infrastructure including water, power, and sewerage facilities
* Providing effective government support for tourism planning and development
* Marketing and promoting the destination in competition with other island destinations
* Attracting outside investment capital for development
* Providing trained or skilled employees for the industry
* Among island destinations, Hawaii's development experience shares many similarities with Okinawa.

Historically, because both Hawaii and Okinawa were independent kingdoms, they had unique cultures which were brought under political and cultural domination through annexation. Geographically, both Hawaii and Okinawa represent isolated island entities—Okinawa being the only island prefecture in Japan, and Hawaii being the only island state in the United States. Economically, the structures are similar with a dependence on tourism, military expenditures, and agriculture. Demographically, Hawaii and Okinawa have approximately the same-sized population, and their residents enjoy the highest longevity in their respective countries. In terms of tourism development, there are also many similarities. Okinawa, like Hawaii is a warm weather destination with good beaches and ocean-oriented recreation which appeal to domestic tourists. Hawaii's largest number of tourists still come from the mainland U.S., and Okinawa's tourists are primarily from the main islands of Japan. For established tourism destinations like Hawaii and Okinawa, a major challenge is to maintain the ability to compete in the global tourism market place. Both must seek continuous reinvestment to support quality and freshness of appeal to maintain their respective market positions and avoid the possibility of decline. In order to remain competitive, they must also continuously review and analyze their tourism markets and their products. The responsibility for tourism marketing and product development are largely a part of the government's role in planning for tourism development and management.

Market Analysis

An important challenge facing Hawaii and other island destinations is to widen the range of tourists both in terms of geographical origin and the type of activities they seek. This requires an understanding of the preferences of today's travellers based on their demographic characteristics including age, gender, income, marital status. It is clear that because of the demographic changes, the attractions and activities offered by tourism destinations cannot remain the same year after year, but will need to adjust to the interests of different groups and preferences. The kinds of activities, accommodations and attractions which are popular today may not be popular tomorrow, and it is important for Hawaii and Okinawa to adjust to these changing market preferences.

Hawaii is currently reassessing its marketing strategy and looking increasingly toward market segmentation. It is looking at both new geographical markets but also special market segments. In terms of market segments, it has also developed new specialized tourism activities for selected markets in areas like ecotourism cultural tourism, sports tourism, and education tourism.

Product Analysis

As a tourism destination, Hawaii has many different tourism products to offer. In order to compete effectively, however, it is constantly examining these products which include the facilities, attractions, activities, and services to tourists and other visitors. The "image" or how Hawaii projects itself and how tourists see it is determined by its different products. Hawaii as an island destination projects an image of a sub-tropical beach resort destination with many ocean-related attractions and activities offering warm climate, friendly people and a unique historical and cultural heritage. A large part of its image as a beach resort is projected through its recreational activities which are primarily water-oriented activities. However, these are not enough in today's competitive market. It is clear that if a beach resort destination is to succeed in today's global tourism market, it must offer other recreational activities besides its water-oriented activities.

In seeking new attractions, events, and ways of packaging its products, Hawaii is seeking ways to keep its repeat visitor market and attract new visitors. Greater emphasis is being placed on improving visitor accommodations, facilities, and transportation systems. In particular, Hawaii is seeking ways to promote a greater role for its unique culture in enhancing the vacation experience for tourists. Increased emphasis is now being placed on protection, preservation, interpretation, and marketing of Hawaii's cultural and historic resources.

Role of Planning and Public Policy

Much of the success with which island economies like Hawaii and Okinawa will meet the challenge will depend on the public policies that will guide the development process and define the relationship between the public and private sectors. The government's interest is generally to develop a tourism industry, generate revenue, provide employment, and stimulate economic growth. The private sector's perspective is to produce a profit and return on investment. But the success of tourism development also depends on a third important element and that is the partnership between the government, the industry, and the community. Community support is essential for any sort of development and the community perspective is critical to success.

Summary

There are many examples of the role that tourism plays in the economic development of small island destinations. It is taking place in nearly every Pacific island destination at the present time. While the volume of tourism arrivals and the scale of tourism development may vary, each island destination is looking to tourism as its primary or at least one of the most important means to achieve economic development and all face common problems. In the case of both Hawaii and Okinawa, the level of development is considerably higher than most other island destinations in the Pacific, but the level of competition and the changing trends in the visitor markets require a good understanding of the process of tourism development to ensure continuing success in global tourism.

Bibliography

Andrew, N; Flanagan, S & Ruddy, J: *Tourism Destination Planning*, Dublin, Dublin Institute of Technology, 2002.

Apostolopous, Y and Leivadi, S: *Sociology of Tourism, The: Theoretical And Empirical Investigations*, London, Retailed, 1996.

Ashworth, G J and Dietvorst, A G J: *Tourism and Spatial Transformations: Implications For Policy and Plan*, Wallingford, CAB International, 1995.

Ashworth, Greg and Larkham, P J: *Building a New Heritage: Tourism, Culture & Identity in the New Europe*, London, Routledge,1994.

Baum, Tom: *We're all Going on a Summer Holiday: Images of Tourism Past and Person*, Buckingham, University of Buckingham, 1995.

Beeho, A & Prentice, R: *Conceptualising The Experiences of Heritage Tourists*, 1997.

Beeton, Sue:: *Film-Induced Tourism*, Clevedon, Channel View, 2005.

Belie et al.: *Tourism and the Inner City: An Evaluation of / Impact of Grant Assist*, London, HMSO, 1990.

Benefice, Brian G, and Cooper, Chris: *Geography of Travel and Tourism*, The, London, Heinemann, 1987.

Bolshevism, Germy: *Coping with Tourists: European Reactions to Mass Tourism*, Oxford, Berghahn Books, 1995.

Boniface, Priscilla and Fowler, Peter: *Heritage and Tourism: In the Global Village*, London, Retailed, 1993.

Bosselman, Fred P: *In The Wake of the Tourist: Managing Special Places in Eight Countries*, Washington, DC, Conservation Foundation, The, 1978.

Briguglio, I. and Vella, Leslie: *Competitiveness of the Maltese Islands in Mediterranean in Tourism*, Chichester, John Wiley, 1995.

Brown, Dona: *Inventing New England: Regional Tourism in the Nineteenth Century*, Washington DC, Smithsonian Institution, 1995.

Brunt, Paul: *Market Research in Travel and Tourism*, Oxford, Butterworth Heinemann, 1997.

Burkart, A and Medlik, S: *Management of Tourism*, The, London, Heinemann, 1975.

Chambers, Erve: *Native Tours: The Anthropology of Travel and Tourism*, Prospect Heights, Waveland Press, 2000.

Chandler, Harry and Carter, John: *Chandler's Travels: A Tour of the Life of Harry Chandler*, London, Quiller Press, 1985.

Clark, Colin: *Tourist Services and Guidance: Heritage and Information*, Strasbourg, Council of Europe Press, 1989.

Coccosis, Harry and Nijkamp, Peter: *Sustainable Tourism Development*, Aldershot, Avebury, 1995.

Cohen, Erik: *Towards a Sociology of International Tourism*, 1972.

Dann, Graham M S: *Language of Tourism*, The, Wallingford, CAB International, 1996.

Davidson, R and Maitland, R: *Tourism Destinations, London*, Hodder and Stoughton, 1997.

Davidson, Rob: *Travel and Tourism in Europe*, Harlow, Addison Wesley Longman, 1998.

Ecotec: *Calderdale: Tourism Impact Study*, Calderdale, ECOTEC/Calderdale Council, 1990.

Edensor, Tim: *Tourists at the Taj*, London, Retailed, 1998.

Edgell, David L: *International Tourism Policy, New York*, Van Nostrand and Reinhold, 1990.

Elliott, James: *Tourism: Politics and Public Sector Management*, London, Retailed, 1997.

Fairgrieve, James: *Geography in School*, London, University of London Press, 1926.

Foster, Douglas: *Travel and Tourism Management*, London, Macmillan Educational, 1985.

Frechtling, Douglas C: *Practical Tourism Forecasting*, Oxford, Butterworth Heinemann, 1996.

Gamble, P. R: *The Educational challenge for Hospitality and Tourism Studies*, Tourism Management, 13, 1992.

Ghimire, Krishna: *The Native Tourist*: Mass Tourism within Developing Regions, London, Earthscan, 2001.

Goeldner, C. R: *The Evaluation of Tourism as an Industry and a Discipline, Paper Presented to*, International Conference for Tourism Educators, Guildford, University of Surrey, 1988.

Gunn, Clare and Var, Turgut: *Tourism Planning*, London, Retailed, 2002.

Hall, C Michael *Tourism Planning: Policies, Processes and relationships*, Harlow, Prentice Hall, 2000.

Hall, Colin and Jenkins, John: *Tourism and Public Policy*, London, Retailed, 1995.

Hall, Colin Michael: *Tourism and Politics*: Policy, Power, & Place, Chichester, Wiley, 1994.

Harrison, Lyndon: *Tourism Means Jobs*, Chester, Lyndon Harrison, 1996.

Harron, S and Weiler, B: *Ethnic Tourism*, Belhaven/Wiley, 1992.

Inkpen, G: *Information Technology for Travel and Tourism*, Harlow, Addison Wesley Longman, 1998.

Inskeep, Edward *National and Regal Tourism Planing*: Methodologies & Case Studies, London, Routledge/WTO, 1994.

Irwin, William *The New Niagara*: *Tourism, Technology, And the Landscape of Niagara Fal*, University Park, PA, University of Pennsylvania, 1996.

Jack, G and Phipps, A: *Tourism and Intercultural Exchange*: *Why Tourism Matters*, Clevedon, Channel View, 2005.

Jakle, John: *Tourist, The: Travel in Twentieth Century North America*, University of North Nebraska, 1985.

Jennings, Gayle: *Tourism Research*, Chichester, Wiley, 2001.

Judd, D R: *Promoting Tourism* in US Cities, 1995.

Karski, A: *Urban Tourism* - A Key to Urban Regeneration?, 1990.

Kotler, Philip et al: *Marketing Places*: *Attracting Investment, Industry & Tourism etc*, New York, free press, 1993.

Labarge, Margaret Wade: *Medieval Travellers*: *The Rich and Restless*, London, Hamish Hamilton, 1982.

Laws, Eric: *Tourist Destination Management: Issues, Analysis & Policies*, Londòn, Routledge, 1995.

Leed, Eric J: *Mind of the Traveller, The: From Gilgamesh to Global Tourism*, New York, 1991.

MacCannell, Dean: *Tourist, The: A New Theory of the Leisure Class*, London, Macmillan, 1976.

Machin, Alan: *Retracing the Steps: Tourism as Education, Janus*, Fin, ATLAS / FUNTS, 2001.

Opperman, Martin and Chon, Kye-Sung: *Tourism in Developing Countries, London*, International Thomson Business Press, 1997.

Patullo, Polly: *Last Resorts*: *The Cost of Tourism in the Caribbean*, London, Cassell, 1996.

Pearce, Douglas: *Tourism Today*: *A Geographical Analysis*, Harlow, Longman, 1995.

Pearce, P L: *Social Psychology Of Tourist Behaviour*, The, Oxford, Pergamon, 1982.

Peters, M: *International Tourism*, London, Hutchinson, 1969.

Ringer, Greg: *Destinations: Cultural Landscapes of Tourism*, London, Routledge, 1998.

Ritchie, Brent: *Managing Educational Tourism*, Clevedon, Channel View, 2003.

Robinson, H: *Geography of Tourism*, A, London, Macdonald and Evans, 1976.

Robinson, M, Evans, E & Chalazion, P: *Tourism and Cultural Change, Sunderland*, Business Education Publishers Ltd, 1996.

Rogers, H Anthea and Slinn, Judy A: *Tourism: Management of Facilities*, London, Pitman: M & E, 1993.

Schwaninger, M: *Trends in Leisure and Tourism for 2000 - 2010*, Prentice Hall, 1989.

Scottish Tourist Board: *Visitor Attractions: A Development Guide*, Edinburgh, Scottish Tourist Board, 1991.

Seaton, A V et al: *Tourism: The state of the Art*, Chichester, John Wiley, 1994.

Shaw, G and Williams, A: *Tourism and Tourism Spaces*, London, Sage, 2004.

Stevens, Terry: *Island Tourism*: Malta, , WTO, 1993.

Trench, R: *Travellers in Britain*, London, Aurum, 1990.

Tribe, John *Corporate Strategy for Tourism, London*, International Thomson Business Press, 1997.

Urry, John: *Tourist Gaze*, The, London, Sage, 1990.

Van den Berg et al: *Urban Tourism: Performance and Strategies in Eight European Cities*, Aldershot, Avebury, 1995.

Van Harssel, Jan: *Tourism: An Exploration*, New York, Prentice Hall, 1994.

Veal, A: *Leisure and Tourism*: Policy and Planning, Wallingford, CABI, 2001.

Wahab, S A: *Tourism Management*, Tourism International Press, 1975.

Walle, Alfred H: *Cultural Tourism*: A Strategic Focus, Boulder, Co, Westview Press, 1998.

Wilkinson, Paul: *Tourism Policy and Planning: As Studies from the Caribbean*, Elmsford New York, Cognizant Communications Corporation, 1997.

Yale, Pat: *From Tourist Attractions to Heritage Tourism*, Huntingdon, Elm, 1991.

Zarkia, Cornelia: *Philoxenia: Receiving Tourists*-but *not Guests-on a Greek Island*, Oxford, Berghahn Books, 1996.

Index

A

Achievements, 140, 157, 171, 229.
Adventure Tourism, 7, 131, 151, 278.

B

Bali Cultural Tourism, 240.
Bureaucracy, 201, 244.
Business Development, 234.

C

Coastal Degradation, 63.
Coastal Tourism, 7.
Commonwealth Games, 278.
Communications, 40, 140, 197, 238.
Crisis in Tourism, 257.
Cultural Environment, 158, 252.
Cultural Impacts, 162, 191, 224.
Customer Service, 112.

D

Definition of Ecotourism, 130, 131, 132, 136, 302.
Destination Management, 196.

E

Economic Development Strategy, 134.
Economic Impacts of Tourism, 2.
Economic Policy, 230, 280.
Ecotourism Management, 300.
Environment Perspective, 222, 225.
Environmental Conservation, 67, 138, 139, 143, 302.
Environmental Management, 135, 156, 157, 169, 194, 195, 217.
Evidence, 18, 19, 29, 31, 61, 70, 113, 234, 266.
Export Strategy, 314.

F

Federal Government, 304.
Freedom, 105, 234, 293, 318.

G

Geographical Phenomenon, 1.
Global Tourism, 4, 210, 278, 336, 337, 338.

H

Heritage Tourism, 199.
Hotel Capacity, 149.

I

Instruments, 72, 104, 117, 118, 311.
International Border Crossings, 300.
International Monetary Fund, 308, 314.
International Tourists, 7, 17, 262.

K

Kangaroo Island Tourism, 104, 109.

L

Labour Market, 161.

Leadership, 7, 25, 183, 290, 297.
Local Economic Development, 75.
Lombok Island, 223, 224.

M

Maintaining Diversity, 172, 176.
Management Decisions, 137.
Marine Environment, 14, 116, 239.
Market Diversification, 192, 198.
Marketing Approach, 245.
Mediterranean Tourism, 171.
Motivations, 2, 269.

N

National Policy, 65, 217, 280.
Nature Tourism, 73, 78, 129, 131, 132, 137, 141, 279.

O

Observations, 134, 289.
Occupations, 22, 54.

P

Performance, 52, 54, 57, 126, 196.
Physical Environment, 131.
Powers, 194, 230.
Promote Sustainable Tourism, 71, 312.
Property Rights, 246, 247, 257, 258, 260.

R

Rafting, 234, 281.
Reservation Systems, 70.
Responsible Tourism, 243, 287.
Retail Sector, 248.

S

Seaside Resorts, 2, 230.
Sex tourism, 272.
Strategic Planning, 230.
Sustainable Management, 182, 198.

T

Tour Operators, 118, 119, 125, 126, 178, 196, 231, 297, 299, 302.
Tourism Demand, 231.
Tourism Environments, 201.
Tourism Flows, 333.
Tourism Income Multiplier, 56.
Tourism Management, 77, 200, 302.
Tourism Market, 132, 143, 145, 148, 150, 197, 238, 249, 336, 337.
Tourism Organisation, 281, 313.
Tourism Policy, 76, 117, 247, 252.
Tourism Product Development, 269, 272.
Tourism Promotion, 7, 278.
Tourism Sustainability, 320.
Tourist Attractions, 7, 9, 82, 106, 185, 217, 219, 221, 312.
Tourist Product, 178.
Transportation, 4, 36, 37, 38, 52, 59, 67, 71, 92, 99, 190, 195, 196, 197, 221, 223, 246, 249, 250, 310, 311, 332, 333, 335, 336, 338.
Travel Agents, 131, 225.
Treatment, 62, 68, 74, 112, 126, 139, 146, 167, 175, 176, 212, 315, 334.

V

Visitor Market, 338.

W

Welfare, 161, 230, 249.
Wisdom, 213.
World Bank, 8, 232, 253, 308, 314.
World Phenomenon, 4.
World Tourism, 4, 228, 237, 240, 245, 262, 281, 313.

□□□